0176006

KT-485-844

SM990032ЧЧ
1- 2000

(Por)

This book is due for return on or before the last date shown below.

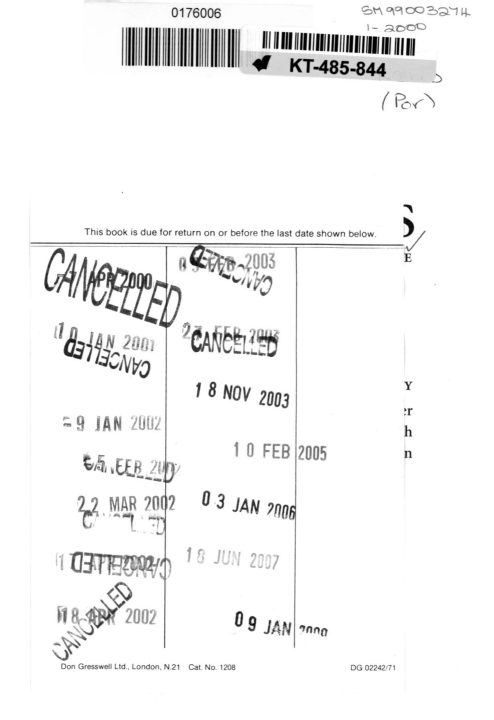

CANCELLED

APR 2000

1 0 JAN 2001

CANCELLED

≈ 9 JAN 2002

≈ 5 FEB 2002

2 2 MAR 2002

CANCELLED

1 8 APR 2002

0 3 FEB 2003

CANCELLED

2 3 FEB 2003

CANCELLED

1 8 NOV 2003

1 0 FEB 2005

0 3 JAN 2006

1 8 JUN 2007

0 9 JAN 2000

E

Y
er
h
n

Don Gresswell Ltd., London, N.21   Cat. No. 1208   DG 02242/71

HARBOTTLES LIBRARY
Oxfam
ST MARTINS SERVICES LTD.
LANCASTER

© Oxfam GB 1999

ISBN 0 85598 407 4

A catalogue record for this publication is available from the British Library.

All rights reserved. Reproduction, copy, transmission, or translation of any part of this publication may be made only under the following conditions:

• With the prior written permission of the publisher; or
• With a licence from the Copyright Licensing Agency Ltd., 90 Tottenham Court Road, London W1P 9HE, UK, or from another national licensing agency; or
• For quotation in a review of the work; or
• Under the terms set out below.

This publication is copyright, but may be reproduced by any method without fee for teaching purposes, but not for resale. Formal permission is required for all such uses, but normally will be granted immediately. For copying in any other circumstances, or for re-use in other publications, or for translation or adaptation, prior written permission must be obtained from the publisher, and a fee may be payable.

Available from the following agents:
for the USA: Stylus Publishing LLC, PO Box 605, Herndon, VA 20172-0605, USA;
tel. +1 (0)703 661 1581; fax +1 (0)703 661 1501; email styluspub@aol.com
for Canada: Fernwood Books Ltd., PO Box 9409, Stn. A, Halifax, Nova Scotia B3K 5S3, Canada;
tel. +1 (0)902 422 3302; fax +1 (0)902 422 3179; email fernwood@istar.ca
for Southern Africa: David Philip Publishers, PO Box 23408, Claremont 7735, South Africa;
tel. +27 (0)21 64 4136; fax +27 (0)21 64 3358; email dpp@iafrica.com
for India: Maya Publishers Pvt Ltd, 113-B, Shapur Jat, New Delhi-110049, India;
tel. +91 (0)11 649 0451; fax +91 (0)11 649 1039
for Australia: Bush Books, PO Box 1370, Gosford South, NSW 2250, Australia;
tel. +61 (0)2 4323 3274; fax +61 (0)2 9212 2468; email bushbook@ozemail.com.au

For the rest of the world, contact Oxfam Publishing, 274 Banbury Road, Oxford OX2 7DZ, UK.
tel. +44 (0)1865 311 311; fax +44 (0)1865 313 925; email publish@oxfam.org.uk

Published by Oxfam GB, 274 Banbury Road, Oxford OX2 7DZ, UK

Printed by Information Press

Oxfam GB is a registered charity, no. 202 918, and is a member of Oxfam International.

Contents

Preface

David Bryer

Gender Works is the latest in a line of publications from Oxfam GB on gender and development issues, charting the ways in which Oxfam GB's staff and partners have taken action to combat women's poverty and marginalisation around the world. This book marks a milestone in the long journey towards our goal of making our work, and our own organisation, work for women. We have a long way to travel still, but the debates included here bear witness to the importance of development workers and their organisations taking seriously the message of gender researchers, workers, and activists throughout the world, who urge us to practise what we preach.

A concern for women's poverty has informed Oxfam's work with communities since early in its history. This was shaped in 1984 into an explicit recognition that we needed to promote women's right to equal access to power, assets, and resources. In the following year, a specialist gender function, the Gender and Development Unit (GADU) was established at Oxfam's head office. It provided support, advice, and training to Oxfam's international programme, while lobbying work continued inside and outside the organisation to ensure that our commitment to gender concerns was rendered sustainable through a formal policy agreement. In 1993, almost a decade after GADU was set up, Oxfam's organisational Gender Policy was agreed. Our organisation was among the first Northern-based non-government funding agencies to embrace a concrete, formal commitment to the rights and welfare of women throughout the world.

During this process, Oxfam GB has become well-known for its commitment to integrating a concern for women's rights and gender equality into its programme work. The stages in our journey have been mapped by a succession of well-known publications, including *Changing Perceptions* and *The Oxfam Gender Training Manual*. *Gender Works*, like its forerunners, is a book of its time; it reflects the current emphasis on institutional analysis, since we are now aware that who 'we' in development organisations are has a direct impact on the value of the work we do. The time is ripe to debate which values need to underpin global development. A value-free, unregulated, 'globalised' economy is never going to deliver the just and fair development that we wish to promote in South and North. The 36 writers in this book, who come from every region of the globe, argue that all involved in development must be aware of the three cultural contexts in which we operate. The first is the geographical and historical location of our work; the second, our own personal experience; and the third, easily overlooked, belongs to our organisation itself. Not only do the underlying values and power relations of our society shape us personally, but they also influence the ethos, assumptions, structures, systems and procedures of our organisations.

The diverse voices in this book provide a wealth of information and a wide array of different opinions on the opportunities, and the obstacles, which writers have encountered along the way to a common goal. This goal is to achieve development programmes which enable women to meet not only all their material requirements in their many roles as producers and carers for their families and the wider community, but the less tangible development aims of freedom, justice, self-determination, and knowledge.

Agreeing Oxfam GB's Gender Policy was the first step our organisation took in mounting a serious challenge to male bias in our development work. This book records key moments in the process of transforming this significant commitment into a living reality. While priorities and approaches to development are continually being re-cast, as a response to new realities, organisations such as Oxfam GB must change, but remain faithful to their core motivation: that of struggling against injustice and its causes. Learning about the successes and failures of our struggle vis-à-vis women, through the insights offered in this book, paves the way for renewing our efforts towards fighting against 'gender injustice' worldwide.

Oxford, 1999

Introduction

Fenella Porter, Ines Smyth, and Caroline Sweetman

This book is a multi-authored contribution to development debates on gender, focusing on the experience of Oxfam GB over the past 15 years. The book has evolved through a participatory process of consultation with staff throughout Oxfam's development programme and beyond. This is described more fully later in the Introduction. Authors include women and men from South and North, based in different locations throughout the world. Most of them work for Oxfam GB and its partner organisations, including other Oxfams from different countries, while a few are former employees of Oxfam or work as consultants. Together, the authors chart their personal perceptions of the experience of Oxfam GB in its progress on turning policy into practice on gender issues: combating women's poverty, and working to promote equality between women and men. The points of view expressed here are those of the individual authors. The fact that this book includes insights from many different perspectives reminds us that no organisation has a monolithic culture; rather, they are contradictory and paradoxical.

The context of this book

Over the past ten years, the attention of gender and development theorists and practitioners has increasingly emphasised the importance of 'getting institutions right for women in development' (Goetz 1995). The rationale for analysing institutions (including not only our own organisations, but also the household, the state, and others) from a gender perspective has been that development can only have a beneficial outcome for women when the working culture, structure, systems and procedures, and underlying values of the institutions which shape women's lives themselves reflect a concern for gender equity. As Aruna Rao and Rieky Stuart among others have asserted, 'we need to think more deeply about organisations themselves. Trying to 'add gender' into their structure and work is not enough; we need to understand and re-conceptualise what an organisation is, and then we need to re-invent organisations and institutions of all kinds in all our societies' (Rao and Stuart 1997, p.10).

This organisational stocktaking exercise in which gender and development workers have been engaged occurs against the backdrop of a long history. Since the UN Decade for Women began in 1975, development practice has been profoundly challenged by feminist thought and action, and significant progress has been made. Feminists are now widely recognised for their work questioning the 'ideal' of the family and household as beyond the concern and jurisdiction of public-policy makers, as a private space where development workers have no business to pry. Paying particular interest to events in the kitchen and bedroom, they identified and problematised profoundly unequal power relations between women and men at the level of the household, which affect and inform social relations beyond it.

Another main line of feminist enquiry and action has focused on recognising the links between what goes on within the household and its implications for women's participation in the 'public sphere' of production and decision-making. Feminist economists have criticised the lack of attention paid by mainstream economists to women's vast and uncounted contribution to economic growth, through the unpaid work of caring for the family, and for ignoring the link between this unpaid work and women's ability to engage in employment, income-generation, and other productive activities. Feminists have challenged received wisdom in many other areas of development, including the segmentation and stratification of the labour market, the dilemmas of reproduction and the controls exercised over women's sexuality and fertility (particularly in population policies), and legislation which precludes women's access to property. However, despite the widespread publicity given to these insights worldwide, it has been a long hard task for feminists located within development organisations to change the design of policy and practice in organisations.

The early 1980s saw an emerging critique of the assumption that NGOs with developmental aims, such as Oxfam GB, were more inherently 'virtuous' than the vast multilateral organisations, including the UN agencies and the international financial institutions (IFIs) (Tendler 1982). At its most simplistic, this stereotype had depicted NGOs as benign deliverers of development to marginalised people. From a feminist perspective, this stereotype has been further challenged: the majority of NGOs reflect 'male bias' as surely as other organisations, and, like them, have largely failed to 'deliver development' to women (Elson 1991).

Building on this analysis, feminist research into NGO policy and practice has paid increasing attention to organisations' cultural contexts, and their internal cultures; tracing how these organisational cultures are linked to procedures and personnel policies; identifying the problem of male bias in all these areas, and the extent to which this undermines women's participation and the perceived value of their contribution. There is a clear link between the participation of women and minorities in organisations, and the success of our work with women in communities. Transforming the lives of women living in poverty will not come about until the male biases inherent in our organisations are identified and addressed.

The articles in this book are Oxfam's contribution to this wider debate, making the connection between the work we do, and who we are. While some articles address these theoretical issues explicitly, others focus more directly on the practical experience of the authors. The many views of contributors to this book form a rich, diverse, and sometimes conflictual set of analytical case studies of the process of getting Oxfam 'right' for women.

Celebrating success and learning from failure

As we discuss later in this Introduction, even when they appear peaceful and unified, in reality organisations are rife with debate, dissent, and conflict. The book as a whole aims to capture good practice on gender issues in our development work, and within Oxfam's organisational structure itself. Many of the articles rightly celebrate successes. Authors from many different parts of the world confirm that gender does indeed 'work', and that Oxfam deserves much of its reputation for innovatory and inspiring work on gender over the years. For example, the article by Visha Padmanabhan tells of the transformation of an entire country programme from reactive technical fixes to a community-based development programme founded on values of equality between the sexes. On the other side of the South-North divide, Geraldine Terry discusses how gender analysis developed in the South is being used to enrich anti-poverty work in Britain. At an international level, gender analysis is used to challenge macro-economic policy through effective lobbying, as the articles by Lucy Muyoyeta and by Lydia Williams of Oxfam America show. Other articles present a more mixed picture, but nevertheless show real progress in the face of enormous challenges.

However, the book also includes articles focusing on what has not worked so well. In doing this, writing and editing this book is a brave (and some may say a rash!) attempt to meet another goal much discussed in development circles — that of organisational 'transparency', in the sense of giving details of failures as well as successes, in the interests of accountability to all who have a stake in our work. This is one of the more unusual elements of the book, and will, we hope, contribute to the development of better development practice both inside and outside our own organisation.

Key issues in this book

Continuous change: the gender perspective

Change is the context for all our work, and a central theme of this book. This book is itself a testimony to the hard work of many committed women and men who have engaged with the threats and opportunities presented by upheavals both inside and outside Oxfam, as well as the slower changes occurring in the wider context of societies in which we work. Writers show that change is both an opportunity for organisations to take on gender issues, or potentially an excuse for gender issues to be 'lost'. For example, as this book goes to press, a new way of working, using common 'strategic change objectives' is being introduced into Oxfam — and an explicit objective on gender issues has been included, despite suggestions from some that the struggle to integrate gender issues into our organisation is now complete. There will be other such moments in future.

On the plus side, change processes can represent opportunities to ensure that gender work remains relevant, innovative and challenging in development processes. Many of the articles here show how gender advocates have transformed themselves and their location to keep up with the constantly changing character of Oxfam and development work, bringing new and challenging perspectives to each 'era'. The current interest in networking and 'harmonising' the work of our organisation with that of others in the family of Oxfams has rejuvenated debates and analysis in each member organisation.

More widely, entering a dialogue with women's movements throughout the world has been an exciting and profoundly challenging process for many within Oxfam. Internationally, the women's movements have been enormously successful in harnessing change to positive effect; this work has brought about transformations in the thought and practice of societies in South and North. The activities of the international women's movement have provided vital support and inspiration for feminists like us working within development organisations as they cope with changing contexts within and outside their organisations. Together, we have engaged in a dialogue which is sometimes difficult, but always creative and challenging.

However, change also presents a potential threat. It is during processes of internal change, such as structural change or cutbacks in resources, that gender expertise and commitment to women's rights is often lost, or at least marginalised.

These changes are most often spurred on by unplanned changes in the external context, such as economic recession or a change of government, which oblige organisations to scale down or modify their activities; development agencies are no exception. Gender-sensitive development or relief work is endangered if gender-related work is seen an optional 'add-on' perspective, which is inessential in situations where resources are scarce. This is a fundamental misconception: good quality development or relief work must be based on an understanding of how social relations operate to disadvantage marginalised groups in society, including women. As Ines Smyth has observed elsewhere, 'insecurity has a personal dimension, in that it is experienced differently and to varying degrees by each individual. But it has also a structural dimension, since the overall conditions under which people live can eliminate or at least reduce such insecurity, or exacerbate it' (Smyth 1995, p.6). Development organisations which successfully work to promote women's rights and interests need to be part of the positive forces which assist women living in poverty to cope, and to harness change.

Some contributors to this book express a profound unease with the outcome of many recent processes of organisational change, viewing these as contrary to the values of feminism and gender equality. Oxfam has attempted to meld the 1980s trend to increased organisational 'professionalism' with the values of egalitarianism, altruism, and commitment to fighting poverty and injustice which have shaped its work since its inception as the Oxford Committee for Famine Relief in 1942. Some writers in this book see the gradual evolution of the specialised team at the centre of Oxfam — which started as an advisory unit formed on co-operative principles and re-formed as a team in a hierarchically-managed structure — as representing these changes in microcosm. Others disagree that there was ever such a 'golden age' of gender in our organisation. What is certain is that, over the past 15 years of Oxfam GB's formal engagement with gender issues, there has been an important shift in the way gender issues are understood and accepted in development work. The principles of equality between women and men, and working with women to promote their rights, have largely been accepted: attention has now moved to putting such principles into practice. Alongside this general acceptance of the principle of addressing the interests and needs of women, mainstream development practice has adopted concepts such as 'participation' and 'empowerment' which are also central to feminist analyses of power and transformatory change. These stress the need to ensure that marginalised groups can gain access to the process of development. However, while celebrating this general interest in the principles of participation and empowerment of communities, we should not lose sight of the fact that women in all social strata and contexts continue to experience poverty and disempowerment differently from men, due to gender-based discrimination.

The role of a specialist gender team

Experience in Oxfam, as in organisations of all kinds throughout the world, indicates that specialist units can be an effective focal point for innovative work on gender equity. While Oxfam has always worked with women, it began its formal engagement with gender issues in 1985, when a specialist unit was set up at head office; subsequently, it adopted and ratified a formal Gender Policy in 1993. A timeline of the 'chronology of gender' in Oxfam as seen from the head office is included at the end of this Introduction; in addition, Oxfam GB's Gender Policy is included as an appendix.

The gender-specialist unit at head office has offered mutual support to over-worked, beleaguered staff both within and outside the unit, acted as a 'task force' to lobby our organisation to take on a commitment to gender issues and put this into action, and has gathered knowledge and experience as a firm foundation for future action. At the same time, a specialist unit can become a ghetto, where individuals are isolated and their work marginalised. In this light, establishing such a unit can be seen as a token gesture on the part of an organisation which tolerates a rhetorical concern for 'women's issues' or 'women's needs', without taking on a real commitment to redressing the marginalisation of women in the organisation and beyond. Discussions in this book of Oxfam's gender-specialist unit is a contribution to this debate. The evolution of the Gender and Develop-ment Unit (GADU) to the Gender Team and finally into its present form, the Gender and Learning Team (GALT) has not been a pre-planned, linear trajectory.

Communicating knowledge and experience

Gender and development, as a political project, has always drawn inspiration from a wide range of practical experiences and academic disciplines. However, it is necessary to balance awareness of diverse voices and points of view, with the need to ensure effective communication through a shared language in order to effect political action (Udayagiri 1995). This book is a result of close communication between people from many backgrounds and diverse contexts. This diversity reflects the nature of many organisations like Oxfam, rooted in the history of Northern Europe or America, but which have evolved into organisations which straddle wide parts of the globe. We have included contributions that explore both the strengths and the challenges of this diversity, and the way in which personal identity can create challenges and opportunities for gender equality and empowerment. Varying in nationality and ethnicity, in class and in religion, in age and experience, they understand a commitment to gender equality differently.

While the terminology of gender and development is Northern, the principles are universal; as Chandra Mohanty (1991) has asserted, it is as a result of bias in communications, the media, and publishing that 'Northern feminisms' are known worldwide and Southern women's independent strategies of resistance to male domination have gone relatively unnoticed. However, our locations are not isolated or static. Engagement with issues of gender equality is informed not only by our own identity and context, but by international thinking and analysis, relationships both locally and across the globe with colleagues and friends, and media including newspapers, books and journals, television, radio, and the Internet.

Ensuring shared understanding of the different experiences in this book was a key issue for us, as editors of this multi-authored book. We recognise that we are ourselves guilty of using words such as 'gender' and 'feminist' imprecisely, and some articles highlight the difficulties presented by this constant slippage in terminology for gender and development work 'on the ground'. A related point is that this book attempts to bridge the 'languages' of theory and practice, and to draw on feminist perspectives as well as those from development studies. The complex interactions and the tensions between knowledge gained from others, and our own experience, as feminists and development workers, is evident in all the articles in this book.

Ourselves and our work

A constant theme in this book is the interconnection between the personal and the professional. Just one example of this is the number of articles included which analyse how women balance productive and reproductive work—both from the authors' own experience, and from that of the women with whom they work. While management theorists are now more widely recognising and appreciating the value of 'male' and 'female' qualities within the workplace, in practice women face both tangible and intangible barriers in their working lives. Who you are, and the responsibilities you carry outside your paid work, definitely do determine how you work and what you can achieve. The linkage between personal and professional is also present in the balance between thought and emotion in some of the articles. In many ways, the writers of this book are telling stories about their own lives, as well as about Oxfam's experience of working on gender. Thus, the articles here can claim only to be versions of events as their writers see it. The truth is that our Gender Policy has been, and continues to be, difficult and challenging to implement. Success and failures, and innovative work and resistance, co-exist.

Another point which resonates from the many contributions to this book is the importance of personal conviction and commitment of staff, including senior management, in ensuring that organisations turn their gender policies into practice. While this needs to be matched by consistent and coherent systems and procedures, it cannot be replaced by them. Personal commitment to the spirit as well as the letter of gender equality is the only means of ensuring that development for gender equity remains a political project.

The process of producing this book

From its inception, *Gender Works* has been seen as both a process and an outcome: the writing of the book has in itself helped Oxfam to take stock of its successes and failures in gender work. The book was conceived as a participatory project, and its outline was shaped by staff from across Oxfam's international programme, who were asked to suggest topics and potential writers, including themselves. Most contributions were instigated at this point, and others commissioned as a result of the debate which started between the editors and other staff members.

Many of the writers have never before recorded their experience in a formal manner, let alone been published; writing in itself has for many been a process of legitimisation of their experiences, and a consolidation of their thinking. Writing for publication is often a means through which commitments are made, both personally and for the organisation itself. In this way, the production of *Gender Works* is a recognition of the work of each writer, a record of their achievements, and a plea to learn the lessons for the future. For some authors, writing was a way of coming to terms with painful experiences.

This book is emphatically not a comprehensive record of Oxfam's work on gender, nor of the many women and men who have worked to make a vision of gender equality a reality within Oxfam and the communities with whom we work. There are many who could not record their stories for a variety of reasons. In particular, the pressures of over-work have been a consistent problem. One author apologised for being late with her final draft, because she had been overseeing emergency work after an earthquake in her region killed 10,000 people. Under such conditions, it is wonderful that this book exists at all. Time for thinking and writing simply is not available to most of the women and men working in development organisations. If we add to this the clash between the demands of our jobs and the other commitments to life beyond the office, it is not surprising that in many cases it had to be contributing to the book that has been squeezed out. We would therefore like to acknowledge the enormous contribution of those women and men who were not able to write for this book.

Conclusion

Gender Works is in no way designed to be the last word on gender issues in Oxfam: as stated earlier, it is clear from the diversity of contributions to this book that the route followed by different advocates for gender equality in Oxfam has been long, sometimes tortuous, and reflects very different ideas on how (and even where!) we should be travelling. There certainly has not been a linear evolution of a single set of ideas about how 'gender in Oxfam' should look, and how to get there — just as there is not, and never has been, one 'position' on gender equality. This book seeks only to be a modest contribution to a dialogue between ourselves in Oxfam, and other organisations and individuals aiming to change gender power relations, focusing on the work in which we all continue to be engaged. In deciding to publish the book, we recognise the importance of the continuous flow of information, experience, and understanding on gender issues between different organisations and individuals working in many different environments.

As we finish editing this book, we would like to acknowledge that however valuable and necessary it is to focus on our own organisation as we have done, this activity has its limitations. The achievement of gender equality in development is not simply a case of institutional learning and change. This book, and other studies of institutions from a gender perspective, can be a contribution to learning about the need for collective action of committed women and men both within and outside our own institutions, in a mutual effort to achieve development which is equal and just for all members of our communities. But we now need to broaden our gaze, away from a narrow focus on our own institutions and their work, to a wider view of the ways in which organisations must work together in different contexts to address women's continuing marginalisation from economic and political power. This implies recasting the terms of our work on gender to remind ourselves that it is a political project, involving people, commitment and power.

References

Elson, D. (1991), *Male Bias in the Development Process*, Manchester University Press, UK.

Goetz, A.-M. (1995), 'Getting institutions right for women in development', *IDS Bulletin*, Vol. 26, No. 3.

Mohanty, C., 'Cartographies of struggle: Third world women and the politics of feminism', in Mohanty, Russo and Torres (eds.) (1991), *Third World Women and the Politics of Feminism*.

Mukhopadhyay, M. (1995), internal paper, Oxford: Oxfam.

Rao, A. and Stuart, R. (1997), 'Re-thinking organisations: a feminist perspective' in *Gender and Development*, Vol. 5, No. 1.

Sen, G. and Grown, C. (1988), *Development Crises and Alternative Visions*, London: EarthScan.

Smyth, I. (1995), 'Gender, change and insecurity: theoretical issues and practical concepts', *Gender and Development*, Vol. 3, No. 3.

Tendler, J. (1982), 'Turning private voluntary organisations into development agencies: Questions for evaluation', Washington DC: USAID.

Udayagiri, M., 'Challenging modernisation: Gender and development, postmodern feminism and activism', in Marchand, M. and Parpart, J. (1995), *Feminism:Postmodernism:Development*, London: Routledge.

Timeline

1984	The Gender and Development Unit (GADU) is established, with a skeleton staff working on a co-operative basis.
1984	The staff network Action for Gender Relations in Asia (AGRA) is established.
1986	A strategy to sensitise staff at all levels through gender training is developed.
1988–91	National and regional policies are developed.
1989	Gender awareness is systematised in job descriptions, grant requests, procedures, and guidelines.
1990	GADU initiates a publishing strategy with books, newsletters, reports, guides, and so on.
1992	The Women's Linking Project — networking as a development tool — is introduced.
1992	GADU becomes the Gender Team, an advisory function, located in the Policy Department.
1993	Oxfam UK/I (now Oxfam GB) trustees agree a Gender Policy.
1993	The International Division Strategic Aim includes gender analysis as integral to programmes.
1994	Women's Linking Conference in Thailand.
1994–95	Twenty-three Oxfam country offices take part in preparatory process for the Beijing Fourth World Conference on Women.
1996	The Gender Team merges with the Programme Development Team to create the Gender and Learning Team (GALT).

I

The challenges of implementation

Introduction to section I

The articles in this section examine some of the many complex challenges faced by development workers who integrate a gender perspective into their work.

Much relief and development work is performed in a demanding external environment of crisis or reconstruction. There are particular concerns in these contexts for gender and development workers who seek to meet women's immediate, practical needs, and the longer-term aims of challenging underlying structural disadvantages facing women, which create these needs in the first place. In her article, Fiona Gell gives an overview of the challenges of adopting a gender perspective as part of Oxfam's international emergencies programme. Countering the idea that there is no time to address gender issues in situations of extreme need, she argues that the consequences of gender inequalities are often exaggerated in situations of upheaval and insecurity, outlining some key problems that arise specifically in emergency contexts. Some of the points raised by Fiona Gell concern the importance of genuine representation and accountability structures among populations affected by disaster. These points are developed further in Judy Adoko's article which focuses on increasing the degree and meaning of women's participation in decision-making, in the context of work with Sudanese refugees in northern Uganda.

Usha Kar's article has similar concerns. She asserts that, in the midst of the need to respond swiftly to life-threatening crisis, there are also opportunities for transformative development work, which should be built upon to pave the way for more gender-fair and just long-term development. Drawing on her experience as a programme representative for Oxfam GB in Bosnia, Usha Kar also focuses on a second challenge for gender and development workers: the contested, and contentious, nature of gender and development practice. Who defines a development outcome which is fair and just for women: the donor, local organisations, or women themselves? Which methods of work are 'correctly' employed to get there? In turn, Martha Thompson grapples with related issues in her article, drawing on her experience of working for Oxfam GB in El Salvador during the liberation struggle. She highlights some central questions about the relevance of a donor's concept of gender to a particular regional context, and what are considered as 'appropriate' modes of struggle in gender and development work.

In contrast to Fiona Gell's and Judy Adoko's examinations of what happens to gender issues when crisis creates a need for immediate life-saving action, Alice Iddi's article draws out the lessons from her involvement in a long-running development project in Burkina Faso. This project saw technical innovation, hand-in-hand with community participation, as the solution to development. The inclusion of women in the programme changed in nature considerably during the life of the project. Alice Iddi links this to the external evolution of women in development (WID) and gender and development (GAD) approaches to development. A key message in this article is that the approaches to WID and GAD are not static, or homogeneous, but dynamic, and sometimes contradictory. The aims of today's gender and development planners and practitioners have developed over the past 30 years, and are continuing to evolve now.

A different set of challenges is encountered by proponents of approaches to gender work developed in Southern contexts, when they try to apply them in the North. Geraldine Terry charts the progress of Oxfam GB's work in the UK in addressing the marginalisation of British women living in poverty from resources and decision-making power. As a new programme working in uncharted territory, the GB poverty programme aims to draw on Oxfam's experience in the international context for its work in the North, providing both challenges and opportunities for the programme.

Challenges for gender work are not only thrown up by the context of the work and by contested understandings of the concept of gender work itself. This section also contains articles which discuss the nature, and outcomes, of the divide between professional and personal commitment. As an issue of culture as well as economics and politics, the concept of gender challenges workers to a change of heart, as well as mind. It is almost impossible to find the vocabulary to discuss this link between the personal and the professional in our organisations, since our working lives are founded on the principle that there is a personal and professional divide, in a post-colonial era where we rightly think twice before challenging the innermost beliefs of 'others'. In her article, Maryam Iqbal looks back at her work in Sindh province in Pakistan, which laid the groundwork for addressing gender issues in Oxfam's development programme in the area. It is clear from her experience that her own identity and personal dedication to gender equality played a large part in her success in advocating gender sensitivity. Feleke Tadele's article focuses on his experience of working as a gender lead person in Oxfam GB's Ethiopia programme, and contributes his analysis of the additional challenges — and opportunities — of being a man working on gender issues.

Much ado about knitting:
The experience of Bosfam (Bosnia)

Usha Kar

Background and context

Although the crisis in Bosnia-Hercegovina broke out into the well-publicised open war in April 1992, internal debate in Oxfam GB delayed the establishment of an operational presence in the country. There were concerns that an Eastern European operation would drain resources away from the development and humanitarian aid programmes in Africa, Asia, Latin America, and the Middle East. Eventually, Oxfam did begin work in the former Yugoslavia, opening a field office in Belgrade, Serbia in April 1993[1] and in Bosnia-Hercegovina in late 1993.[2]

Tuzla, a town located in government-held territory in northeast Bosnia, was assessed to be a suitable base for the Bosnia programme, for a number of reasons. The local authorities upheld an explicit commitment to multi-ethnicity in the town: many Serbs had fled at the beginning of the fighting in Tuzla, leaving a Muslim majority, but an ethnically mixed population remained. Although under frequent shell fire, working in Tuzla did not expose staff to the consistent high levels of physical risk that Sarajevans underwent. Logistically it was feasible, though difficult, to operate from there, and to have tangible impact.

And needs were high: at that time thousands of people had been displaced by the fighting and by 'ethnic cleansing' from Eastern Bosnia into Tuzla Canton. The luckier ones had joined friends or relatives living in and around Tuzla, but many were housed in shoddy, hastily prepared 'collective centres' in schools, factories, and other inappropriately equipped public buildings.

Tuzla region was framed by three front lines. Tuzla town, the principal urban centre, was accessible only from the southwest. The fighting between the Bosnian government army and Bosnian Serb army forces in the nearby Majevice hills was often audible in the towns on either side of the line, causing fear and distress in the hearts of non-combatant relatives as they went about their daily business. To reach Tuzla safely involved journeying from the south through territory which was the subject of vicious and continued dispute between Bosnian Croat and Bosnian government forces. Importing goods into government-held Bosnia from the outside was difficult, sometimes treacherous. The blockade of the Tuzla region in the winter of 1993 led to rocketing inflation.[3]

For the general population, both local and displaced, in Tuzla region, the situation was desperate (as in other regions in all parts of Bosnia-Hercegovina). Everyone was affected by outcomes of the conflict although effects varied in their intensity according to the sex, physical ability, age, ethnicity, degree of displacement, and wealth of the individual.

Flour and oil and other staples, in desperately short supply, were imported into the town by international donors. As raw materials ceased to arrive and electricity supplies fluctuated, factories, coal and salt mines, and other production entities in the heavily industrial town and surrounding region closed down or reduced output to a minimum, creating widespread unemployment. Workers were kept on retainer agreements, those who were not mobilised working without pay (except for occasional humanitarian aid packages) on the understanding that they would have post-war employment.

Clothing factories, formerly major employers of female staff, closed down, reopening only for production of army clothing by workers mobilised to produce goods without wages. The ground floor of a factory near Banovici, previously a gynaecology/women's health clinic and crèche, was converted into a hospital for soldiers injured at the Front. The largely female work-force of this previously thriving business therefore lost their incomes, regular health checks, and child-care support.

Many men faced the fears, boredom, and dangers of life on the front line. Those from displaced families often spent their leave from the line in comfortless, poor housing separated from their families.

Unable to finance social services as well as the war effort, the Bosnian government ceased to prioritise education, health-care and social services in favour of military expenditure. Women's workloads increased as a result.

Where possible, women continued to work in their pre-war roles, whether professional, technical, or manual, as well as maintaining their domestic roles — cooking, cleaning, raising children. Their home-management workloads were compounded by increased nursing responsibilities, queuing, budgeting, economising, having to clean their homes without access to convenience products, and so on.

Poor women and men, often those displaced from rural areas, fetched water from springs and stand-pipes, and collected firewood from the hills around the towns. Without access to land and often lacking the formal skills or connections to enable them to compete for the rare waged jobs in the urban areas, they were particularly disadvantaged.

Urban residents, generally less affected than displaced rural people, also had to adjust to extreme changes in lifestyle. Not only electricity[4] but water supplies were drastically reduced. Candles lost any romantic associations, and washing machines laboured at unfamiliar times of the night as women leapt from their beds to switch them on when power supplies resumed.

When Oxfam GB began operations in Tuzla, thousands of displaced people were housed in 57 collective centres. Most of them had left their homes hastily with only the possessions they could gather up and carry with them. Sanitary facilities were inadequate, privacy was non-existent, and shocked, often recently abused and bereaved people slept on donated mattresses in overcrowded rooms. Physically fit younger men of 'fighting age' had been mobilised into the armies, taken prisoner, killed, or injured. Thus the vast majority of these displaced people were women, children, disabled people, sick people, and elderly men. Largely dependent on imported humanitarian aid for warmth, food, and clothing, they sought or awaited news of missing relatives, coped with the experiences of violent displacement and continued miseries of family separation, injury, and poverty, and faced the daily struggle to survive by queuing for aid packages or finding other sources of income or goods. This was compounded by continuing fear — of unending poverty, of continuous social disruption, of shelling, of losing relatives on the front lines or in detention camps, or losing children to shells while they were playing outside.

Oxfam's analysis and response

Oxfam identified isolated, displaced women as among the least powerful and living in the worst circumstances. In addition to daily fears and hardships, they bore the primary responsibility for support of elderly, young, disabled, and sick relatives, friends, and community members. Later, Roma people, especially women, were also recognised to be among the poorest and most marginalised in the community.[5] Disabled people, especially those disabled before the war or born with disabilities before or during the war, were also identified as intensely disadvantaged. A programme was developed to work with disabled people, later targeting disabled women to encourage their involvement in defining and managing the programme.

Many international NGOs were present in Tuzla when Oxfam arrived. In other countries Oxfam generally works with local counterpart organisations or groups, but in Bosnia at this time there were only a few identifiable local organisations. Thus Oxfam in Tuzla began an 'operational' programme with a concomitant, explicit agenda to support the development of local NGOs. The long-term aim was to fund local partners and leave sustainable local organisations behind.

The elements of the programme initially developed in some isolation from each other, with more coherence emerging as the programme matured. Contacts with associations of disabled people and ideas for projects and programmes supporting disabled adults, children and their carers were developed. Large relief-distribution mechanisms and programmes were also devised and implemented. After consultation with displaced women, funds were obtained in negotiation with UNHCR to establish 'knitting corners' in all the collective centres. This venture was founded upon the clearly expressed desire of women, particularly displaced rural women, to knit, an activity in which they frequently engaged before the war.

The knitting corners were to fulfil multiple functions. Primarily they were intended to provide displaced, vulnerable, or disadvantaged women with wool and occupation, to produce good-quality relief items for other poor people, and to promote an anticipated, though ill-defined, corresponding increase in the knitters' sense of 'well-being'. No indicators were set in advance, however, which made subsequent qualitative evaluation of the impact on women's lives difficult. The knitting project was broadly summed up as a 'psycho-social' intervention.

Other organisations in Tuzla were also supporting women through knitting projects under the category of 'psycho-social rehabilitation', although approaches differed. Psycho-social interventions were almost exclusively targeted at the displaced female population. 'Psycho-social' became a key phrase in applications to donors, although there was no consensus or working definition — inside or outside Oxfam — of its precise meaning. It is debatable whether 'rehabilitation' was a feasible or likely outcome, when the war and suffering continued as a present reality, with all the associated loss and misery. Semantics aside, though, the general idea was that through activity and mutual support (in some projects with additional formal individual counselling), people would identify and strengthen their own ways of coping with the difficulties they faced. Their sense of community, community networks, and support mechanisms that had been disrupted by displacement and loss would be rebuilt or replaced to some extent.

Eventually Oxfam obtained further funding from UNHCR to establish and open a programme of eight 'workshops'. Spread throughout Tuzla region, they were to offer alternative spaces in which women could gather.[6] Women could escape the overcrowded, stressed atmosphere of their collective accommodation and support each other through conversation and companionship while engaged, if they wished, in an activity — principally knitting. Workshop locations were therefore chosen for their proximity to collective centres. Women were able to gather there and exchange information with other women from other collective centres — which was vital in the search for missing relatives and friends and crucial for maintaining contact with wider developments in the war. Women from the local community and those housed in smaller privately-run collective accommodation were also encouraged to participate.[7] In response to the wishes and skills of the displaced women, the activity-base was broadened to include sewing and weaving, and the items produced were distributed as relief supplies.

Once the workshops were established, women brought finished knitted goods to them, were paid with wool, and given more to produce the next item; the items were distributed by Oxfam staff in liaison with local logistics centres. Eventually, workshop staff and participants organised the distributions themselves, drawing up their own criteria for prioritising recipients, and publicising the distributions. Knowing the recipient communities, they were able to identify those most in need.

The workshops quickly attracted a large number of participants, principally in the knitting scheme: 3,500 were involved after 6 months' operation, compared with a projected figure of 1,000. Workshop staff were largely drawn from the displaced community and were therefore able to influence the shape of the programme, informed by a genuine understanding of the needs and situation of displaced women. They encouraged the involvement of women living in the collective centres, many of whom were lethargic and depressed as a result of their displacement and the struggle for daily survival in inadequate communal spaces without independent sources of income.

Some questions and dilemmas

Oxfam's aim was to enable women to come together, and to give them some respite from the collective centres, in a supportive, companionable atmosphere where their children could be cared for in the 'children's corners'. The women themselves could be warm and drink coffee (increasingly becoming a luxury greatly valued as a symbol of the former quality of life), watch television or listen to the radio (for vital information about the progress of the war), knit, sew, weave, talk, and … and what?

Within Oxfam, it was periodically suggested that the activity-base should be phased out and the programme re-focus on providing advice, information, and advocacy services for women, encouraging them to redefine future gender relations. But programme staff who worked closely with participants insisted that women would not participate in such a project: the activity-base was the main reason for women's initial and continued participation, with company, coffee, and child-care all attractive bonuses. At this point in the war, they argued, women were primarily interested in earning wool as remuneration for their work, occupying themselves in a welcoming environment, and experiencing a sense of an altruistic satisfaction in making goods to relieve the poverty of others. No wool, no women.

This did not sit comfortably with ideals of empowering women to challenge gender stereotypes and transforming gender relations through programme work. There was a constant tension between the aspirations of the staff (mostly expatriates), and the aspirations often expressed by programme participants.[8]

The sensibilities of some Oxfam staff in Oxford and in the field were ruffled. Should Oxfam, an agency widely perceived as a leader in gender-policy implementation and gender analysis, not only support but *manage* a project so conventionally feminine in nature? The knitting programme evidently responded to women's expressed immediate, practical needs, but how was it to advance their strategic interests? Could women sitting, women *knitting*, really be considered an acceptable and appropriate Oxfam 'intervention' in fulfilment of its mandate to relieve 'poverty, distress, and avoidable suffering'? Could knitting enable women to move towards liberation and self-assertion, rather than reinforcing their traditional roles? In other words, did the programme have enough radical potential to bring about positive change in women's lives?

These troubling questions reappeared throughout the development of the programme. Yet, as Martha Walsh found after interviewing women who took part in the subsequent programme, 'Many of the women enrolled in the project are either widows or have male relatives among the missing. Desperately they wish to return to "traditional" family life' (Walsh 1996). Within the context of the war and their personal experiences, many women wished, above all, for unconditional reunification with their families. This very understandably took precedence over concerns for the transformation of society and of gender relations.

Beginnings of an organisation

The workshop programme, though popular and successful in terms of participation, production, and its original short-term aspirations, lacked longer-term objectives or direction, was totally dependent on continued external funding and thus unsustainable in the long term. Its dependence on wool for its main activity (costly even when bought locally) undermined its sustainability. There was not, at this time, any internal open market for the goods produced.

Aside from international agency staff, few people had spare cash to spend on hand-knitted or craft items. There was no realistic possibility of identifying and serving an export market. To some extent this short-termism in programme planning was inevitable, in a highly unpredictable political/ military context with heavy reliance on external donor funding, which was available in large quantities but for only for brief planning periods.

The vulnerability of the programme was dramatically underlined in early October 1994, when UNHCR announced that it would no longer fund international NGOs' programmes beyond December 1994. It would, however, consider funding local organisations to implement the same programmes.

The UNHCR decision coincided with a new confidence and team spirit among the workshop staff. Oxfam's Zagreb-based Regional Representative, who had developed many fruitful contacts with women's groups there and in Belgrade, had visited Tuzla and questioned the short-term aspirations of the programme. Her observations and discussions with participants and staff resulted in a visit by women from the Zagreb-based Centre for Women War Victims (CWWV). Courageously, two Croatian women travelled into Bosnia (at a time when the war was active and political relations between Croatia and Bosnia were strained), and led a two-week training course, sharing their experiences and training workshop staff in group-leadership techniques to provide group support for women facing particular difficulties in coping with their experiences.

These training sessions were a turning point for the programme. The workshop staff who day to day worked in relative isolation from each other[9] had their first opportunity to develop as a team, share personal and professional experiences and build their confidence in a supportive environment. Aside from their personal courage and dedication, the women from Croatia also brought the first war-time contacts with other women from the Former Yugoslavia, a glimpse of life beyond the confines of war, and the clarity of their vision. The training sessions concluded with a morale-boosting party with dancing — the first such occasion for many of the staff since the war began.

Following the CWWV training course, Oxfam in Tuzla assessed that the workshops' programme staff were ready and able to take a far greater role in managing the programme for themselves. Oxfam would support the process by helping to build administrative and management capacity. The end goal was an independent, sustainable organisation.

This decision coincided with UNHCR's decision to fund local organisations, and led to the first step — both legally and symbolically important — towards building an independent organisation. Workshop staff and participants met to choose a name for the organisation and began the complex process of registering as a separate legal entity.[10]

The first shock to some Oxfam staff, keen to see the programme progress towards independence and democratic self-management, was the women's choice, proudly announced, of the name 'Bosfam'. Walsh notes that 'Bosfam is actually short for Bosnian Family, an indication of the primacy of family life in Bosnian culture which was widely expressed …'[11] (Walsh 1996). The name, of course, compounded several meanings, not only reflecting Bosnian family values, the group's pride in their attachment to Oxfam, and their pleasure in the play on words, but also (despite their excitement and commitment to the idea of independence) their lack of confidence in their ability to act autonomously, despite Oxfam's assessment that the time was right.

From this point onwards, joint planning took place to develop staff and organisational capacities towards independence. Oxfam trained Bosfam staff and trustees in financial and narrative reporting to donors, equal opportunities principles, and strategic planning skills, facilitated networking with women's groups in other parts of former Yugoslavia, and gradually handed over decision-making and financial control. Core costs and a variety of activities were funded by Oxfam (until UNHCR became involved). Bosfam was encouraged to make needs assessments, write funding proposals and submit them to Oxfam as training for later applications to other donors to strengthen and diversify the funding base.

Thus Oxfam continued to fund knitting and sewing activities, while supporting Bosfam to plan ahead to explore possible routes to future sustainability. Crucially, Bosfam had to develop the confidence to take control of its own programme, and Oxfam was keen to avoid unnecessary interference in Bosfam's organisational decision-making.

Feminine, feminist, or frivolous fashion?

By early 1995, in addition to the daily activities and group-support sessions, Bosfam was tentatively taking more control over its own management and organising events such as *dernik* — celebratory cultural parties with traditional Bosnian food and dancing, organised and attended by hundreds of women   from collective centres throughout the region. In a growing spirit of creativity and a desire to demonstrate the participants' skills and achievements, Bosfam women developed new ideas and initiatives. The decision was taken to stage a glitzy, high-profile fashion show in Tuzla town — with funding support from Oxfam!

Oxfam in Tuzla faced a dilemma. It could justify funding a programme based on 'feminine' activity, ostensibly addressing primarily 'practical' gender needs, but could it reconcile itself to funding an event that could even be interpreted as *contrary* to the advancement of women's strategic gender interests? The fashion show might be seen as reinforcing conventional prejudices about women's pre-occupation with their physical appearance, their excessive interest in fashion, and other frivolous diversions.

Preparations began. Against the backdrop of a freezing winter, with a sporadic cease-fire in place, and young men shivering in their positions in the hills until the spring, a date was set for the show. Bosfam issued invitations not only to women from the collective centres and local women, but also to local dignitaries, the press, representatives of international NGOs, local TV stations, and so on. A venue was reserved in the Hotel Tuzla. Frantic knitting, sewing, weaving, cooking, and other activities ensued.

Senior Oxfam staff, visiting from Oxford, were invited as guests of honour. One later remarked:

> While appreciating the invitations, we almost *begged* them not to send a copy of the video to Oxford! Who knows what people at home would have made of Oxfam funding a women's fashion show… On the one hand we wanted Bosfam to become independent of Oxfam, and on the other we were rather worried by all this.

Oxfam in Tuzla faced a second dilemma. Even if funding a fashion show was considered inappropriate, a funding agency must accept that if a newly created organisation is to be truly independent, it may get co-opted or go off on tracks contrary to, or at least not entirely in line with, the organisational principles and aims of the funder. At what point is it appropriate to withdraw support funds? How can the development of democratic decision-making structures within a new organisation be encouraged, if the funding agency then effectively vetoes a collective decision by refusing to fund the activity proposed?[12]

Preparations continued. Finally, despite reservations, Oxfam funded the fashion show. Fiona Gell, Deputy Country Representative at the time, recalls:

> It was incredible and fantastic, a sort of glittering parade, in total contrast to all the gloom outside. Shells still pounded the wrecked city intermittently. But inside Hotel Tuzla something else was going on. In the Crystal Ballroom, which had seen no gathering or celebration since the start of the bombardment, the Oxfam-funded fashion show was underway. Young refugee women, ground down by bereavement and violence, their futures bleak and hopeless, were striding up and down a catwalk, tripping up and down playfully in silken evening dresses and gorgeous woolly jumpers. The atmosphere was bursting with self-confidence. They were lovely, exciting, sexy, had the audience rapt.
>
> The place was packed, with the buzz of local people, families, friends, staff, political leaders; even the Mayor of Tuzla was there; everyone was welcome. A local band boomed rock melodies, the atmosphere was electric — a great show.

The event involved women from all corners of Bosfam's work. The garments were designed by Bosfam and Oxfam staff, made up by women in the workshops, and displayed by modelling students from the Youth Centre. Different groups were brought together to help survive the emotional horror of war.

In the Crystal Ballroom I learned the meaning of 'psycho-social rehabilitation'. (Fiona Gell, personal communication 1997)

Some outcomes

The fashion show was a huge success, and attracted enormous local attention. It was a uniting and morale-boosting experience, not only for the women involved in staging it, but also for the audience and local community. It established Bosfam's independent name and reputation as a Bosnian women's organisation. It celebrated and displayed some of Bosnian women's traditional skills. It created opportunities for Bosfam to begin to move towards income-generating as well as psycho-social activities.[13] In one evening, this celebration of 'feminine' skills significantly advanced the development of Bosfam as an organisation. The training and organisational development work that had begun was accelerated by the spirit of common accomplishment and pride that was established. The planning of the event had utilised and developed women's skills in publicity, promotion, financial management, managing media and public relations, and massive organisational co-ordination. Far from being perceived locally as a conservative product of 'feminine' activity, the show was interpreted by a prominent local politician as a reflection of Bosnian women's determination not to accept fundamentalist restrictions on their freedom to dress as they pleased, and to unite with women from different ethnic groups.

Contrary to the expectations and concerns of some external observers, Bosfam, which was based on 'feminine' activities, epitomised in the staging of a fashion show, and addressing the very immediate and practical needs of women, was an organisation strengthened and encouraged by the success of these activities. The outcomes of this essentially 'feminine' activity also strengthened the organisational identity.

Conclusion

The supposed transition that takes place from practical interests to strategic interests through feminine and feminist activity respectively is explored in Walsh's paper. She hypothesises that this is too simplistic an analysis to 'capture the interplay between women's identity and agency' (Walsh 1996).

> Feminine/feminist rubrics, which have been widely applied to characterise women's organisations and movements, tend to envisage women's empowerment in terms of the realisation of their strategic interests through the politicisation of their practical interests. (Walsh 1996)

The danger in using such 'binary constructs' (Walsh 1996) is of automatically assuming that 'feminist' activity is superior to 'feminine' activity and women's 'strategic gender interests' more important than their practical needs, when women themselves may weight the importance of these differently according to the changing context in which they live. It was meaningless to emphasise 'strategic' interests at the expense of practical needs or 'feminist' rather than 'feminine' activity and organisation, in a context where women's daily struggle was about basic psychological and physical survival. This was particularly the case when such values were not rooted in the women's own analysis and experience of their situation. Interventions designed without listening to women's analysis and identification of their own needs, whether practical or strategic, are likely to be inappropriate and unsuccessful in their own terms.

The Bosfam example illustrates that while traditionally 'feminine' activity is often seen as retrogressive, the time, place, and context of a project determine the degree to which it is able to be (or should attempt to be) transformative. In the context of Tuzla in early 1995, the fashion show arguably furthered Bosnian women's strategic gender interests. In another context it might well have undermined such interests.

Oxfam learned that it is counterproductive to push women towards activities considered suitably 'feminist' or 'strategic' according to predetermined, imported, abstract, and subjective definitions and measures, unrelated to the local culture, and to a community's own values and understandings. Interventions must be paced according to what is actually happening in women's lives, encouraging but not forcing the building of confidence and identification of goals. The training provided by representatives of the Centre for Women War Victims was a successful example of one such intervention which created opportunity for women to explore new approaches and ideas in relation to their social context and the continuing war, without imposing a pre-set agenda on them. 'Empowerment' is wholly dependent on the situation, experiences, emotions, and motivation of the women involved, and, while encouragement can be given, women cannot be accelerated to a state of 'empowerment' by an external agent.

As the war continued, when the peace agreement was signed, and as the uneasy peace unfolded, Bosfam developed and responded to the changing situation and consequent changing needs and aspirations of its female constituency. It has evolved into one of the leading Bosnian women's organisations and continues to grapple with challenging issues faced by many emergent organisations.

Bosfam has expanded into activities which more explicitly address women's practical needs and their strategic gender interests, with projects such as literacy and vocational training courses,[14] a women's advice and information centre, income-generating and marketing activity, and (with a sister organisation, 'Zena 21') the organisation of a women's conference 'Women Transforming Themselves and Society'. Bosfam has also taken a prominent role in advocating with and on behalf of the families of men missing from Srebrenica in eastern Bosnia.

In July 1996, on the anniversary of the Srebrenica tragedy, Bosfam and the Association of Women from Srebrenica organised a high-profile public meeting to ensure that international attention remained focused on their situation. Powerfully and poignantly, the venue was adorned by thousands of hand-embroidered cushions, each bearing the name of a missing person. While Bosfam's activities are increasingly based on 'feminist' strategies of building women's capacities in decision-making and taking control over their lives, the organisation continues to gain strength from, and to be rooted in, its base of 'feminine' activity.

About the author

Currently Regional Programmes Manager for Children's Aid Direct in Asia and Eastern Europe, Usha Kar has worked in community development, tourism, refugee-reception programme management, and as Country Representative for Oxfam in Bosnia 1994–96. She holds an MA in Gender Analysis in Development.

In her early years she harboured a deep dislike of knitting, owing to the interruption of her television viewing by the clacking of her mother's and sister's needles, and her own inability to succeed in the craft. Her attitude mellowed in later years when, following the death of her father (from a small town in central India), she witnessed her mother (from a small town on the Norfolk coast in England) knit her way through the crisis. Final conversion came in 1995, during convalescence after a car accident in Bosnia, when she managed to produce a single fluffy bootee. She is 37 and single, and the bootee has yet to come in handy!

Bibliography

Hastie, Rachel (1997), *Disabled Children in a Society at War*, Oxford: Oxfam.
Huremovic, Damir (1996), 'Independent Sector in Bosnia-Hercegovina: A Personal View of the Sector', unpublished draft.
Walsh, Martha (1996), 'Beyond Feminist and Feminine: Unpacking Women's Initiatives in Ex-Yugoslavia', unpublished dissertation.

Men in the kitchen, women in the office? Working on gender issues in Ethiopia

Feleke Tadele

In this short article, I attempt to assess the opportunities and constraints that exist for men who work on gender issues. In particular, I wish to share my own experience as a man employed by Oxfam GB in Ethiopia. I particularly examine the challenges and the opportunities that I have experienced over the last four years, during which time we have formally engaged in the promotion of gender issues in development projects and the formulation of gender strategies and policies.

Oxfam GB began its field operation in Ethiopia in 1974; the operation was scaled up after the famine of 1984–85. We presently run programmes which address three key issues: food security and livelihoods, civil and human rights, and social-service provision. We aim to promote gender equity across all these three areas of work. In 1997, we started to develop a women's rights strategy to use during the next period to 2000. The Addis Ababa office has begun the process of training its staff in the tools of gender analysis, and attempts are being made to incorporate gender-related aims in routine objective-setting and work-planning. Beyond Oxfam, there are opportunities to address gender-related issues in Ethiopia, in the policies and programmes of government and non-government organisations.

In comparison with many other African countries, statistics on gender-related issues look bleak in Ethiopia. Despite their equal share with men in socio-economic life, Ethiopian women have little decision-making power and a smaller share of resources and benefits. Eighty-seven per cent of women in Ethiopia are engaged in agriculture, contributing about 50 per cent of income based on subsistence agriculture (UNICEF 1993). However, little attention has been given to involving women in rural development efforts and enabling them to benefit directly from agricultural extension services. Girls make up only 33 per cent of school enrolments, and the drop-out rate is very high. Among educated women who work in the formal labour force, only 11 per cent have management posts, and most are engaged in manual and clerical jobs. The average number of children born to Ethiopian women is currently estimated at 7.7 (CSA 1993), and the rate of contraceptive use is about 4 per cent among women of child-bearing age (CSA 1993). This is a very low rate in comparison with other African countries such as Kenya (23.2 per cent), Botswana (29.7 per cent), and Zimbabwe (32.2 per cent).

Such statistics offer compelling evidence for the need to work on gender-determined power relations and to promote women's rights. Such work has begun, at least in theory, at government level and within the NGO sector. Ethiopia has a national gender policy in place, and women's desks have been established within various government departments. A number of local and international NGOs have been encouraging debate and the development of subsequent action to address women's needs. However, at present, these policies are still a long way from succeeding in delivering their goals of affirmative action by a strong women's movement, one that is able to address gender issues effectively. In the past, women's organisations been part of the state political apparatus, and a civil movement has not yet become apparent.

Some people still associate women's issues with the negative experiences under the socialist regime in Ethiopia. The Revolutionary Ethiopia Women's Association was established at a national level during the revolution in the mid-1970s. Despite the association's effort to promote projects which directed resources at women, more attention was given to the political position of women. As socialism rooted its philosophy in the question of class struggle, gender issues were considered only as a factor that contributes to class differentiation. 'Power' was the main question, and radical change for women's position was promoted. As a result, there is a popular perception that some women abused their rights within their families, trying to achieve a radical exchange of roles with their husbands. This is believed to have included rejecting the role of child-care, showing disrespect for existing family rules, and spending too much time at political meetings away from home. The current interest in gender relations is thought by some people to be no different from those days. Working on gender issues is therefore difficult, because some think that the same things are being propagated in a different format, as part of the new political agenda in Ethiopia. In relation to this, there is a tendency to assume that the women who work in the gender movement are 'Westernised', with a weak relationship with their culture and religion. This, it is alleged, is proved by their 'lack of commitment' to going and working with rural women. Working with urban middle-class women's groups and organisations is considered fashionable, or Westernised, and irrelevant to the 'needs' of grassroots women.

The comparative rarity of women employed in the workplace in Ethiopia makes it particularly noticeable that one sector — gender issues — is dominated by women. In the Ethiopian context, women's educational opportunities are low, and this practical constraint on women's employment is a major reason why the vast majority of formal-sector posts go to male employees. In 1997, Oxfam itself had 70 staff in Ethiopia; only five were female, and one of these was the expatriate Director. Yet, because people assume that gender is a women's issue, it is assumed that a post concerned with gender should be filled by a woman. The overall scarcity of educated women in paid employment, and the fact that gender is seen as a women's issue, can lead to a ghettoisation of gender concerns.

My own experience works against this trend. I started to work as the contact person on gender issues four years ago, as part of my responsibilities for advising Oxfam's Ethiopia programme on community development and civic/human rights. I was happy to accept the responsibility for gender work, for three reasons. First, as a sociologist, I believe that gender inequalities in Ethiopia are mostly the result of the norms and values with which our society defines the roles and responsibilities of women and men. Action to redress this problem is, therefore, the duty of sociologists like myself; and this action is the responsibility of both women and men. Second, in my view little attention has been given to the task of involving Ethiopian women in development initiatives, and enabling them to benefit from such programmes. Thus, I feel that my action on gender issues could contribute to increase the involvement of women. Third, NGOs like Oxfam GB and its partners, given their resources and commitments, are among the main agents working for the promotion of women's rights. Hence, my position within Oxfam means that I am in the right position to act.

Opportunities and disadvantages for men who work on gender

One advantage for me as a man working as a lead person on gender is that my responsibility gives me dual positions in debates on gender. I speak both as a man — a gendered person — and as a 'gender specialist'. Provided that men recognise that gender issues the ways in which power relations between women and men are played out, it should be obvious that they are as close to the issues as women are. I am in a good position to influence the attitudes of other men. Pragmatically, my identity as a man can be used to further the agenda of women's rights, as I am likely to be listened to by both women and men.

Another pragmatic advantage of being a man working on gender issues in Ethiopia is that, at the current time, men do not face the same problems as women face in jobs where they are required to travel extensively in remote areas, sometimes alone. I wish to emphasise that this does not mean that women staff do not travel; but that, due to a mixture of cultural and practical factors, there are constraints on women's mobility at work. First, most educated Ethiopian women are still chiefly responsible for domestic affairs, so women are expected to fulfil their responsibilities at home. As a result, women find it difficult to travel for extensive periods away from home. Many find themselves limiting their work to that which can be done around their home areas. Second, even if a woman is well educated, when she travels out alone she has a greater chance of being harassed than men. We know that these issues are two of the reasons that explain why women are less likely to apply for posts in rural projects than in urban ones; and, as the statistics indicate, Ethiopia is a country where rural development initiatives are a very significant part of NGO work. The majority of women who do apply for employment on rural projects are either single, divorced, or widowed; the married women who apply tend to live in the specific project area.

However, pragmatism apart, men also face significant disadvantages when working on gender issues; my role as a gender lead person has not been as easy as I was expecting. The main challenges I have encountered are outlined below.

The first challenge comes from the fact that women and men experience gender relations so differently. As stated above, gender issues are misunderstood and assumed to be the same as women's issues, and working on gender is therefore assumed to be a woman's job. Thus, many women take it as a joke when they see me in meetings and discussion forums. Even if a man is sympathetic to the cause of gender equity, and has knowledge of the practical and theoretical issues, he may encounter prejudice from those who feel that, since women lose most through gender-determined disadvantage, only women can sense the real issues and can plan necessary changes properly. Some may perceive men who are interested in gender issues as simply joining the gender specialists because gender is a fashion, and it is advantageous to be part of a new movement. These people see development organisations involved in gender issues as simply taking advantage of funds offered for gender-related activities, and individuals working on gender as following a lucrative career path. For some, this is certainly true. Some 'women's' and 'women-oriented' organisations use the current concern for women's rights and gender issues to their own advantage to gain funding, by using the rhetoric only. In my work I often find local NGOs which note gender issues a key concern; some even derive the name of their organisation from gender and development terminology, calling themselves names such as 'Organisation for Women and Development', 'Aid to Women', 'Forum for Women', and the like. As a representative of a Northern funding agency, one faces challenges when one starts to consider partnership with such organisations. In these organisations, the number of women engaged on the board or in senior management positions is very small; sometimes almost non-existent. When one attempts to analyse the organisation from a gender perspective, ask about more action on gender equality in planned projects, or suggest that more women should be recruited to the organisation, those at the top of the organisation often take it as a real threat to their power. In this way, one discovers that they are not committed or serious about the issues.

Another challenge comes at a personal level. Some people, particularly men, question one's own gender identity. They think that if a man works on gender issues, he must lack a strongly 'masculine' identity. Ironically, the other side of the coin is that if a woman performs the same role, some men will question her gender identity. Because of her pioneering position, she may be seen as a protester, revolutionary, or a woman who has excluded herself from her culture. It is inevitable that gender work has a significant personal dimension, and we cannot reverse entrenched attitudes on the roles of men and women overnight. Our work can only hope to create an enabling environment, where some perceptions are changed, and the ground paved for more work tomorrow.

For instance, in the case of *injera* (Ethiopian bread) baking, this is a duty which is entirely assigned to women. However sensitive I am to gender issues, and however committed my wife is to achieving gender equality, in our cultural context, I feel I am prevented from doing the baking. Instead, I sit with my wife and hand her the necessary materials for baking. This might sound amusing or irritating to people who do not know our cultural background, but this is in itself a big shift of role, as compared with my father, who has never been in the kitchen. I am sure that in future our son will share responsibility with his wife more fairly, having been socialised differently by his parents (and of course improved technologies will make the baking business simpler for everyone). Here we can see that there are practical as well as cultural constraints which mean that men find it hard to work on gender issues at a personal level, and that linking one's personal experience into one's professional work becomes difficult.

Finally, there is an issue about ideas of power-sharing. Just as some men consider gender to be a 'women's issue', some 'gender-aware' women consider gender movements only from the view-point of women reversing traditional roles or gaining power over men. In my experience, most gender-sensitive men, including myself, feel that gender work should bring equity between women and men. It should not be a process that ultimately creates a different set of power-losers and power-gainers. Men will find it difficult to work on gender issues if women assume that men should be working for their own immediate loss of power, as women gain in power. Instead, both women and men need to be persuaded that gender equity would mean the equal participation of men and women in decision-making.

Conclusion

In the foregoing sections, I have attempted to assess the opportunities and constraints that exist in working on gender issues as a man. I have stated that, while there are relatively few women in employment in Ethiopia, the posts that they do take are often the gender-specialist posts. Only a few men deal with gender issues as their prime responsibility in Ethiopia. There are some good reasons for employing men, from a pragmatic perspective. However, only a few women consider that gender issues could equally well be addressed by men and women specialists. Some women I have encountered also allege that if a man works on gender issues he may intensify male power over women, in the sense that women will be perceived as having to speak and act through a male advocate, unable to defend or extend their rights by their own efforts.

However, as other articles in this book argue, gender is about power relations, not about women's status and needs only. Experience teaches that if women alone work for greater equality in gender relations they face difficulties. If positive changes are to be achieved in gender relations, women, especially the prime movers in the movement, should be convinced that men can play a positive role. As development workers, we can conclude that if we are working towards gender equality and development, we have to exert a greater effort to win the trust and better involvement of men.

About the author

Feleke Tadele is a sociologist and an anthropologist by profession. He has extensive experience in community development, participatory development, gender analysis, micro-finance, and civil-rights issues. He is currently manager of urban programmes for Oxfam GB in Ethiopia.

References

Central Statistical Authority (CSA) (1991), 'The 1984 Population and Housing Census of Ethiopia: Analytical Report at National Level', Addis Ababa.
CSA (1993), 'The 1990 National Family and Fertility Survey', Addis Ababa.
National Office of the Population (1994), 'Population Situation in Ethiopia and its Impact on Major Socio-economic Sectors', Addis Ababa.
Oxfam UK/I (1996), 'Strategic Plan for Ethiopia: 1996–2001', Addis Ababa.
Oxfam UK/I (1996), 'Women's Rights Strategy', Addis Ababa.

Gender concerns in emergencies

Fiona Gell

It is well recognised that the needs and interests of women and men differ in times of peace; but that they perhaps differ more during periods of emergency, disaster, and conflict is less acknowledged. In addition, women and children make up the majority of refugees and displaced people, and the proportion of widows and female-headed families is significantly higher in this population. They are often particularly disadvantaged in disaster situations because they are likely to be vulnerable to increased physical and sexual violence, to lack resources to fulfil their reproductive roles in the family, and often to lack the support of men to help provide for the family. Gender relations can shift and change rapidly during emergencies, and both women and men often have to come to terms with new roles and responsibilities almost overnight. Emergency responses can either ignore these gender dynamics and risk further marginalising women, or address them by putting gender at the heart of assessment and planning processes. If this is done, women not only benefit from immediate practical support on an equal footing with men, but their longer-term interests can also be safeguarded.

Oxfam GB's mandate is to alleviate distress and suffering through emergency work as well as to reduce poverty through development work. Its 'one programme approach' attempts to integrate a range of development, emergency and advocacy programmes. The Gender Policy, agreed by Oxfam GB in 1993, was one of the first tools which attempted to ensure the application of Oxfam's thinking on gender across the whole range of its work, including emergency response.

The urgency, the political complexity, the large number of organisations involved, logistical constraints, and the high turn-over of specialist contract staff in emergency work, mean that these programmes are implemented in a top-down manner. The pressure for rapid response is intense, not only for humanitarian reasons but also because of media pressure and competition for funds. This is particularly so in acute emergencies: the urgency of limiting mortality and morbidity tends to focus the response on technical solutions, such as setting up water treatment and distribution systems, building shelters and latrines, or distributing food and clothes. However, these strategies will only reduce morbidity and mortality across the population if they are based on some degree of social analysis. This does not imply the need for detailed socio-economic research, but it does require a broad understanding of the following: the demographic profile of the population; the roles played by women and men in the family and community; who has access to and control of what resources; and coping mechanisms employed by women and men to survive.

In the early 1990s, while there was widespread acceptance that gender sensitivity was crucial to effective and equitable development work, the debate on the importance of gender roles in emergency work was little developed. The question then was: is gender a concern that can and should be dealt with in emergency situations? In the last few years the debate within Oxfam has moved on. There is now an awareness that if an emergency response is planned without regard to gender relations, the inequalities between women and men are likely to be deepened. Women's vulnerability can actually be increased, their status further eroded, and their capacities diminished rather than enhanced. The question we are now asking is: given the importance of a gender sensitive approach to effective emergency work, how do we analyse and address gender issues?

The employment of Gender Advisers as emergency support staff who are deployed rapidly to the field from Oxfam's head office has provided one mechanism for promoting good field practice on gender and pushing forward institutional learning. As one of the two Emergency Gender Advisers recruited in 1994 I travelled, over the course of two and a half years, to diverse emergency situations in West Africa, South America, South Asia, and Eastern Europe. Many of the examples used in this article come from that experience, attempting to capture some of the key lessons that Oxfam has learned on gender and emergencies over the past few years.

Key issues and responses

Representation and participation
In order to maximise the impact of emergency programmes across a population, you must ensure that women and men both get access to resources, which means consulting women as well as men from day one. This is often a challenge under the

constraints of emergency conditions. It is particularly hard to find the space to talk to women alone. Women may lack access to public forums, lack the necessary negotiation or linguistic skills to participate, or simply be over-burdened with the daily business of sustaining their families. Their needs are often invisible, unless emergency workers make systematic efforts to identify and listen to women from all sectors of the population, and to find ways of working with them.

It is not only a matter of asking women and men about their immediate practical needs, but understanding who the population is, and how gender dynamics have changed during the emergency. Disaggregating demographic data by gender is essential, as well as looking at the distribution between women and men of roles, authority in the family and community, skills, and access to and control of resources.

Much of this information can be gathered by talking to key informants and grassroots leaders, through group discussions and participatory[15] exercises with representative groups, or from local experts or researchers.[16] Clearly certain concerns cuts across social groups: for example, disabled women will have different concerns to both able-bodied women and disabled men, as they may have to cope with marginalisation on two accounts and may need particular support to ensure their access to the benefits of relief interventions.[17] Working through existing or newly formed women's groups or committees is an effective and practical way of engaging women; it also helps to strengthen women's organisation and collective voice, and to rebuild their support structures.

Strategic concerns of women and opportunities for change

It is often argued that emergency situations are not the proper place for attempting to reassign gender roles. In fact, it is often precisely during emergencies, conflict, and social disruption that opportunities emerge for women to take on new roles, learn new skills, and assume positions of influence at the level of the household, the community, and nationally. The absence of men during a war often means that women assume traditionally male roles in the family and community and gain entry to the public sphere. During Peru's civil war, thousands of women organised in Mother's Clubs to distribute milk for children, and many of them went on to assume positions of authority and leadership in their communities. Taking on new functions, the Clubs lived on long after the distribution of milk had ended.

The organisation of women to manage distributions of clothing and household items in emergencies often acts as a building block for the development or reconstitution of a women's community organisation which goes on to address longer-term concerns and tackle issues of gender inequality. In the northern Bosnian town of Tuzla, such a group developed among displaced women from various regions; it later became the independent NGO 'Bosfam' (see Usha Kar's article in this book). In Sino County, a conflict-stricken area of Liberia, Oxfam worked on a distribution with the Sino Women's Association (SWA) who, before the arrival of international agencies, had provided poor families with food from their own resources. SWA worked with Oxfam to register displaced and disabled people and identify women leaders across Sino County — who were hiding in the bush, having fled the fighting — and then to facilitate a large distribution of clothes and soap. The relief programme encouraged SWA to increase their membership, to better organise themselves, and to strengthen their leadership and as a result, when Oxfam was forced to leave the area due to an upsurge in the conflict, SWA continued with the distributions themselves.

The strength and solidarity built up between women in this way during emergencies can also contribute to peace-building and reconciliation. The Union of North Caucasus Women, through whom Oxfam distributed clothes to Chechen families in the war with Russia in 1995–96, played an important role in peace-building. Not only did they monitor the abuse of human rights and directly challenge military leaders, but in a March for Peace, Chechen mothers whose sons had died in the war marched together with Russian mothers who had also lost their sons, in a public demand to end the war.

When peace or normality returns, women often face the difficulty of how to retain the gains they have made, and they face pressure to resume the typically patriarchal relations of the status quo. Aid agencies can play an important role in supporting women so that they do not slip back into old patterns of vulnerability, by recognising and supporting their new areas of skill and authority, and their organisations. These will afford women greater control over their lives and increase their capacity to insure both family and community against future crisis.

Vulnerability to violence and the protection of women

Although men may also be subjected to sexual violence, the vulnerability of women to this form of abuse is widespread and frequently reported during emergencies. The war in Bosnia was a tragic example of how rape is increasingly used as a weapon of war: a means to control, violate, and terrorise women into submission. Women and young girls who lose their source of income, as a result of displacement or loss of home and possessions, are often forced into sex work. Those without the protection of adult males in refugee camps may be forced to pay for adult male labour with sex. In camps for Sierra Leonean refugees in Guinea, I met single mothers desperate for adult male labour to help construct their houses, as only those who could prove their refugee status by constructing a house were entitled to receive food rations. With no source of income to buy labour, and with hungry children to feed, these women were extremely susceptible to sexual coercion. It is not infrequent that camp officials, whose mandate includes protecting women, actually abuse them, and that men responsible for distributions demand sex in return for rations.

Oxfam attempts to address these issues in its technical programmes, first of all by talking directly to women, without any men present. Wherever possible, we try to implement food distributions through women directly into the hands of women in order to reduce the risk of sexual harassment, and to provide water and sanitation facilities at a safe distance from camps. These choices are not always easy: latrines which are lit or placed too close to the camp can either protect or expose women. Shelter for female-headed families and widows must also be provided in a way that protects rather than isolates or exposes women.

Emergency situations can sometimes provide new opportunities for women as they find new positions of influence in the community. As gender roles begin to shift, giving them more authority and control, they may face a violent backlash from men who feel that their power is being usurped. Women may also face increased violence within the home, as men struggle to cope with the indignity and frustration of enforced inactivity, and the loss of authority, earning capacity, and their ability to fulfil the role of provider. If agencies' interventions are based on sensitive consultation with both women and men, they can help to reduce these tensions.

The loss of public and private space

The loss of home and private space, and the over-crowding which often occurs in disaster, can cause acute stress and sometimes danger for women and girls. Dealing with menstruation can become problematic and stressful. In Sri Lanka, urban women displaced to rural areas are concerned for the safety of their daughters who now have to leave the vicinity of the home to wash during menstruation. Oxfam is helping these communities to construct menstrual shelters where they can wash in privacy and safety away from the home. Men are also affected by this loss of private space. In Ingushetia, a state in the Northern Caucasus, the cultural taboo on contact between a married man and his parents-in-law was threatened by displaced families having to crowd into one-roomed accommodation in shelters, causing some men to spend all their waking hours outside the home.

On the other hand, women also struggle to survive if they are confined to their homes in emergency situations. In Taliban-controlled areas of Afghanistan, women are struggling not with the loss of private space, but with the loss of access to the public domain. As part of their strategy of control in their struggle for military and ideological supremacy, this extremist Islamic militia has imposed severe restrictions on women's participation in the public domain. Women are in the main confined to their home, and education or employment outside the home are banned; as a result, social networks are breaking down. Those women who do not have adult male relatives employed outside the home have few means of financial support, and used to survive on bread rations distributed by the World Food Programme; when the Taliban decreed that women could not even go to aid agencies pick up relief goods and bread, but had to send male blood relatives, those without adult male relatives were seriously threatened.

Supporting women's domestic/reproductive role

The reproductive work of women (provision and preparation of food, collection of water, health of children, and so on) is usually where the impact of disaster and displacement is first felt. With the loss of home, women may lose cooking equipment, washing, food and water storage, and bedding. Water sources are likely to be further away, and may involve queuing for long periods; fuel and cooking pots will be scarce; it may be necessary to queue for food rations; camp environments can be hazardous for children. The time involved in this reproductive work — and the stress involved in doing so under the emotional burden of having lost possessions, home and perhaps family — increases enormously. Men often face the opposite problem, a lack of work, in situations of displacement. They rarely take on much of the burden of reproductive work, and resources and opportunities may not be available for finding productive work, especially if they have lost land, equipment, and capital. They often suffer from boredom and a loss of sense of worth, which can lead to anti-social behaviour, and increased levels of violence.

The way that relief programmes are organised can either help to overcome these problems or exacerbate them. If men are given responsibility for distributing food, clothes, and household items, but women have prime responsibility for their management at the household level, women's control over their situation is diminished. Women are often bumped out of distribution lines through violence or sexual harassment; pregnant, lactating, or elderly women may have difficulty waiting in long queues. Single mothers are often at a disadvantage as they may be unable to leave their shelters to collect relief items. If they rely on men to bring rations to them, they may be short-changed. If women are in charge of distribution, they have better access to information about their entitlements, are better able to arbitrate in disputes, and are more aware of those women who are being denied access. Consulting men on the siting, design, and management of water sources where women are the main managers of water at household level is unlikely to result in tap stands of an appropriate height, containers of an appropriate size, or mechanisms for community control of the water source which are suitable to women. Working with men to establish mother-and-child health clinics may result in arrangements which do not suit the daily routine of women who are most likely to take children to clinics. Much evidence suggests that the distribution of resources through women, and their involvement in planning, is likely to be more equitable and effective than through men. Many of Oxfam's programmes now have clear mechanisms for distributing relief items through women directly to women.

Supporting women's productive role and economic rights

During an emergency, the number of households primarily or exclusively dependent on women's labour for survival is likely to increase. This places an additional burden on women at a time when they are experiencing emotional and economic stress. Relief and rehabilitation interventions can provide opportunities to support both women and men in their productive roles. It is crucial that women as well as men be able to benefit from these opportunities both in the short-term (for example, digging wells and latrines), and in the long-term (through employment with aid agencies, technical training, credit facilities). They may need special social support (such as child-care facilities) or economic support (for example, through gaining legal ownership of land) in order to be able to take advantage of these opportunities.

There are three important factors in ensuring that production work benefits both women and men: understanding the sexual division of labour in the population; having implementation teams made up of both women and men; and closely monitoring the gender dynamics of the process.

A distribution of seeds and tools in Liberia addressing a food security crisis in an isolated rural area clearly exemplified this. An analysis of the sexual division of labour in rice production had found that women and men made separate farms but helped each other with gender-specific tasks: men cleared land, women planted and weeded, and both harvested. While produce from the women's farm was mainly exchanged for goods, that from the men's farms was mainly kept for planting the following year. We therefore understood that seed rice had to be distributed to both women and men. Although we knew that about half the farming population were women, the number of women arriving at the distribution point was far lower than men. When we monitored the percentages of women in the population, of women registered as farmers and of women collecting seeds and tools, we discovered that a high percentage of women had not been registered. They had not been informed or were busy caring for the family during registration, and of those who had registered, many did not go to the distribution point because, as they said, 'only male farmers had been called'.

The root of the problem was that there were no women on the registration, distribution, and community mobilisation teams. We called in the Sino Women's Association, who were busy in the area identifying displaced and disabled people for a distribution of clothes, and the word quickly went out to women through the networks they were building up.

Another example comes from the Peruvian Andes, where Oxfam was helping displaced people who were returning to their rural homes after many years of civil war to regenerate their agricultural production. In the first phase of the project local NGOs (heavily dominated by men) distributed seeds for cereal and potato crops for which men are responsible, and distributed llamas to men to restock the community herd. Women's needs, roles, and areas of expertise in animal husbandry and agricultural production had not been considered — yet 40 per cent of the returning families were thought to be headed by women. They had actually become passive recipients of a rehabilitation programme entirely managed and controlled by men. Consultations with women clarified that they needed support for their own area of expertise, which included raising small livestock such as guinea pigs (a traditional source of protein in the Andes) and chickens to support the household economy through the rapid rearing of high-protein animals with a short life-cycle. A new phase of the project addressed these and other concerns of women directly. The project did not aim to work exclusively with women, but to work through women's organisations so that there was a strong nucleus of women from both local NGOs and communities managing the process. In this way, the women's 'petty cash' (small fast-breeding animals) and the men's 'strong safe' (large slow-breeding animals) comple-mented each other, both of their coping strategies were strengthened and the whole community's food security was improved.

The pressure on women's time is an important consideration. If women take on new productive roles without any change in the sexual division of labour, they may be no better off. In the Peruvian example, women suggested that they could save time by replacing manual grinding stones, which only women used, with mechanical grinders that men were prepared to use. Mechanical grinding stones were distributed and the transference of domestic labour from women to men freed up women's time for productive activities.

Humanitarianism versus women's rights: a new dilemma

One of the complex questions facing both Oxfam and the international aid community today is how to respond to the plight of women living under Taliban rule in Afghanistan. When the Taliban took over Kabul in September 1996, they abolished women's rights to education and employment. The impact on the lives of urban women, many of whom were well-educated, professional women, was devastating. Oxfam felt unable to continue its community-based programmes in Kabul as it no longer had access to women workers or women beneficiaries. While the level of humanitarian need in Kabul is evidently high (chronic poverty, poor public health, virtually non-existent state services) programme work in this context would mean working through men rather than women, and being unable to ensure that women benefit from the programme; it would also signal an acceptance of the Taliban's abolition of women's rights.

International agencies debated the dilemma in many fora and responded in a variety of different ways. Oxfam felt that the most effective way in which it could address women's long-term strategic needs was to support the recovery of their rights to education and employment through a sustained programme of witnessing and influencing: witnessing the impact of the restrictions on their lives and trying to encourage change. Our work switched focus accordingly and we took a strong public stand against the Taliban policies on women, which continues today. We suspended our community programme, although we have remained ready to intervene with emergency response in the case of life-threatening circumstances. The Taliban have presented us with a situation in which the principles of the humanitarian imperative and women's rights have clashed. There are no easy answers, and together with the international community Oxfam continues to struggle to identify and develop the most effective response.

Some conclusions and a look ahead

There is still a long way to go to ensure that a gender perspective is systematically incorporated into all emergency programmes. This chapter has identified some insightful and creative responses to addressing gender inequalities, sometimes on the back of mistakes made and lessons sorely learned. An awareness of gender issues in emergency work is certainly growing, the debate on how to implement programmes in a gender sensitive way has been stimulated, tools have been developed and tested, and efforts are being made to develop minimum standards. There is at least a widespread recognition of the basic requirements for a gender-aware response.

Increasingly, we need to be raising the issue of gender in emergency work at policy level between agencies and funding bodies. We need to continue to search for common mechanisms to set and follow minimum standards and best practice guidelines on gender, and to train emergency staff accordingly. Sustained advocacy work on women's rights, particularly on their right to protection from violence, must support our humanitarian response. Our local partners' gender awareness must continue to be stimulated, because they are the ones who most often have to scale up their capacity to respond to disaster: gender-insensitive development work will breed gender-insensitive emergency work. And finally we need to continue to monitor and evaluate our emergency work with a gender perspective, and to document and share this across programmes and cultures. Gender-aware responses in emergency work remain an enormous challenge, but one that we ignore at great cost to the lives of both women and men.

Endnote

Much of the work on gender and emergencies on which this article is based has been done by Oxfam's Gender and Learning Team, its Emergency Department, and by individuals in the field. In particular I would like to acknowledge the contribution and support of Bridget Walker, who is responsible for much of Oxfam's internal documentation on the subject and who edited the 'Women and Emergencies' edition of *Focus on Gender* (1994, Oxford: Oxfam).

About the author

With a background in development and anthropology, Fiona Gell joined Oxfam GB at the end of 1994 and worked as a Gender and Representation Adviser in the Emergency Department until 1997. She has worked in various emergency situations around the world, concerned particularly with issues of gender, social diversity and community participation. For the past year she has been Programme Management Assistant on Oxfam's South Asia team with a particular focus on the complex emergencies in Afghanistan and Sri Lanka.

Gender in times of war (El Salvador)

Martha Thompson

Introduction

When members of the Association of Salvadoran Women (AMS), one of Oxfam GB's counterparts in El Salvador, went out to hold a workshop on gender with women in a co-operative in San Miguel on the southern coast in 1988, they noticed that the men were hanging around the building, listening to them through the open windows in the adobe walls. When they finished the workshop, one of the AMS women started to talk with the men outside and asked what they thought about what they had heard. The men hemmed and hawed and finally, several admitted that they had been worried. When they had heard that women were visiting from San Salvador that day, the men had been afraid that the AMS visitors were going to teach the women in the co-operative that if their husbands hit them they should hit them back. 'But you didn't say anything about that,' said one of the men, 'so it's ok for you to come here.'

This incident reveals the kind of thinking which was typical for many of Oxfam's counterpart organisations in El Salvador during the war; work with women that focused on the imbalance of power between men and women was seen as potentially divisive, and threatening. The deeply rooted social, political, and economic injustice in El Salvador had finally erupted into civil war in 1979. The brutal 11-year war, fought between the Farabundi Martí Liberation Front (FMLN), a socialist revolutionary force with significant popular support, and the government and military trying to maintain the status quo which was biased in favour of the élites, claimed 80,000 lives (mostly civilian), displaced half a million people, and forced 800,000 to flee the country.

Oxfam's programme in El Salvador before and during the war focused on strengthening the popular organisations in their work for structural change. These grassroots organisations from the marginalised sectors — farmers, co-operatives, unions, slum-dwellers, women, displaced, returning refugees, and human rights workers — were allied with the Catholic and the progressive Protestant churches and a group of progressive Salvadoran NGOs.

These groups, including the co-operative organisation which the AMS visited, generally shared a common analysis. They believed that the conflict had its roots in the dramatically skewed distribution of economic, social, and political power in the country. They defined their work as transforming both structures and themselves into agents for change. The men in this community were committed participants in a process of transformation, based on a class analysis formed from their own experience of powerlessness and victims of violence, but which did not include the specific need to transform the underlying roles of men and women.

This was in many ways a strategic choice. The war and the government repression were the defining parameters of everyone's life. Gender analysis — an analysis which saw gender as integral to overall oppression, and women's oppression as rooted in the unequal power relationships between men and women[18] — was not seen as instrumental in the task at hand. During the war, most of our counterparts were under extreme and constant harassment by the government and military which saw them as subversive; many members of these organisations were arrested, tortured, harassed, and often killed. Their priorities included surviving the war, dealing with repression, and organising against it. As a consequence, none of our counterparts considered gender inequality to be the central injustice in their lives, although some women's groups saw it as one of the inequalities they were dealing with. Most counterparts saw the inequalities based on gender relations as a Northern concern, and not one of their priorities.

This is not to say that women's groups did not exist, with their own agenda for change. El Salvador had a long history of women's organisations, many of them part of progressive churches or parishes. Many of these groups disappeared due to the widespread government repression against the popular movement from 1978–83. Ironically one of the first groups of the popular movement to re-form and take to the streets in 1985 were the Mothers of the Disappeared. By 1988 there were several women's organisations, including a women's labour union, the Movement for Salvadoran Women (MSM), the Institute for the Union of Women (IMU), the Coordination of Salvadoran Women (CONAMUS), and the Association of Salvadoran Women (AMS). Most of their work was based on an analysis of the obstacles women faced as a result of the skewed political, economic and social situation in El Salvador, the war, and the repression. They focused on getting women together to talk about their problems, provided counselling and set up some income-generation projects. Only IMU and CONAMUS began to integrate feminist thinking into their work, but stopped short of actively raising the matter of power imbalance between men and women within the popular movement, or making gender inequalities the central axis of their work. During the period of extreme repression, there was a strong current among people in the popular movement, particularly the leadership, to see any 'special interest' groups within the movement as secondary and potentially divisive.

Gender becomes an element of Oxfam's programme

Oxfam, and other funding agencies with a long history of work in El Salvador and with close ties to the popular movement, began to include elements of gender analysis in their programmes in the late 1980s, during the latter half of the war — a time of upheaval and transformation. Our development of gender work in El Salvador was greatly influenced by the context described above. This paper is my reflection on the process by which the funding agencies introduced gender as a programmatic element in their work in El Salvador, the difficulties posed by the context and the mistakes we in the funding agencies made. We learned many lessons through this process, including which problems were due to the situation, and which were made worse by our own attitudes.

As a project officer in El Salvador from 1988–92, and part of the regional Oxfam team for Mexico and Central America, I was an active participant in that process. By 1995 Oxfam GB had decided to incorporate gender work into all its overseas programmes. As in many other agencies, Oxfam's field staff in Central America offered some resistance, because we perceived gender as a theme imposed by the head office, not raised by our counterparts. From 1985 onwards, Deborah Eade, the Deputy Representative, pioneered work on bringing an understanding of gender issues to the regional team in Central America; but for many years, team members held a range of opinions on what emphasis should be given to gender analysis.

Mistakes made

Given the tendency to live from day to day in an emergency or a situation of conflict, the civil war was not an easy time to introduce gender work. This difficulty was even exacerbated by the fact that in my opinion, we in Oxfam made four basic mistakes in trying to incorporate a gender analysis into our work.

The first mistake was to throw money at the issue without understanding the analysis of gender inequalities and deciding how best to address these through our work and that of our counterparts. Most of our counterpart organisations in El Salvador, with the notable exception of IMU and CONAMUS, also knew very little about gender analysis, other than that Northern funding agencies kept mentioning it. Unfortunately, we were bringing it up with dollar signs written all over it. The word 'gender' attached to a project increased the probability of its being funded. Funding agencies told counterparts that they had money for gender projects, and of course, the counterparts (no fools they) soon produced lots of 'gender projects'. One colleague remarked that if we could only get projects with women collectives planting trees we would be able to cover both gender and environmental issues.

Local NGOs without a real understanding of gender analysis often guessed it had to do with women's development, and they would write up projects to train women in tailoring or baking so that the women could set up micro-enterprises. Many funding agencies went along with these projects because they needed to include a certain number of 'gender projects' in their programme to gain the approval of head office.

The second mistake is interwoven with the first: many agencies saw gender inequalities as an issue of funding rather than awareness. We did not really understand gender analysis, nor how it might 'fit' with the context in which we and our counterparts were working. The discussion was not about whether or not women had particular needs, but about how gender could inform the overall analysis of the struggle for social transformation and the pressures of war and repression. Yet even more experienced women's organisations were proposing work that focused much more on class analysis and the immediacies of war than on gender analysis. Rather than fully explore the tension between the gender analysis and class analysis, we settled for an uneasy compromise which included continuing with our work as before, but incorporating several additional measures under the general rubric of addressing gender inequalities. These included enhancing women's opportunities or improving their situation, supporting the five or six women's organisations in the popular movement, expressing concern for women's needs in projects with mixed groups, and trying to ensure that our work did not affect women negatively.

In common with most funding agencies, we in Oxfam did not really incorporate gender concerns into our class analysis; nor did we make gender inequality one of our priorities during the war. By limiting our own education on gender concerns, we did not emphasise education on gender as a way of starting the discussion with our counterpart organisations. If we had introduced a gender analysis into our programmes through broad discussion with our counterparts and with local women's organisations before we began to fund 'gender projects', I believe that we would not have contributed, as we did, to the distortion of the concept.

Since many of us did not understand gender analysis, we did not necessarily explore other experiences of introducing a gender perspective into development work in other parts of the world. When we in the Oxfam regional team began to discuss gender issues in our team meetings, it would have been particularly helpful to have information on how gender work had been introduced into other programmes working in conflict situations similar to that in Central America in the late 1980s. It would also have been very useful to look at experiences in other societies in transition, where funding agencies introduced gender concerns into the work of counterpart organisations which saw their role as leading a process of social transformation, and which had not previously seen gender analysis as key to that transformation.

The third mistake the agencies made was not to recognise the gains which women had made during the war; nor did we understand how transformation of gender roles could be integrated into the general process of social transformation. Women had gained an impressive visibility during the war: they were in the leadership of the FMLN, in the leadership of sectors of the popular movement, and in the organisations that repopulated the conflict zones. Many of those killed and revered as models of courage and commitment were women. As the war progressed, women played an increasingly important role in defending their communities. When the military entered the community, the women would gather with their children, and confront the soldiers, planting themselves in their paths, challenging them, and reproaching them for their actions.

The most dramatic change in women's roles outside the armed movement was visible first in the refugee camps and then, from 1987 on, in the communities which repopulated the conflict zones (many of which were composed of people from the refugee camps.) Women were elected to community councils, and trained as health-care, education, and human-rights workers. Most importantly, not only were they given the training and opportunity to take on these new roles, but the communities also created support systems to free them from other work. Because they were supported by funding projects, these communities often had running water near the house, there was a guaranteed supply of food, there were child-care centres, and there was access to health-care. As a result of the relative security, these communities grappled more closely with the differences between men's and women's roles than the agencies, which tended to assume that because women were taking on new roles, becoming leaders, and gaining recognition, gender issues were being addressed. In many ways this was a gender work laboratory, but we did not study it closely enough.

We failed to realise that the root of all this change in gender roles was not an analysis of gender relations or a questioning of the division of power between men and women. The root was the condition of war, the needs of the community, and women's willingness to take part in a struggle with which they identified. At the end of the war, when the struggle for change no longer required that women assume these roles, women were supposed to relinquish them for 'the greater good', just as they were supposed to assume them in the first place for 'the greater good'. That notion of the greater good, however, was not cynical or shallow. The members of the popular movement (both men and women) were deeply committed to a valid idea of change that was both personal and political.

It was precisely the validity of the popular movement's struggle in El Salvador, reinforced by the exigencies of working in an environment where one's colleagues are in constant danger of being detained, tortured, and killed, that made funding agencies reluctant to force the issue of gender equality with counterparts. During the war, funding agencies' work depended above all on the level of confidence their staff were able to develop with local counterparts, and most of them saw concerns of gender as either not at all important in the context of the war, or as potentially divisive. In a war, transparency is often seen as a threat to security. A discussion of gender roles would ultimately create conflict between people in the popular movement, and men were afraid that conflict would lead to a contest of leadership and differences of priorities. Our fourth mistake was not to risk the relationship with our counterparts by pushing the discussion.

Lessons learned

Change is not a straight line that goes from A to B in a synchronised sequence of events. It is made up of many strands moving at different rhythms, intertwining, and bending back on each other. The funding agencies' mistakes in approaching gender issues impeded their ability to discuss with partners how a gender analysis might be fully integrated into programmes. However, our emphasis on women's projects, and on support for women's organisations, set processes in motion; willingly or unwillingly, we all learned from those processes. Gender work that was clearly flawed (in an extremely difficult context) still provided lessons which helped many of us to understand gender relations in El Salvador better.

In some cases, women taught us by pointing out how small details of projects created problems because of gender roles. For example, one project funded by Oxfam was a revolving credit fund for fertiliser in the war zones of the province of Morazan. The highly successful project enabled the 27 communities which had repopulated the war zones to buy fertiliser to grow subsistence crops. The communities themselves managed the project, and people could pay their loan in money or in produce. I had checked several times with the leadership whether women had equal access to the loans and they showed me women's names on the registers. On one visit, I stopped in an old woman's house to avoid the rain and we chatted about her participation in this project. During the discussion, I realised that she, like all elderly women and single mothers with young children, could not cultivate by herself, and hired men to do so. They usually ended up paying a third of the harvest to the worker and a large part of the remainder to repay the loan. The problem was not access to the benefits of the project; but for women, access to those benefits was not sufficient to solve problems related to their gender.

This brought home to me the importance of disaggregated data in looking at beneficiary communities. 'The community' is not made up of a series of identical individuals. Ensuring that projects benefit women equally must go beyond simply checking that men and women receive the same benefits. One must take gender roles into account, which determine how those benefits can be used.

Looking for gender projects to fund, as a way to integrate gender into a programme, obscures the fact that funding is not necessarily how one promotes a change in thinking, and a change in thinking is the beginning of gender awareness. I realised this when I attended a community meeting in one of the repopulated villages in Chalatenango. The community had taken the decision to take responsibility for those women abandoned by their husbands. If a husband left his wife and children and took up with another woman, the community would give the family food from the common harvest. Everyone tended both their own plots and the common plot to provide food for those who could support themselves. The men who were staying with their wives and children were complaining about the burden of supporting abandoned wives and families and proposing that the community reduce the food allotments, when one of the abandoned wives got up to address the crowd. She scolded the men for blaming the women and children and said that the problem was not their fault, but caused by the men who had left their families. She argued that a man who had abandoned his family and lived with another woman in the community should be obliged to divide the harvest from his plot between the two households. This woman had never been to a gender seminar, but she had an acute grasp of the gender issues involved in the abandonment and their relationship to the community's good. In a few sentences she elevated the abandoned women from objects of pity and charity to people who had the right to a share of the goods produced by the fathers of their children.

For me, it is humbling that neither the woman's intervention nor her proposal had anything to do with funding a project. If funding agencies were trying to support the development of gender awareness in counterparts, this example showed that raising people's consciousness, facilitating awareness, and providing education were more key than funding for 'women's projects'. Doing the former meant putting a lot of creative time and energy into talking to counterparts, building links with other women's organisations, looking for educational materials, and promoting seminars or exchanges. Some people did that, but they had to do it over and above the rest of their work. Most of us, myself included, often felt too many other conflicting priorities to put in that amount of time. It was an investment that did not necessarily result in projects, or funding work.

Steps towards change

As stated earlier, an analysis of gender relations in El Salvador had begun to emerge in the Salvadoran women's organisations during the war, although they had made a strategic decision to prioritise class over gender analysis in their work as part of the popular movement. In 1987, several women from Salvadoran organisations participated with other women from countries in Central America in a gender workshop in Mexico, held by the Mexican women's organisation CIDAHL. Leaving the everyday hardship of the war enabled Central American women involved in political and military struggles to overcome some of the isolation caused by their national contexts. For the Salvadoran women it was key to have the opportunity to discuss with other women engaged in political struggles the tensions between their commitment to a political struggle and their concerns as women which they felt were not being addressed in that struggle. As a result of the 1987 workshop, the Salvadoran participants invited the Mexican women's organisations to do gender training of women's groups in El Salvador.

It took until the end of 1990 for the five or six Salvadoran women's organisations in the popular movement to incorporate fully a gender analysis into their vision and try to address gender inequalities as the primary focus in their work. These women's groups faced a very difficult choice: if they tried to push for the inclusion of gender issues in the platform of the popular movement, they would be accused of dividing the popular movement. The more the women insisted, the more they were in danger of becoming estranged from other groups. If they desisted, none of their concerns about gender would really be addressed. In the polarised society of those years, to abandon the popular movement would have left the women's groups completely isolated, without the solidarity, connections, and support that had helped all the groups survive the war. Most women's groups tried to find some compromise and not bring the discussion to a breaking point. Most believed that gender issues would be dealt with when the war was over. Even so, some of the women's groups, particularly CONAMUS, took their work on gender inequalities further in 1990 by introducing violence against women and women's health as key themes in their work.

In 1990–91, a new women's organisation was formed by women with a long-standing political commitment to change, *Mujeres para la Dignidad y la Vida* (Women for Dignity and Life) or *las Dignas*, as they were popularly called. As 1991 progressed, they played a strong leadership role in the women's movement; in many respects, *las Dignas* were bolder than the older women's groups in placing gender issues on the table within the popular movement. The stronger they became, the more they clashed with the political leadership of the popular organisations. 1991 was a pivotal year for the popular movement, because the Archdiocese of San Salvador called together different sectors of society to discuss the divisions in Salvadoran society and to formulate proposals on different issues to be addressed in the peace process. The national debate was a way of making the voice of civil society heard in the peace negotiations between the government and the FMLN. In the section for women's issues, the women's groups came together to formulate common proposals and began dealing with how to raise some gender concerns within the popular movement.

At this time, although the women's movement was becoming more active and raising gender as an issue to be discussed seriously in the popular movement, one sector was conspicuously absent in such debates: rural women. Ironically the most visible changes in women's roles had taken place in the rural areas, in the war zones; yet the membership of the Salvadoran women's organisations was basically urban or led by urban women. Although the women's groups all had rural outreach activities, this never resulted in a significant representation of rural women or their concerns.

When the war ended on 1 January 1992, everything seemed to change so fast that the familiar world disappeared before the new one was built — so many of the skills which people had developed to deal with the war seemed useless in peacetime. Three factors accelerated the way in which Salvadoran women's organisations began to succeed in prioritising a gender analysis. First, the FMLN did not incorporate any gender awareness into their electoral agenda but insisted that the women's organisations garner support for the overall FMLN political agenda, rather than push their own. Many of the women's organisations began to question the worth of subordinating their concerns and needs to the overall political plan once again, because the argument for putting aside possible divisive issues for the common good had lost its immediacy with the end of the war. Second, women who were ex-combatants in the FMLN were re-integrated into society. Some of them joined the women's movement and provided both a new energy and a political legitimacy to challenge the leadership of the FMLN on issues of gender equity. They could not be easily dismissed since they had carried weapons and had lived and fought in the mountains for years. The third factor was that roles had changed for many women during the war. Although those women had taken on new roles because they felt that the struggle in which they were engaged demanded it, this did not imply a fundamental shift in gender relations; their experiences had simply changed them.

A particularly clear example of this was the case of women in the repopulation communities in the war zones. They had played a very important role in their communities because they had had particular opportunities for training in refugee camps, and chances for leadership due to the shortage of men. These communities needed women to assume leadership roles and consequently took on some of these women's domestic responsibilities such as child-care. When men began returning to these communities to take up their familiar roles, these women did not want to relinquish their responsibilities. These women had gone through a transformation process, had discovered new capabilities ; they could not just retreat to their pre-war domestic life. One woman said to me, 'My companion wants me to go back to gathering firewood and washing corn as if I never carried a gun or worked as a radio operator or participated in an attack.'

As 1992 wore on, the frustration of the women's movement was exacerbated as many did not see that positive changes, a better life, and more justice, were forthcoming very quickly after all the suffering and sacrifice. On the other hand, the danger that had made the popular movement work in unity had abated. People were no longer getting picked up in the night, offices were no longer bombed, communities were no longer being attacked. Unity was no longer so essential to survive. From 1992 to 1993, the changes in El Salvador made it easier for the women's organisations to redefine their commitment to the overall political struggle. Women began to feel new confidence in raising their concerns, and the number of women's groups multiplied. They began to speak on all kinds of issues from a strong and independent gender analysis, and entered into painful and difficult debate with the leadership of the popular movement and the FMLN. The possibilities to develop gender work took on new and wide horizons. By 1995, the Salvadoran women's movement was completely different from what it had been in 1988, in terms of its breadth, depth, the issues it addressed, and in the underlying analysis, the number of organisations, and their approaches.

Concluding reflections

The work on gender by funding agencies in El Salvador during the war posed several questions for reflection, because the war imposed real limits for developing this work. The agencies made some real mistakes, most of which were rooted in our lack of deep understanding of gender relations in El Salvador. Linked to this, we would not or could not really integrate a class analysis and a gender analysis in a time of war and in the face of resistance from partners, or lack of a clear direction from Salvadoran women's organisations. How can funding agencies try to introduce strategies of work that are not seen as priorities by the actors in that situation? How can funding agencies promote gender analysis before women's organisations in the country have made it a fundamental part of their work? Indeed, how can funding agencies introduce strategies without the power of money distorting the work? I believe that the Salvadoran experience shows that until counterparts themselves prioritise an issue, it is hard for the funding agency to develop real work on it. The truth is that funding agencies can push their own agendas because they have the money to do so, but the possibility of producing any real change is limited.

It is significant that the opportunities the Salvadoran women's organisations had during the war to learn about gender and reflect on it were locations physically removed from the war, such as Mexico. I am struck by a dichotomy: when the popular movement in El Salvador was strong, the development of gender work in member organisations was very weak; it became much stronger in the post-war period, when the popular movement was weaker. I feel that, in funding agencies, we have a long way to go with our counterparts to hammer out an integration of class and gender analysis in the middle of a war.

About the author

Martha Thompson is a Canadian who began working in Latin America in 1979. She holds a MPH in International Health and worked in Mexico and in Honduras from 1983–86. In 1986 she went to work in El Salvador for Catholic Relief Services, and later for Oxfam GB. She became Oxfam's Deputy Regional Representative for Central America and then worked as a consultant on refugee repatriation in Guatemala. In May 1995, she began her present job with Oxfam Canada, job-sharing with her husband Minor Sinclair the post of Field Director for the Caribbean, based in Cuba.

Bringing it back home:
Gender and poverty in the UK

Geraldine Terry

A brief history of Oxfam's poverty programme in Britain

Oxfam GB decided to develop a poverty programme in Great Britain (GB) in 1995, after over a year of action-research and internal debate. It was a momentous step; apart from a small grants budget for anti-poverty organisations in and around Oxford, this was the first time Oxfam GB had turned its attention to poverty and social exclusion on its home ground. The decision was taken for a number of reasons, the most important of which was the increase of poverty and inequality in Britain and the moral imperative to respond. We also increasingly recognised poverty as a global issue, cross-cutting traditional divisions between developed and developing countries. Some of Oxfam's partners in the South were questioning why Oxfam GB was working to reduce poverty abroad but not in its home country. Consultation with British anti-poverty organisations suggested that Oxfam GB, with its extensive international experience, had something unique to offer them. Oxfam could help to introduce an international perspective on the causes and effects of poverty, and facilitate learning from the anti-poverty work of its partner organisations overseas; in particular, some British anti-poverty organisations were recognising that communal self-help approaches developed in the South might be useful in the British context too.

The programme views poverty in several different ways. There is no doubt that *absolute* poverty — material deprivation — exists in Britain, and is on the increase, although the problem is not as widespread as in many other countries where Oxfam works. Every day people go hungry in Great Britain, and every day thousands sleep on the streets. Many more people, however, suffer from *relative* poverty. Being poor in an affluent society creates its own, non-trivial, problems, such as how to make sure your children have a balanced diet if the only shop selling fresh vegetables is an out-of-town supermarket which can only be reached by car. Relative poverty also has damaging effects on psychological well-being, health, and even life-expectancy. The concept of social exclusion, developed in Europe, is also important in the British poverty discourse. It tries to capture the way sections of the population are barred from society's mainstream through discrimination, early-life disadvantage, lack of resources, and other handicaps.

Oxfam GB's national programme was started in 1996. At first the emphasis was on building partnerships with organisations working at the national level, but soon a regional programme was initiated in the north of England. Here, the focus is on working with grassroots anti-poverty organisations. De-industrialisation in the region, as a result of economic globalisation and unsupportive government policies in the past, has produced long-term mass unemployment, poverty, and a plethora of related problems such as poor health, crime, and high levels of drug abuse among young people. A programme is also now underway in Scotland. Eventually the Poverty Programme (GB) will work with local anti-poverty organisations all over the country, while continuing its existing work with lobbying and campaigning bodies and coalitions at the national level.

Working on gender in a post-industrial, comparatively rich country is a new challenge for Oxfam GB. On the other hand, as staff search for ways to incorporate gender into the new programme from scratch, they benefit from ten years of institutional experience. The idea of 'learning from the South' — in terms of concepts, strategies and practical initiatives — underpins the whole programme, although it remains to be seen how much of Oxfam GB's experience of gender work overseas can be transferred directly to Britain.

Women, men, and poverty in Britain

Women are over-represented in many of the social groups affected by poverty and social exclusion in the UK: lone parents, the low-paid, elderly people dependent on means-tested state benefits, and people who care for elderly relatives. Women make up 59 percent of people who depend on income support, a basic means-tested benefit (Oppenheim and Harker 1996). As elsewhere in the world, the causes of women's poverty in the UK are complex. Its roots lie in the family:

> Many women's lives are still shaped by the family responsibilities they have
> traditionally been expected to take on — the tasks of child-care, caring for the
> elderly and maintaining the home. These tasks shape women's work patterns, the
> type of occupations they work in, their earnings and their social security benefits.

They push women into financial dependence upon men or upon state benefits. It is often assumed that women do not need an income of their own and that money, food and other resources are shared evenly among the family. For many women neither employment nor [welfare benefits] can keep them out of poverty. (ibid.)

However, the female face of poverty in Britain is largely unacknowledged in both official studies and in public and political debates.

Unemployment and homelessness are good examples of how gender differences tend to make women's poverty less visible than men's. Women's unemployment has, until recently, been under-recorded because of gender-bias in the methods used to collect official unemployment figures. Women with partners in work, and single mothers who might nevertheless have wanted paid work, were generally not included in these figures. In Britain, homelessness tends to be seen as a male problem because most people who sleep on the streets are young men. Because of their vulnerability to sexual violence on the streets, women and girls tend to find other ways of dealing with homelessness or the threat of becoming homeless, using street-sleeping as the last resort. They may bed down on friends' floors, exchange sexual favours for a roof over their heads or put up with damaging relationships with men, rather than live on the street. Images of young men sitting on the pavement begging — a commonly-used visual short-hand for poverty in Britain — distort perceptions both of who suffers from homelessness in Britain and what forms homelessness can take.

The exception to the rule of poor women's invisibility is the case of lone parents, most of whom are women. But although the 'problem' of lone parents is incessantly discussed in the media, in this case visibility often means stigmatisation. Female lone parents tend to be characterised by the right-wing press and some sections of the public as feckless and irresponsible. The social ills which beset poor communities, such as high rates of crime and vandalism, are sometimes laid at the door of single mothers, whose 'poor parenting skills' are blamed. Perhaps more than any other social group in poverty, working-class lone mothers are likely to be branded as the so-called 'undeserving poor'.

The political context of gender work in Britain

The contemporary British women's movement — if it can be said to exist — dates from the early 1970s. The movement in Britain has always been amorphous and diverse. Even at its height, there were no strong centralised feminist organisations as in the USA. Despite or because of this, the movement has had some striking achievements, one of the best-known internationally being the campaign against the siting of US nuclear missiles at Greenham Common in the early 1980s. In its first stages, at least, this campaign brought together women of many different backgrounds, ages, and political convictions. Since then the women's movement has expressed itself in a wide range of interest groups and single issue campaigns. African-Caribbean and Asian women's groups have been influential both within and outside their own communities. Some of the strongest and most successful feminist campaigns have focused on violence against women, for instance the women's refuge movement, rape crisis centres, and, in the 1990s, the Zero Tolerance campaigns against domestic violence. Although the women's movement in Britain has always been dominated by middle-class women, a large number of working-class women became involved in political activity for the first time during the bitterly-fought Miner's Strike of 1984, when miners' wives organised in order to defend their husbands' jobs and their communities. Some went on to get involved in other areas of political activity.

There is another sphere, not generally regarded as 'political' or part of the women's movement, in which women dominate. This is the sphere of grassroots community politics, in which working-class women often get involved through their roles as mothers. Throughout Britain, women run after-school clubs, play-groups, mother and toddler clubs, community cafés, and a range of other community initiatives. These are sometimes linked to local campaigns for improved facilities and environments, such as campaigns for traffic-calming measures and better playgrounds. Ruth Lister argues that this type of informal politics is 'women's citizenship in action' and should be given greater recognition by those involved in formal politics (Lister 1998).

It is certainly true that, despite the richness of women's participation in civil society and women's activities in the community, our voices continue to be weak where formal politics and public policy are concerned. However, there have been some positive developments since the general election of May 1997, which should make it easier to raise gender issues in public policy dialogue. One of the most important of these was the election of an unprecedentedly high number of women MPs, although the proportion is still small. Likewise, the establishment of a government women's unit in 1997 — despite its under-resourcing — should help to push to the foreground the needs of women living in poverty.

Yet at the level of government policy, the picture still looks bleak in terms of gender inequality. Policies range from the gender-blind to those which, although they are gender-aware, in fact exacerbate women's disadvantage in relation to men. One example of gender-blindness is the failure of central and local government to take men's and women's different roles and needs into account when planning the regeneration of impoverished areas. Some gender-aware policies actively work to the detriment of women, such as the decision to remove the extra welfare benefits paid to single parents.

On the other hand, the exclusion of young, working-class men from jobs, and the resulting anti-social behaviour of some men, is now seen as one of the most pressing social problems of our times. The demise of traditional male-dominated industries is one important cause of this exclusion, as is the changing nature of work in Britain. There has been a shift from secure, full-time jobs for men to insecure, part-time, and often low-paid jobs for women, encouraged by government policies designed to create a more 'flexible' labour market. One aspect of male exclusion is the the feeling of detachment from their communities which unemployed men experience, and which at its extreme can turn into active hostility on their part to community activities, carried out in the main by women (Campbell 1993).

Insofar as it addresses the gendered nature of working-class masculine identity, political and public concern with male exclusion is welcome. However, there are two risks associated with it. First, however well-intentioned they may be, policies and initiatives which attempt to address men's gender needs might simply perpetuate existing gender assumptions, divisions, and inequalities. For instance, a church organisation has opened a small resource centre for local unemployed men in a socially deprived neighbourhood in the north of England, hoping to overcome their reluctance to get involved in community activities. Church staff describe the centre as being 'free from women's and children's activities', where men can learn 'men's work such as craft skills'. Cookery classes are also planned, but these are targeted at men living on their own rather than unemployed men whose partners might be engaged in the familiar double-shift of work inside and outside the home. Church staff involved in both the men's centre and in projects for local women and children recognise that they are re-inforcing gender stereotypical behaviour. However they argue that such an approach is necessary, at least initially, in order to draw men in.

The other risk is that the new concern with male exclusion may be co-opted by the anti-feminist backlash — laughably known as 'post-feminism' — which has been a significant feature of British society since Prime Minister Thatcher's era. If this happens, 'male exclusion' could become a smoke-screen to obscure the needs of women in poverty, or be used as a spurious rationale for once again concentrating on men's needs at the expense of women's.

Working on gender in the Anti-Poverty Programme (GB)

As might be expected, there is a wide gap in gender-awareness between main-stream community practitioners and social policy academics specialising in gender analysis, although the picture may be different in the black and Asian voluntary sector, where organisations such as Southall Black Sisters are active in raising issues of gender and race. In the white mainstream voluntary sector, it is rare for gender considerations to be made explicit in anti-poverty work. There are, of course, exceptions to this generalisation, notably women's centres, which provide services to meet women's practical needs, and the small but increasing number of initiatives which set out to address men's gendered needs.

Oxfam's Poverty Programme (GB) has attempted to mainstream gender into all aspects of the programme as well as to prioritise it as a specific area of work. It is conducted at a variety of levels, involving government departments, local authorities, academics, and the voluntary sector, and includes both funding and non-funding support. The aim is to build up a critical mass for gender work. In order to do this, the Poverty Programme (GB) must be proactive, but it must also react quickly and take advantage of opportunities as they arise.

The programme's gender-related work has a number of advantages. One of the most important is Oxfam GB's status as a well-known national institution, literally a 'household name'. In addition, Oxfam's decade of experience in gender-related work overseas gives us the legitimacy to raise the issue in Britain. Partly because the programme is relatively young, the team has taken a very proactive approach to gender, as to other programme priorities. Having access to gender specialists in Oxfam's head office has helped them to do this, but it is also true that many general programme staff in Oxfam now have a commitment to and under-standing of gender, which informs any work they do for the Poverty Programme (GB). Lastly, Oxfam's gender materials — such as the Links newsletter and *The Oxfam Gender Training Manual*—are useful tools for creating initial interest and strengthening partner organisations' work.

This is still a young programme, but already there have been achievements. Some of the programme's most successful gender initiatives to date are listed below. These examples have been chosen to give an overview of the different levels the programme is working at, and the wide range of activities we are supporting.

Urban regeneration policy and the Joseph Rowntree Foundation

Following an approach by the Poverty Programme (GB), the Joseph Rowntree Foundation (JRF), a respected social research body based in the UK, commissioned Oxfam to produce a report on gender considerations in urban regeneration schemes. These schemes, mentioned above, are important vehicles for delivering statutory sector funds to economically disadvantaged areas. In general, they are gender-blind, directed at environmental and economic regeneration rather than social needs, and they do not use gender-disaggregated indicators or outputs. The programme employed a consultant with extensive overseas experience of gender-related work to produce the report, which was later published by the JRF as *Challenging Assumptions — Gender Issues in Urban Regeneration*. It included recommendations for all stages of urban regeneration programmes, including needs assessment, design and implementation, capacity-building and evaluation.

In addition to its value as a research project, *Challenging Assumptions* has proved a useful tool for raising gender issues with other organisations. The interest it has generated among staff of local authorities, women working in urban regeneration bodies, and academics, has enabled Oxfam to forge new alliances. Several seminars have been held to discuss the report's implications, and an entire issue of *Housing Agenda*, the magazine of the National Housing Federation, was based on it. The report was also used by Oxfam (working together with the Barrow Cadbury Trust) to lobby the Department of Environment, Transport and the Regions on urban regeneration policies. We are now looking at ways of building on this work.

Incorporating domestic issues into the 'Clothes Code' campaign: the National Group on Homeworking

An example of the programme's gender-related public campaigning is its work with the National Group on Homeworking (NGH). This partnership is interesting because it gave Oxfam an opportunity to integrate domestic gender issues — in this case, the low pay, poor working conditions, and job insecurity of British homeworkers — with the global objectives of its 'Clothes Code Campaign', which aims to secure improved conditions for garment-workers world-wide. This was the first time Oxfam incorporated British policy issues into its campaigning. Since then, Oxfam GB's Policy Department has worked with NGH on lobbying the government to ratify the 1997 ILO Convention on Homeworkers. In this way, Oxfam has brought an international perspective to bear on the situation of British homeworkers.

Learning from micro-financial initiatives overseas: the Full Circle Fund

As in many developing countries, women on low incomes in Britain who want to start up small businesses are often prevented from doing so by banks' reluctance to lend money to them. The Full Circle Fund, a pilot scheme run by the Women's Enterprise Education and Training Unit in Norfolk, is attempting to overcome this problem by providing credit to women in three communities, as part of a support package including business training, and help with child-care and transport problems. The credit element will be administered by small groups of women who will take on joint responsibility for assessing each other's loan applications and meeting any liability from repayment defaults. The project emulates features of the well-known Grameen Bank of Bangladesh and the

Women's Self-Employment Project in Chicago, USA. It is an example of how models developed overseas, including the South, can be adapted and applied to tackle women's poverty in Britain. Oxfam provided funds to help the project get off the ground, prior to its receiving large grants from other sources.

Using drama to explore the exclusion of young men: 'Wise Guys' by the Red Ladder Theatre Group

The Poverty Programme (GB) has made a grant to the Red Ladder Theatre Group, who take theatre to young people, to fund resource packs to support their play, *Wise Guys*. This is a powerful, highly professional production about a group of young men in London's East End. The play shows how their family back-grounds, and the lack of alternative opportunities, push them into a life of crime, drugs, and violence. It is particularly strong in depicting how a culture of male violence in the home can be passed down from father to son. The resource packs are designed for both youth workers and young people, and will be used to stimulate and guide post-performance audience discussions. Red Ladder used material from the *Oxfam Gender Training Manual*—including gender awareness exercises developed in Africa and Asia — in the resource packs.

Integrating gender awareness into participatory research: the Community Council for Berkshire

The Community Council for Berkshire approached Oxfam for help in assessing community needs on a large housing estate. They had heard about Participatory Appraisal (PA) methods and wanted help to try out this approach. The Poverty Programme (GB) paid for a consultant with experience of using PA in Africa to carry out research involving over 250 people, most of them estate residents, in July 1997. This was an unusual community research project in the British context, because women/mothers and men/fathers were consulted separately, along with other social groups. Although there were many similarities between women's and men's concerns, they tended to stress different sets of problems in their commu-nity. On the whole, men emphasised security and the physical environment while women were more concerned with social issues such as debt and isolation. The researchers noted that they found it easier to involve women in the assessment than men, partly because many local men work away from the estate during the day; this differs from the experience of many participatory researchers in the South. But although women were strongly involved both in the analysis and in drawing up a subsequent action plan for the estate, it remains to be seen whether their voices will be heard by local decision-makers, most of whom are men.

Despite these and other successes, programme staff have encountered diffi-culties in raising concerns of gender, especially with grassroots mainstream organisations. It is much easier to include gender-related work in projects which are already gender-specific than to introduce it into our work with mainstream projects such as community centres. Where gender-specific projects are directed towards gendered practical needs, such as women's centres, it has sometimes been hard to promote work on gendered strategic needs.

There are several reasons for these difficulties, both external and internal. An important external factor is that men continue to hold most senior posts in both the public and voluntary sectors, which makes it difficult to get gender recognised as an issue. The voluntary sector in particular suffers from a lack of resources. Many projects have to limit themselves to providing services, as this is all that government is prepared to fund. Shortage of funds also means that staff and volunteers spend a large proportion of their time fund-raising. With so little energy to spare, they may see work on gender needs as at best a luxury, and at worst a waste of time. Their crying need for resources makes it more difficult for them to benefit from the non-funding support that the Poverty Programme (GB) offers. Lastly, the gulf between the black, Asian, and white voluntary sectors means that it is difficult for them to learn from one another.

Many of the internal problems are also linked to limited resources. The team that co-ordinates Oxfam's Poverty Programme (GB) is very small, and gender-related work is only one of several programme priorities, so resources have to be obtained from elsewhere — sometimes from the Gender and Learning Team (GALT), sometimes from outside Oxfam. However, GALT is itself over-stretched, and skilled gender consultants are in short supply and can be expensive to employ. The programme's slender resources and its newness tend to limit its influence on a scene where most of the large funding organisations show little interest in gender issues.

The vision for Oxfam's gender work in Britain

The next stage is for programme staff, with the help of GALT, to reflect on what has been achieved so far and identify opportunities for gender work. On this basis we can draw up a strategy for taking gender forward more systematically, perhaps seeking external funding for a gender programme within the overall programme. It is clear is that there are many possible ways of raising gender-awareness with partner organisations, despite the barriers. For instance, programme staff are planning regional gender-training workshops in partnership with sympathetic voluntary organisations and local authorities. Other ideas include facilitating a regional conference of women's centres and adapting *The Oxfam Gender Training Manual* for use in the British voluntary sector.

The programme's work on gender has only just begun. During the next five years, staff hope to build strong links with organisations doing gender-related work at a variety of levels, from national advocacy organisations to small community-based projects. We need to work with these partners to develop our conceptual understanding of gender relations in Britain. Learning from the work of our partners in the South will be vital. Some of the ways we can encourage this are involvement in more projects such as The Full Circle Fund, investigating the potential of North-South community linking and exchange programmes, and exploring the potential of Oxfam's publications to introduce new ideas to the British voluntary sector. We aim to reach a position where Oxfam is recognised in both the voluntary and statutory sectors as the leading British agency working on gender issues. More importantly, however, we aim to deepen the programme's impact on poverty by incorporating a strong gender dimension into our work.

About the author

Geraldine Terry worked as Programme Development Officer for Oxfam's Poverty Programme in Great Britain, based in the north of England, from 1997–98, after carrying out action-research to assess the feasibility of such a programme. She was previously employed as Communications Officer on Oxfam's Asia desk. Before joining Oxfam, Geraldine was a neighbourhood advice worker, an English lecturer, and a designer of computer-based training, based mainly in Britain, with several years in Italy and Papua New Guinea. She is currently completing a Master's degree in Development Studies at the University of East Anglia, UK.

References

Campbell, B. (1993), *Goliath, Britain's Dangerous Places*, London: Methuen.

David, R. and Craig, Y. (1997), 'Participation begins at home: adapting participatory development approaches from Southern contexts', *Gender and Development*, Vol. 5, No. 3.

Oppenheim, C. and Harker, L. (1996), *Poverty: the facts*, Child Poverty Action Group.

Lister, R. (1998), *Citizenship: a Feminist Perspective*, London: Macmillan.

Pearson, R. and Watson, E. (1997), 'Giving women the credit: the Norwich Full Circle Project', *Gender and Development*, Vol. 5, No. 3.

Representative systems and accountability structures in refugee settlements in Ikafe, Uganda

Judy Adoko

Background

The massive influx of Sudanese refugees into Arua District in north Uganda in 1993 prompted a search for longer-term solutions to the protracted refugee problem. It was finally agreed to set up settlement programmes that would work towards refugees' self-reliance. In contrast to transit camps, which emphasise care and maintenance, settlement programmes aim to help refugees become more independent, by providing them with opportunities to develop their own livelihoods; and by helping them to integrate within the official structures and systems of the host population. Refugee representation is key to both of these. Oxfam GB was invited by the office of the United National High Commissioner for Refugees (UNHCR) to become the implementing agency for a settlement programme in Ikafe, which was eventually home to about 55,000 refugees.

As Programme Officer responsible for gender issues in Uganda, I arrived two years after the programme's inception to investigate the different ways in which men and women were being affected as refugees, and to try to uncover some of the less obvious cultural aspects that were likely to affect programming in Ikafe.

The significance of gender in refugee settlements

Becoming a refugee affects men and women in many different (and often hidden) ways.[19] It was important that Oxfam worked with men and women refugees to identify difficulties and opportunities for both, along with ways of overcoming, or possibly building upon, some of the enforced changes in their lives. Ensuring that the different voices of men and women were able to be heard was obviously vital to this process. With male and female populations in Ikafe almost equal during the time that I was there — 21,036 women to 25,231 men — it was only fair that their interests were equally represented and heard.

Gender-related concerns in refugee situations are many and complex. For example, as refugees in Ikafe, women were often unable to meet some of their basic needs (food, water, shelter), because of delays in the delivery of food, poor water supply in many parts of the settlement, or long queues at scarce grinding mills — issues that are no doubt common to many refugee situations. This meant that there was less time for them to get involved in community activities. At the same time, it caused additional strains within the home and an increase in domestic arguments. Men had lost access to paid work and their ability to provide for the home in other ways, and there were fewer opportunities for them to be involved in community affairs, because traditional structures had collapsed. This compounded their loss of social and economic status, and with it their reduced levels of self-respect and motivation.

It had not originally been the intention to have someone on the programme solely responsible for gender, because it was expected that each sector of the settlement programme (food and land distribution, water and sanitation, etc) would address gender concerns independently. We were concerned that gender issues should be integral to every activity — not something added on as an after-thought. However, with the pressures on humanitarian agencies to perform in the emergency environment of the early Ikafe days, programme priorities were inevitably focused on addressing tangible basic needs within a very short time. Ensuring the integration of gender-fair practice in a settlement programme such as Ikafe is an extremely complex task, and the short training given to staff to upgrade their understanding was not sufficient to provide the level of analysis required. As a result, gender issues were addressed on an *ad hoc* basis.

With hindsight, having somebody solely responsible for gender issues from the programme's inception might have succeeded in ensuring a holistic approach to gender concerns from the beginning of the settlement. It was always the expectation that every activity would be carried out with a thorough understanding of cultural and political issues, gained through research, but inevitably there was never sufficient time to do this properly. A Gender Officer could have given on-going training at a range of levels, and worked more closely with managers in planning and monitoring activities with a thorough gender analysis. In Ikafe, the additional training I was able to give to extension staff to enhance their abilities to gather information and to analyse data was a first step which remains important to programming today. This is now evident at field level, where extension staff — who are all refugees — have a much greater understanding of gender concerns, and are much more receptive to the need to identify and overcome cultural prejudices related to gender.

Establishing representative systems

One of the starting points in Ikafe was to put in place a system for representation that would give refugees who felt disempowered a sense that they had some control over events. But we were immediately faced with a dilemma. Should we recreate systems that were already familiar, something that may be valued by a displaced and disoriented people? Or should we seize the opportunity to establish new systems, which may be more equitable or fully representative; and which are likely to be more sustainable within the new environment, especially where parallels and links with the systems of the host population are made?

South Sudan has a strong hereditary chieftain system. The representative structures are largely hierarchical and tend to be dominated by men. These structures continue to enable communities to function, despite years of social and economic destruction as a result of war. The chief (or, through him, his headmen) deals with civil and criminal issues related to law and order, mobilises for communal activities, and gives spiritual and political guidance. It was immediately obvious that these tribal and clan linkages remained important to the refugees within Ikafe. Imposing a Ugandan system on a people who have very little tradition of an active and vocal civil society might then have met with a degree of resistance. On top of this, we had to ask ourselves to what extent we wanted to make special efforts to promote women, who are traditionally not represented in Sudanese administrative and political systems.

Women often find themselves in new positions of authority as refugees, taking over responsibilities within the home and community from men, who are either absent or unmotivated to get involved. We had to ask ourselves whether we wanted to use this opportunity to redress culturally imposed roles; or whether it would be better for the representative systems to focus on recreating familiar institutions — where women have little voice in politics and administration.

After some discussion with refugee and local (host population) leaders, it was decided from the start of the programme to set up structures in the settlement that would be similar to those of the Ugandan nationals, so that when Oxfam left, the refugees would be well positioned to integrate within the national structures of the host society. The Ugandan Local Council (LC) administrative structures were introduced into the refugee settlement, with only a few minimal changes to cater for the specific needs of refugees.

The Ugandan system has tried to involve women by creating one mandatory post for them in each LC, leaving the eight remaining posts open for both men and women to compete for. Yet in reality, when it comes to voting, communities will often assume that the eight posts are reserved for men, and only one position remains left for women. When it comes to leadership, our culture automatically assumes that a man should take this role. Even when there is democratic voting, both women and men will vote for men. The Sudanese culture is very close to that of the Ugandans in this respect. Alice Jabe, a Sudanese in Ikafe camp confirmed this: 'We were not brought up in the Sudan to talk when men are around. We are afraid that we would not be able to defend ourselves. They also say that a woman cannot be a leader, because she cannot command respect.' As a result, when elections took place in the refugee settlement, like the Ugandan nationals, the refugees assumed that women had one mandatory post and that the remaining 12 were reserved for men. The attempts to involve women in the running of camps, just as in the Ugandan system, had worked to exclude women even more.

These early representative structures set up by Oxfam had failed to accommodate women because the constraints were not properly understood. Because women were unhappy with the fact that they were not well represented, one year after the first elections, Oxfam set out to find out how the representative structures could better accommodate women.

Why women were not well represented

We found that the mandatory women's post had certainly created some problems. Although the (often uneducated) chiefs and elders continue to have considerable influence, playing an important part in social and political affairs, it is almost always the educated who are voted in for administrative structures, and in 80 per cent of the cases, these are men. In the case of the refugee settlement, the uneducated felt even more excluded, because they assumed that agencies wanted only those who could speak English, and most of the educated refugee women had been recruited as teachers by another agency within the settlement. As one Sudanese woman once said: 'We thought we needed to elect those who speak English, so that they can communicate with agencies' staff such as Oxfam.' Another woman had this to say: 'Oxfam, you surprise us by asking us why we are not well represented on the structures. It was your staff who informed us that women had one post only.'

When we looked further, we found a number of other reasons why women were being excluded, many of them linked to cultural taboos. A number of women said that their husbands did not want them to participate in public meetings because 'a woman who always joins the company of men will fall in love with other people's husbands'. There was also on the surface an apparent lack of interest from women. Many women said that the meetings were not relevant to them. They were mostly concerned to get their practical needs addressed, and when there was no immediate result, the less educated especially tended to lose interest. Rachel Nyanwich complained: 'When we speak up, we never see any result. We usually ask for things like saucepans, jerrycans, and boreholes, but nothing ever comes of it. We spoke in the past, but now we have given up with it.' Veronica Gubo added: 'Women hear, but they do not come. Meetings are announced through churches but you find women sitting instead of attending. They think they are not for them. They think they are only for men.'

Another fact which limited women's participation was simply that they were too busy elsewhere. As another woman refugee put it: 'I do not go, because I spend all day waiting for water or lining up at the grinding mill.' Some people also felt that women could be represented through their own separate bodies, whether church associations, income-generating groups, or women's unions.

Introducing changes

When men and women were actually asked, many did not oppose the idea of equal representation. The community was often ready to listen to women's voices, as two women, Martha Angera and Margaret Nyoka, explained: 'We are given equal chance to talk at meetings. Men do listen to women, and they respect our work if we do it well. Men do not always stop women from going to meetings. Though I am not educated, I get a chance to speak up at meetings, and the men do listen to me.'

Having identified some of the constraints which prevented women's participation in representative structures, we then turned our attention to exploring different ways of overcoming some of the more hidden obstacles.

Organisational awareness-raising and training
The first thing we did was to look into our own institutional systems. We found that women's failure to turn up for meetings had often been interpreted as a lack of interest — even by our own community development workers (CDWs), who had often themselves subconsciously excluded women. We carried out workshops and training to raise awareness among the refugee extension workers — and the CDWs who managed them — of their own inherent cultural prejudices. As they became aware of these, it became possible for them to target women more specifically.

Raising awareness among the refugees

It took us a month to go round the camps and talk to people about the need for a gender-balanced representative structure. Our purpose was to get the community to look inward and admit that women and the disadvantaged were excluded because of cultural prejudices of which they were not even aware. After asking mainly the leaders why women were not represented, we would then start the process of logical thinking aloud. For example:

> 'So why are there no women on the representative structures?'
> 'Because we are not educated [or because women are not educated].'
> 'Do you need education before you can become a leader?'
> Some would say 'Yes', some would say 'No'.
> 'Are your chiefs educated?' …
> 'How come that they are your respected leaders?' …
> 'Do you still think you need education to become a leader?' …
> 'Then why do women need to be educated before they are elected on the structures?'

At this stage, there is usually silence, which can be followed by another excuse for excluding women, such as that they form their own associations. We again encouraged a process of self-questioning to overcome this:

> 'What are the representative structures and committees for?'
> 'They are for water, education, food, and so on.'
> 'Are women not interested in these items?'
> 'They are. In fact, they are more interested in these items.'
> 'If they are in their separate women's groups, how will they know what goes on in the water, education, and food committees? Are there no women in the camps?'
> 'There are.'
> 'Do you now agree that women should be part of the committee?'
> 'Yes!'

Through logic we challenged the myths that a woman cannot represent herself; or that a person needs education before he or she can become a leader. We also argued that the minority tribes such as the Dinka, and also the disadvantaged members of the refugee community, should elect their representatives, since no one else would be able to represent them any better.

Picking the best from different cultures

With a much better understanding of the culture of the people we were working with, and having raised their awareness of the need for better representation of women, we then concentrated on re-designing the system in a way that would accommodate the traditional leaders and systems, and at the same time address gender-related concerns and ensure women's participation and representation.

In order to do this, three different structures were developed. The Ugandan system has been incorporated and adapted for administrative purposes, so that the settlement's administrative structures are standardised with those of the local population. However, traditional Sudanese systems (based on the chieftain system) have been kept for judicial purposes. A third and new system has been designed for integrating activities and delivering services within the settlement. For the first time there is a structure for co-ordinating the bodies and activities initiated by all the implementing agencies within the settlement. Two members from this are then put forward to form the Council, which represents the whole refugee community in Ikafe. There is also provision at this level for two representatives each for the Dinkas, a large 'minority' tribe, and for the disadvantaged groups.

Equal representation

The numbers of men and women in the settlement are virtually equal. We proposed therefore that they should be equally represented. On all new structures it was stipulated that if the Chairperson was a woman, the Vice should be a man, and so on. Re-elections were held for water and grinding mill committees, with men, women, the host community, and refugee populations all equally represented. Through discussion, communities began to acknowledge that there was no reason why women, who were as many as the men, could not represent their own interests. We were able to argue that, since the systems were anyway imposed and not necessarily traditional or wholly familiar to the Sudanese, there was no justification for perpetuating cultural inequalities where women's representation was concerned.

Terminology

Careful use of language in developing activities, we believed, could work to enhance women's involvement in running the settlement. For example, if we say that we want to elect 'pump mechanics', the assumption is likely to be that women are not eligible, because men are the ones who are good with 'machines'. Yet women are the ones fetching water, and if there is a pump breakage, they suffer more than men, because it is they who have to walk long distances and waste time queuing. In this case, for example, we tried saying things like Oxfam needs 'to elect five women and five men to learn how to repair and maintain the water pumps'. Many words carry male connotations, so in Ikafe we changed titles to employ words that were more neutral. For example, 'chiefs' became 'elders', because chiefs are always male, but not all elders are men. There are female elders as well. This tunes the mind to include women.

Conclusions

The Ikafe experience has shown me that people are deeply prejudiced without knowing it. This bias is revealed in the form of excuses, which are mistaken for reasons, to exclude women. If deeply analysed, these excuses do not hold water and can be overcome.

Because of cultural assumptions and inhibitions, purely democratic elections tend to perpetuate an undemocratic process, because they exclude women and the disadvantaged, keeping them always marginalised. I believe that having a framework within which fair voting must take place is the only way of encouraging and sensitising communities in a way that would ensure a gender-sensitive representative structure.

From the start of a programme for newly settled refugees, a framework should be worked out that openly acknowledges cultural aspects and the demographic profile of the refugee population. At this stage, things should not be left totally to democratic elections. After a more solid framework has been established, democratic elections can then take place. Women's workload should be recognised, and attempts made to reach them, especially in the early days of settlement, when work burdens tend to be even greater. Careful use of language can also enhance women's involvement. Most importantly, in all our work in Uganda, we should be aware that any leadership elections will always operate to the advantage of educated men — unless there are specific measures to combat it. A carefully designed, gender-fair election framework is the only way forward for women and the disadvantaged.

About the author

Judy Adoko, a Ugandan, is a lawyer who qualified from the University of Dar-es-Salaam. She worked with the Ministry of Lands in Tanzania and subsequently with two other advocate firms. After ten years as a refugee in Tanzania, Judy returned to Uganda in 1981. She joined Oxfam in 1988 as a gender and development programme officer (refusing the title Women Project Officer), and is now Deputy Country Representative for Oxfam in Uganda. Her main interest of late has been working on land issues, especially on understanding the effect of new concepts of economic growth on vulnerable men's and women's access to land. Judy is a convert from project-oriented support to broader policy work.

Mind the gap:
How what we do differs
from what we say (Burkina Faso)

Alice Iddi

Introduction

This article raises issues about the implementation of strategies for achieving gender equity, drawing on lessons learned from a well-known soil and water conservation project (Projet Agro-Forestier — PAF) in Burkina Faso, and my ten years of working with Oxfam GB staff. I explore how Oxfam's good intentions regarding gender equity have been translated into concrete actions. The example shows that these actions often do not adequately reflect the complexity of gender relations, because they fail to take account of the relationships between men and women and the ways in which they make decisions, but rather address women and men as separate entities. The issue is further complicated by the need to understand and address gender relations in the cultural and social realities in which programmes and projects operate. I compare the Gender and Development approach (GAD) with Women in Development (WID) and discuss the need to understand the social and cultural context of each intervention.

The Projet Agro-Forestier (PAF)

An overview of the PAF experience
The initial aim of this project was to address the widespread deforestation and environmental degradation in the drought-prone Yatenga region, by developing micro-water catchments to encourage tree-growth. It involved determining the contours of the land with the help of a simple water level (made of plastic tubing)

and then building lines of stones (*diguettes*) along these contours. It soon emerged, however, that farmers were more interested in this technique for growing food crops than for growing trees. Oxfam reoriented the project to respond to this need, and by 1983 farmers and technicians alike considered the techniques they had jointly developed an effective soil and water conservation (SWC) technology.

In technical terms, PAF was considered one of the most successful SWC projects in the West Africa region. The technology it developed and promoted has been shown to be capable of generating significant increases in crop yields and natural vegetation cover, is ecologically sustainable, and requires little external input. Thus, in Burkina, PAF has had a tremendous impact on SWC in particular and natural-resource management in general. PAF also enjoyed a high level of recognition and reputation for several years within Oxfam and associated development agencies in the UK and elsewhere.

Given this glowing picture of the project's impact, PAF seemed to have achieved its objective of researching and offering farmers a simple, affordable SWC technology. This, as well as a concern to reinforce local capacity for self-development and sustainability, led Oxfam to terminate its funding for PAF in 1996.

Impact on women

In comparison with its technical achievements, PAF's success in promoting gender equity is, at best, mixed. To be fair, an assessment of PAF's record on gender equity must take into account the context in which it started and evolved. At the time of its initiation (1979) and during its early years, issues such as access to and ownership of land and other resources in the family or community were not raised. Nor did the project examine questions such as who benefited from the increased yields from 'treated' land; or how the new technology affected the roles and responsibilities of women and men in a household, and their multiple needs and priorities. Such questions were just not raised. The assumption was that women would, of course, also benefit when family food production increased.

This assumption seemed to be confirmed by research carried out as part of an evaluation of the socio-economic impact of the project in 1992, which recorded women's own testimony. However, a deeper analysis suggested that women lost more than they gained from PAF. It was evident that the technology promoted by PAF consumed a significant amount of women's time and energy. Consequently, they had less time for other activities directly beneficial to them. For example, women had less time for tending their personal fields (yes, women also have their farms to look after!) and for undertaking income-generating activities. Most women were not given access to the 'treated' (improved) land for their personal fields, nor did the women have direct access to the resources and inputs provided by Oxfam, such as barrows and carts.

It is difficult to determine precisely to what extent the women benefited from the increased crop production that their labour helped to generate. In Mossi society, women are responsible for providing the ingredients and processing all raw / primary food stuffs into an evening meal, as well as breakfast and lunch, in most cases. They are also responsible for providing and managing all the 'small' things that make a big difference to the survival, production, and reproduction of the family. These responsibilities include caring for the health and well-being of the family, providing water, producing food, raising and educating children, cleaning the house, and clothing their children.

The man, as the head of the family, has primary responsibility for relations with the wider community (arranging marriages, funerals, religious affairs, community relationships, and so on). He is traditionally responsible for providing the cereal grain for the evening (main) meal, at least. This is usually a standard measure dished out to the woman/women for several evenings at a time. The measure may change if there is an increase in the number of mouths to feed for a considerable length of time. It does not change if there is an increased crop yield.

The man as head of the family decides on the use of any surplus production from the family farm. The women, who contribute their labour to the family farm, are not consulted. He can use surplus grain for buying animals (as security for lean years), assets such as bullocks or donkey and plough, settling dowry/marriage expenses for a son, settling disputes involving family members, buying roofing sheets, a bicycle or mobylette, or marrying a second or third wife for himself. The family head may, and often does, consult with important family members, including senior wives and older women, but the final decision is his.

Therefore, the benefits for women who invested time and labour in the building of the *diguettes* that helped to generate the surplus vary greatly and depend on decisions taken by the men. It is not certain whether the sum of these benefits outweighs the opportunity cost of the women's invested time and energy measured in terms of their reduced personal time and restricted income. What is clear, however, is that whatever benefits women derive from the SWC work are indirect. There is a high probability that these are minimal in relation to the time and effort they invested.

Mind the gap

Women/gender in theory and in practice
What does the PAF experience have to say about the effectiveness of Oxfam's attempts to promote gender equity in projects and institutionalise gender analysis in its procedures? The context in which PAF was initiated and evolved

must be taken into account. Oxfam initiated PAF as a technology-transfer project. The focus was to develop a low-cost but effective soil and water conservation (SWC) technology for improved agricultural production in dry-land areas. Men farmers were the target group. This shaped PAF's planning and implementation process and, subsequently, its outcomes for women.

As it turned out, the technology required a huge amount of labour from women, especially in gathering and transporting the rocks to the field to be 'treated'. The men did most of the digging up and piling of the stones at the source. They also determined and demarcated the contour ridges and did the actual construction of the rock bunds. The women (and children) brought in the stones, mostly on head pans. They also were responsible for providing food for the work groups, and water for the animals and the compost pits in the later phase of the project. It was obvious that the women took on additional tasks and responsibilities, adding to their already heavy workload.

Oxfam subsidised the purchase of modest tools and equipment such as pick axes, shovels, wheel-barrows, and carts. These were made available to farmer groups in order to reduce the workload. A revolving stock of grain was also provided to village groups, to enable poorer families to borrow cereal to feed work groups when they came to help build *diguettes* on their farms. Invariably, the equipment and grain went to men. In other words, there were very few obvious ways in which women benefited from this project.

It is important to note that Oxfam did support projects with women's groups in the area (and elsewhere), and, indeed, PAF staff provided follow-up support to these groups, such as the dynamic Titao Women's Group. But these projects were separate and independent from PAF. As in PAF, gender analysis was not an issue. Staff (myself included) asked no questions about the impact of these women's initiatives on their menfolk, or on the relationships and decision-making processes in the family. This was the 'women in development' (WID) approach.

The concept of gender analysis which gained currency within Oxfam in the mid-1980s, and the creation of the Gender and Development Unit (GADU) in particular, were critical to the shift from a WID to a GAD approach (in other words, from looking at women as a particular group to looking at the relationship between women and men). A gender perspective became an important yard-stick for assessing people and programme proposals. But most project staff did not (and still do not) know what this really means. Unlike WID, a gender perspective includes both women and men. Gender analysis puts (or should put) emphasis on the social realities in which roles, responsibilities, and expectations are assigned to men and women. It assesses the differences, constraints, and trade-offs between men and women, which should then inform policy and programmes. However, despite all the ink that has been expended in the name of gender, GAD remains largely a theoretical, abstract concept which has yet to replace the WID approach in practice. Oxfam has made little headway in enabling staff and partners to carry out gender analysis which is inclusive of both women *and* men, taking the social realities into account, and informing programme planning accordingly.

Add women and stir

Despite the ambiguity, the winds of change swept across Oxfam in general, and field programmes in particular. Women's Projects Officers were recruited. When new women staff were recruited to other field positions (including my own), their job descriptions stated explicitly that they were also responsible for gender issues.

Similar measures were taken at the project level. In the case of PAF, women were simply 'added' to the existing project activities. A female field worker (*animatrice*) was recruited to be responsible for women's affairs; the project's budget then included funding for women's initiatives, which PAF had responsibility for implementing.

These measures were based on the assumption that female programme staff would be better able to appreciate women's needs, interests, and concerns than their male counterparts who were already in post. Paradoxically, in its strict division between the sexes, this perception was still rooted in the WID perspective.

In the case of PAF, this state of affairs became particularly problematic for the *animatrice*. Her job became more and more unclear and difficult to manage, as the existing way of working in the project did not change, except to accommodate a woman staff member. While her male colleagues divided up and each covered five to six villages, she was expected to cover more than 20 villages. Her task was to work with all the women involved in the SWC, which was still the principal activity. It became very difficult, if not impossible, for her to do meaningful work.

Hopping on one leg: women-only projects

At the beginning of the PAF project, it was very clear when Oxfam talked about women in development (WID) that its aim was to promote the needs of women, who had been left out in past development programmes. This was simple and straightforward. There was no ambiguity, and actions corresponded with the language. They also stemmed from the conviction that benefits to the woman automatically benefit the whole family, and that her role is crucial for positive social change and development.

In the case of PAF, taking women into account was a positive step forward. However, the fact that activities relating to women were merely tagged on and carried out exclusively with women, with little effort to apply a gender analysis, jeopardised their potential for positive change. More importantly, the gender issue remained on the periphery.

It was essential to understand that decisions affecting husband and wife, men and women, are negotiated. Credit loans are an example. In general in West Africa, a woman has to consult with her husband and obtain his approval before contracting a significant loan. This may seem unacceptable, as it 'impinges' on the woman's decision-making powers. But one of the main reasons for it is that the husband could legally and morally be held responsible for paying the debt if she defaults. It is not uncommon for the whole family to contribute to pay for an individual's debt, in order that he/she does not undergo public humiliation.

Although the language of Oxfam has changed, the actual work in West Africa has remained in the WID mode. This generates the mistaken impression that 'gender' means the same as 'women'. When one hears Oxfam's partners and collaborators refer to 'gender projects', meaning projects with women, it becomes clear how far this misunderstanding and confusion has gone. It is no secret that project partners, whether potential or actual, throw in all sorts of proclamations and rhetoric about women in their project proposals, in order to impress funders who, they know, aspire to promote 'gender-sensitive' programmes.

It is indisputable that women play a vital role in development. It is also true that women-only projects bring significant and direct benefits to women and their families. However, women-only projects do not usually change the relationships between women and men, and may even lead to further marginalisation of women. Moreover, excluding men from income-generating activities, for instance, may lead to the woman assuming family responsibilities which otherwise should be the man's.

In sum, the active participation of men is vital if women's needs and concerns are to be addressed effectively and gender equity is to be promoted. Failure to include both women and men in a holistic approach to social development is like trying to progress by hopping on one leg. Sustainable development and gender equity will advance more quickly and further if both legs are used together — difficult, slow, or painful though it might be at the beginning to make progress.

Understanding gender relations in context

The example of PAF demonstrates that Oxfam faces the complex challenge of adapting its philosophy to the realities of different socio-cultural contexts.

In many West African cultures, the woman belongs to two families. She has a strong allegiance to both, and she has different duties and responsibilities within each. Although her husband's homestead is (or is supposed to be) hers, she is at the same time considered a 'stranger' there. Her home is her parents' homestead; that is where she belongs. She feels a much stronger sense of belonging to and consideration from her own parents and siblings; there she has more (legal) access to and control of resources as well as decision-making, the last of which increases with age. She can and does go back there, if and when things get difficult.

Taking the household as the decision-making unit can, therefore, be problematic. In the Yatenga religion in particular and the African context in general, patterns of residence, production, consumption, and investment do not tally with the Western view of a household. In many western perspectives, a household is a corporate unit. In other social realities, consumption units often cross residential boundaries but do not necessarily form co-operative units for production, pooling resources, or investment. Networks of interdependence within and beyond domestic (household) units are prevalent and very important.

Given these realities, the current approach, in which the woman is seen either as an individual or merely as an integral part of her husband's household, misses essential considerations. The problem is further complicated when concepts such as production, consumption, income, and investment are used to evaluate processes and outcomes of projects and programmes.

The challenge is to develop culturally appropriate and context-specific strategies for promoting gender equity in general and in projects such as PAF, in particular. Within Western feminist thinking, men are often perceived as oppressors, which implicitly promotes a confrontational approach. In my experience, women in West Africa often do not favour such an approach, because (unintentionally perhaps), it attacks core values of these societies. Thus, it often puts people, indeed women, from these societies on the defensive. Personally, it awakened in me a critical consciousness that resulted in a more cautious approach to embracing the ideal of gender equality.

Concluding remarks

Oxfam has made significant progress in promoting women in the development process over these past ten years. However, there is a yawning gap between rhetoric and reality concerning gender and development.

In the case of PAF in Burkina Faso, this gap is due (at least in part) to an insufficient understanding of the difference between women in development (WID) and gender and development (GAD). Although the rhetoric tells us that Oxfam's work is addressing 'gender issues', what is actually happening is the implementation of 'women's activities', which are treated as a separate sector, rather than a theme which cuts across the entire programme. In reality, Oxfam has made little progress beyond the WID perspective. PAF (like many other projects) was never designed in the initial stages to understand and address gender issues. The response to the imperative to 'include gender' resulted in simply adding women activities to the existing project work, with no gender analysis to inform and effect change in planning and implementation.

Operating in different cultural contexts complicates the issue, because it is vital to understand gender relations within a particular context in order to be able to effect positive change in addressing inequalities between men and women. Although the rhetoric of gender analysis gives the illusion of universality, when applied to complex local situations, it can lead to inaccurate understanding and inadequate (or even counter-productive) interventions.

To 'mind the (gender) gap' properly, it is essential, first of all, to recognise its existence and importance. Oxfam needs to assist its staff and partners to invest more time and effort, despite the existing daily management pressures, into developing a better understanding of the social and cultural realities in which they work. It should also encourage dialogue and open debates within Oxfam, with partners and with local people themselves, on their understanding and strategies for implementing gender-balanced programmes.

Such measures would encourage and enable field staff to derive context-specific insights which would inform programming and enable them to address gender inequality more adequately, with a better chance of effecting positive change.

About the author

Alice Azumi Iddi is a Ghanaian who has worked in development programmes and projects at a range of levels and in a variety of capacities over the past 18 years in West Africa. She led a community-based health programme in northern Ghana and Togo, acted as a family health adviser, and was the deputy representative and later representative for Oxfam/UK for ten years, based in Burkina Faso. Alice holds a Master's degree in Social Development Planning and Management. She has a wealth of experience in sustainable development and gender-equity issues, and is now based in Canada.

The spaces between the weave: Building alliances at the grassroots (Pakistan)

Maryam Iqbal

Introduction

I started working for Oxfam GB in Sindh Province, Pakistan, in April 1993. I was 25 years old and keen to be back in Pakistan to work in the development field. Although born in London, I had spent roughly half my life in Sindh, and the local language, Sindhi, is my mother tongue. I had not come on a mission from Oxfam to instil notions of gender equity in the Sindhi masses — quite the reverse, in fact! I was back because I had grown up there, and I wanted to work with Sindhi women in my chosen field of development. At the time, Oxfam had an all-male staff whose area of specialisation did not include working with women or on gender issues. With a background in gender studies, I was keen to work on such issues. I was given an initial three-month contract — there was evidently little expectation that I would stay longer in this chauvinistic and sometimes hostile climate. This article is about my work in what sometimes felt like the front line of the struggle to promote gender equality in Oxfam's work in Sindh. I felt alone, and I later learned that many programme officers feel the same isolation in this kind of work.

The political landscape and the history of NGOs

I arrived with Oxfam in Pakistan during a period of relative calm, shortly after a time of prolonged political unrest which frequently erupted into violence and a general breakdown of law and order. Some of this unrest was attributed directly to rival ethnic factions drawing attention to their marginalised and impoverished populations. There was also a strong current of public feeling that the government was in fact contributing to this violence as an opportune political distraction.

To make matters worse, the NGO sector was lurching from one crisis of legitimacy to the next: the newspapers made allegations about squandered funds and the antics of 'five-star NGOs',[20] and questioned the role of bilateral and other donors, who funded city-based organisations working on rural poverty in four-wheel drive vehicles. While many NGOs were in fact working legitimately, it was at times difficult to answer the very searching and valid questions of our partners and other observers who could not reconcile the two images. In addition, Sindh has a long tradition of voluntary philanthropic and self-help organisations, 'local *tanzeems* and *sudhar sanghats*',[21] but a fair number of these were what are locally termed 'paper organisations', formed in hurried anticipation of legitimate (or illegitimate) funds from 'friends' in transient business or government postings. Of course this dealing and hustling in the public sphere was entirely a man's *forte* and not in the realm of the average Sindhi woman's knowledge.

In this political and social landscape, my brief was to identify and develop a number of local groups who had ventured into working with women. While I could see the beginnings of a gender-sensitive analysis of poverty and an awareness of the need to incorporate this analysis into the voluntary sector's work, the notion of women as a special interest group (such as farmers or artisans)[22] was still far more common. My job was to weave my way through the lively arena of voluntary groups, and take forward the agenda of gender equity in development.

Getting into the spaces between the weave

I arrived in the office, aware that as a young woman development worker, I might have a high, although possibly fleeting novelty value. How to sustain the initial interest long enough to engage my colleagues and Oxfam's male project partners in gender-sensitive poverty analysis, needs assessment, and response would be my challenge for the next four years. A vital factor, which did not enter anyone's understanding immediately, was that Sindh was home to me. This was to be an important element in grounding my gender analysis in the everyday fabric of life in Sindh and in helping other actors in the local environment to get away from the prevalent notion of sexual equality as women's desire and demand to behave like men. The concept of gender and feminist theory were often seen as imports — like a Datsun car, but without the benefit of being so useful.

Over time and during my travels, I learned to detect almost imperceptible hints of opportunities to push the discussion, debate, and even practice of gender equity in many unlikely situations. I was able to create, use, and sometimes just plain exploit such opportunities. This was almost invisible work, and vastly under-valued in 'development' plans and programmes, but it was vital to develop fora for discussion about gender-fair development in order to make change sustainable. What follows are some examples of my work in building up these opportunities at the local level in Sindh. A distinction may be made between those strategies that were actively followed, constituting a 'grassroots advocacy' strategy, and some of the challenges which I faced unprepared, 'on the frontline'.

Building alliances

As the vast majority of women with whom Oxfam wanted to work in Sindh had low public visibility, finding the right man, or men, to work with was very important. If I wanted to reach women's spheres of influence, I would have to be invited in through the male public sphere.

I was surprised to realise how much of my time I spent with men's groups to facilitate women's gradual participation in the local development process. Men's role in the move to a gender equitable society was not mentioned in the gender literature that I had come across. Yet without this aspect, it was only half the story. In the short term, it was vital to build strategic alliances with rural men's groups and to support their work: they must feel that you understand the issues in their particular area and that you will therefore take them into account. These alliances were also important for my work as a channel for communication through which the stark division between the public and private sphere could be challenged. A very real sense of male fear about all manner of extreme calamities which might follow once women became organised had to be addressed and put into perspective, based on what women's real needs and aspirations were.

This was in no way to detract from the need to initiate and maintain links with the Pakistani women's movement. But most women's organisations which had experience of social mobilisation were city-based and, if anything, were looking to Oxfam to introduce them and provide systematic access to rural women. In order to widen their constituency to include rural women, we first had to establish the habit of networking. We did this by inviting members of Pakistani women's organisations to a number of training sessions and workshops, which then opened up spaces for our women partner groups in which their experience could grow.

What does this have to do with the price of tomatoes?

A deep knowledge of the region and an ability to talk fluently on a wide range of subjects became key to making the unlikely alliances referred to above. Information that might seem entirely irrelevant to advancing the cause of women in Sindh suddenly became essential nuggets. They were the hooks in dialogue with those people for whom this information was essential knowledge in its own right.

I was to spend endless evenings, maybe on the porch after dinner, talking with my uncles about all manner of things, many of which were really only of local concern. Regular items of such discussions included the state of the tomato market; the extent of pesticide use on okra; the price of agricultural inputs such as fertiliser and tractor time; and the timing of the seasonal closure of river gates for desilting and dredging the Indus and her tributaries. All the while, I assimilated the richness and depth of rural language, with its references to the great Sufi saints.[23] At the same time, I would be finding out about the division of agricultural labour between the sexes; through chats with casual labourers working in agriculture and construction — about where there was a bumper crop of roses or melons this season, or which abandoned aspect of the Indus Highway was being reconstructed — I would learn about workers' migratory patterns. I was trying to get to know as much as possible about those matters close to the hearts and minds of the people with whom I was working, and of whom I was, in some way, a part.

I made a studied attempt to refamiliarise myself with Koranic references to women and interpreting them in the most liberal, if not feminist, sense. The Prophet Mohammed married Bibi Khatija, a strong independent woman who was 25 years his senior[24] and worked in the transport business (she owned several camel caravans[25]), a fact that would probably make the leaders of the ultra-conservative Taliban movement shrink in horror, should they choose to remember it. Quotes or incidents retold in the Koran would help me reassure and equip others to take forward the issue of educating daughters in their village, or lobbying village elders to take a stand for women's rights.

Wide-open door policy

I felt that I should talk about gender to anyone who paid a visit to the office, planned or unplanned, or to people I met during the course of a project visit. Some of this is an inevitable part of a programme officer's work. However, in a society where the pace of life and people's approach to networking are different, and where gender equity is a sensitive issue, many people wanted to see what I was like before arranging any specific meeting. I was not simply a visiting environmental resources specialist, with whom farmers may book time to discuss their crop rotation. This meant that I spent a vast amount of time in impromptu meetings. Whether I seemed approachable,[26] informal, rooted in the local context, whether I spoke Urdu (the national language) or Sindhi (the local one), whether I seemed enthusiastic or tired, were all factors that would count in my attempt to advance dialogue on gender.

These factors seem small, and are indeed almost imperceptible. But they did influence the efficacy of grassroots advocacy work to promote gender-fair development, with a particular group, on a particular day. It was hard to absorb how such little nuances of behaviour and circumstances on that day would gain points in 'advocacy credit' or erode tenuous gains. By 'advocacy credits', I don't mean that anything tangible had changed but that hopefully, in some small way, the groundswell of opinion had shifted a little. This kind of grassroots influencing precedes changes at the programme or policy level and needs to be recognised as an essential activity. It goes largely unnoticed, yet the amount of time that staff in field offices spend on influencing suggests that the essential basis of goodwill upon which Oxfam's reputation and efficiency depends is built in this way.

Some challenges

In some NGO circles, the view was held that in order to work with women, and to encourage them to take part in the development process, the most essential input was a four-wheel drive car — the logic being that this would protect women from the unwanted gaze of men. Unsurprisingly, Oxfam was not going to entertain such ideas. When people realised this, their emphasis would shift and they would then view me as a conduit through which other funds could be attracted. I wanted to make sure that I was not seen simply as a channel through which small rural organisations could gain further access to funds under the various banners of 'women in development', 'gender and development', or simply 'women'. What I did want was for people to enter into dialogue on gender inequality.

I was aware that some people viewed me as part of an experimental and innovative approach to development. I had applied initially to work as a volunteer, at a point when the historically strong spirit of volunteerism for welfare and development in Sindh was at a low ebb. The work of volunteers was not considered serious. In the end, I never actually was a volunteer with Oxfam, but the initial impression that I might be on some kind of placement stayed for a while, and it didn't help to enhance commitment to the issues that I was working on. My initial three-month contract did nothing to alleviate Oxfam's image as a wacky and experimental organisation (in contrast to Oxfam's preferred image of itself as innovative and cutting edge). My terms of employment gave my colleagues an impression of transience, which probably felt more comfortable to some of the men. However, while many male peers and potential partners in the NGO movement met the idea of *auratun ji tanzeem*[27] with broad smiles and an amused exchange of glances, a minority welcomed me and the nature of my work with all the relief and excitement of seeing a long lost friend. Regretfully, they were few to begin with, but their number increased and they remained true throughout.

Being the first member of staff with specific responsibility for qualitative programme development issues, my brief was not to spend much money, but to work towards developing the capacity of a few of our partners. This kind of work involved training, workshops, a lot of visits, close monitoring and follow-up activities, and small group work. At the time, however, there was a noticeable bias in Oxfam towards spending money and dispersing funds as a sign of success in managing programmes. A high number of counterparts in a portfolio was considered a sign of effective work. At training sessions and workshops, Project Officers would ask each other: 'So how many grants do you manage?' It was far less usual to hear people ask: 'What is the level of women's participation in the groups that you manage?'

Final reflections: more spaces between the weave

Over time, small changes in people's attitudes made me realise that a new reality had begun to take shape in the landscape I had first encountered. When I joined Oxfam, there was never any correspondence from men's organisations requesting assistance to form a counterpart female organisation in their village, and none from any women's organisations. By the time I left, there were far more requests for assistance with women's group formation than the existing structure of the Oxfam office could effectively deal with.

In the year after I joined Oxfam, another female colleague was hired, and during an extended period of emergencies work we had an additional three women on the team. During that time, when it felt like there were a lot of us, it seemed crazy that it hadn't always been like this. The novelty value was all but gone, and in its place was an acceptance that everyone on the team, both male and female, should play a role in achieving a gender-sensitive, effective programme.

To really bring about change, advocacy for gender-fair development must be home-grown. It is not just a matter of entering the spaces between the weave, but also of growing in that space, and evolving from the vast and rich fabric of everyday life. In the context of Sindh, this meant really getting to know the communities' concerns and aspirations, so that people did not feel the need for hard-line attitudes and behaviour, and thus achieving the desired result through skilled persuasion. Mastering this meant only asking for things which could be immediately granted, and constantly giving evidence and influencing informally in favour of the argument. This work involves a great deal of fluidity and flexibility, and almost imperceptible strategies and responses which are vital to prepare the ground on which Oxfam's work and reputation depends. Advocating for gender equity is not only about research and policy papers; it is also about the time that Oxfam's field staff spend making contacts and forming opportunities for change in local communities, which is crucial to its success at all levels.

About the author

Born in London, Maryam went to live in Sindh, Pakistan when she was three months old. She was brought up speaking Sindhi, Urdu, and English. She holds a BA in Economics and Industrial Relations and a MA in Development Studies, specialising in education in national development and gender and development. For Oxfam, Maryam worked as Programme Development Officer in the Sindh Office, as an Emergencies Officer in Pakistan and Afghanistan, and in Oxford as Researcher for the Strategic Planning and Evaluation Team and the Policy Department. With a strong interest in working at the grassroots level as well as at the national and international level, Maryam has worked as a consultant and is presently based in London.

Notes to section I

1   The Serbia office was established largely to respond to the needs of the inflowing Croatian Serb and Bosnian Serb refugees following the turmoil that ensued after the international community's recognition of Slovenia, Croatia, and then Bosnia-Hercegovina as independent states.

2   A further office was opened in Zagreb, Croatia in 1994. Programmes and offices were also established in the Caucasus region of the Former Soviet Union and in Albania.

3   In the Bosnian Serb-held areas, prices rocketed as sanctions prevented import of raw materials and goods. A typically Bosnian way of measuring 'essentials' is to quote the prices of coffee and cigarettes at a given time. Stories abounded: as cigarettes hit 100 Deutsche Mark a packet, one entrepreneur allegedly stood outside the Hotel Tuzla charging 2 DM a puff to desperate nicotine addicts! On the front line, it was rumoured that young men, charged with the task of fighting each other, sympathised sufficiently with the human desire for a cigarette to fire them across the front line to the opposing forces, who returned their fire with money attached. And in detention camps around the country, cigarettes represented one of the most desired sources both of comfort and currency.

4   TV Tuzla provided programming on a two-day rotation, as electricity supply schedules meant that half the town could view on a given night.

5   A community which included the temporarily resident international aid community.

6   The workshops programme also included establishing a youth centre in Tuzla town; a children's centre for the children of displaced people, freeing up the mother's time to attend the workshops; a support centre for disabled children and their parents — later to become the *Koraci Nade* (Steps of Hope) Centre documented in Rachel Hastie (1997), *Disabled Children in a Society at War*, Oxford: Oxfam.

7   One of the explicit aims was to ease growing tensions between the displaced, largely rural population — for whom material living conditions were often hardest and to whom humanitarian aid was mostly targeted — and the local

urban population, many of whom also suffered poor living conditions but felt marginalised by the distribution of aid.

8   A further debate centred on how to ensure that women received fair remuneration for their labour, and that Oxfam was not exploiting them (what is a 'fair wage' in a context where no one except the very fortunate are being paid at all?).

9   Workshops were miles apart, and travel between them difficult and often dangerous owing to shelling, poor road conditions, and lack of transport.

10   At that time Bosnia-Hercegovina lacked a clear legal framework for registering NGOs, and the situation is still not fully resolved.

11   Huremovic notes ironically 'what never ceases to impress me is the vivid imagination employed in generating names for [international agencies' projects becoming local self-sustaining NGOs] — it is almost impossible to guess that Bosfam is actually Oxfam's brainchild, and Terre des Enfants was once a children's program started by Terre des Hommes' (Huremovic, unpublished, undated).

12   There is insufficient room here for discussion of a third crucial dilemma which faces Oxfam and similar organisations: how to prioritise programmes at a global level, and how to prioritise and assess concepts of 'distress and suffering' in varying cultural contexts. As one Oxfam staff member questioned: 'Should Oxfam have been funding a fashion show as part of its relief and development work? Should this "psycho-social work" have been allowed to compete for funds with saving lives in Rwanda?' (Fiona Gell, personal communication 1997). In reality of course, prioritisation is not a straight-forward issue, with funds allocated regionally by major donors and so on, but the underlying dilemmas and debates remain.

13   As Fiona Gell noted: 'the show provided great marketing publicity for the stylish and quality goods produced by the workshops ... more importantly, it showed that creativity and skill were still thriving even in the midst of war.' (Fiona Gell, personal communication, 1997)

14   Particularly for rural women, who are at a great disadvantage in the urban labour markets in the areas to which they have been displaced.

15   For example, Participatory Rural Appraisal (PRA) methods.

16   'Representative' groups refers to those which carry the voice of all community members, particularly the most vulnerable: this includes both women and men, children and the elderly, ethnic and linguistic minorities, disabled people, lower castes, and so on. For a full discussion of this, please refer to Judy Adoko's article in this volume.

17   See Lina Abu-Habib (1997), *Gender and Disability*, Oxford: Oxfam.

18   I am using this definition of 'gender analysis' throughout this article,

emphasising the analysis of gender inequality as a primary point of understanding in social relations.

19 See also Fiona Gell's article on gender and emergencies.

20 NGOs for whom such hotels were the most obvious venues for seminars on poverty.

21 Translation from Sindhi: development organisations usually village- or community-based.

22 This is in no way to suggest that farmers and artisans are a homogeneous group, but rather, that they are subject to certain common influences due to their trade.

23 Such as Shah Abdul Latif Bhittai, Sachal Sarmast, and Watto Faqir.

24 Koran / Hadith reference.

25 Hadith reference.

26 It was usual for a senior or otherwise respected working woman to be addressed as 'Madam' in conversation, even if the discussion was in Sindhi. This had all the connotations of an unwanted colonial hangover and one that Oxfam of course sought to avoid. It was so ingrained in local use that the only way we succeeded was to point out that the only person called a Madam in England, was the woman in charge of a brothel. It worked.

27 Women's development organisations (*aurat* means woman).

II

Organisational culture and procedures

Introduction to section II

> The inclusion of women is never a simple addition; a fundamental
> rearrangement of some kind is always needed. (Eisenstein in Dean 1997, p.34)

As stated in the main Introduction to this book, research into integrating gender issues into organisations has proliferated over the past decade, showing us that putting in place a policy on gender is only a first step to transforming working practices, and the end results of the work itself. Articles in this section consider the links between Oxfam GB's organisational culture, systems and procedures, and good development work for women — both outside and within the organisation.

One of the great debates for gender analysts is to what extent work on gender issues can really achieve greater equality between women and men without a change in organisational culture which goes beyond a gender policy, to an explicit commitment to feminist and transformative goals. The languages of 'feminism' and 'gender' are examined in this light by Ines Smyth, working in Oxfam's specialist gender unit at head office; in her article, she argues that the choice of language indicates a fundamental difference in political stance. In many development agencies, gender issues are regarded as an important 'technical' area of development, but the use of the more transformative and political language of feminism would mean that accepting a depoliticised notion of women as the 'poorest of the poor' would not occur so easily.

The barriers to gender equality that are part of organisational culture are explored further in the article by Wendy Carson, who carried out research in Oxfam in 1995, using a psychological approach. She argues that in Oxfam, organisational norms reflect archetypal 'male' values of efficiency and results-orientation, at the expense of 'female' values of co-operation and process-orientation. Wendy Carson argues for a more even balance between the two sets of values, as the language and ideas of gender equity must be supported and legitimated by organisational culture as well as systems and procedures.

Elsa Dawson's and Bridget Walker's articles give insights into the way in which different systems and procedures, particularly planning and impact assessment, can be used as a lever to achieve successful implementation of an organisation's gender policy, and to take a step along the route to social transformation. In addition, both emphasise that policy development, and use of systems and procedures to enforce policy, must be accompanied by change on a third level: individual change in the form of personal commitment of development workers to gender equality and organisational change.

In line with this, many development organisations which have engaged with gender issues have found that the commitment of senior level staff is an essential element of success. Oxfam GB is no exception. The commitment of senior staff gives authority and legitimacy to gender issues, while a high percentage of women at senior level indicates the organisation's willingness to change its ways of working. For many women managers in non-profit-making organisations, as well as for those in government and the private sector, promotion to senior office has amounted to a struggle for their own legitimacy as post-holders, as well as for the legitimacy of the policies they promote.

While not all women are advocates of gendered approaches to development, and men can support them too, the contribution of women managers who are committed to gender equity must not be underestimated. In Oxfam GB, women managers have often used the power and opportunity given to them to pave the way for an understanding and acceptance of gender concerns in many different contexts. This is clearly demonstrated by Visha Padmanabhan, whose article discusses her efforts to transform the programme in Cambodia from a technical relief programme to a community-based development programme with gender equity central to its work. In turn, Sue Emmott looks at the strategic decisions that upheld Oxfam's commitment to women's rights, and at the implications of such decisions. Parallel to this, she analyses her own role as a woman manager, guiding Oxfam staff in the complex and dangerous environment of Afghanistan.

At what cost are such contributions by women managers made? The article by Dianna Melrose examines at the way in which Oxfam GB's organisational culture and her own personal and professional commitments have interacted, putting enormous pressure on her and other women managers as they ascend the organisational hierarchy. In Oxfam GB, as in other development organisations, the imperative 'to change the world' demands a commitment of time which is difficult to balance with the dominant social norms in most cultures which expect women to take on the role of primary carers for their families. In his article, Norman Clift, of Oxfam GB's human resources department, looks at the way in which a facility such as a workplace nursery can further equal opportunities between women and men. Oxfam GB should demonstrate its commitment to its Gender Policy by providing facilities to ensure that women and men with caring responsibilities have these recognised and their practical needs met.

Changing the rules: Implementing a gender policy through organisational procedures

Bridget Walker

Don't change your body, change the rules.   (Jackie Fleming, Leeds Postcards)

The study of organisations, their structures and processes has always been of concern to those interested in social change, and particularly for women: organisations are usually in the public domain, from which women have been so often excluded. Even if women are permitted to enter and participate in organisational life, this does not guarantee entry into the forums where policy is made, nor does it guarantee the formulation of policy that takes women's interests into account. Often, it is in procedures for policy implementation that the match or mismatch between policy and practice becomes evident. Examining the 'rules' of institutions — both written and unwritten — from a gender perspective has therefore been an important area for feminist enquiry into women's subordination. For organisations with a mandate to promote equitable human development, this kind of enquiry is an essential task.

This contribution is a personal account of my own experience within Oxfam GB over the past seven years. It speculates about the extent to which changes to the organisational structures, and the stresses on these structures at a time of substantial change, have affected the way in which gender issues were introduced and perceived in Oxfam, and the opportunities that were taken or missed.

I arrived in Oxfam at a time when management was being more clearly defined as a line stretching from the Oxford head office to the country offices, with the aim of creating clearer levels of accountability and coherence in the vertical relationship. However, Oxfam failed at that time to establish meaningful links between posts *across* the organisation. For an issue such as gender relations, which cuts across all of Oxfam's concerns worldwide, this presented problems. Obtaining programme information on which to base decisions about issues such as gender was surprisingly difficult. It was not easy for one office to learn from another's experience of working on gender issues, owing to an existing organisational weakness in the recording, storage, retrieval, and exchange of information.

I was faced with the task of managing from Oxford, for a temporary period, a large country-programme at a time of emergency. The problems of communicating about work on gender outlined above were compounded by a feeling on the part of some staff that gender issues were an 'add-on' concern, for which there was no time during a disaster. In situations where working on gender was not prioritised by staff or their managers, there was no way for other staff to challenge this, since gender was seen as a management responsibility.

Using systems and procedures for feminist ends

Handy (1988)[1] points out that 'the more differences you have to take account of in your structure ... the more you will need to find ways of integrating the different parts ... there are three main ways of holding an organisation together: the hierarchy of command; rules and procedures; co-ordinating groups.'

In Oxfam, the hierarchy of command was strengthened through the formalisation of the line-management structure. Subsequently, strategic planning was introduced in the early 1990s as a mandatory procedure for all parts of the organisation. In contrast to these developments, the Gender and Development Unit (GADU) had been set up in 1985 with a co-ordination function, as an advisory unit for the international programme. GADU lacked the authority which is a feature of hierarchies of command, governed by rules and procedures; consequently, when I subsequently joined GADU as an adviser to the international programme, I encountered problems similar to those encountered in my previous role.

The culture of Oxfam at that time meant that there was considerable ambivalence about codifying procedures, and a fear of imposition from the centre. When the subject at issue for codifying good practice and minimum standards is a highly personal one, concerning gender roles and relations, attitudes and behaviours, seeming ambivalence on the part of colleagues may mask substantial levels of personal discomfort or resistance. This ambivalence seemed to pervade the context in which GADU's gender advisers operated. The unit had been in existence for some four years when I joined Oxfam, yet there was no organisational policy on gender. This lack conveyed a mixed message: on the one hand, Oxfam had devoted human and financial resources to work on gender, and this was clearly an exciting and pioneering initiative which was evidence of commitment at the most senior levels. On the other hand, the unit's purely advisory role meant that programme managers were under no obligation to consult gender advisers for support on their work, or, if they did so, to follow the advice that was given. Staff in some areas of the world which fell within my geographic responsibility as a gender adviser did not converse readily with GADU — a group described by one colleague as the 'feminist thought-police'. (Policing, of course, is ideally carried out by consent.) The position of GADU within the International Division led to a focus on gender concerns in the over-seas programme only, to the exclusion of other parts of the organisation. Links with Oxfam's other departments were largely informal; in particular, there were no clear mechanisms to ensure that gender issues were considered by staff responsible for personnel and human resources. Thus, there were no ways of creating and enforcing gender-aware strategies for recruitment, selection, and staff development, although an equal-opportunities policy covered some areas.

However, theories of organisational culture point to the existence of sub-cultures alongside the dominant cultures. Within Oxfam, personal contacts were the key to gaining entry to territories which were sometimes described as 'hill-top republics' by those to whom the structures gave the role of gate-keeper. Cultivating relationships with individuals who shared a commitment to gender issues was critical to GADU's work. Staff searched out others who were in sympathy with aspirations to gender equity, forging alliances and networking across programmes and hierarchies. This horizontal linking created a critical mass of people and data from which to work for change.

Uncovering the rules to achieve change

A first step in thinking about change is to discover what the rules actually are. This is not always straightforward. It was not easy when I joined Oxfam to identify where policy was made, by whom and how, or indeed what constituted policy, and how it derived its authenticity. It can be argued that this lack of clarity was a feature of Oxfam at that time of change from a 'family firm' to a multinational corpora-tion; the organisation had yet to institute systems and procedures which would promote information-sharing, and adequately manage such a large, diverse body.

Two key processes and procedures — strategic planning, and monitoring and evaluation systems — will be discussed here, as a route through which gender concerns were introduced into Oxfam's programme mandate. Strategic planning is tracked over two phases: 1990–91, and 1994–95. In the process of developing these procedures, Oxfam's organisational Gender Policy was formulated and approved, providing an extra impetus for the incorporation of gender concerns across Oxfam's programmes. By working with these processes and procedures, significant progress has been made in changing Oxfam's 'rules'.

Strategic planning

It was the introduction of strategic planning in the wake of restructuring in 1990/91 which made gender issues into an institutional priority in Oxfam's international programme. Strategic planning was intended to be a tool to help implement organisational change and strengthen new ways of working. It was mandatory for all, and gender was one of the themes that had to be addressed. The planning process began at programme level: each country office was asked to produce a situational analysis, including an internal critique of Oxfam's strengths and weaknesses in that context. From this, a set of aims and strategies had to be agreed, to shape the office's work for the next three years. These aims and strategies were synthesised with those of other countries and regions, and fed into the same process at cross-divisional and corporate level. This work led to a summary of how Oxfam's work with communities contributed to the overarching aim of achieving universal 'basic rights' and 'sustainable livelihoods'. In this way, the language of 'rights' entered Oxfam's everyday vocabulary, and the concept formed a rationale for work to promote women's basic rights and livelihoods.

Strategic planning was regarded with some ambivalence in some quarters; fear was expressed that a chain of 'command and control' would be established, since strategic planning was a tool developed in the military and commercial sectors of the industrialised world. A review of the first round of strategic planning frankly acknowledged some of the teething problems.

But for me, and others seeking knowledge of how gender issues were being addressed in country programmes, it was a breakthrough. For the first time, it was possible to have an overview of gender work across Oxfam's programmes, in a consistent and systematic format. The poverty analysis included data disaggregated by gender, which revealed the particular condition and position of women — for example, numbers of female-maintained households, teenage mothers, vulnerable girl-children; women's lack of civil and legal status, property and inheritance rights, and access to resources; the economic and political trends leading to women's further exclusion and impoverishment; the effects of these on gender relations, and of male exclusion / unemployment. The strategic planning process also ensured a new profile for issues such as violence against women, and the causes and effects of conflict.

Critics have argued that the strategic planning process merely revealed the lack of gender awareness in many programmes, and did not in itself lead to more gender-fair programme implementation. I would suggest that it served a similar function to legislation. Like the UK's 1975 Sex Discrimination Act, it has been a necessary but not sufficient reform, from which to build up a body of case law.

In the first phase of strategic planning, gender was described as a theme. It became evident that this approach did not capture the totality of what was needed, but a new rule had been established: gender was no longer an optional extra, but central to programme planning and implementation. The International Division's strategic plan addressed the crucial issue of personnel procedures, proposing that gender awareness be included in all 'Overseas and Marketing Division recruitment/selection, and other personnel procedures and practice, and ... management induction and staff training'.

However, the ID strategic plan did not mention the recruitment of women managers as part of the gender strategy; this was a serious omission. The need for this, and enabling procedures to encourage women, had previously been discussed and documented on the Africa Desk:

> At a discussion of gender at an Africa Strategy meeting in September 1991 it was recognised that programmes were most committed to gender ... in those field offices where the staff worked well as a team, where there were gender-aware male managers and women in the team at a senior level who were committed to gender justice. The seniority of the women concerned was a key issue.[2]

This illustrates the complexity of policy implementation: appropriate procedures are not enough. While procedures supply a clear operational framework, and rules of engagement and minimum standards, people always provide the driving force.

By the time that the second phase of strategic planning began in 1994–95, Oxfam's Gender Policy had been agreed. After wide consultation across the organisation, the policy was approved by Oxfam's Council in May 1993. The programme of implementation for the Gender Policy was subject to delays, so strategic planning — at least in the International Division — was the chief driver of Gender Policy implementation. It was now part of the mandate. The second phase of strategic planning built on learning from the first; there was wide consultation over the draft guidelines. These were introduced at regional planning meetings. A Strategic Planning and Evaluation (SPE) team had been created, and I had joined the team as SPE adviser to the Asia and Middle East programmes. The new matrix management structure — designed to enable cross-programme exchange and thus address some of the problems that resulted from the failure to create these linkages in the first round of restructuring — meant that, in addition to being part of a central team, SPE advisers with a geographical responsibility were full members of the management teams of the areas to which they had been assigned. As a gender adviser, I had seldom been invited to these forums, and I certainly did not have a place on them by right. Yet I found that my background in gender-related work was welcomed by the Asia / Middle East management team, and I was asked to take a 'lead role' on gender in the area. Often, gender advisers and SPE advisers worked hand in hand.

Gender was no longer seen as an issue to be addressed in isolation from other issues, but as a defining perspective on development. Staff were asked to look critically at the use of data, and sources of information for situational analysis; and to think how gender issues informed their vision and values. The process, designed from the start to be participatory, was to consult women, and women's organisations were seen as important stakeholders.

What difference did this make? In the Middle East, a consultant was commissioned to produce a paper on poverty and gender issues in the region. Violence against women emerged as an important issue; research has continued, and support has been given to new partners. In Indonesia, Oxfam convened a gathering of a wide spectrum of women's organisations and networks for a discussion day, whose conclusions formed part of the country situational analysis. In Oxfam in Bangladesh (a country office which had already drawn up its own set of project criteria from a gender perspective), the Gender Policy was examined as part of the organisational mandate, and 'customised' for the country context. This included stressing practical ways of ensuring the safety and mobility of women workers—and consideration of the implications of this for resources. An analysis of activities was carried out as part of an organisational self-assessment exercise by the office in December 1997; this made a comparison over a five-year period, and showed that there had been important changes in staffing, with increasing numbers of women in management positions, and shared approaches to work on gender. In all these instances the initiative came from the managers concerned, both male and female. It was their commitment, together with the specialist advice that they commissioned (both within and from outside Oxfam), that turned paper procedures into human realities.

Monitoring and evaluation

In my view, the other key procedure to assist the integration of gender concerns into Oxfam's programmes has been monitoring and evaluation. Documentation of programme experience has enabled women to articulate their interests and needs, and provided evidence of the gender-determined impact of development processes. Externally, it was evidence that women were not benefiting from development that provided the initial drive for resources for women in development (WID) and gender and development (GAD) initiatives. The UN Conference in Nairobi in 1985, and the resulting Forward Looking Strategies, created an international environment of support for work on gender.

Within Oxfam at that time, committed women staff in Latin America and East Africa, and women's networks in India, were challenging Oxfam to take account of gender issues. Subsequent work in Oxfam has explored what women want from the development process and asked whether that is being delivered. (The most formal example of this in Oxfam was the consultation process of the Women's Linking Project, discussed in Candida March's contribution to this volume.) Oxfam has been generally weak in the area of monitoring and evaluation from a gender perspective; successive evaluations have shown that much work needs to be done on integrating gender issues into the process. This has been particularly the case in the evaluation of emergency work. Currently, the organisational policy on evaluation is changing, with increased emphasis on continuing monitoring and assessment during the life of an intervention. Nevertheless, it is likely that external evaluation of major programmes will continue.

Work needs to be done to ensure that terms of reference for monitoring and evaluation consistently include gender-related criteria. It is not enough simply to include women on the evaluation team: both they and the other team members need to have an understanding of gender issues, and expertise in enabling women (and children, where appropriate) to contribute effectively to the evaluation processes. Women may use different indicators to assess the success of a project from those of the NGO engaged in the project: in Chad, an evaluation of urban income-generating projects for women-maintained households was successful from the point of view of simple quantitative measures of repayments schedules and sustainable small business enterprises. However, the assumption of planners that women might use the income to pay for health and education services was not entirely borne out. For the women, the success of the project lay in the fact that it provided resources which enabled them to buy pots to cook extra food for other members of the community, to contribute to community celebrations, helping to end their enforced exclusion from society.

Here, the outcome may have been slightly unexpected for the funders, but seemed ultimately beneficial to the programme participants. In other income-generation projects, the same cannot be claimed: in Bangladesh, quantitative indicators may suggest success, but the reality behind the repayment figures may be less optimistic. It is the degree of women's control over resources within the household which determines whether women are themselves benefiting from development interventions; they may simply be acting as channels for resources to men, with more responsibility for repayment, and no more authority than before. Such research would suggest that a pretty wide net needs to be cast in assessing the outcome of our work, that the unpredictable is what should be expected, and that, with multiple actors and competing interests, there will always be the likelihood that someone's gain is someone else's loss. We need monitoring procedures and practices which can identify qualitative indicators, which take account of the different stakeholders' interests, and which can become part of a learning process for all involved.

Developing and using tools

In both strategic planning and monitoring and evaluation, a gender-aware approach to analysis is an important starting point. At project level, analytical tools (the various gender frameworks, the 'People-Oriented Planning' framework for use in refugee situations, the 'Capacities and Vulnerabilities Analysis') are used widely by programme staff. In Oxfam, use of these tools in emergency programmes in Asia has significantly increased understanding of the issues and interests involved. However, programme staff have also increasingly worked on developing appropriate tools. For example, in Pakistan and Bangladesh workshops on 'lessons learned' are a regular follow-up to relief programmes, and a workshop in Bali in 1996 drew on the experience of programme staff to identify models of good practice and establish standards. At the same time, the SPE team at head office has been working on guidelines for programme and project management and support, drawing on checklists, guidelines, and materials produced and tested in the country offices.

Conclusion

Despite the positive achievements mentioned above, a tension remains. How should organisational procedures for policy implementation agreed and implemented? Are guidelines to be developed and adopted collectively, or disseminated from the centre? The Project and Programme Management Support Guidelines developed by the SPE team are available for use in each office, and training workshops have been initiated by many (but not all) managers. It is too early, as yet, to assess how effective these guidelines may be in providing a systematic and consistent approach to improving programme quality; but, like the strategic planning guidelines before them, they should provide an opportunity for looking at gender at project level across the programme.

What is certain is that no procedures can be effective without the commitment of people — both women and men, and at every level. And commitment alone is not enough. Yayori Matsui[3] talks of the 'need to have a global perspective, a structural analysis and long term strategies. We must begin by listening to the voices and hearing the pain of the most victimised and oppressed women in our own countries ...' Learning how to listen to women is a first and essential step to developing strategies for change, but sympathy and solidarity need to be accompanied by analysis of political, economic, and social structures, from the most personal levels, where gender relations are learned, to the international level, where the development discourse has yet to incorporate gender in a systematic and meaningful way.

I have suggested that the introduction of planning and evaluation procedures which develop an analysis requiring the participation of all stakeholders has the potential to transform organisational understandings and actions on gender and development. However, commitment is needed from staff with the authority to take this forward. There remains organisational weakness in sharing knowledge, and remembering and rewarding programme experience. In developing the Gender Policy and devising means for its implementation, Oxfam's organisational rules have been exposed to critical consideration. The jury has yet to reach a verdict on the extent to which, in consequence, they have been changed.

About the author

Bridget Walker has worked in development with several different organisations in Africa and the UK, in programme management and support. She joined to Oxfam in 1990 as a regional manager, and subsequently was employed as a Gender Adviser and most recently as Strategic Planning and Evaluation Adviser for programmes in Asia, Middle East, Eastern Europe, and the former Soviet Union. She will take up the post of Deputy Director of Responding to Conflict, based in Birmingham, UK, in 1999.

Two steps forward, one step back: Experiences of senior management

Dianna Melrose

Introduction

I write from the perspective of a feminist, who is also a working mother and one of the relatively small but expanding number of women senior managers in Oxfam GB. As the member of the international programme's Senior Management Team charged with responsibility for gender issues, and head of the department in which the organisation's gender specialists are located, my aim is to share some reflections on what has and has not worked in implementing our Gender Policy.

By sharing this experience, hopefully others will avoid some of our mistakes. I feel that the more open we are with each other about the huge obstacles to pursuing gender equity and meaningful organisational transformation, the more we can pool ideas on solutions to common problems and feel a much-needed sense of solidarity. By basing this article on my own experience, I also bring out the particular obstacles faced by a woman senior manager who has broken through the glass ceiling of an organisation,[4] and I outline some of the lessons to be learned.

At least on paper, Oxfam GB is a feminist[5] organisation. Our Gender Policy commits us to a radical and ambitious agenda in pursuit of gender equity and women's human rights. However, in reality there is a considerable gap between the policy's ambition and its patchy implementation, with much to celebrate and much to lament. Despite the extensive discussion that took place before the policy was adopted, it is clear — with the benefit of hindsight — that part of the problem lies in the very different understanding of what the policy means.

This gap in perceptions first dawned on me soon after I took on responsibility for gender issues in the International Division. A few of us were trying to persuade a key trustee and senior manager of Oxfam to invite some representatives of Southern women's organisations to the forthcoming Oxfam Assembly meeting to help cement new alliances in pursuit of women's human rights. Our efforts failed: we were told that if any of us thought the Assembly was going to give time to gender issues, we were wrong. Its purpose was to talk about what we mean by poverty, about our development approach, and to discuss whether Oxfam should work on poverty in the UK. Nothing to do with women's or gender issues, of course!

This is not to suggest that Oxfam trustees and top managers are anything other than fully in agreement with the need to achieve greater gender equity, and for Oxfam to do more to help some of the world's most disadvantaged women attain their human rights. The issue is where this goal fits with other goals, what priority should be given to specific gender work, and what it implies in terms of governance, working culture, human-resources policies, and resource allocation.

Some historical perspective is also needed. Oxfam in 1998 is a very different organisation to the one I joined in 1980. Then, overtly sexist behaviour was not only tolerated but openly exhibited by some, but by no means all, of the almost exclusively male managers. It would not be tolerated today. Oxfam does a great deal of innovative work on gender issues, with whole programmes turned around through the sort of transformational leadership described in other chapters.[6]

Multiple realities

Reality — past and present — is rather more complex than a linear progression from sexist organisation to one active on gender equality. Multiple realities have and do coexist. In 1979, the male manager who recruited me to Oxfam went out of his way in taking positive action to avoid ending up with an all-male three-person fledgling public-policy/lobbying unit, then called the Public Affairs Unit. Having failed to attract suitable women candidates, he went round the building asking for ideas on who to approach and was given my name as a failed candidate for a Desk Officer post on the Latin America desk. When I joined, I encountered sexual harassment which was mild by the standards of the City of London, where I started my career; however, it was all the more shocking given Oxfam's values.

When I became head of the Public Affairs Unit a few years later, the (male) recruiting manager, before offering me the job, launched into a long preamble on how he was going against his better judgement in not appointing one of the two 'chaps' who, despite their management experience, had none whatsoever in advocacy. On another occasion, when I was considering shortlisting a man for a vacant administrator post (having recruited two feminist women as researchers/lobbyists) the same manager rebuked me for trying to subvert 'the natural order'.

Today Oxfam still has at its apex a Corporate Management Team of five men and one woman, with men disproportionately represented in other senior management posts; but the culture is so changed, at one level, that success in recruiting women to top posts is prized. However, having been involved in recruiting for the current director and other top posts, it is painfully evident that, whereas relatively inexperienced men do apply, few women will.[7]

These contradictions — particularly our failure to challenge the prevailing gender-biased, anti-carers' working culture — make one feel that in terms of effective Gender Policy implementation, for every two steps forward, we take at least one, sometimes several, steps back. This was brought home to me most vividly in the recent discussion on Oxfam's values, conducted as part of a fundamental review of Oxfam's future direction. In a meeting of influential trustees and staff, I argued for gender equity being central to our values and beliefs, in line with the agreed organisational Gender Policy. I was reduced to stuttering, inarticulate disbelief when asked: 'why gender?'.

Given the prevailing attitudes in British society, and the anti-feminist backlash to which Ines Smyth refers in her article, perhaps it is hopelessly optimistic to think that we should be able to build on what is there, rather than to keep rehearsing first principles? Gender specialists have rightly identified the recruitment of gender-aware staff, particularly managers, as potentially the single most effective transformational strategy. The job descriptions say all the right things, but although some key appointments were delayed because the best candidates lacked skills in gender analysis, this is more the exception than the rule. I know that I have recruited advocacy staff for their knowledge of key targets, political skills, and macroeconomic analysis, and been prepared to give them the 'benefit of the doubt' on gender analysis and commitment to gender equity.

Leadership: what are our real priorities?

All our experience bears out the critical importance of strong and consistent leadership. Some of the best examples of transformational leadership in Oxfam are found at the level of programme officers and middle management, rather than at the top (myself included), especially in terms of a consistent prioritisation of gender concerns.

Part of the problem is that in a large and complex organisation such as Oxfam, senior staff inevitably have multiple roles. As we wrestle, not that effectively, with multiple priorities, gender concerns fairly consistently get squeezed. Critical here is what is most valued at the top. I have not conducted an opinion poll among trustees or the Senior Management Teams, but I know what they value me for: of my multiple roles, what is valued by most are the Policy Department's advocacy achievements, my leadership on engagement with the private sector or UK government, my role as a media spokesperson — not my lead role on gender issues in the International Division.

Our experiment with asking a senior manager to take on the gender lead role for the Corporate Management Team ran into similar problems. Bottom line for the deputy directors of the organisation (as we are constituted today) is our income, the performance of shops and Fair Trade activities, overall programme impact and speed of response in emergencies, effective human-resources policies, and sound financial management.

With no critical mass of gender enthusiasts at the top, Gender Policy implementation tends to be approached as one more item on the list of competing priorities, to be ticked off every so often, rather than as a perspective which should inform every decision we take and be integral to everything we do. As one organisational development consultant put it: 'The people at the top need their outlook transformed. This usually does not happen. Therefore gender is not institutionalised. This has become a cliché: but unless it happens organisations will continue to struggle with "add-on" management of gender'.[8]

Oxfam's gender specialists have long been aware that some of our pioneering work on gender has tended to be more valued outside than within the organisation. Why do we undervalue gender work? Part of the answer must be that we remain a male-dominated organisation at the top decision-making levels. But it is more complex: as Suzanne Williams argues in her article, there is a desire at the top of the organisation (which I share) for Oxfam to be able to state more clearly what difference we are making to the lives of poor women and men — in other words, to be able to demonstrate visible results. The problem with the struggle for gender equity is that we are in for the long haul. It is harder to demonstrate tangible, immediate impact, and it involves a process of change which necessitates investing resources in changing Oxfam itself (through capacity-building, developing tools for gender analysis, investing in an exchange of learning across programmes, and so on).

Oxfam is at the moment in a critical phase of transition. Our role for many years has been that of a Northern funding agency (transferring resources from North to South). The values governing this role have been simply to relieve poverty, not to 'interfere' with more complex issues of human rights and social justice. However, as Oxfam has evolved we have become a more complex and relevant organisation committed to working in alliance with others to promote social justice and protect human rights (through a range of strategies, including advocacy and building local capacity). The problem is that the values shared by many (but not all) of our most influential trustees and senior managers are that of the funding agency. In other words, money spent on ourselves, on processes such as facilitating networking between women's organisations to build common advocacy agendas, or investing in developing staff competencies in gender analysis, is money diverted from 'the poor'.

With some of the sceptics, a rights discourse will get us nowhere. It is more effective to emphasise the 'efficiency' argument, which is more acceptable to those who are rooted in Oxfam's original 'funder' role, and who resist our adoption of a more complex role in social justice and human rights. This involves citing the uncontested fact that women make up 70 per cent of the world's poor, and giving out the message that if we are serious about tackling poverty, then on efficiency grounds we have to be serious about gender.

At the same time, the more strategic approach of many trustees and senior-level decision-makers in Oxfam accepts that it is more cost-effective to promote far-reaching policy change of potential benefit to millions of poor women, men, and children than to fund atomised community-level projects. But the legacy of suspicion of money spent on organisational transformation, to equip us to act as an effective change agent on gender equity, remains alive and kicking.

Performance management

There is a lack of consistent leadership which is necessary to bring about a more holistic approach to gender issues, and this explains what we see in Oxfam: centres of energy and best practice in some places, inaction in others. We lack incentives to reward best practice or to impose sanctions against managers who fail to incorporate a gender perspective. We are still in the process of defining quality standards, as is evident from the lack of clear benchmarks documented in the gender mapping exercise. In recognition of the problem of lack of consistency in management approaches to gender, we have drawn on the suggestion that managers include an appropriate objective on gender-awareness in individual performance objectives. The Corporate Management Team agreed to manage performance on incorporating gender in one's work in this way, but their decision was not followed through. In the International Division, an edict was issued, but it descended like a 'lead balloon' (as one colleague put it) and sunk into oblivion, amidst a welter of competing messages.

Our experience suggests that edicts count for little unless managers are resourced and supported to follow through on them. As Visha Padmanabhan comments in this book, some of the more lasting change has been stimulated through investment in horizontal exchanges on best practice such as the staff network AGRA,[9] which can have an invaluable demonstration effect on others.

Gender specialists and senior management

The single most important resource for ensuring that gender issues are integrated into Oxfam was the energy of the pioneers during the 1980s, and the subsequent investment in a specialist gender unit (initially called GADU), which was set up in 1985. As the person who wielded the axe in what Suzanne Williams calls, in her article, the 'institutional execution' of the Gender Team in 1996, and who acted as midwife in its rebirth in the merged Gender and Learning Team, I fully agree with her that it remains essential for Oxfam to have a core of gender specialists.

We need gender specialists to support managers, programme staff, and partners, and to keep challenging us by bringing in fresh and innovative thinking. But managers must take the lead, not abdicate responsibility to the experts, and create an environment where the specialists can engage productively with others to bring about change. It is clear that to be able to do this effectively they need to feel trusted, not constantly threatened by repeated restructuring and the need to 'justify their existence', which can lead to unhelpful cycles of blame and mutual recrimination. With the benefit of my experience of managing gender specialists, I can say categorically that none of us should underestimate the sheer exhaustion, emotional scarring, and the potential for long-term burn-out as a result of fighting recurring battles on gender issues. At their best, the gender specialists have been creative, strategic, supportive of colleagues and quick to seize new opportunities (such as advocacy and networking around the Beijing conference, strategic planning, innovative publishing and cross-programme learning initiatives). At their worst, they have been conflict-ridden as a team to the point of paralysis, much given to blaming others and feeling victimised.

My experience is that the gender specialists generated mixed emotions throughout the organisation, ranging from strong appreciation and admiration to resentment. For some colleagues, especially isolated women programme officers and country representatives, the gender team could never deliver enough; as a result, these colleagues in the field alternately felt supported and let down as the Gender Team did or could not meet their needs. At the other end of the spectrum, some managers resented their intrusion; and even colleagues in their own department working on advocacy have been dismissive or angry as their attempts to integrate gender analysis into their work were dismissed as not good enough.

Differences in working culture have added to the problems. Lobbyists, working to immediate deadlines imposed by government, parliament, or the media, have been dismissed by gender specialists as task-obsessed, remote from the field, and have had their values and identity challenged. Lobbyists, in turn, have under-valued the gender advisers' knowledge, dismissing them as process-oriented, out of touch with the real world of Northern decision-makers, and low on visible results. The atmosphere of low levels of trust and high levels of mutual suspicion and miscommunication that can ensue is not a fertile one for moving forward on gender issues, and personally challenging to me as their department head.

The most challenging aspect of being responsible for the integration of gender issues in the International Division has been learning how to work productively with gender specialists, whose frustration with slow progress and with the organisation for not living up to its ideals needs to be channelled somewhere. My first mistake was to underestimate the legacy of low levels of trust and the emotional damage that tended to make the team to close in on itself — a natural defence mechanism. Most difficult for me as a feminist was to have my motives constantly questioned and my performance always found wanting. I drew some comfort from the literature and from a consultant who had worked closely with the gender advisers; she reassured me that women gender pioneers always expect more of other women. Having lived through the depressing years of Thatcherism which yielded nothing for women, intellectually it is easy to understand other women's profound mistrust of the few women who do become senior managers: have they not 'sold out' to the prevailing culture and started behaving like men in a man's world? Was I really just another of these 'femocrats', with no real commitment to organisational transformation? At an emotional level, this was hard.

Motherhood and the glass ceiling

The crisis hits when the personal comes up against the demands of a seemingly immutable organisational culture. It is here that our fine words about commitment to gender equity ring most hollow.

Motherhood is said to be the largest single determinant in the failure of women to achieve parity with men.[10] Women throughout an organisation such as Oxfam suffer the consequences of working long and unsociable hours, and the effects of this on family life. For many women in Oxfam this means sacrificing your children by not being there for them, or so preoccupied with work, that you're there in body, but not in mind. Promotions do not make the situation any easier, and my experience has been that each promotion has significantly increased the pressure on my family life. Who would want to be an organisational media spokesperson if every phone call in the evening or at the weekend might send you rushing around organising complex child care and 'dumping' on your partner yet again? I am haunted by the memory of leaving my youngest son to scream as I tried to sound 'professional' on the phone to a trustee who caught me at home in the evening. How can we talk of lofty ideals and working for a 'caring' organisation as we damage those who are most vulnerable and precious to us?

I am grateful that Oxfam's top management in 1987 responded positively to a staff initiative and set up a workplace nursery. I benefited directly, secure in the knowledge that my two sons were being well looked after, that they were near me and also part of Oxfam, given its centrality to my life. I can think of at least a dozen women colleagues who have made very major contributions to Oxfam's strategic direction in recent years who had or have their children in the nursery. It was an important factor in encouraging a number of us to continue working for Oxfam.

The nursery's success has meant that almost since its inception, demand for places has far outstripped supply, limiting its potential in attracting new staff. While on maternity leave in 1990, I gained direct insight into the barriers to actively discriminating in favour of women as I drafted the allocation policy for nursery places (having volunteered, not disinterestedly, to speed things up). I have doubts that we have managed the nursery as the strategic asset it is. We started it in a tentative way, restricting it to small premises that have made it less economic to run. As a result, the fees are prohibitively high for some of the least well-paid staff. At times it has been managed alongside the car park and print room, not as an integral part of a human-resources strategy designed to attract and retain working mothers. Moreover, the workplace nursery, invaluable as it has proved for some, is of course only part of the solution. It raises issues of fairness, because most Oxfam staff—especially those not based in Oxford—cannot benefit. It eases the practicalities of going back to work after maternity leave, but it does not help women regain confidence in getting back on top of a job after an extended absence.

For many of us, the real tensions between work and home only begin when our children start school. Then, their emotional and practical needs — to be fetched and carried between different carers and activities, especially during the school holidays—really make life the sort of challenge that too few men have ever experienced. This is an important gender issue, because it primarily affects women's career opportunities, but also a growing number of men's. More and more men, particularly those who are attracted to working in a not-for-profit organisation such as Oxfam, want to share the demands of parenting and give quality time to their children. A number of senior male managers in Oxfam are very much victims of its working culture and the expectations of their peers. Some are acutely aware that their wives are sacrificing their careers, but have not yet reached the critical mass needed to effect change. For women, the strains on personal relationships can be even worse. If you are fortunate enough to have an exceptional partner who is prepared to take on the lion's share of looking after the children and sacrifice his prospects of interesting paid work, you run into additional problems. In going 'counter-culture', a man takes on a considerable burden, because so much of male identity and esteem is tied up in the world of work. Every additional demand to accommodate your job can add significantly to stress levels.

Oxfam GB will continue to find it hard to attain the diversity among senior management through recruitment, with a better balance between women and men and people of various ethnic backgrounds and nationalities. I believe that this will block our effectiveness as an organisation. Having been the only woman on the International Division's Senior Management Team for a number of years without making a perceptible impact on its working culture, I see major differences now that we have achieved a critical mass of three women in a team of seven. Among these is the additionality brought by women's emotional intelligence: the newer women members of the team actively challenge us and are succeeding in 'outing' some of the emotional undercurrents that have blocked our effectiveness as a team.

Conclusion

Implementing a gender policy which necessitates organisational transformation is fraught with difficulty and requires strong and consistent leadership. Gender specialists have a vital role to play and need effective support in their inherently challenging role. Oxfam can rightly celebrate some pioneering work on gender. At the same time, we have a lot to gain by owning up to and reflecting on our failures. 'Success has many parents, failure is an orphan', as it is said.

Arguably the biggest challenge facing us is one that faces society at large, to which there are no easily palatable solutions: How do we transform our organisational cultures to be more family-friendly, to create an environment in which more women and people of a diversity of ethnic origins can succeed as senior managers? Moreover, how do we create a better balance between the demands of work, our responsibilities as carers and our desire to participate in our children's early lives, and the need to have time for personal relationships?

Having just experienced the sense of deep loss after the death of a very dear colleague, Christine Whitehead, who felt that the stress of being pulled simultaneously in these different directions contributed to her illness, I know I for one owe it to her to do my bit to find some answers.

About the author

Dianna Melrose is Oxfam GB Policy Director and gender lead person for the International Division, currently on a two-year secondment to the British Foreign Office. She joined Oxfam in 1980 as a researcher/lobbyist, and became one of the small but expanding number of women senior managers. She is a mother of two sons, both of whom spent their earliest years in the Oxfam workplace nursery.

From infrastructure to people: Experiences from Cambodia

Visha Padmanabhan

Introduction

When I look back at the history of Oxfam GB's Cambodia programme, it is not surprising that it was difficult to address gender issues. When I arrived in 1993, in an intensely political environment, the emphasis was still on relief and reconstruction, with a male-dominated government institution as Oxfam's counterpart which placed a heavy emphasis on technical work (often seen as a male forte). This was not a congenial environment in which to promote gender issues. A gender perspective was missing not only in the technical programme, but within the overall management perspective.

Over time, Oxfam's programme in Cambodia moved from high-profile relief and reconstruction work to a longer-term approach with a focus on community development. This paved the way for the introduction of a gender perspective into our work. This article considers some of the challenges of introducing gender concerns into a very male-dominated technical programme, and some of the strategies through which this was achieved in Cambodia.

I started in Oxfam GB as a Programme Officer in South India in 1985. It was a new experience for the staff of the then South India (Bangalore) Office to see a woman in a role which had formerly been taken exclusively by men. There were doubts about my ability to cope with stressful travel schedules, to deal with drivers, to stay alone in a hotel, or simply to deal with project partners, who were then mostly men. It was also a challenge for me to establish my own working style without being undermined by the dominant culture of the India programme. There were four women programme officers in India then, and we felt the need to start our own support group. Thus the Women in Development group was set up, which was later broadened to address gender issues not only in the programmes but also in the workplace. This group was the beginning of Action for Gender Relations in Asia network (AGRA), which was to become a crucial source of support for me, particularly when I took on the management role of Regional Representative; the first Indian woman among six male representatives at that time.

In 1992, I was the first (Indian) woman to move to Oxfam in Zimbabwe as Deputy Representative. Appointing a Southern woman from another developing country to a senior management position was a breakthrough for Oxfam. We had come far from the days when one of my male colleagues in India told me that if we kept talking gender, we might not be promoted: instead we would be isolated!

The path has been hard. I was either branded as 'too strong', or made to feel that I was not an easy person to deal with. But I have learned from a wide base and gained a good understanding of gender issues in development work from a broad cross-cultural perspective. It has given me an insight into the attitudes of a range of staff. For me the need to take on aspects of the gender and development debate is clear, and it is this commitment that gave me the energy to take on the challenge of the Cambodia Programme when I became Country Representative in 1993.

Background to Oxfam's programme in Cambodia

Cambodia during 1979–85 was marked by the end of the Pol Pot era, famine, the trade embargo by the West, and only limited aid from the Soviet block. This all led to strong control by central government. There was no free contact between Cambodians and foreigners. The very contact between people which is so vital for good development work, and particularly for an understanding of the intricate gender relations, was not available. Oxfam's intervention in Cambodia was unique and challenging. Up to 1985, Oxfam supported government-implemented infrastructure construction, provision of food aid, emergency supply of seeds and agricultural tools, and a rural water programme. However, in 1986–89 the government implemented economic reform. This was a major change in the environment in which Oxfam pursued its work. The infrastructure work continued, with major rehabilitation of irrigation canals, drilling wells as part of the rural drinking-water programme, emergency aid to displaced people, support to a technical training college, and so on. The earlier approach of support for the rehabilitation of the war-torn economy, and international campaigning to change policy towards Cambodia, was still of major importance.

Between 1989 and 1991 the fighting continued. However, after the signing of the Paris peace accord, various agencies started to deliver aid. An important addition to Oxfam's programmes was support for the first local organisation (KHEMARA) to be headed by a woman, and support for the health projects of another international organisation. A major breakthrough was employment of Khmer staff and consolidation of the country office. The year 1992–93 was crucial, in that it marked the preparations for elections and the return home of refugees. Sporadic fighting continued, and the economy continued to be unstable, but the influx of multilateral and bilateral aid and aid personnel continued.

There are many key issues to address from a gender perspective in Cambodia, including mental health, violence against women, and women's participation in politics. Cambodia's active adult population has a high proportion of women, but they have been conspicuous by their absence from politics. Following the 1993 elections, there are only a handful of women in the national government, and almost no women representatives at provincial and district level.

Managing the Cambodia programme

When I took over in Cambodia, one embassy official commented, 'You are a woman, you are Asian and from a developing country, how did Oxfam appoint you?' At times I had to use subterfuge to be involved in the technical discussions dominated by male colleagues. Since I knew that my predecessor had had a hard time (even as a man) with the technical team, I thought it was best to approach the problem in a positive way. For example, during a group discussion on the integration of infrastructural work into community development work, one of the senior technical staff started explaining some of the finer details of the work to another male programme officer, while others were left out. When I asked what they were discussing, the answer was 'Oh nothing, some technical stuff.' Although I was angry, I kept cool (with great difficulty) and said 'Very good, then you need to explain to the group, as the purpose is for all of us to learn'. This not only made him repeat what he had said, but it also ensured that women were included in discussions about technical issues. This way slowly we became more interactive, although of course every now and then we had these minor confrontations, which strengthened our commitment to address gender concerns.

Similarly there were occasions when the UN consultants or World Bank consultants, along with a Cambodian government ministry, would invite international organisations for consultation. Once when I raised a question of women's role in the socio-economic survey form, they responded with laughter, and the minister of planning said, 'Oh, in Cambodia, women are the home ministers and they handle the cash, we do not have any say …'. Everybody laughed. I was hoping that the so-called high-profile consultants would explain, but to my surprise they also stayed quiet. When I took a second opportunity and asked another question concerning women, they said that they would follow it up and get back to me. What I found is that, if one asks too many questions (particularly if they are gender-related), one is either made to feel isolated and stupid, or given a false assurance of future consultation — but nothing happens afterwards.

One of the key lessons from my experience in India had been the importance of forming a peer-group support network (such as AGRA) to withstand some of the resistance or hindrances encountered when trying to address gender issues. Informally I started building a support group of women who headed agencies in Cambodia, and we started listening to each other and sharing some of the management problems. This confidence-building and mutual understanding helped a lot, especially because all agencies attended the same meetings and worked with the Cambodian government or communities on similar projects.

For management purposes, Oxfam's organisation-wide Gender Policy was essential in Cambodia. It was translated into Khmer, and all staff were given a copy along with their job descriptions. In addition, a letter explaining the nature and role of AGRA (East) was written in Khmer as a hand-out for new staff and provided along with the contract. This was a very useful way to make it clear that managers had a responsibility to incorporate a gender analysis into all their work. I used this fact as the trump card with resistant project partners and government counterparts (who were mostly men), to explain our policy, beliefs, and under-standing of development work from a gender perspective. If the partners were not in tune or did not make an effort, I did not hesitate to intervene and impose conditions on the provision of financial or non-financial support.

Within Oxfam, I felt that the male technical staff were less resistant once they were made to understand that addressing gender relations is an institution-wide mandate. The Gender Policy, and the training and research work subsequently undertaken by the Cambodia office, helped a great deal. A programme officer was given responsibility to ensure that matters concerning gender relations were followed up, and that staff were kept informed about the activities of AGRA East. Maybe my own presence as a woman also helped.

Given the shortage of local staff, priority was accorded to basic investment in staff development and capacity-building, in order to increase the number and quality of national staff. Recruitment processes, including advertisements and interviews, all included explicit gender-related questions. Specific time was devoted in staff meetings to helping everyone to understand the Gender Policy, and gender training for all staff became a crucial starting point. Besides this, assertiveness training and training in negotiating skills were also provided, so that women staff (who outnumbered men in the office) were provided with appropriate support. Monthly staff meetings became the place for raising issues and discussing problems and concerns related to gender in the workplace. Similarly at social events we made a point of including male and female relations of members of staff, and this also became a way of creating awareness.

Working relationships for women staff responsible for supervising or managing the male staff became a regular point of discussion. It was necessary to think critically about cultural assumptions about authority and gender. Also, since respect for older people is an important feature of Cambodian culture, these discussions enabled younger Cambodian women to be assertive without feeling that they were failing to respect their elders.

Transforming the programme

When I arrived in Cambodia, I found that the planning and implementation of large-scale rehabilitation projects was undertaken at the national level, with little or no participation of the actual beneficiaries. There had been little analysis of gender issues in Cambodia at the time. In spite of the process of political and economic liberalisation, which has enabled development agencies to work at province and commune levels, programme planning has largely remained top-down, with a continued focus on material aid and technical development.

I do believe that unless women are fully involved in and benefit from projects, there is no meaning in the work. This business is serious: studies of the situation in Cambodia show that 65 per cent of the adult population in the post-war years was female. A large number of households were headed by widowed or single women. In 1989 and 1994, the study of a canal-building project highlighted the specific and different problems of women, especially single or widowed women, who were shown to be among the poorest. It showed the double burden of women, who had to support their families economically as well as caring for their households. It is Oxfam's responsibility to make sure that women are included in the development process and benefit from the programme, and also own and decide the future of it.

With the change in the working environment in the early 1990s, Oxfam's programme began to shift towards development of the community. Khmer staff now included a couple of women, and gender training was held for the first time for all staff. Through these efforts, the approach became more strategic in operation and response, with a longer-term focus on incorporating a gender perspective into programme and planning.

From 1992 to 1996 Oxfam adopted a three-fold strategy in Cambodia: a small operational community programme was implemented in a few villages in two provinces; financial and intensive technical support was given to other local-level organisations; and training was provided for staff, drawing on the lessons from the operational community programme, in order to strengthen the team's analysis of poverty. The community-development projects brought staff into direct contact with poor villagers (many of them women-headed house-holds) and their problems related to food provision, income, and indebtedness.

However, it was not easy for Oxfam in Cambodia, when refining its whole programme, to translate the information and knowledge it had acquired about gender relations into programme work. A study was initiated to gather gender-focused data at different levels (from government and multilateral donors, from international and local organisations, and from the communities) in order to improve our understanding of the critical gender issues related to poverty, and how people cope with them in the Cambodian context. This gender-focused data enabled us to integrate the gender issues better, through problem analysis and programme planning. The study also provided the opportunity to understand how other NGOs in Cambodia were addressing gender issues, and their different approaches to integrating gender-related criteria into their programmes.

Through these processes, staff developed a clear idea about the concept of gender and about the link between gender and development in Cambodia. This understanding was strengthened in a workshop which provided all staff with feed-back from the study, and gave a gender analysis of the programme. In addition, all the government counterparts, men and women — mostly men — received gender training in Khmer from the community development staff. This training was very effective, because it addressed the Cambodian situation and made a lot of sense to those working on projects in which Oxfam was involved.

The incompatibility of the established technical programme with the newly initiated social component was the major dilemma. For example, putting in pumps and reaching targeted numbers of pump installations lends itself to short-term aims and objectives, but education about water use involves community organisation, which requires substantial time. In order to develop a gender perspective in the Cambodia programme, the decentralisation of the technical programme became necessary.

The community development programme had to focus carefully on ways of providing space and support for emerging local organisations, without making it seem that Oxfam was competing with them to implement the project. Nurturing and supporting community initiatives in a country where there had been no history of local organisations was a great challenge. Often the work had to be done within the limited human-resource capacity available in the country. There was a lot of apprehension among expatriate colleagues (particularly while the major water programme was being handed over) when expansion and funding of local organisations was gradually increased. This approach required careful planning and nurturing through funding and non-funding support services from Oxfam. In this way the so-called technical intervention was integrated into an approach based far more directly on an analysis of community needs, with full community participation.

It is also important to recall the South-South linking initiatives of Oxfam's Gender and Development Unit (GADU), which were part of the Women's Linking Project, discussed by Candida March in her article. These links helped boost gender issues in the programmes and at the office level, and we were able to share the experience with our Cambodian counterparts, with the wider NGO sector, and with the Cambodian women's ministry. This gave Oxfam the opportunity to contribute to the preparation of the Cambodian government's documents for the Fourth World Conference on Women in Beijing in 1995. In a way, the changes that I was making in the programme and management style in Cambodia coincided with pre-Beijing events, which helped to further the positive change towards enhancing gender issues in the programme and at a personal level.

Conclusion

It is now one year since I left the Cambodia office, but I feel very proud that the staff have continued to be committed to the organisation's approach. Sustaining progress towards gender equity is a great challenge in the constantly changing and complex environment in which development work is to be carried out. I strongly believe that there must be mechanisms and appropriate institutional structures to suit the changing needs of each situation.

From my very first day I stated to staff that I was an outsider who could share ideas and help them to think through issues, but ultimately making a choice to change the situation was the responsibility of Cambodians. The responsibility to address gender concerns is now a part of each individual's job in the Cambodia programme. The programme has laid the foundations for a central gender perspective by changing the programme to make it appropriate to the changing needs of men and women. This perspective has added value to the programme itself, and I don't see the issue of gender equity disappearing in Cambodia — although of course the intensity of the team's commitment may be modified.

About the author

Visha Padmanabhan is Regional Representative, Caucasus, for Oxfam GB, based in Tbilisi. Over the last ten years she has worked for Oxfam in various capacities in India, Zimbabwe, and Cambodia. She has a continuing interest in gender perspective in both development work and management structures.

Gender: Assessing the impact [11]

Elsa L. Dawson

Introduction

The evaluation of Oxfam GB's multi-million pound Great Lakes emergency programme argues that, given the lack of data on the actual impact of our interventions, nothing can be said about impact. (This is not to say of course that impact did not occur. We just have no written record of it.) The evaluation goes on to state 'it seems reasonable to conclude that the speed of the Oxfam water response in providing clean water in adequate quantities had a marked impact on the well-being of beneficiaries, particularly in "saving lives"' (Collins et al. 1997).

The question to be addressed in this article is: how do we know we are actually achieving positive changes, or at least contributing to changes, in the lives of the women we are trying to benefit? Do changes in the gender division of labour and in the relationship between men and women lead to improvements in their well-being? How do we know that such improvements are really occurring?

Central to our strategies for changing gender relations are the notions of empowerment and building up the capacity of women and the organisations representing them. But can such things actually be measured? How do we know whether any of the changes we note in the lives of women beneficiaries are really attributable to Oxfam? Changes in their lives are part of complex wider processes that surround our projects and programmes, and it is often hard to distinguish what is due to our interventions and what is due to other changes.

Within Oxfam GB, we are increasingly asking these questions. Our major institutional donors, such as the UK Government's Department for International Development, are also making mounting demands on us for evaluations which include an assessment of impact achieved. In addition, the rising competition for public donations, and the ever more critical eye of the media, combine to produce escalating pressures on organisations such as Oxfam to come up with concrete evidence of benefits accrued as a result of the funds entrusted to us.

What is impact and how do we measure it?

We have defined impact as 'sustainable changes in living conditions and behaviour of beneficiaries and the differential effects of these changes on women and men' (Oxfam and Novib 1994). However, we have also noted that the sustainability of changes cannot be guaranteed, especially in complex political emergencies. It is generally agreed, nevertheless, that impact is more than immediate outputs and effects.

Oxfam has supported a number of initiatives in Kenya promoting conservation or 'organic' agriculture. A review in 1997 to assess the impact of this approach on food security and the livelihoods of rural people found that the sale of vegetables and milk had an important effect on the income and position of women in households. Less expenditure for vegetables meant that women had less reason to ask men for money, and there were many indications that women kept at least some control over the money they earned from the sale of these products. 'Some women had also gained status and confidence through their involvement in the training of other farmers and the management of the community groups through which the work was carried out.' (Neefjes et al. 1997)

Accurate assessment of impact is dependant on a number of key tasks being implemented effectively throughout the life of a project. For example, if a baseline study has not been carried out at the beginning of a project, changes occurring as a result of the project will be more difficult to establish. If no clear objectives have been set, or if the ones set do not correlate with the problems identified, defining impact will be impossible. If no information about the indicators which were identified in accordance with the set objectives was gathered during the project's implementation, again the job of impact assessment will be more difficult, relying on interviews of beneficiaries and staff after the activities have taken place.

Adopting a gender perspective to impact assessment means examining these changes through a 'gender lens', determining which of them have had a positive effect on women, and on their unequal relations with men. Negative change is also important to consider and learn from, as are unintended and unexpected changes. Recording and using negative or unexpected change can often present problems of honesty and transparency, particularly when reporting to funding bodies, but both form an essential part of impact assessment.

In this article we consider some of the constraints we have encountered in measuring impact involving benefits for women and girls (many of which are equally a problem in assessing change of benefit to men), and the ways in which Oxfam has addressed these constraints.

The challenges of assessing gendered impact

Measuring the intangible

Measuring impact in relation to women is particularly difficult, because we lack clarity about what we are hoping to achieve in the longer term. What is our vision of the role of women in an ideal world? Our Gender Policy states that we have an explicit commitment to address 'gender-related inequalities' as a prerequisite for 'achieving sustainable development and alleviating poverty' (Oxfam 1993). But is this sufficiently clear to all our staff as a basic direction for their work?

Our projects often aim to achieve the complex goals of women's empowerment and participation, and the fulfilment of their rights. But how do we measure such intangible elements as empowerment? There is confusion about what 'empowerment' actually is. It is an abstract concept, capable of being interpreted in many ways. When we attempt to translate the word into other languages we realise the complexity of the notion. Rowlands (1995) has described it as follows:

> Bringing people who are outside the decision-making process, into it. This puts a strong emphasis on access to political structures and formal decision-making, on access to markets and incomes that enable people to participate in economic decision-making.

She also provides a definition with a more developmental focus:

> A process whereby women become able to organise themselves to increase their own self-reliance, to assert their independent right to make choices and to control resources which will assist in challenging and eliminating their own subordination. (quoted from Keller and Mbwewe 1991)

Rowlands points out that the empowerment process is not necessarily linear, but more like a loop or a spiral. Certain activities may be empowering in one way and disempowering in another, especially if the different kinds of power she mentions (power over, power to, power with, power within), and the two spheres of individual and collective power, are taken into account. There are also many different areas of life in which women can become empowered — the political, the economic, health, education, the home. Significant changes often take place within people's homes and are thus difficult to observe.

Whose reality counts?

However, what do empowerment and participation signify in the vast range of contexts in which Oxfam-funded empowerment initiatives are carried out, particularly when we take into account our women beneficiaries' own perspective? We have learned to be keenly aware that theirs may be different from our own.

What actually constitutes impact varies markedly depending on who you are talking to. We have found significant differences between what Oxfam staff and our public supporters consider to be impact, and what women beneficiaries see as changes in their interest. We also find variations between the perspectives of our beneficiaries themselves, and between them and the women of other sections of society in their countries, who may belong to different classes, ethnic groups, castes, and even age-groups, or even play different roles, such as daughter-in-laws and mother-in-laws, carers of the infirm and small children.

But whose opinion really matters? Obviously, it is the women beneficiaries of a particular project to whose views most significance must be attached, since the project is intended to assist them. Where our systems are not sufficiently participatory, our beneficiaries' views are inadequately involved and recorded, and outsiders' views may be artificially imposed. We must always ask prospective women beneficiaries about their criteria for well-being, which might well be different from our expectations, and might not necessarily include participating in a women's organisation — as our project proposals so often seem to assume.

Other interests, such as those of a partner organisation implementing a project, other NGOs working in the area, other communities not directly targeted by the project, and those of local government agencies, also have legitimate claims to be taken into account. It is not easy to develop systems which can identify and recognise differing points of view, and to assimilate them into the final assessment.

Problems with participation

Participatory approaches are important in order to gather accurate information on the complex process of development. This is particularly vital in the case of women, whose views may not have been picked up in written descriptive studies or whose voice may not have been heard in community meetings. Talking to women in small groups, or on an individual basis, can ensure that their views are heard. Such groups can take account of the various views which we have noted within different groups of women (women of different ages, levels of education, marital status, class, and so on), and according to their roles in society.

But many of our projects now go beyond seeing 'participation' as merely consulting women on their 'problems'. Ways are being found to ensure their 'full participation in the analysis' (Roche 1993), in order to record their problems from their perspective.

In many development projects, empowerment seems to mean merely participation in communal activities. Although inviting women's participation seems ideal in principle, we always have to be aware that we are taking up their valuable time, time that might otherwise be spent earning an income, looking after children, and perhaps most importantly, relaxing! Many development interventions ostensibly aimed at assisting and empowering women actually increase women's burden of work in encouraging them to participate in communal activities. It is only where such activities are actually increasing women's active participation in decision-making, that empowerment could be said to be occurring.

For example, as a mother of one child working full-time, I certainly have no time or energy for political campaigning or any extra work. And I am lucky enough to have a flexible employer and workplace nursery care for my child. Does this make me an 'unempowered', 'non-participating' woman, unconcerned about her rights? Who is to look after children in the ideal world we are working towards? What about their rights, for example, to adequate care, especially in the case of girl children, who in developing countries so often end up looking after siblings while parents are at work instead of receiving an education or playing? What would the women we are trying to assist really consider to be a step up the ranks of well-being?

Sustainable change

How sustainable are the positive changes brought about by our projects? An important element of the word 'impact' is something that is 'durable', and impact assessment includes the search for changes which will be sustainable over many years after the completion of an initiative. But how can this be measured in the short-term? If we carry out measurement during or immediately after completion of a project, the future of the process is uncertain. If we go back and do so after a certain number of years, much information may have been lost in the meantime, and the causal relationships will have become more complex and more difficult to identify. What can be attributed to the project, and what is rather due to other contextual factors becomes much harder to distinguish.

Practical solutions

Many staff running Oxfam-funded projects now aim to collect information throughout the implementation by monitoring the indicators set in the project design, so that impact can be judged. Some establish new indicators together with women beneficiaries to reflect the empowerment process and positive changes which are being brought about from their point of view. However, this task is cumbersome, because the amount of information amassed is often beyond the capacity of staff to deal with and analyse.

The use of 'frameworks'[12] has in many cases enabled staff to collect and organise relevant information for monitoring and analysing impact quickly and efficiently. It must be emphasised that frameworks are tools to be adapted in various contexts, not a replacement for commitment to gender equity and an understanding of gender inequalities. One such tool is the Gender Analysis Matrix, a simple, systematic instrument for determining the different impact of development interventions on women and men, developed by UNIFEM. This matrix is easy to use with participatory techniques, and covers the main areas of information required in order to detect gender-specific impact, including women's empowerment. Applicable at different stages in the project cycle, it has proven an especially useful tool for our project staff and counterpart organisations.

The Capacities and Vulnerabilities Framework, although designed specifically for use in emergencies, goes beyond such contexts in its emphasis on thinking about the capacities of potential beneficiaries, not only their vulnerabilities. Many project staff have put to use the ideas developed by Naila Kabeer in the Social Relations Approach (1994), which emphasises the culturally and contextually defined structures of gender relations. The Harvard Framework for gender relations (Overholt et al. 1985) contains a checklist of questions regarding women's and men's activities, access, and control, and influencing factors which Oxfam staff have found useful.

The time and resources available to Oxfam for carrying out impact assessment activities are limited, especially if a project or programme is small in terms of budget and staff, and/or of short duration. Development projects funded by Oxfam tend to last between three and ten years, have relatively low budgets compared with those implemented by the large international agencies, and have limited numbers of immediate beneficiaries (apart from our large-scale emergency and advocacy work). Systems and frameworks which are easily and rapidly applicable, and cheap to implement, have been useful in developing methods of monitoring the impact of our work. They are not, however, an infallible panacea and must be used with awareness and analytical ability in order to be successful.

Fundamental questions ...

Ironically, a fundamental constraint on measuring the impact of our work is our staff's intense moral commitment to their activities aimed at the relief of poverty and distress. This leads them to see such routine tasks as measuring their work as an administrative task of lesser importance, understandable when they are faced with situations of acute human suffering. Tasks related to project activities and funding administration are constantly given greater priority. They do nevertheless feel acutely the need to learn from experience, and seek methods that can efficiently provide them with greater possibilities of doing so.

We may actually be over-complicating what is actually a very simple question which we need to ask different stakeholders — 'What has changed in women's lives and why?'— and to record the answers. Perhaps the biggest stumbling block to assessing our impact is monitoring, gathering, and documenting information on preset indicators. John Rowley et al. (1997) have hypothesised that managing ongoing work in Oxfam does not receive the same rewards as starting new initiatives, and that this why, for example, we do not have properly documented information about the impact that our Great Lakes programme has had on women's lives. We need to develop new and effective methods of monitoring our programmes, and ways of supporting and motivating staff to do this.

We are aware that we will never be able to report with absolute accuracy on the achievements of our work in relation to women and gender. All we can provide is our best judgement, and continually learn about what seems to have benefited women and girls, and what has not, or produced negative effects. Nevertheless, the discipline of having to report this may force us to be more rigorous in our efforts to seek out projects which will achieve more real positive change for women and girls, of direct relevance to their everyday lives.

About the author

Elsa Dawson is a strategic planning and evaluation adviser for Oxfam GB. Before joining Oxfam, she worked as Latin America Programme Officer for World University Service UK. Previously, she was Save the Children's Field Director in Peru for eight years, and carried out research on the role of NGOs in development. She is an active member of the Development Studies Association, co-ordinating the NGO Study Group. Her current research interests are impact assessment and social auditing for NGOs.

References

Collins, Steve, McKenzie, Shona and Weaver, Sue (1997), 'Draft: An Evaluation of Oxfam's Field Programmes in the Great Lakes Region of Central Africa, 1994–97', unpublished paper, Oxfam.

Keller, B. and Mbwewe, B.C. 'Policy and Planning for the Empowerment of Zambia's Women Farmers'. *Canadian Journal of Development Studies* Vol.12, No.1, pp. 75–88.

Kabeer, Naila (1994), *Reversing Realities: Gender Hierarchies in Development Thought*, London: Verso.

March, C., Mukhopadhyay, M. and Smyth, I. (eds.) (1999), *A Guide to Gender-Analysis Frameworks*, Oxford: Oxfam.

Neefjes, Koos, Mafongoya, Paramu, Mwangi, Muthoni with Ngunjiri, Eliad and Mugure, Esther (1997), 'Conservation Farming, Food Security and Social Justice', internal report, Nairobi/Oxford: Oxfam.

Overholt, Catherine, Anderson, Mary B., Cloud, Kathleen, Austin, James B. (eds.) (1985), *A Case Book: Gender Roles in Development Projects*, Boulder: Kumarian Press.

Oxfam UK/I (1993), 'Gender and Development: Oxfam's Policy for its Programme', internal policy paper, Oxfam.

Oxfam UK/I and Novib (1994), 'Terms of Reference for Research on Impact Assessment', internal paper.

Roche, Chris (1993), 'Some Ideas on PRA meets GRAAP: A Research-Action Proposal', internal document, Acord.

Rowlands, Jo (1995), 'Empowerment Examined', *Development in Practice*, Vol. 5, No 2.

Rowley, J., Harding, D., Malena, C., Mowles, C., Nichols, P. (1997), 'Oxfam Program Standards Review: Report of First Survey', internal report, Oxfam.

A rose by any other name:
Feminism in development NGOs

Ines Smyth

Introduction

Since arriving at Oxfam GB over two years ago, something has struck me about the way we work: the ease with which we use the term gender, and the reluctance to employ the terms 'feminist' and 'feminism' in our work. As is the case with most development agencies, much of the writing and discussion within head office are notable for the absence of these words. We have a Gender Policy, agreed in 1993. We write and talk about gender-sensitive policies and strategies, of gender work and gendered activities or approaches. But on feminism, feminist policies and strategies, or on feminists, there is a resounding silence. This is despite the fact that, to different degrees, staff in the various regions where Oxfam works engage with feminist ideas and bravely attempt to translate them into practice.

In this article, I argue that 'most development agencies shy away from the language of transformation' (Parpart and Marchand 1995, p.15). Not only the language, but the substance of feminism as a transformative project, seems to be misunderstood, feared, and thus shunned.[13] I recognise that an explicitly feminist language is not always appropriate or useful in our work, and that, in most communities and environments, it is possible to 'use feminist concepts with the language of the people we are working with' (Becky Buell, personal communication 1997). However, development organisations which value learning must consider the insights which feminist concepts offer. In my view, their neglect to do so is linked to their failure to interact with local women's movements. As a result, Oxfam and other donor organisations are not aware of how relevant these groups' thinking is to development debates.

A personal and professional dilemma

This reluctance to speak of feminism worries me, because I joined Oxfam partly in the hope that this would solve a personal and professional dilemma. In common with many western feminists, I saw in feminism the possibility of making the personal political. In my previous job, as an anthropologist working in the field of development, I had come to realise the dangers of analytical and political generalisations which take as their starting point the experiences of western, often white and middle-class, women. Perhaps the most challenging contemporary feminist debate is that on the dominance of 'western feminism'.

Chandra Mohanty (1988) makes one of the best-known contributions to this debate. She asserts that western feminists depict all women in developing countries as forever poor, oppressed, and passive. By perpetuating negative stereotypes, western feminists become part of the oppressive systems they denounce, and undermine the possibility of alliances between feminists of a range of identities and backgrounds. The 'gender experts' in development organisations are under fire from similar analyses: they are seen to be complicit in the denigration of indigenous knowledge, for example by accepting planning frameworks as universally applicable and as superior to any other form of problem-solving. The hegemony of western feminism, and its consequences for women's equality throughout the world, presents perhaps the greatest personal and professional challenge to those in the North who, like myself, work on gender and development.

It has been pointed out that individual feminists can seek a solution to this dilemma by engaging in various forms of micro-politics (Parpart 1995). This means being active in struggles which are 'embedded in the daily lives of individuals', in order to redefine the practices and discourses of the institutions they inhabit. This form of feminist activism can involve individuals in all aspects of their identity, such as gender, class, race, and so on. This position is adopted by those who are attempting to bring gender 'home' to development institutions. Micro-politics are said to offer the possibility of avoiding feminist post-colonial domination, and to be valid cross-culturally. Presumably micro-politics are not proposed as an alternative to 'collective action by women' (Parpart 1995, p.19) which many, including myself, believe to be one of the fundamental tenets of feminism, despite its conceptual and practical difficulties.

Another answer to the problem of western feminist hegemony argues that women's groups and movements in the South have their own voices, through which they are able to 'resist and delegitimise dominant discourses' (Marchand 1995, p.71). This resonates with proposals by feminists from the South to establish alliances of women's movements that span differences of geographical location and power (Sen and Grown 1987).

The two answers are obviously complementary. But while the first is open to me as an individual, the second must be adopted by the organisation I work with, by recognising and fostering the potential of women's organisations in the South. In my view, Oxfam has been slow to support, financially or otherwise, the practical, analytical, and conceptual work of feminists and their organisations. I consider that this is one of the main reasons why, at least at head office, many find it hard to speak of feminism. As one colleague pointed out, 'the language of feminist thought is tough to get through if you are not accustomed to it, and it is hard for non-feminist organisations to translate important concepts into their policy and communication work' (Becky Buell, personal communication 1997).

Fear of feminism

Currently, most people in Oxfam seem to be more comfortable to speak of 'gender and development' (GAD) than of feminism. Of course there has already been a shift from the less political language of 'women in development' (WID) which preceded it. In many parts of the organisation, the demise of WID and the rise of GAD have been accepted, and the limitations of isolated 'women's projects' acknowledged — as can be seen from many articles in this book, including Alice Iddi's. But even if a gender relations analysis is now recognised as an indispensable tool for understanding inequality in our societies, this does not necessarily mean that people embrace the political agenda of feminism. Feminism, in its many variants, is rooted in the recognition of women's oppression at all levels (Moore 1988); 'feminism is not a one-dimensional social critique, but a multi-layered, transformational, political practice and ethics' (Wieringa 1995, p.3). I think it is from this notion of feminism as political practice, as well as from the language of transformation, that most development organisations—including Oxfam—shy away.

Feminist debates
Publishing in Oxfam has provided notable exceptions to the silence on feminism in Oxfam generally: *The Oxfam Handbook of Development and Relief*, *The Oxfam Gender Training Manual*, and the recent book on women's empowerment by Jo Rowlands (1997) all present strong challenges to this pervasive caution, while Oxfam's international journal *Gender and Development* has consistently engaged with feminist debates, their relationship to development, and to Oxfam's work.[14]

Yet internal reports, correspondence, and much unpublished 'grey literature' which circulates in Oxfam are mostly silent on the subject of feminism. Within the Policy Department, where I work, a recent catalogue of internal papers on a range of subjects lists 192 documents; of those, only two mention feminism. Similarly, in my experience, feminism is not really discussed in corridor, telephone, and e-mail conversations, correspondence, and at meetings, while people are relatively at ease with terms such as gender, gender policies and strategies, and even with the new usage of the verb 'engendering'.

Oxfam's projects

A search of the Oxfam database, which lists all projects supported by the organisation since the early 1990s, is also instructive. It reveals that less than 100 out of over 15,000 entries use the terms 'feminism' or 'feminist' (or equivalents in other languages).

The projects database has obvious limitations as a source of information on attitudes at Oxfam House, because most entries are based on proposals submitted by partner organisations — but the summaries are written by staff in Oxford. I suggest that Oxfam staff perceive a dominant non-feminist stance in the organisation, and conform to it by opting for the less confrontational language of 'gender' and 'women'. I have confirmed that proposals employing controversial language are re-phrased and toned down in order to secure approval for funding. How often this self-censorship goes further than merely the choice of wording and affects the actual choice of partner organisations or project activities, probably depends on a variety of factors. But this phenomenon will certainly have a profound impact on the nature of Oxfam's work.

Other issues follow from the results of my database search. First of all, the degree of Oxfam's overt engagement with feminist practice and ideas varies considerably in various regions of the world. For instance, the Latin American and Caribbean region appears fully conversant with, and active in, explicitly feminist initiatives. This may be due to the region's vigorous tradition of feminism, but it is also due to programme staff who responded sympathetically and creatively to particular opportunities.[15] In other regions and countries, for example in India and Lebanon, an equally challenging dialogue with local feminist organisations and fora appears to be taking place. Elsewhere, there is less overt engagement, although individual members of staff were, and still are, deeply committed to feminism and active in feminist initiatives, networks, and organisations.[16]

Oxfam has engaged in some explicitly 'feminist' initiatives as an organisation. Before and after the Fourth UN Conference on Women in Beijing in 1995, there were considerable exchanges and discussions with women's organisations on the themes of the Platforms for Action, in many countries where Oxfam works. However, these various forms of engagement have not all been recorded centrally, and the ideas which sprang from this engagement with the international women's movement have rarely been followed up fully (see Candida March's article on Oxfam's Women's Linking Project), nor have they become common currency in the organisation as a whole in an explicit and influential manner.

Entering the household

The projects database reveals another sign that many in Oxfam — at least at Oxfam House — are uncomfortable with feminism as a concept. I perceived reluctance to look at the household in our development work. It is generally agreed that feminists have made the personal political, and extended the boundaries of what constitutes social reality and policies into the private sphere (Clough 1994). It is also acknowledged that even after the importance of this sphere of social life has been formally accepted (UNDP 1995), most northern NGOs, including Oxfam, have been unable or unwilling to enter it. As White (1997) points out, so-called 'women's programmes' often extend women's working hours. Yet organisations which promote such programmes do little to encourage men to relieve their wives, sisters, or daughters of this increased burden by sharing responsibility for housework or other traditionally 'female' tasks. This neglect demonstrates development agencies' unwillingness to challenge norms and practices dominant within the household, especially when doing so would question male roles and privilege.

Violence against women

Another illustration of development organisations' unease with feminism is the long period of time that they have taken to recognise violence against women as a development issue. Oxfam's mandate is to 'alleviate poverty, and relieve distress and suffering'. Statistics and qualitative information about the universality, incidence, and severity of domestic violence (UN 1989, Caputi and Russell 1992) document the scale of the distress and suffering it causes to vast numbers of women. In several countries, Oxfam supports activities and organisations which work with survivors of domestic violence, often addressing legal and welfare aspects of the problem.

In various parts of former Yugoslavia, during the recent war and its aftermath women have been subject to intensified violence. One of Oxfam's strategic aims in former Yugoslavia is 'to empower women to challenge the causes and alleviate the effects of gender-based suffering caused by patriarchal structuring of society and exacerbated by armed conflict'. Oxfam has also gained experience in combating violence against women in South Africa through supporting programmes such as People Opposing Women Abuse, which provides services to women who have experienced sexual, physical, and psychological abuse. More recently, Oxfam has supported the Programme for the Survivors of

Violence in KwaZulu Natal, which confronts men's violence in the community and seeks to educate the perpetrators, rather than only target women.

Unfortunately, Oxfam supports few programmes which, in my view, explicitly address gender-related violence. Our work on domestic and other gender-related violence is not the outcome of a systematic analysis of its causes and consequences, nor of an organisational strategy, which would ensure that priorities and directions are set, and impact is measured. Formulating a strategy on gender-related violence appears all the more pressing in the light of Oxfam's growing interest in post-conflict concerns such as rehabilitation and re-integration of soldiers into communities.

Reasons for rejecting overt engagement with 'feminism'

Defence of local culture

One of the most frequently voiced concerns within Oxfam about gender equality is that this perspective imposes priorities and world-views which are at odds with local values and cultures.[17] I cannot fail to note a double standard here. As Metha puts it: 'Why is it that challenging gender inequalities is seen as tampering with traditions or culture, and thus taboo, while challenging inequalities in terms of wealth and class is not?' (1991, p.286) Despite the paradox, in my experience the fear of imposing inappropriate, western views and practices on gender continues to be keenly felt in Oxfam's head office. The absence of feminist language implies that this would be even more unacceptable in ethical terms than the language of gender, and more dangerous in terms of programme strategy.

Acceptance of 'pop-feminism'

I suspect that development agencies' reticence to use feminist terms and ideas is partly a result of their unconscious acceptance of what Eisenstein (1997) calls 'pop-feminism'. In most western countries, many of the issues which, 20 years ago, only concerned the women's movement — a sizeable, but still comparatively limited number of women — are now widely discussed. Equal opportunities at work, sexual harassment, and violence against women have become 'mainstream concerns' (Mann 1997). However, according to Eisenstein, their popularisation occurs hand in hand with an extreme simplification and misrepresentation of feminism. 'Western feminism' has been depicted globally in a way that ignores its diversity and its complexities. Ironically, pop-feminism both sanitises feminism's radical roots and demonises them, by presenting to global audiences skewed versions which emphasise individualism, female supremacism, 'victimhood', and an over-preoccupation with sexuality. I am not denying that variants of western feminism may suffer from these flaws, nor am I rejecting the validity of some of the criticisms of western feminism mentioned earlier. I am merely suggesting that some of our organisations, in their reluctance to consider feminism seriously, appear to have accepted such myths.

Perhaps the most detrimental aspect of such perceptions of feminism is that they ignore feminism's rootedness in women's specific experiences: 'Feminism itself refers to political movements that emerge in specific historical conjunctures, and we may expect various forms of feminisms to bear the mark of their political, cultural and historical context' (Gal 1997, p.31). It is obviously wrong to assume that western feminism is applicable and relevant to other contexts, especially when we consider the unequal power relations between western countries and the developing world. But, as Gal's statement indicates, there are many feminisms, each with its distinct history, problems, and achievements.

Anxiety over feminism as a political project

Resistance to feminist thinking and language is often justified by saying that Oxfam, as a charity, cannot embrace any overall political project. In fact, all of Oxfam's work recognises a political element in the complex causes of poverty, and addresses this in its advocacy and community-development work. But the thinking is that by grounding our work in our own experience of the complexity of women's and men's poverty, and its causes, we will stay within the boundaries of the laws governing charitable activities. Moreover, while this reason for refusing to debate feminist ideas using feminist language might be understandable as an explanation of the less than wholesale acceptance of feminism as a political agenda, it is not sufficient to justify the uninformed dismissal, fear, and scorn of feminist ideas which I have encountered in Oxfam.

Closet feminists

I suspect that in many cases, individual staff members are reluctant to debate feminism in the office because they have made a tactical decision not to do so. This is because they wish to carry out work which may be inspired by feminist principles and practices, in an environment inimical to them. Sadly, the earlier practices of the specialist unit in Oxfam's head office (the Gender and Development Unit, later re-named the Gender and Learning Team) may have contributed to the problem. By claiming for itself exclusive expertise and responsibility for feminist analysis, it may have stifled the emergence of creative, open debates from other locations within the organisation.

Staff members have sometimes solved these situations by becoming 'closet feminists', who continue working and interacting with feminist organisations and ideas, or who support women to gain a stronger voice and increased legitimacy within social movements, but who avoid the overt language of feminism. In these cases, the neutral terminology of gender has helped otherwise more radical thoughts and initiatives gain acceptability. A gender discourse can offer both a valid set of tools for the analysis of social relations, and the possibility for feminist practice and thinking 'in disguise'. For some Oxfam staff, this has created the space to develop feminist practice, in ways which are both relevant and acceptable to different external and internal contexts.

However, this strategy is not without its price. One of the consequences has been to allow the organisation's dominant anti-feminist culture to remain largely unchallenged. In addition, work carried out firmly within feminist principles and practices has not been acknowledged as such, and important learning opportunities have ben lost. Similarly, the practice of 'closet-feminism' within Oxfam has at times alienated feminists outside the organisation, and discouraged those inside it. For instance, Oxfam's Middle East office in Beirut organised a recent workshop for staff and partner organisations to explore the concept of gender, and gender-planning methods. Participants from local women's organisations perceived this approach as an anti-feminist ploy, aimed at validating and strengthening—in theory and practice—dominant gender roles.

Conclusions

Organisations such as Oxfam find it safer not to use the language and practices of feminism. One possible explanation for this is that most development organisations are not engaging with the 'feminisms' represented by women's organisations worldwide; another is that they may be reacting to mass-marketed pop-feminism. Anti-feminist attitudes within development organisations, and the belief that feminist language and thought would clash with local cultures, also provide an explanation. The reaction is to remain safely within the boundaries of the less contentious gender and development discourse.

I do not propose that development agencies such as Oxfam should become 'feminist organisations', with the sole goal of struggling against patriarchal structures and norms. Also, I do not deny that a gender discourse can be radical and transformational: gender and development can be about strategies to redress gender based inequalities and hierarchies of power (Macdonald 1994). In my opinion, the language of gender and of feminism are complementary, rather than either antagonistic or synonymous.

But a rose by any other name may not smell as sweet. I maintain that the lack of explicit and critical engagement with feminist terms and ideas in development organisations inhibits them from participating fully in debates about different forms of social mobilisation. At the practical level, their attitude means that they fail to give sufficient support and opportunity to individuals and groups among their own staff who are dedicated to feminism in its many forms. Similarly, it prevents agencies such as Oxfam from working together with the feminist organisations in the South which are formed as a result of local analyses of women's circumstances - however different their feminism may be from western feminism. These are also the very organisations which develop powerful critiques of local culture, and who would thus offer a way out of the 'gender and culture' dilemma in which so many development organisations seem to be stuck.

About the author

Ines Smyth is a social anthropologist with a PhD from University College London. She taught development studies in several academic institutions before joining Oxfam in 1996. Her areas of expertise and interest are gender theory, gender and industrialisation, and reproductive rights. Among her most recent publications are *Searching for Security: The Impact on Women of Economic Transformations* (edited with Isa Baud), Routledge, 1997.

Bibliography

Caputi, J. and Russell, D. (1992), 'Feminicide: Sexist terrorism against women' in Radford, J. and Russell, D. (eds.) *Feminicide: The Politics of Woman Killing*, Buckingham: Open University Press.

Chigudu, H. (1997), 'Establishing a feminist culture: the experience of Zimbabwe Women's Resource Center and Network', *Gender And Development*, Vol. 5, No. 1, pp.35–43.

Cleves Mosse, J. (1993), *Half the World, Half a Chance*, Oxford: Oxfam.

Clough, P.T. (1994), *Feminist Thought*, Oxford: Blackwell's.

Eisenstein, Z. (1997), 'Feminism of the North and West for Export: Transnational Capital and the Racialization of Gender' in Dean, J. (ed.), *Feminism and the New Democracy*, London: Sage Publications.

Gal, S. (1997), 'Feminism and Civil Society' in Scott, J.W., Kaplan, C., Keates, D., *Transitions, Environments and Translations, Feminisms in International Politics*, New York: Routledge.

Jahan, R. (1995), *The Elusive Agenda: Mainstreaming Women in Development*, London: Zed Press.

Macdonald, M. (1994), *Gender Planning in Development Agencies: Meeting the Challenge*, Oxford and Euro Step.

Mann, P. (1997), 'Musing as a Feminist on a Postfeminist Era' in Dean, J. (ed.), *Feminism and the New Democracy : Resisting the Political*, London: Sage Publications.

Marchand, M.H. (1995), 'Latin American Women Speak on Development: Are We Listening Yet?' in Marchand, M. and Parpart, L. (eds.), *Feminism Postmodernism Development*, London: Routledge.

Mehta, M. (1991), 'Analysis of a Development Programme' in Wallace, T. and March, C .(eds.), *Changing Perceptions: Writings on Gender and Development*, Oxford: Oxfam.

Mohanty, C. (1988), 'Under Western Eyes : Feminist Scholarship and Colonial Discourses', *Feminist Review*, Vol.30, pp.61–88.

Moore, H. (1988), *Feminism and Anthropology*, Cambridge: Polity Press.

Parpart, J. and Marchand, M. (1995), 'Exploding the Canon: An Introduction' in Marchand, M. and Parpart, L. (eds.) *Feminism Postmodernism Development*, London: Routledge.

Rowlands, J. (1997), *Questioning Empowerment: Working with Women in Honduras*, Oxford: Oxfam.

Sen, G. and Grow, C. (1987), *Development, Crises and Alternative Visions: Third World Women's Perspectives*, New York: Monthly Review Press.

UN (1989), 'Violence Against Women In The Family', New York: United Nations.

UNDP (1995), 'Human Development Report 1995', New York: United Nations.

Wallace, T. and March, C. (1991), *Changing Perceptions: Writings on Gender and Development*, Oxford: Oxfam.

White, S. (1997), 'Re-thinking gender and development: The challenge of difference', paper presented at the DSA Conference, Norwich, 11–13 September.

Wieringa, S.(1995), 'Introduction: Subversive women and their movements' in Wieringa, S. (ed.), *Subversive Women, Women's Movements in Africa, Asia, Latin America and the Caribbean*, London: Zed Books.

Personnel management in crisis: Experience from Afghanistan

Sue Emmott

Introduction

In September 1996, the Islamic fundamentalist Taliban forces took control of Kabul, Afghanistan's capital, and immediately prohibited women from working and girls from going to school. Oxfam GB was thus faced with an extreme and direct challenge to its institutional Gender Policy. The abrupt change from a situation where women were actively involved in the relief and rehabilitation process in their country both as employees and beneficiaries, compromised Oxfam's principles to the extent that the programme was suspended.

The main focus of this case study is on human-resource management. I describe the attempts to develop a gender-sensitive programme with both men and women, and the response of agencies and individuals in the wake of the Taliban take-over. In an Oxfam programme, teams are multi-cultural, composed of both national staff and expatriates, and the issues affecting them are often very different. Balancing the varying needs and the power relations in such a team is one of the most difficult tasks facing a manager (especially a woman manager), and there are no easy solutions on offer here.

Oxfam's mandate and Gender Policy

The fact that Oxfam GB had a Gender Policy placed it in a unique position among international agencies in Kabul when Taliban forces took over the city. Although the effects of an extreme form of Islam were felt by all agencies, it was only Oxfam which had both a desire and an obligation to address the issue of gender directly. Within Oxfam, this was also the first time that the Gender Policy would be tested in such a public way.

The Oxfam Gender Policy states that sustainable development and the alleviation of poverty cannot be achieved unless gender-related inequalities are addressed. It acknowledges that gender-related oppression varies according to context, as do women's opportunities for involvement in development, and indicates that Oxfam's responses to the issues will be sensitive to local circumstances, respecting the capacity and strategies of local women for change. Of the five objectives of the Gender Policy, two are particularly relevant to the Afghanistan programme. One commits Oxfam to developing positive action to promote the full participation and empowerment of women, in order to ensure that men and women benefit equally in development. The other commits Oxfam to confront the social and ideological barriers to women's participation and encourage initiatives to improve their status and basic rights.

At field level, having established a programme in Kabul based precisely on those objectives, it was clear that we could not ignore Taliban's edict that women were not allowed to work and girls not permitted to attend school. Within a few days we had suspended the programme, pending negotiations with Taliban, on the grounds that we could not achieve our aims without female staff. In addition, after full discussion with all the male staff, we requested them to stay at home until such time as their female colleagues were permitted to return to work. In Kabul such an action was possible, because women have long been active in the workforce at all levels, and all our male staff had wives who worked and daughters who attended school. A capital city is very different from the rural areas, and one of the main problems of Taliban's edicts was the imposition of rural, tribal norms on an urban and often liberal-minded population.

Having worried about their future during 17 years of war, and seen women play a crucial role while many men were fighting, many Kabulis realise that the country cannot recover without the participation of women. However, under recent regimes, it is a rare person who feels able to speak out against abuses of basic rights, so there was a sense that Oxfam could and should say what local people themselves would like to. During the following months, all aspects of policy development were fully discussed with all staff, to ensure that it was their needs which were being met and not the organisation which was pursuing its own agenda. This was important because, in the NGO co-ordination forum, there was a dominant tendency for aid workers to speak about what they thought Afghans wanted, rather than what they actually wanted. This was particularly true of cross-border agencies, hostile to, but ignorant of, the previous communist regime in Kabul.

Although the decision to suspend the programme was taken quickly, it was discussed in fine detail both in Kabul and in Oxford. From the outset it was known that, although we wished to negotiate with Taliban for the return of women to work, the cultural and religious distance between such a fundamentalist movement and a liberal Western aid agency was likely to render negotiations impossible. Therefore, we had to agree that, in the absence of a change in the situation, Oxfam would either withdraw from Kabul or maintain the suspension of its programme. Given that Oxfam's mandate is to relieve poverty, distress, and suffering, we also had to be confident that a long suspension would not harm the very people we were aiming to assist.

In terms of the programme, although we had conducted a very successful winter relief programme, which had proved that it was possible to reach women beneficiaries through women staff with the full co-operation of men, the main strategic aim was sustainable rehabilitation, rather than emergency relief. There were other agencies who had greater capacity in relief work and had been in Kabul longer, so Oxfam had decided to focus on restoration of the city water supply, which would have long-lasting benefit for a large number of people. Essential community-level surveys, communication and education work with and through women would be impossible under the Taliban regime, and, as water had not flowed through the mains for four years and the programme was proceeding very slowly anyway, a suspension for a few months was felt to be relatively harmless. In line with the Gender Policy, and on the basis of sound experience, Oxfam believed that a water programme could not succeed without the participation of women. Furthermore, Oxfam was likely to be the only agency willing to speak out, and it seemed to be important that someone did.

Communicating the reasons for suspension was very difficult. With Taliban it was almost impossible, because their beliefs about the role and status of women are at opposite ends of the spectrum from Oxfam's. But it was also very difficult to communicate our policy to other agencies. The decision to suspend work was greeted with both admiration and distaste. Among those who attended co-ordination meetings there was a wide variation in understanding of development issues in general, and gender-related concerns in particular. The quality of debate was therefore often poor. Some agencies, having accepted the conventional view that it is difficult to work with women in Islamic societies, employed few or no women. Some did employ women, and regretted the ban, but did not see it as in their interest or within their power to contest it. At first some quietly defied the ban. With such a wide range of views and responses, it is not surprising that agencies were variously grateful to Oxfam for raising the issues they themselves preferred not to, or resentful that attention was being drawn to them if they carried on as normal.

The debate in Afghanistan has been a muddled one. For most agencies and aid workers, the gender debate is about women and women's programmes. When the subject of women's rights is raised, other agencies usually respond by arguing that men as well as women are affected by Taliban policies, being forced for example to grow beards and pray in the mosque. Gender, it is argued, cannot be viewed in isolation from human rights in general. For Oxfam, gender is about the relations between men and women. In some Islamic societies, it is impossible to work with women and men together, but that was not the case in pre-Taliban Kabul. In our programme, although only women were able to gain access to homes and to women, they could not work effectively without the support of male colleagues for logistics and security, nor without the facilitation of their work by male community leaders. The programme in Kabul was about meeting the needs of women and families by respecting and working within the roles they define for themselves. It is only after trust is developed that it is appropriate to work sensitively in a way which furthers empowerment.

Gender and human-resource management

In all Oxfam's work in Afghanistan, gender relations had been a key theme. From the beginning of the programme in Kabul, it was the intention to ensure that women and men had equal opportunities to work with us. Although many women had paid work in Kabul, and would like a job with an international agency, it was not easy to recruit women with relevant skills and language capability. Therefore, in addition to advertising it was necessary to make special efforts to 'headhunt' suitable women, using whatever networks were available. Rather than require experience for a particular job such as administration, which would exclude women candidates, the criteria were set as a good standard of English and an aptitude to learn. For programme staff, although communication was difficult and their own learning hindered because materials are in English, we recruited capable, skilled women with little or no English, and a translator to assist them. In many agencies, the women who are employed are those with good English who often have no work experience. It is also the case that translators, by virtue of being able to communicate with expatriates, are often promoted to powerful positions, while more senior women are by-passed. For work with communities, the most important characteristics are empathy, sensitivity, and maturity. Of course, this can mean that standards have to be relaxed, for example in report writing, but it is important when recruiting to remember whose needs are really being served. Many a potentially good programme for women fails because programme officers are recruited on the basis of fluency in English rather than experience.

Because the programme in Kabul was new, it was possible to achieve a good gender balance among the staff. In established programmes, where men are predominant, it is very difficult to alter the balance, and it is usually possible to recruit women only when male staff leave. Some agencies in Kabul had set up programmes during hostilities, when it would have been impossible to employ women, and this created a situation which made gender-fair recruitment later on more difficult. A feature of countries in conflict is that paid employment is scarce, and those fortunate enough to have jobs with well-paying agencies tend not to leave, so male domination can become entrenched. Even where a positive effort is made to recruit women, it is critically important to provide the kind of environment in which they feel comfortable. A lone woman can feel alienated and unsupported — a point which applies equally to Afghan women and expatriates.

Not only women were recruited to work for Oxfam on the basis of an Equal Opportunities Policy. We made efforts to recruit disabled people, also successfully. We hired a woman teacher, severely disabled during a rocket attack, who had begun a very promising project with disabled women. But it was Oxfam's effort to recruit women, and the success of their involvement as programme staff, office staff, cooks, and cleaners which strengthened the desire to protect their rights by suspending the programme rather than see them so disenfranchised. In the early days, word spread very quickly that Oxfam had sent the male staff home because the women had to stay home. There is no doubt that Oxfam's women staff felt enormously supported by this move, and women in other agencies also felt encouraged that such a stand was made on their behalf. In my opinion, it was an essential part of communicating the message that our women staff were genuinely equal to the men, so much so that the programme could not run without them. In the early days it was not difficult to adopt such pure principles. In contrast, some other agencies immediately recruited men to take women's jobs.

The genuinely gender-friendly environment in the Oxfam office had been enjoyed by all who worked there, so the absence of the women was sorely felt. Although the women were the main sufferers, the male staff in the office felt the absence of their female colleagues acutely and were very genuine in their praise of the women's roles. One of the male staff poignantly observed that men and women in society were like the wings of a bird. Without one wing, a bird cannot fly.

Expatriate aid workers and gender issues

Most aid workers in Afghanistan are men, and they are generally reluctant to attach particular importance to women's involvement in the relief and rehabilitation process, for fear that it will damage co-operation with the authorities. This has been the case since the early 1980s, through the long 13-year *jihad* (Holy War) of the *mujahideen* against the communist government. Soviet forces occupied various cities of Afghanistan from 1979 to 1993 and, although the position and status of many women improved greatly, the introduction of education for women had been at the heart of the resistance. Among the three million Afghan refugees in Pakistan, education programmes for women were fiercely resisted at first; but gradually they became accepted, and female expatriates have been able to design and manage programmes with some success. However, men's perceptions of what types of project are possible with women still tend to determine what programmes are attempted. Perhaps one of the main obstacles to a good gender-oriented programme is the tendency of male aid workers to make assumptions about limitations, rather than to test those assumptions carefully and gently push the boundaries. In the worst case, this means that women are effectively excluded, a point which applies equally to Afghans and expatriates. In the case of internationally recruited women staff, it has often been their male colleagues who exclude them from certain postings or refuse to allow them to meet with the authorities. Yet, even in Afghanistan under Taliban, it has been the exception rather than the rule that women have been rejected by male colleagues.

These points have major implications for the management of programmes in Afghanistan. My appointment, as the first female representative in Afghanistan, was the result of enlightened management at headquarters and the rejection from the outset of the predominant view that a woman could not do the job. One of the advantages of an Equal Opportunities Policy is that it shifts the responsibility for deciding whether or not a woman can do the job to the woman herself, rather than the appointing manager. In other less enlightened or less professional agencies, women would not be considered for senior management positions. Indeed, in Kabul during co-ordination meetings, some men were quite open in their view that, if Taliban refused to meet women, the agency should send men in their place. In fact I was never denied the opportunity to meet Taliban authorities (although some women have been excluded in some locations), and I worked to ensure that my male colleagues would support me in the event that I was asked to leave a meeting. There had been an unfortunate experience in Herat in which the one woman Programme Manager was requested to leave a meeting by Taliban, while her male colleagues remained silent and continued without her. Taliban have never prohibited expatriate women from working, provided that they adhere to a modest dress code.

Male expatriates tend, therefore, to accommodate restrictive views almost automatically, and fail to push the boundaries of acceptability unless they have no choice. In that respect the presence of increasing numbers of women working in Afghanistan, regardless of the regime in power, has the potential to make a lasting impact on Afghan women. One of the most rewarding aspects of my role as Representative was to be seen as a role model by aspiring Afghan women. They would observe, from experience with other agencies, that Oxfam was different, in that it did not just talk about gender, but made real efforts to involve women beyond those recruited specifically for a women's programme. These effects are far-reaching, as evidenced after the suspension when, it would seem, my name and Oxfam's became well known as the supporters of women. (After women were ordered to stay at home, their sources of news were male family members who went outside, and the radio, which reported intensively on the situation of women in the early days.) In advocacy terms it is highly likely that a woman manager has more power than a man.

The most difficult aspect of being a woman manager in Afghanistan was not the constraints imposed by fundamentalist Islam, as most people imagine. It was the difficulty of managing expatriates, and men in particular. My perception of Afghan Islam is that the criteria for acceptability are one's competence in the job and one's perceived sincerity and integrity. Male or female identity is then less important. However, where Afghans are accepting, expatriates may reject, and some of the most difficult challenges to my authority came from older expatriate men who had difficulty in being managed by a woman. They seemed to be from a different 'gender generation', and they justified prejudices which would be unacceptable in a Western context by arguing that Equal Opportunities had little place in a fundamentalist environment.

Although there are certainly difficulties in being a woman manager, there are also some advantages. My impression, in dealing with government officials or checkpost guards or warlords, is that they are less suspicious and do not expect women to have ulterior, political, motives. They also seem more prepared to discuss failings in the system which prevent aid being effective, without feeling that they are losing face. I was always received very politely in contrast to the experience of some of my male colleagues, especially the younger, more aggressive ones, who often found doors closed to them. The main disadvantage for me was my relative lack of access to informal tea-room discussions, but this is not so different from the old-boy networking which goes on in bars in the West. What is interesting, however, is that male aid workers' perceptions of the difficulties of being a woman manager are different from the reality; and their perceptions can be easily translated into unequal opportunity.

In terms of threat to my authority, the greatest challenge came in the management of security. At Oxfam headquarters there is a belief that security guidelines can be drawn up and implemented through a rational process which everyone agrees to. This is far from being the case, and human nature is such that people deeply resent curfews, dress codes, or alcohol restrictions and will flout them regardless of the risk to themselves or others. Men, in particular, often have a fascination with war and guns, and an almost naïve belief that they can do as they please without coming to any harm. As a manager, with attacks on aid workers becoming increasingly common, it is highly stressful to be responsible for staff security in such conditions, and the antagonisms which develop can find no outlet for safe expression in such confined environments.

In complex emergencies, especially those such as Afghanistan which are not highly publicised, it is extremely difficult to recruit experienced aid workers. The restrictions of lifestyle, especially for women, are a major deterrent, and job advertisements yield a very poor response. Far from making ideal appointments, agencies often find themselves scraping the barrel. It is often argued at headquarters that recruitment procedures should be improved, but the reality is that, with increasing numbers of conflict-related emergencies in the world, there are simply not enough experienced aid workers to go around. Although there are many things which would improve retention of staff, the bottom line is that the abnormality of the lifestyle and the stress mean that few remain more than two or three years. One of the main lessons I learned as a first-time senior manager, following two particularly problematic appointments, was that it is probably better not to appoint at all, to the extent that a planned project cannot go ahead, than to appoint inappropriately. The current debate about the need to professionalise emergency aid recognises the problem, but any possible solutions would require investment of resources — which the donors to the voluntary agencies are unlikely to support.

Ultimately, as foreigners in a country, we are symbols of our culture. In the tense and enclosed environment of Kabul, living under curfew, some expatriates need to seek release through parties and risky activities. In positions of far greater power than they could attain in their own countries, they feel they can behave as they wish, ignoring cultural norms and security guidelines. The partying behaviour of Western women, for example, out and about in the company of many different men, may not attract undue attention in some other cultures but, in fundamentalist Afghanistan, where women are always escorted by a male relative, they are perceived to be 'loose', and this can compromise a whole programme and create a highly antagonistic situation. Where they work with local women, they do not seem to understand how their own reputations may reflect negatively on their staff and possibly endanger them.

International women in Kabul were of two types: there were the party animals, often very young and on short-term assignments, and those who observed the restrictions and developed a commitment to the cause of gender and development; this often went beyond professional responsibilities to become a deeply held personal conviction about what is right and just. For my own part, having established a new country office, recruiting all the staff and playing a key role in the development of a programme, my relationship with those colleagues and with the long-suffering citizens of Kabul went beyond the professional into the personal. It was therefore extremely frustrating that most aid workers found gender issues to be of marginal importance.

Not only do most aid workers have a limited understanding of gender, they also know little of the universal standards regarding equality and women's rights such as the UN Declaration on Human Rights and the Convention on Elimination of all Forms of Discrimination against Women. Where these are known about, as in the UN agencies, there is no mechanism for translating standards into action on the ground, and most field workers have felt ill-prepared for challenges such as the Taliban decrees on the status of women and girls. The result is that, rather than being guided by agreed principles, actions result from simplistic and frequently uninformed notions of cultural specificity.

Conclusion

Having a Gender Policy in Oxfam was invaluable in clarifying strategy and response when women's rights were restricted in Kabul. Although many people would not know the content of the policy exactly, every employee is bound to it in his or her terms of reference for the job. The framework for response was therefore set, in contrast to most other agencies, who struggled with the issue in a relative vacuum. For Oxfam, all that remained was to work on the detail of *how* to respond, rather than *whether* to respond. In human-resource terms, the appointment of a woman Representative, committed to maximising the involvement of women and supported by the Gender Policy, meant that the Kabul programme was gender-sensitive from the outset. In an unfavourable environment, special efforts had to be made to recruit, train, and support women and then to remain supportive of them when they were prohibited from working. It was important that Oxfam not only advocated gender-fair development, but was seen to be practising it.

As a woman manager I encountered many difficulties over and above those faced by men. Many are no different from those facing women managers in the West. However, the management of expatriates, both male and female, in a fundamentalist Islamic society which was a very restricting and very insecure environment, was extremely stressful and made me feel very isolated.

The Oxfam programme in Kabul remains suspended, more than a year later. During that time the Gender Policy has been subject to continuous challenge, but, in defining a set of core principles for Oxfam, it has helped to focus the debate on those principles. The suspension has been both admired and criticised. The main criticism is usually that suspension helps no-one and may worsen the situation of those who most need help. In the end, much of the focus on gender is about strategic rather than practical gender needs, and women's rights have been so severely eroded in Kabul and other parts of Afghanistan that at least one agency has acknowledged the need to look beyond the short term and to face the challenge of the future.

About the author

Sue Emmott was the Oxfam Country Representative in Afghanistan in 1995/96. She is a nurse and midwife with a first degree in Social Policy and a Master's degree in Health Education. Much of her professional work has been in situations of conflict, always with a focus on gender issues. Following her management experience in Afghanistan, she studied for her MBA at Cambridge University and is now working as Health Systems and Institutional Development Adviser with the UK government's Department for International Development in India.

Rhetoric to reality:
A psychological approach

Wendy Carson

Concepts of 'gender relations' instil fear and evoke resistance among both men and women. Perhaps this resistance evolves from the definition of gender itself.[18]

> People are born female or male, but learn to be girls and boys who grow into women and men. They are taught what the appropriate behaviour and attitudes, roles and activities are for them, and how they should relate to other people. This learned behaviour is what makes up gender identity, and determines gender roles. Gender describes those characteristics which are socially determined, as opposed to those which are biologically determined. Socially determined characteristics can and do change over time and according to social and cultural factors.
> (Williams 1994)

Change is a theme throughout this definition. Integral to change is the element of uncertainty, invoking fear and anxiety of the unknown. When fears and anxieties are not acknowledged, they may lead to resistance toward changing the familiar. Organisational change toward greater gender equality must acknowledge and address these blocking agents: uncertainty, fear, anxiety, resistance, and sabotage.

In this article, I will present from a psychological perspective examples of these agents at work within the organisational life of Oxfam GB, and how they affect the goal of changing it. Through the words of both present and past Oxfam employees, the article illustrates the dichotomy between the rhetoric of gender equity within Oxfam, and a rather different reality.

The basis for this contribution is information collected in 1995 for a case study of gender relations within Oxfam GB (Carson 1995). The study focused primarily on Oxfam's International Division. Participants were present or former employees in the Oxfam UK/I head office and one of the African country offices. They included both men and women, with occupations ranging from country office watchman to corporate director.

Oxfam took a lead among NGOs in establishing a gender and development unit in 1985; it was also among the first agencies to institute a formal Gender Policy addressing both programmatic and organisational gender issues. This reflects Oxfam's awareness that, to provide a quality emergency and development programme, programmatic gender policies must be mirrored in organisational structures and processes. It is not sufficient to address gender relations in development work alone; promoting gender relations must be an integral component of organisational development.

A psychological approach to organisational culture

Examining the culture of Weber in Oxfam

In the nineteenth century, Max Weber developed a bureaucratic model of organising which has dominated organisational and managerial thought throughout this century. His writings were born out of the growing capitalist value systems of maximising profit by impersonalising the system. Thus, his description of 'rational' organisational excellence specifies a rigid hierarchy, top-down communication, specific role definition, rationality, and the separation of the public and private spheres of life. It is devoid of love, hatred, and 'all purely personal, irrational, and emotional elements which escape calculation' (Weber 1978). Weber maintains that this method of organising is the epitome of efficiency resulting in technical superiority.

Jargon such as 'strategic management', 'minimum standards', 'rational arguments', 'workforce productivity', 'delivering', 'defending your corner', 'results-oriented', 'task-driven' and the 'non-professional connotations of emotion', which dominates the language of Oxfam staff, suggests the integration of some of Weber's bureaucratic principles in Oxfam's organisational culture. Compounding this impression is the view that being more effective at achieving operational goals at the expense of employee well-being is acceptable. This is reflected in this corporate manager's words:

> When you look at what, over the last two years, we've managed to achieve in our programme overseas and in our fund-raising, we're now in a position where we continue to expand and, I believe, be more effective in fighting poverty ...
>
> I think part of the price that Oxfam has paid is that we haven't spent as much time and attention on ourselves, internally, on our own human-resources aspects. That is why people are feeling the stress of change. But if you say that we're

actually here to fight poverty as the primary objective, then that's why I would say I believe, having the same decision, I'd do the same again, because we have been more effective at fighting poverty.

Many contemporary organisations continue to rely on rational scientific management or the 'machine model' of organising (Bowles 1990), having adopted, to a lesser or greater extent, Weber's theories. Rather than recognising the limits of rationality, the pattern of organisational development appears to be moving towards achieving greater rationality, systematisation, tightening, and codification. In other words, we are moving towards the Weberian ideal.

Explaining Weber with Jung

Rationality is a key element in Jung's theory of the personal unconscious. It is one feature in the description of the *animus*. The *animus* or 'masculine' aspect is defined by Jung as the rational, analytical, objective, and logical aspect of the human psyche. Conversely he describes the *anima* or 'feminine' aspect as the intuitive, social, feeling, and irrational aspect. These psychological elements are independent of biological sex and all individuals, male and female, have both the *animus* and the *anima* in their psychological make-up. In most individuals' psyches, however, either the *animus* or the *anima* assumes a more dominant position, leaving the opposing element to be pushed into the unconscious.

The second component of Jung's theory of the unconscious is referred to as the collective unconscious, which is the hereditary blueprint of the human mind's evolution. According to Jung, the collective unconscious represents the sum of human thought as it has evolved throughout human existence. Jung articulates the collective unconscious through archetypes, which, he argues, developed as a tool to structure our understanding of the world in manageable ways. Some organisational theorists have adapted Jung's theories of the personal and collective unconscious to describe and understand the behaviour of organisations (Handy:1991 and Bowles:1993).

Rhetoric versus reality

Despite a liberal and innovative policy rhetoric on gender explicitly outlined in the Oxfam Gender Policy, the perspectives of employees, both women and men, describe a reality not different from what research has found in other organisational sectors. Patterns of gender relations in the workplace such as vertical and horizontal segregation; the 'glass ceiling' at the level of middle management; the 'double shift'; equity models of equal opportunities initiatives; and an imbalance of confidence between men and women, are equally prominent in Oxfam.

Vertical and horizontal occupational segregation

Occupational segregation explains the division of paid work on the basis of sex. This can occur both within organisational sectors (vertical segregation) and between organisational sectors (horizontal segregation).[19]

At Oxfam's UK headquarters, 63 per cent of total employees are women, yet most of them hold lower-graded posts. This invariably translates into lower remuneration, less responsibility, lower status, and less influence on decision-making. Figure 1 compares the grades of women and men throughout Oxfam's UK headquarters. This figure clearly represents vertical segregation in Oxfam.

Figure 1: Oxfam staff distribution (staff grade by sex)

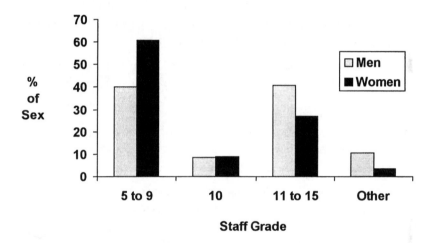

This phenomenon is often referred to as the middle-managerial glass ceiling: a barrier which allows women to see what occurs on the other, higher level, but which prevents them from ascending to those higher organisational positions. In essence, the glass ceiling effectively prevents women from participating in senior decision making. The glass ceiling in Figure 1, representing Oxfam as a whole, occurs at grade 10 (Oxfam GB's grading ranges from grade 7 to 15). For the International Division taken in isolation, the glass ceiling has shifted to grade 11.

Men and women interviewed for the study recognised that women could be found in the 'usual sectors such as personnel', indicating a form of horizontal segregation. 'Women's departments' tend to be those departments which are removed from any genuine decision-making power. They are often service- and people-oriented departments, rather than strategic, task-oriented departments. Tasks performed in these departments tend to mirror women's unpaid domestic and caring work in the home.

The double shift

One of the factors contributing to the strength and integrity of the middle-managerial glass ceiling is the prominence of the 'double shift'. The term describes how women engaged in full-time paid work outside the home are often expected by their partners and society to carry the 'lion's share of domestic responsibilities', leaving them less 'space to just sit and think about work'.

Unpaid domestic and child-care work in the home was identified as one of the most common and strongest barriers to gender equality in Oxfam. Women are expected to fit their career schedules around the demands of child-care. Conversely, men do not perceive the need to alter their schedules. If women want to work outside the home, they are often given the choice; however, it remains their responsibility to ensure the smooth functioning of home life (Newell 1993).

One employee described his distaste for unpaid work in the home when his partner's temporary illness necessitated his involvement. He expressed a reluctance to become permanently involved with this type of work.

> In fact sometimes she is sick, the children are sick, I had to do the washing and the cooking all week and I didn't really like it … Perhaps I was not used to it. But I didn't like it.

Other men recognise the inequalities present in parenthood and domestic work when it is considered 'women's work', and are committed to contributing 'their share'. One man describes his arrangement with his partner:

> I have a rotating system of child-care with my partner, so I do Mondays, Wednesdays, Fridays, and Saturdays and have Tuesdays, Thursdays, and Sundays free … Romantically you might sort of think 'Well, we'll do everything together' but practically we're just desperate to try and get a bit of time to do something …

Workload and the double shift

Ninety-six per cent of respondents were acutely aware of the quantity of work in their jobs. This was especially true for respondents based in the UK whose jobs required them to travel. The way in which respondents at head office approached their high workload was different from those in the African field office, where expectations tended to be more realistic (Carson 1995), but there is no doubt that workload is problematic for both men and women in both offices.

An indication of the workload is given in the daily routine of one woman who goes on to contemplate the effect on the personal relationships within her family:

> Is it possible to do these jobs and stay sane? Because what I have been doing for the last six months is to go home between 5pm and 7pm. I then look after my kids until I get them to bed at 8pm. I then eat some food, very fast, prepared by my partner. I

then work from half past eight until midnight, or one in the morning, and sometimes two in the morning ... I think my family takes the pressure. The implication for my relationship is that I almost never speak to my husband, because he's a poor third after working. He's third after kids, work, relationship.

Women's attempts to juggle excessive workloads and domestic responsibilities lead to misconceptions and criticism regarding their commitment and choice. Our study found that women were often viewed as being less committed to Oxfam's goals as a direct result of their having to fulfil certain domestic and child-care responsibilities. One man's perception was that 'women would see work as less of a priority than men. Women tend to prioritise relationships over work ...'. Working the double shift means that women are unable to extend their working hours as much as men, who don't have the same burden of domestic and child-care work. One woman's comment supports this, revealing how Oxfam, unconsciously, values women's contribution less:

> Rushing off to collect children from school is seen as a lack of commitment. If you look around the organisation, it is quite often the men who are seen to be committed and working late. And it is quite often the women who are absent because of their domestic responsibilities.

One policy-maker suggested, with respect to the very high workload which potentially disadvantages those working a double shift, that people have choices, to which there will be advantages and disadvantages:

> Life is always a trade-off between any one individual's values, beliefs, what they want to do, what they don't want to do ... I make a choice to do something and there's pros and cons to it ... It's just choices people make. That doesn't mean to say that the organisation can't try and create a better environment but I think that at the end of the day, part of it is individual choice ...

Often organisations do not acknowledge the compromised choices in workers' lives, nor do they recognise that workers can be committed to their personal relationships *and* to their work. The rhetoric of being organisationally committed to improving gender relations in the workplace means compensating for the realities of inequalities, particularly the inequalities of unpaid work in the home.

Equal opportunities: Are they really equal?
The aim of equal opportunities initiatives is to ensure that the structural barriers preventing women, ethnic minorities, and people with disabilities from participating in paid work are removed. With regards to women, these initiatives have generally focused on positive action models to improve women's representation at all levels of economic activity.

Two models have predominated positive action initiatives: the equity model and the complementary contribution model (Adler and Izraeli 1988). By far the most popular model has been the equity model, in which women are assumed to be professionally identical to men, and effectiveness is measured against long-standing male norms. It is under this model that activities such as assertiveness training and career development have been designed to help women compete in the job market on a more equal footing to men. The message underlying this model is that for women to be successful in organisations they must display masculine values and behaviours. The phrase 'equal opportunities' under the equity model therefore is a contradiction in terms.

The less popular complementary contribution model makes the assumption of difference. Women's and men's contributions to organisations is assumed to be different and equally valuable, leaving the potential for women to make a unique, different, and valued contribution. Although proposals to re-examine job descriptions and recruitment qualifications to encompass women's potential had been made by Oxfam, the prevailing approach remains the equity approach. The emphasis here is on identifying 'the best qualified candidate', and equal-opportunities energies are channelled into developing strategies to improve women's competitiveness, as explained by this senior manager:

> Selection for jobs has to be on the basis of the best qualified candidates.
> Therefore, the challenge on implementing the Gender Policy is in what support
> the organisation can provide to enable women to stand a better chance of getting
> to be qualified applicants for a post.

What is overlooked in this analysis is that the definition of 'qualified applicants' has been constructed from male perspectives and norms. In this light, 'support' must therefore be translated as: 'How can we make women more like men?'

Confidence: Issues of invisibility, isolation, exclusion, and role modification
The final factor seen to perpetuate the existence of the glass ceiling is self-confidence.[20] This factor manifests itself by blocking women's attempts to break the glass ceiling, and by undermining women's chances of success if they do manage to break through. In Oxfam, self-confidence is clearly an issue. Sixty-five per cent of women in the study revealed that they suffered low self-confidence and self-esteem themselves, as well as observing it in other women. Despite the fact that men and women participating in the study were encouraged to discuss the same themes, none of the men expressed a lack in confidence or self-esteem.

The feeling of visibility seemed to be a contributing factor to levels of self-confidence. Ninety-three per cent of women interviewed for the study recounted their experiences of invisibility. Their stories told of not being taken seriously, of being ignored, unheard — or not even bothering to try to get their voices heard, and 'suffering with it quietly'. Apart from a few men who recognised the visibility of their own sex in certain situations, none mentioned the kind of invisibility that almost all of the women described.

Not recognising and valuing women's different and unique contributions to an organisation, and expecting them to behave according to male norms, not only blocks their chances of breaking the glass ceiling. It also undermines the chances of success of those women who do manage to reach the other side. This often results in debilitating feelings of isolation, exclusion, and in role modification.

Women who have broken the glass ceiling are often perceived by their former peers as having abandoned women, contributing to their feeling of isolation. A manager describes this resentment and tension:

> There's a couple of women who I've had explode at me and shout at me and in a sort of fit of rage say 'Well, we all know about you and managing women, you're terrible at it' and I suddenly thought, 'Well, my God, is this really the case?'

Resentment also manifests itself through the exclusive behaviour of male colleagues. According to one woman, male colleagues regularly engaged in making a 'whole new range of decisions' either in the pub or during weekend activities from which she was excluded. Many women who find themselves working in a 'masculine' environment feel the pressure to adopt a more 'masculine' role in an attempt to become more credible.

The phenomena of glass ceiling, double shift, and pressure to conform to male values are particularly apparent in organisations which have developed their culture based on Weber's definition of organising. Rational, logical arguments rooted in well-defined principles dominate Oxfam's value system, leaving little room for other, equally valid methods informing decision-making, such as intuition. The priority placed on the ability to work long, uninterrupted hours, and the complete separation of work from domestic life, ultimately rest on a Weberian understanding of organisational 'efficiency'. Understanding the organisational culture of Oxfam with the view to finding change means understanding the unconscious nature of the processes dominating Oxfam's organisational life.

The processes of universal reason, characterised by judgement, rationality, discrimination, and objective interest, are reflected in the accounts of Oxfam employees. Conversely, attachment, relatedness, friendship, and subjective intuition were markedly lacking from the voices of Oxfam employees in their accounts of gender relations in Oxfam. Qualities which are essentially 'masculine' are dominant over 'feminine' qualities.[21]

It is clear that reconciling the rhetoric of gender equality in Oxfam with the reality presented is not simply a matter of restructuring or grafting new initiatives onto the old culture, because such approaches tend to retain and reinforce the status quo. Nor is it a matter of abandoning scientific rational action in favour of intuitive relatedness. According to Jung, this strategy would only tip the balance towards the other, equally ineffective, extreme. The answer lies in the search for the right balance, in integrating the clearly absent 'feminine' qualities with dominant — and increasingly domineering — 'masculine' qualities.

Unfortunately, there is no 'magic bullet' strategy in achieving that integration. Bowles (1993) proposes a fundamental shift in organisational values and beliefs that requires a conscious confrontation with the ethic of mechanistic thinking and rational action.

> It might suggest a flattening of hierarchies and dispersion of power in order to reduce distance between people, fundamentally an empowerment of all individuals in an organisation … It might include use of human 'feeling' to dictate ethical action … moving the organisation into relationship with the community as a whole.

Fear, anxiety, and resistance to change

Fear and anxiety are normal responses to the prospect of change. This was reflected in one man's perceptions of the kinds of changes involved in achieving greater gender equality:

> On gender, generally I see one problem … Are you going to start talking in terms of different roles for men and women? People think men should now do what women are doing and women should do what men are doing … If people start picking up that gender is all about exchanging roles, problems might come in. People are trying to change things which have always been like that.

Resistance and sabotage, on the other hand, are destructive responses to the fear and anxiety of change. When fear and anxiety are channelled towards creative ends, the transition towards change is healthy and positive. When they are allowed to degenerate into resistance and sabotage, debilitating consequences can result for both individuals and the organisation.

Failure to take action is one form of resistance and has been described by Critchley and Casey (1989) as resulting from internal organisational fear. In Oxfam, there appeared to be a general failure to take action on issues regarding gender equality. A policy is instituted but implementation is delayed for one reason or another as observed by one man in Oxfam House:

> If you look at the gender policies, how much they are implemented? They're always seen as, 'Oh, yes, we are forgetting about gender', and we add them at the end.

Resistance can also be construed in the subtle, intangible way in which gender discrimination manifests itself in Oxfam: as 'assumptions about the sort of person we need to do this job — aggressive, self-starter, the sort who can make hard management decisions. Someone, unconsciously, sees a man as the person they want, even if they haven't actually formulated it.' In a politically correct environment such as Oxfam, where it is no longer acceptable to be 'outright sexist or racist', discrimination becomes entrenched as an unconscious resistance strategy, which is more difficult to eradicate.

Resistance, in itself, is a mild form of sabotage towards change. Male back-lash (Smith 1982) is a more aggressive form of sabotage: it is a destructive response to intense fear. It occurs when men perceive their position threatened by efforts to enforce policy encouraging women into more senior, influential positions. It is a protective yet destructive response, often directed at women's competence, working style, and knowledge, and designed to undermine their confidence. (It should be noted that both men and women can engage in destructive interactions.)

One woman member of staff describes how her self-esteem was undermined after she perceived a male colleague to be questioning her competence:

> I felt close to tears at that point, because I was confused: what if he is right? What if it is my job and I just don't know how to do it and that's why I'm failing? …
> I would feel that I wasn't doing my job and I was failing and I was the weak member of the team.

Women begin to feel like the 'embattled minority' and the consequences can be severe as evidenced by one senior manager who chose to leave her position with Oxfam for health reasons related to the efforts to sabotage her. The poignant metaphors she uses to illustrate the consequences are very revealing:

> I had no choice but to leave Oxfam in terms of personal health, but should I actually have left? … It gives 'the chaps' the excuse to turn around and say 'Women aren't up to it'. It's like they define the arena, they define the size of the lion, then they crow when you get chewed up.

These responses to fear and anxiety effectively comprise an approach to gender equality where people perceive themselves either as winners or losers. It is important to stress that the perpetuation of gender inequality in Oxfam is an unconscious process. Understanding that this perpetuation is not due to individuals consciously and maliciously plotting to sabotage efforts of change is the first step in developing strategies to overcome the pattern. Conscious efforts to recognise this unconscious nature and to design a win-win approach are essential if the creative channelling of fear and anxiety is to be achieved.

Conclusion

Few if any organisations have truly attempted the radical destructuring and reconstructing process necessary to achieve fundamental shifts in values and beliefs. Providing a step-by step-manual of the initiatives necessary in this process is, therefore, extremely difficult. Exposing the unconscious behaviour potentially blocking organisational change towards greater gender equality, however, is an important first step to improving the organisation's effectiveness.

Oxfam's dominant organisational ethos has become preoccupied with enhancing performance to the extent that human consequences, particularly for women, are neglected. The pathway to greater rationalisation — where, in the words of the men and women interviewed, 'strategic management', 'minimum standards', 'rational arguments', 'productivity', 'defending your corner', 'results-oriented' and 'task-driven' management are the valued norm — often requires managers to suspend personal and ethical involvement in the pursuit of organisational performance and profitability, fitting with Weber's concept of efficiency.

In subjecting Weber's theories and Oxfam's dominant organisational culture to a Jungian analysis, it becomes clear that the rational bureaucracy is one with a highly dominant *animus* and a grossly underdeveloped *anima*. Jung maintains that only through the recognition and integration of an individual's unconscious can that person be considered 'well-adjusted'. It follows that a 'well-adjusted' organisation would strike a balance between *animus* and *anima*. Taking it one step further, for Oxfam to become a 'well-adjusted' organisation, integrating the *anima* into organisational processes appears to be of paramount importance.

For organisations such as Oxfam, whose objectives and rhetoric clearly indicate a concern for a more humane world, where exploitation of humans (regardless of sex, race, class, or socio-economic situation) or the environment is deemed unacceptable, adopting these principles might present a way forward in closing the gap between rhetoric and reality.

About the author

Wendy Carson, a Canadian, graduated from McGill University, Montreal, in 1990 after working for three years in South Sudan in a primary health-care project. She holds a MSc in Mother and Child Health from the Institute of Child Health, University of London. Her dissertation, on which this article is based, focused on gender issues in international NGOs. She has since worked in Rwanda, Burundi, and Somalia, and is particularly concerned with the link between gender issues, poverty, and disease. (She would like to acknowledge the Canadian Federation of University Women for their contribution in making this chapter a reality.)

References

Adler, N. and Izraeli, D. (1988), 'Women in Management Worldwide', in Adler, N. and Izraeli, D. (eds.), *Women in Management Worldwide*, New York: ME Sharpe.

Bowles, M. (1990), 'Recognizing Deep Structures in Organizations', *Organizational Studies*, Vol.11, No.3, pp.395 412.

Bowles, M. (1993), 'Logos and Eros: The Vital Syzygy for Understanding Human Relations and Organizational Action', *Human Relations*, Vol.46, No.11.

Carson, W.J. (1995), '"Rhetoric vs. Reality": Gender and Other Organisational Issues', MSc thesis, Institute of Child Health, University of London.

Clarkson, P. (1995), 'The Differential Outcomes of Organisational Change' in *Change in Organisations*, London: Whurr Publishers Ltd.

Critchley, B. and Casey, D. (1989), 'Organisations Get Stuck Too', *Leadership and Organisation Development Journal*, Vol.10, No.4, pp.3–12.

Hakim, C. (1979), 'Occupational Segregation: A Comparative Study of the Degree and Pattern of the Differentiation Between Men and Women's Work' in 'Britain, The United States and Other Countries', Department of Employment Research Paper No. 9.

Handy, C. (1991), *The Gods of Management: The Changing Work of Organisations*, London: Business Books.

Newell, S. (1993), 'The Superwoman Syndrome: Gender Differences in Attitudes Towards Equal Opportunities at work and Towards Domestic Responsibilities at Home', *Work, Employment and Society*, Vol.7, No.2, pp.275–289.

Smith, J.M. (1982), 'Avoiding the Male Backlash' in Cooper, C. (ed.), *Practical Approaches to Women's Career Development*, Sheffield: Manpower Services Commission.

Stover, D.L. (1994), 'The Horizontal Distribution of Female Managers Within Organizations', *Work and Occupations*, Vol.21, No.4, pp.385–402.

Tanton, M. (1994), 'Developing Women's Presence' in Tanton, M. (ed.) *Women in Management: A Developing Presence*, London: Routledge, pp.7–26.

Weber, M. (1978), in Roth, G. and Wittich, C. (eds.), *Economy and Society*, Berkeley: University of California Press.

Williams, S. (1994), *The Oxfam Gender Training Manual*, Oxford: Oxfam.

Wilson, F. (1995), *Organisational Behaviour and Gender*, Maidenhead: McGraw-Hill Book Company International (UK) Ltd.

Setting up the Oxfam nursery

The editors with thanks to Norman Clift

Nurseries have offered parents invaluable child-care facilities for some time, and, in Britain, can be found in churches, public meeting places, and recently even in shopping centres. But despite their obvious advantage for parents, they are still the exception rather than the rule. This is also the case in the workplace. Child-care for children below school age still takes place primarily in the home, with women taking on most of the child-rearing. This means that women give up their formal (paid) work, at least for a few years, at what is often an important point in their own careers. This has long been considered unfair: the assumption that women will take on the reproductive role of child-carer in the home disadvantages them in the workplace, and denies them equality of opportunity with men.

As employers, many development organisations aim to ensure that job applicants, staff, and volunteers do not suffer unfair discrimination. They believe that following a policy of equality of opportunity will benefit not only the individual but also enrich the whole organisation. A major concern of any equal opportunities policy is to address the difficulties faced by mothers of young children. There is an argument for the costs of child-care being borne to some degree by the employer, as these costs represent an investment in the productivity of the employed parent. A workplace nursery can be regarded as a legitimate production cost in the same way as the provision of a cafeteria, desks, chairs, and so on. This thinking was recognised at the time of setting up the Oxfam GB nursery:

> Women are essential to the success of any enterprise. They occupy key jobs requiring talent, skill and commitment, yet even so, many employers evade the question of what their response should be to providing essential child-care facilities, without which women cannot work on an equal footing with men. In

focusing their attention on the costs such provision will entail, employers fail to recognise the enormous benefits to be derived from such provision by both employee and employer. (report made to the Oxfam Executive in 1986)

Workplace nurseries have often been assumed to have benefits only for women employees; but their benefits apply equally to women and men. A nursery enables both male and female employees to accept and carry out reproductive care, alongside their productive (formal) employment. Thus, the gendered division between productive and reproductive work can be challenged by both women and men.

The Oxfam nursery has been in existence now for ten years. The thinking behind its inception was, first, that a workplace nursery demonstrates the employer's acceptance of employees' need for child-care, and also of their role in providing it. A further rationale was that organisations such as Oxfam are committed to promoting social justice and gender equality through their development work internationally, and a workplace nursery reflects this wider support for equal opportunities and gender equality. In other words, a workplace nursery was seen as an important part of practising what we preach. Suzanne Williams, co-ordinator of the Gender and Development Unit in 1985, recalls:

We saw the nursery as a fundamental building-block in the struggle for equal opportunities and particularly access for women to demanding and senior jobs in Oxfam — and indeed, it has made an enormous difference to so many people's lives, enabling us to work in the confidence that our young babies and children were close at hand, safe and happy. (internal Oxfam document, 1998)

A central part of equal opportunities

The greatest obstacle to many women's employment and promotion prospects is still a lack of adequate child-care. Women with children form a substantial part of the labour force, but they do so against tremendous odds. In the UK, discrimination against women in the workplace is illegal, yet national statistics provide incontrovertible evidence that women with young children are still effectively discriminated against, because they are expected to take most of the responsibility for child-care. Little consideration is given to the fact that good-quality, reliable, and affordable child-care services are in short supply, and that this shortage results in unequal opportunities for women with young children.

Rona Alexander, Programme Manager in the Marketing Division, states that,

the rationale in the beginning was Oxfam's commitment to equal opportunities, which was heavily invested in at the time. David Jones, the then Deputy Director, did a lot to get it going — with constant pressure from the union and vociferous activists. (internal document, 1998)

A positive investment for employers

Providing facilities for child-care can be a positive economic investment for employers. For example, many women who leave work on maternity leave are unable to return to their jobs because they cannot find adequate and affordable child-care facilities. This is not in the employer's interests, and it undermines the progress which has been made in establishing better employment rights for women on maternity leave. These women may have worked for many years; they are experienced employees with skills and training in key areas of an organisation's work. Their loss is a major loss for their organisation, because time and capital spent on training and maternity pay cannot be recouped if the woman is unable to return to work after having a child. Other costs incurred, for example in employing temporary staff for up to six months (or in some cases, up to a year), also cannot be recovered. Unsatisfactory child-care arrangements might force parents to leave their employment, which means added expense in recruiting new staff. A workplace nursery also benefits employers when recruiting new staff. Many candidates who are highly skilled and have knowledge of direct relevance will have young children. An organisation which is offering just conditions of employment can expect to attract the best staff and will be respected by the public and other organisations alike.

While the initial cost of setting up a nursery may seem high, the return for the employer more than justifies this expense. To quote Helen Auty, Personnel Manager of London Weekend Television (long recognised as an equal opportunities employer):

> Some of the direct results of the provision of child-care facilities have been a reduced turnover of staff, a reduction of recruitment and training costs, and an increased stability among our staff, who are employed in a highly competitive environment. It is an integral part of our Equal Opportunities policy and has helped us to retain, among others, producers, casting directors, production managers, accounts assistants and photographers. This benefit has also increased our profile as a 'good' employer, enhancing a substantial list of desirable benefits in service.

Child-care in Oxfam: A case study

The nursery was opened in Oxfam House in Oxford in 1987. It was not feasible to set up nurseries in other locations; so, to ensure equality of treatment in all offices, a child-care allowance is available to staff in the UK and Ireland. But no provision was made for women working in country or field offices; in the case of more remote field offices, it is often considered unsuitable for children to accompany their working mothers—although many men working in the same situations will be accompanied by wife and children (Carson 1995).

The experience of contributors to this book, including Dianna Melrose and Suzanne Williams, indicates that providing child-care for staff has benefited Oxfam GB by widening the field of personnel at head office and in regional offices in the UK and Ireland, enabling Oxfam to gain access to expertise among women and men with young children which would otherwise be denied. This point is also echoed by Susie Smith, now Deputy Director of Oxfam's International Division, who states:

> The nearby provision of good quality child-care was a huge plus for me. It made Oxfam a particularly attractive employer, and enabled me to continue working throughout the early childhood years with as little disruption and difficulty as possible. It was a huge help in enabling me to pursue my career with Oxfam, and it was part of what made me want to do that. (internal document, 1998)

Child-care allowances and places in the Oxfam House workplace nursery have been made available to both men and women in the organisation, making the point that it is equally feasible for men to take responsibility for their children's care, and helping to break down the divisions between men's and women's established gender roles. However, in 1997 only women applied for the child-care allowance.

Parental involvement in the nursery

Oxfam's nursery was established on the initiative of a small group of staff members, and the involvement of parents has continued to be an important part of running the nursery. The thinking behind this was that a workplace nursery can benefit enormously from parental involvement: their ideas, concerns, and support are an important contribution. Parental involvement encourages a relationship of trust between parents and child-carers and ensures that parents feel comfortable with the surroundings in which their children are developing.

Perhaps most importantly, the relationship between parents and the organisation keeps open a line of communication between the organisation and the nursery. Issues of importance to the nursery are thus treated as central concerns in the organisation, ensuring that it takes continued responsibility for providing child-care. Parents are involved in the Oxfam workplace nursery through a voluntary management committee. This committee not only allows parents some involvement in the running of the nursery in which their children are being looked after, it also ensures that they (as representatives of the organisation) maintain a link between the organisation and the concerns of the nursery.

Allocation of nursery places

Because the demand for places far exceeds supply, allocation of places has been a consistent problem for many nurseries. A total of 663 of employees in the Oxford head office qualify for a nursery place, but there are only 23 places in the Oxfam nursery. This means that there is one nursery place available for every 28 eligible staff members. Clearly not all staff members will require nursery places, but there is considerable demand. This has been a cause of considerable anguish among staff and the nursery management committee, who decide how to allocate the very few places available. Allocation of places for the nursery must be regulated, but in doing so it is clear that some priorities must be established, compromising the ideal of fully accessible child-care for all employees with young children.

In discussions over allocation, some groups of employees can be prioritised over others, but it is important that no group is excluded. Priorities for the Oxfam nursery were initially identified in terms of the needs of the organisation, the children, their parents, and the nursery. For example, it was considered to be in Oxfam's interests to ensure that people taking up 'hard-to-fill' posts have priority access to nursery places. For the children, and particularly the parents, it is important to have siblings together. Children with disability or special needs and parents with disability were also put forward as priorities, as were single parents.

Inevitably, some issues that can be seen as very important can also be seen as beyond the scope of a nursery-places allocations policy. For example, the issue of parents on low incomes brings up problems of assessment: how does one take into account total household income, and how does one avoid the pitfalls of 'means-testing'? Yet the complexity of such issues should not be used as an excuse to ignore the problem, but as a reason for examining it on a much wider organisational basis. This example illustrates the importance of ensuring that discussions about the nursery maintain a central place in organisational priorities, as many of the issues that arise contain fundamental problems for the organisation.

Nursery places are allocated within the principles of a commitment on the part of Oxfam to be an equal opportunities employer. From the start, Oxfam based its provision of nursery places on the principle that no child, individual, or family should be excluded from the nursery activities on the grounds of gender, sexuality, class, family status, means, disability, colour, ethnic origin, culture, religion or beliefs. However, allocation of places in such an over-subscribed facility remains an area for discussion and debate. This is also connected to the next problem area — the thorny question of funding.

Funding

Despite the obvious advantages of a subsidised workplace nursery, the allocation and use of donated funds for child-care has to be very carefully considered. For a variety of reasons, a workplace nursery that is self-financing is very difficult to achieve in any context. In particular, there must be a desire to maintain a nursery charge which is affordable for lower-paid staff.

Given that one of the purposes of a nursery from an organisational point of view is to help women continue in their jobs, affordable child-care is particularly important, because women are predominantly found in the lower-paid posts. There is often a delicate balance between buying child-care with a salary from (formal) paid work, and giving up paid work to look after children at no (formal) cost. Once the line is crossed, and the cost of child-care exceeds the salary from paid work, the whole idea of the workplace nursery is undermined, and access is denied to those women who are often in the greatest need. There is therefore a need for continued investment from employers. It has been argued that the level of funding has to be measured against the value of nursery provision to an employer. The British Civil Service now accepts this, based on a calculation that the cost of replacing a staff member is approximately one year's salary. The provision of child-care for working parents represents real 'value for money' for the organisation, and campaigners have argued that both the government and employers can do more to share the costs and benefits of child-care.

For a time, Oxfam used an innovative scheme to facilitate a reduction in nursery fees, involving a salary sacrifice/tax-reduction arrangement. Nursery users agreed to have their annual pay package re-allocated, which gave a smaller amount of taxed salary, and Oxfam was able to use the remainder to cover the costs of nursery provision. The effect has been that staff save tax and National Insurance on their child-care costs. The scheme was initially cleared by the Inland Revenue as legitimate, but subsequently this agreement was revoked, and we had to revert to the original arrangements. Schemes such as this should receive wider consideration as a means of encouraging improved child-care provision.

Practising what we preach

It is clear that a workplace nursery not only is a positive investment for employers and an important facility for the organisation and its staff, but also is highly relevant to organisations that are committed to promoting gender equity through their work. When the nursery was set up in 1987, it was seen as an essential part of the implementation of Oxfam's Gender Policy, which states a commitment to gender equity both throughout our programme work, and within the organisation. As Dominic Vickers, a fund-raiser in Oxfam's Marketing Division, observes, 'we can't ask governments, corporations, and our partner organisations to take gender issues seriously unless we also take them seriously in the workplace' (internal document, 1998). It was felt that a commitment to gender equity in organisational programmes must be mirrored by the organisation's commitment to its own staff by providing a genuinely gender-equitable working environment. Ensuring that women are not constrained in their careers by child-care responsibilities goes a long way towards promoting a more equitable professional structure.

Provision of a workplace nursery could also be seen as part of a larger process of changing assumptions about gender roles. By providing necessary facilities for child-care in the workplace, we are enabling both men and women to take responsibility for their domestic lives as well as to be full and valued productive actors within the organisation. This responsibility is further enhanced when parents and staff are able to collaborate in the running of the nursery, as an organisational priority.

It is no longer necessary or expected that domestic (reproductive) tasks are separated from the (productive) workplace, with women taking on the unpaid responsibility for the home and children, leaving men free to operate as professional, paid, members of a workforce. A genuinely equitable workplace should begin a process of breaking down the barriers between reproductive and productive roles. The Oxfam workplace nursery, although over-subscribed and challenged in providing affordable child-care, especially for the lower-paid, has enabled women to continue with their professional lives as well as ensure that their children are cared for. But, perhaps more importantly, it has enabled both men and women to take responsibility for child-care without compromising their place in the workforce.

About the authors

Norman Clift joined Oxfam in 1981 following a working life in commercial organisations. While with Oxfam, he has been engaged, both as a volunteer and a member of staff, in a variety of human-resources roles. He is currently assisting in the work of Corporate Human Resources on a part-time basis.

References

Carson, W.J. (1995), '"Rhetoric vs. Reality": Gender and Other Organisational Issues', MSc thesis, Institute of Child Health, University of London.

Notes to section II

1　Charles Handy (1988), *Understanding Voluntary Organisations.*
2　Bridget Walker (1994), 'Towards a Gender Strategy for Africa', internal discussion paper, Oxfam.
3　Yayori Matsui, 'Violence against women in development, militarism and culture' in King, Ursula (ed.) (1994), *Feminist Theology from the Third World.*
4　Please also refer to Wendy Carson's article in this volume for a discussion of the glass ceiling, and the experience of women who break through.
5　The *Concise Oxford Dictionary* defines 'feminism' as 'the advocacy of women's rights on the ground of the equality of the sexes'.
6　For example, see the article by Visha Padmanabhan in this volume.
7　See Wendy Carson's article for further analysis of this phenomenon.
8　Margaret Legum, 'The Right Time to Institutionalise Gender'.
9　Action for Gender Relations in Asia: see the article by Kanchan Sinha in this volume for more information on this Oxfam staff network.
10　Aminatta Forna (author of *Mother of All Myths*), 'Go Girls', *The Guardian*, 16 July 1998.
11　Some of the material contained in this piece has been published as a chapter entitled 'Assessing the Impact: NGOs and Empowerment' in Afshar, H. (ed.) (1998), *Women and Empowerment*, London: Macmillan.
12　'An analytical framework sets out different categories of elements / factors to be considered in an analysis; it draws attention to the key issues that have to be explored. A framework may outline a broad set of beliefs and goals, or it may be more prescriptive and give a set of tools and procedures.' See March, C., Mukhopadhyay, M., Smyth, I. (eds.) (1999), *A Guide to Gender-Analysis Frameworks*, Oxford: Oxfam.
13　Many thanks for the invaluable comments and suggestions given by Becky Buell, Deborah Eade, Francine Pickup, and Caroline Sweetman and Fenella Porter.
14　The implications of feminist debates for anti-poverty organisations was discussed particularly in the introduction to *Gender and Development*, Vol. 5, No. 1, February 1997.
15　It is worth mentioning by name at least some of those who pioneered feminist

work in the region: Suzanne Williams and Celina de Godoy in Brazil, Audrey Bronstein in the Andean region, Luisa Maria Rivera and Deborah Eade in Mexico and Central America and, more recently, Jenny Vaughan, Fifa Stubbs, Becky Buell. It is also indicative that those mentioned are all women, in positions of authority in the various country programmes.

16 That they are not mentioned here by name is due in part to practical considerations, and in part in respect to the fact hat they may want to continue to work 'in disguise' (see below).

17 See *Gender and Development*, Vol.3, No.1 (1995) for various perspectives on this issue.

18 This definition of gender is only one definition of many. It should be used as a working definition to be referred to throughout the article. It is by no means intended to be universal or exclusive to all other definitions.

19 For further reading on occupational segregation please refer to Hakim (1979), Wilson (1995), and Stover (1994).

20 For further reading on this topic see Tanton (1994).

21 It should be noted that 'masculine' and 'feminine' are defined in the Jungian sense and should be thought of in terms independent of biological sex.

III

The role of a specialist team

Introduction to section III

The articles in this section reflect on the advantages and disadvantages of having a specialised team working on gender concerns in a large development organisation, and on the enormous personal cost of this work. Suzanne Williams records her experience as a member of Oxfam GB's Gender and Development Unit (GADU), and the struggles that were a part of its inception. Tina Wallace, also a member of GADU in the early years, remembers this period, focusing on the team's innovative ways of working and on the message of co-operation and participation both within Oxfam GB, and with groups and agencies external to it.

In addition to telling the story of GADU's birth, Suzanne Williams also looks forward to 1996, when the unit was merged with another, retaining gender-specialist staff but losing much of what had made it unique. She questions whether the transformative vision of the pioneering era was swept away by these structural changes, or whether GADU was always perceived as a unit which was 'born to die' once it had performed its role as a catalyst. Questions remain as to whether the 'mainstreaming' of gender — i.e. the move to make a focus on gender issues mandatory for all staff in all activities — and the loss of a specialist unit in an organisation inevitably reflect a certain loss of commitment to a transformative vision of equality between women and men.

In her article, Alison Farrell looks at her experiences as a young feminist in the specialist gender unit at head office in the mid-1990s, and records the excitement and sense of personal satisfaction, as well as the challenges that this work still holds for the women who are the future of gender work in development. She also raises the issues associated with working as a volunteer, both from an organisational and a personal point of view.

It is commonly accepted that our understanding of gender is closely linked to our identity, and the way in which we locate ourselves personally and politically in our professional context. In the final article in this section, Chris Roche, the first male manager of Oxfam GB's specialist gender unit — now called the Gender and Programme Learning Team — explores the scope that men have for participating in dialogues about feminism and gender and development, in solidarity with women, and their scope for action as professionals in development organisations.

Chronicle of a death foretold:
The birth and death of Oxfam GB's
Gender and Development Unit

Suzanne Williams

There never was a death more foretold ...[1]

Preamble

My story is that of the founder of Oxfam GB's Gender and Development Unit (GADU),[2] and I therefore claim some historical authority — but I do not claim the only truth. In writing this article, I feel a little as though I am writing an obituary for a beloved, but estranged, daughter, with whom I have had a long, sometimes close, at other times hostile, relationship; a daughter who I abandoned shortly after giving birth, and who in her teenage years was often glad to keep me out of her life; and one whose days, it seems to me, were always numbered. It is true that in the end we were in a sense reunited, and something of her now continues in a new form; it is still too early to tell what our chances of survival will be. But my aim here is not to be prophetic; it is to look back and to tell the story of an end foreseen, and a death foretold. Doubtless many will disagree with me, but my view is that GADU's fate was sealed from the beginning. She lived on borrowed time, for a number of reasons which I will sketch out in this article.

The core and the periphery

This account is a mixture of unashamedly personal memory, and an attempt to be a little more objective. I see the GADU's life-cycle in the context of a question about what is perceived as permanent and what is seen as temporary in an organisation, what counts as 'core' and what as peripheral. GADU was set up at a time when Oxfam's Overseas Division, as it was called then, was debating whether to set up a system of 'core' and 'flexible' staff. Core staff would be those long-serving trusted individuals on permanent contracts, who could be moved from one overseas posting to another, building up experience and expertise over time. The rest would be on temporary contracts, called in as necessary. Those of us concerned with gender equity protested that this could be profoundly discriminatory to women, far fewer of whom at that time had longstanding field experience than men, and who, unless they were single, would be far less likely than men to be able to move their families around. For 'core permanent staff', we read 'the chaps'.

I believe that this thinking has never quite gone away—this is what a 'gendered archaeology'[3] of Oxfam might disinter — and the story of GADU can be understood in the light of what is considered to be 'core', and what is flexible, peripheral, and inevitably the first to go when it comes to the crunch. Experiences of Women in Development (WID) or Gender and Development (GAD) machineries in NGOs and government-funded donor agencies, as well as states, show that these tend to have an advisory and catalytic role in both policy and operational functions in the institution. Their success depends upon the extent to which managers take on the agenda, and integrate it into the core functions and ethos of the organisation; but most organisations lack the mechanisms to ensure compliance with their own gender policies. In Oxfam GB, even now, for all the intensive work on gender over the last decade, and the institutional commitment to its Gender Policy, the question of whether gender equity should be a core value for Oxfam has recently been raised.

Passion and porridge

So, if this the chronicle of a death, you ask: is GADU dead?

Yes, GADU herself is dead. In the mid-1980s, when the women's movement and feminism were struggling against new enemies, GADU represented a vision and a challenge. The 1980s heralded the culture of self-enrichment, the rise of monetarism, and the collapse of socialism. The mid-decade UN Women's Conference in Copenhagen produced evidence of the decline in the status and well-being of women around the world, in spite of policies and strategies to enhance women's development. While gains had been made in relation to employment and remuneration, far more women had become poorer, and the 'feminisation of poverty' was a trend in both the poor and richest countries. The few advances women were making began to be subject to male backlash.

Feminists were demanding a new agenda, not the integration of women into dysfunctional structures and systems. Gita Sen and Caren Grown wrote in 1987:

> We want a world where inequality based on class, gender and race is absent from every country, and from the relationships between countries. We want a world where basic needs become basic rights and where poverty and all forms of violence are eliminated. Each person will have the opportunity to develop her or his full potential and creativity, and women's values of nurturance and solidarity will characterise human relationships.[4]

During the 1980s, many of us in Oxfam joined in protests with the women at Greenham Common, supported the miners' strikes, went to rallies and vigils for South Africa, Nicaragua, and Guatemala. And it was the same passionate belief that we brought into the conception and early days of GADU — and, it should be said, into other parts of Oxfam.

But over time, the vision and passion were too hard to sustain. GADU was a women's organisation within a men's organisation, with all the consequent tensions. Dealing with the same resistances and obstacles over and over again was like being force-fed cold porridge. At first, it was unpleasant but manageable, because Oxfam was growing rapidly but had not yet lost its sense of excitement and direction. It was certainly full of contradictions and erratic behaviours, of machismo and discriminatory and patronising attitudes towards women, but there was nonetheless still a strong belief in human development. Oxfam was prepared to share the risks which poor people take every day, and support their organisations over a long period of time, accepting that many hoped-for outcomes could not be guaranteed, and would not be apparent in the short term.

However, during the 1980s and 1990s competition in the marketplace brought pressure to bear on NGOs to demonstrate quantifiable results. While this was part of the professionalisation of NGOs, and indeed essential to define what impact they were having in tackling poverty and injustice, it also spawned shallow or one-sided interpretations of accountability, and an anxious short-termism in relation to development processes. Indicators were *in*, solidarity and commitment to partners were definitely *out*. The need for visible results was seen in the positive explosion of graphics — flow charts, matrices, pie charts, webs, you name it — in NGOs' presentations of their work. But in all of this, some things which were central to the vision of gender equity and the work of GADU began to be discredited and lost. These were the perceptions that social processes are long-term, complicated, and difficult to understand and measure; that they need careful and sensitive scrutiny; that gender and other identities, and social relationships critically determine the course of development interventions; that partnerships must be built on mutual trust, and that this doesn't happen overnight.

The inquest …

Perhaps it is as a coroner rather than as an archaeologist that I pose the question whether, during the late 1980s and the early 1990s, GADU and the rest of Oxfam were going in different directions which eventually, inevitably, brought them into head-on collision; or whether there were simply too many accidents along the way.

Looking back now, I'm not sure exactly when GADU died — was it the moment of 'institutional execution', when it was merged with another team, or before then? Was it a slow death, a death by a thousand cuts? Did GADU die when the vision which nurtured her died, as the new corporate culture began to stifle her? Some would say that she had been suffering from a terminal illness for some time and that, in her weakened state, she was an easy target when financial cuts had to be made. They might argue that the illness was partly of her own making; that she was riven by internal conflicts and mismanagement; that in spite of continuing support from many quarters in Oxfam, she had alienated too many of her friends and allies. Others would maintain that she did not die at all, but has instead been brought from her crumbling outpost into the bosom of the family.

The myths abound, and will doubtless alter with each retelling, in the best of oral tradition. In my view, the most cruel myth of all is that gender in Oxfam was mainstreamed to the extent that GADU was no longer needed; that it had done its job, just as had been envisaged; and that merging it with another team was a way of 'mainstreaming' gender more effectively. This myth, like a pale spectre, hung over GADU's head all her life. She was always under pressure to justify her existence, every fault magnified by her detractors. It was a hard life: we know that specialist knowledge on gender will always be needed and that the forces against women's equality with men are not diminishing. Fighting those forces takes energy, time, and resources; as the literature on the adoption of gender concerns by organisations indicates, it is essential to have a well-resourced specialist structure *as well as* individuals throughout the organisation to advance and monitor the process.

But let me go back to the historical record, and lay out the bare bones of my memory, and what I have gleaned from the recollections of others who were there at the time. This is only an account of the beginning and ending of GADU, and an attempt to make sense of it.

The rest is history

In 1984, after I had been back from my posting as Deputy Country Representative for Oxfam in Brazil for just over two years, I was asked by the then Overseas Director to be the 'focal point' for gender in Oxfam. This was in response to my having raised the question of women in development and gender inequality while still in Brazil, and expressing the view that Oxfam was lagging terribly behind Brazilian NGOs and feminist organisations working in the development field. Oxfam had a lot of catching up to do. I had written a chapter on women and development for *The Oxfam Field-Director's Handbook*, and Maitrayee Mukhopadhyay was commissioned to write *Silver Shackles*, an account of the oppression of women in India, for the end of the UN Decade for Women in Development, marked by the Nairobi Conference in 1985. It was the first of Oxfam's long list of publications on women and gender.

In the UK, women and women's organisations were mobilising for the Nairobi conference, and we also had to get moving. In Oxfam at the time, the organisational culture made the field office — especially the (usually male) field director — king, and only endorsement by field staff gave legitimacy to any endeavour. Of course, having come into Oxfam through the field, I subscribed wholeheartedly to this article of faith. I knew that the field offices in Latin America, Africa, and Asia had to be behind any initiative on gender at the centre. I wrote up proposals that went to the various field staff meetings, and on the strength of the positive responses from all of them, I formulated the proposal for GADU.

In the meantime, I had been networking in Oxfam House, setting up a steering group on gender to take the work forward. We were concerned that this group include not only staff from the area desks in the Overseas Division, but from key departments in the other divisions — such as Education, Campaigns, and Personnel Division, and the campaigns offices throughout the UK — in order to ensure consistency in policy and practice between our field programme and home operations, including the recruitment, selection, and working conditions of staff. We made strong links with the Oxfam Women's Group, and were active on the nursery committee and the Equal Opportunities Working Group.

But all of us were doing this work during time snatched from our full-time jobs. GADU had no fixed abode, so we had to meet in offices temporarily vacated by absent staff, carrying our boxes of books, journals, and a growing volume of correspondence around with us; we had no budget, so we pinched stationery and borrowed typewriters from our respective departments.

Then, on the strength of the field offices' support, and the clear interest from Oxfam in the UK (especially from the campaigns offices) I proposed the formation of a specialist unit on gender to the new Overseas Director, David Bryer, on his first day in office. David was enthusiastic, having been at the Latin America meeting where the issue had been discussed. It would be a 'ginger group' I remember David saying, and he suggested that it be established on a trial basis for a year, because soon enough, gender would be part of everyone's job, and integrated into all policies and procedures. Later, the period was extended to three years.

So right from the start, GADU was conceived of as a temporary structure, a means to get gender going in Oxfam, get it taken up by all of the organisation, and make itself redundant. The unit's greatest indicator of success would be to have worked itself out of a job.

David wrote his first memo to the Overseas Division, announcing the setting up of the new Gender and Development Unit, and he continued to give it his support. I started out as the Co-ordinator of GADU, working half-time on it, and continuing half-time on the Brazil Desk. I was thus only a part-time mother, of a child who was to have accomplished her life's purpose within three years. I didn't for a moment believe that we would achieve the transformation of Oxfam in those three years, but I had no idea of the depth and breadth of the resistance we would encounter, and which GADU would face all through her life. Nor was I able to predict the changes Oxfam would undergo during the 1980s and early 1990s.

GADU's life was extended; but I still believe that her early death continued to be envisaged, and there were many foretellings of it. Some of the views expressed at the beginning — for example, that to establish a specialist gender unit would create a ghetto, and marginalise an issue which needed to be centralised and integrated — continued to be made to her dying day. These also became self-fulfilling prophecies, when GADU put up barricades and later on failed to build on the growing network of support in other parts of the organisation. But these are not simple cause-and-effect dynamics; while many of GADU's friends in Oxfam tried to 'mainstream' gender in a way which did not imply the extinction of the specialist group, others polarised the issues.

In 1985, GADU was established. We had our own, albeit temporary, office (oh the joy of putting up shelves for our books and papers! — the significance of this is discussed in this volume by Sue Smith), and a full-time and a part-time post. I was the full-time Co-ordinator, appointing an officer to work on the resources. We had help from volunteers from the start. We insisted that GADU should have no hierarchy, and that paid staff would be on the same grade. This persisted for some time, and was a point of principle (see Tina Wallace's contribution). We believed in co-operative and open ways of working, and were trying to set an example within a hierarchical and male-dominated organisation.

The steering group became the GADU committee, which was invaluable in maintaining wide support across the organisation. The committee, composed of women and men, met regularly; its members' responsibilities included working on gender in their departments, whether by commenting on project applications, publications, or promoting training courses. The members were conduits of information in both directions, and at the time essential to our survival in the unit: the GADU committee was the only forum in the Overseas Division which offered staff from different area desks the opportunity to meet on a regular basis and discuss organisation-wide issues. This was one of the great strengths of GADU in its early days (Tina Wallace's article discusses this in more detail). Had the model been sustained and developed over the years, GADU's story might have had a different outcome, and we might be fully in line with current developments in Oxfam. But this is in the realm of speculation; back to the history.

A joyous reminiscence: an anonymous well-wisher sent us £400 just after GADU was founded. We never discovered who it was, but the committee met in high excitement. We bought the first model of the Amstrad PC with it. If our donor is reading this — the Amstrad saw the unit through many years of work!

We were committed to change within the organisation as well to change in Oxfam's development programme, and by the time I went on maternity leave in mid-1986, GADU had been a key player on the nursery committee, and the Oxfam nursery had been established after much negotiation, and with the support of the Deputy Director of Oxfam. We had good relationships with staff in field offices and the GADU Newspack was beginning to circulate, with information about gender issues in the various parts of Oxfam's international programme; we also had a strange role in commenting on grant applications, as and when the Desk officers chose to send them to us. Mostly, they only sent us projects which targeted women — projects to get women sewing, knitting, or boiling water — of course, gender only concerns women!

I take up the story again from 1996, after a restructuring in the Overseas Division had created the Policy Department, with several 'teams', including GADU, renamed the Gender Team, and the Programme Development Team (PDT) — the other team in the Department which had a brief for direct programme support and for enhancing programme learning to improve the quality of Oxfam's work. When the PDT was created in 1993, GADU had begun to feel that her position was threatened. The discourse of mainstreaming was in the air, turned to suit different purposes. It was mooted that it was time to mainstream gender and really integrate it into the organisation. It was said that GADU had largely achieved its objectives — and indeed, the achievements were substantial. Oxfam had a Gender Policy, a commitment to gender equity was required in most (but not all!) job descriptions, gender objectives featured in strategic plans, and gender was a required variable in project appraisal, monitoring, and evaluation. Oxfam had developed its advocacy work in relation to issues such as debt and human rights, and participated actively in European and international women's fora, notably Eurostep and the Nairobi and Beijing conference processes.

When I first named GADU, a staff member said mockingly that it sounded like a device for sexing baby chickens — gender was not part of Oxfam's vocabulary in the mid-1980s. Now gender is no longer a strange term, although still a frequently misunderstood one (but less likely to be applied to chickens ...).

Surely, with all these successes, some people argued, the time was ripe to merge the two teams with similar mandates to improve programme quality — the Gender Team and the Programme Development Team, in which I was, at the time, Basic Rights Adviser. The merger actually happened while I was on secondment as Country Representative in South Africa; I returned to find that my job title had become Gender and Human Rights Adviser, and that, in the merger, three colleagues had left the Gender Team, one was made redundant, and the contract of the fifth was not renewed. The remaining two staff members were effectively absorbed into the PDT, which became the Gender and Learning Team (GALT).

The epitaph

Personally, I have come full circle. What we have now is a new configuration, a number of gender specialists within a multi-disciplinary team. We can't be accused of ghettoisation. We have the advantage of a team with wide-ranging skills and experience, and the potential to advance gender work on a broader front. But, from my position now, and remembering the beginnings of GADU, I see that the same challenge and problems remain. Gender work is still catalytic and advisory; peripheral, not core. Gender specialists are still expected to monitor progress in the organisation, and maintain a role in internal policy and external advocacy, as well as to offer direct programme support, through training, impact assessment, planning, and evaluation. The new team has an important function in research and learning. Yet we still, frequently, find ourselves in the sidestream, battling to get gender into the mainstream, rather than determining the course of the stream itself.

There are many versions of why the Gender Team was merged into the PDT; but why not the other way around? There are different levels of explanation. On the level of organisational culture, it was never envisaged to have a permanent specialist group working on gender, and setting its own agenda; I do not doubt that this is because gender equity is still not perceived to be a core value throughout Oxfam; I fear that although Oxfam now has a Gender Policy, there are still considerable obstacles within the organisation to implementing it comprehensively and effectively, and that the organisational culture, while far more aware of gender differences, is still by and large male-defined, particularly in relation to working patterns.

On the level of institutional management, I also do not doubt that the internal divisions and tensions within GADU, by no means exclusive to the unit, were subjected to particular scrutiny and sanction within Oxfam, because the unit worked on gender-related issues and was staffed mainly by feminist women.

Rounaq Jahan, in her study of four institutions (two international donors and two governments) points out a number of shared features of their gender 'machineries'. She also observes that:

> … in most organisations, solutions to the structural problems of the machineries were sought in individual personalities: individuals holding WID/GAD positions were either acclaimed or blamed for their personal traits rather than their professional qualities. In the early years of the Decade, agencies recruited feminists from outside to fill WID positions, but later the agencies turned to 'managers', as it was believed that feminists were confrontational and pushed their male colleagues too hard![5]

We must conclude that if GADU had really been intended to last, as a central and permanent part of the organisation, and if gender had indeed been taken on as a core value in Oxfam, it would not have been disbanded, with the result that fewer gender specialists have been available to Oxfam. It would have been recognised that the organisation could ill afford this loss — too much remained and remains to be done. Other solutions would have been found. But as GADU's death had always been foretold, it was only a matter of fulfilling the prophecy. It now remains to be seen whether the existing capacity on gender in Oxfam will be strengthened or weakened by the latest round of institutional restructuring, and whether Oxfam's commitments to tackling the causes of poverty and distress will be effective for both men and women.

About the author

Suzanne Williams joined Oxfam in 1977 as Deputy Country Representative for Brazil. In 1985, back in Oxford, she founded the Gender and Development Unit, and was its first Co-ordinator. She was active on the workplace nursery committee, and her daughter benefited from its care. After a journey through Oxfam's Information and Campaigns Departments, she co-authored *The Oxfam Handbook of Development and Relief* and *The Oxfam Gender Training Manual*. While Oxfam's Country Representative in South Africa, she initiated strong support for organisations working on violence against women. This remains a key issue in her work in the Policy Department as Gender and Human Rights Adviser.

GADU remembered: Some reflections on the early years

Tina Wallace

Introduction

My first day of working for the Gender and Development Unit (GADU) was also my first day of working for Oxfam GB. On the way to work I had a minor car accident. Not serious, but my fault, because I was distracted by thoughts about how it would be in a new job, and by the tears of my small child over a minor incident as I was leaving. I never arrived the first day at all. When I reached work on day two, brimming with apologies, I found there was no desk for me and no clearly designated space for the small gender team — myself, part-time; a full-time temporary staff member; and a volunteer.

It was over a year before the gender unit was given administrative support, yet the job was vast. Originally it included working with the Overseas Division on development work, tackling the needs of both Oxfam staff and partners in over 70 countries; working with Oxfam's UK Divisions on campaigning and fund-raising; and working to change attitudes towards gender and the personal behaviour of Oxfam staff.

During the first month I deleted swathes of my job description, eliminating work in the UK. This had consequences later, because gender issues within the institution proved as important as gender issues in the overseas programme, but just getting to grips with the Overseas Division was a massive task. Working with a large, dispersed staff from diverse cultures, and trying to reach partners as well as staff with only two people in GADU, was a problem exacerbated in the mid-1980s by the difficulty of communications, especially in much of Africa — there were only telexes, not faxes, and phone calls were nightmarish and expensive.

In addition, my job was part-time. I applied because I wanted to combine the work with child-care and other commitments outside Oxfam. However, going home around 5.30pm remained problematic, because the workload was so high and the organisational culture equated commitment with long hours spent at work. It seemed so important to defend both spaces, given my role as a gender officer. Yet for precisely the same reason it seemed harder to do: I felt that I had to impress others in order to interest them in gender issues, and to get gender accepted. Some GADU staff, over the years, felt that this pressure 'to prove ourselves' outweighed the demands of trying to combine caring for a family with working.[6]

Our task was unbounded, the resources limited, and the space inadequate. GADU worked against what, at times, felt like impossible odds to achieve recognition for gender issues, for the role of the unit, for resources, and for the time to bring a gender perspective to Oxfam's work.

Initially, GADU staff experienced much overt verbal hostility from staff in the UK and overseas (the most hurtful, sometimes cruel comments came from European staff, not all male). We could be discussing the provision of wells and the need to look at women's role in water collection, and then be asked, 'Well, my wife looks after our children while you are here lecturing us. What about your children?' Similar comments were made at a summer party: 'Your daughter seems normal enough for a child that is left by its mother.' Very few women with children worked at programme level in the Overseas Division (only five in the mid-1980s), and the vast majority of programme staff had no dependants; the organisational culture was male dominated. Taunts such as 'Is it true you are all dykes in this room?' or 'What are the ladies plotting today?' were sometimes thrown at us as people passed; when we objected, the riposte was 'Can't you take a joke?' Telexes arrived accusing us of interfering with the natural order of life, although very few staff from the countries where Oxfam worked were openly abusive in this way: indeed, they raised many challenging and complex questions for GADU.

I had a second minor car accident after a colleague and I had run a gender training session for new staff. One man had sabotaged the entire session, reducing us to pulp; we had sat like rabbits staring into the headlights of an on-coming car as he whipped up the group into a mode of hostility and non-co-operation. Those organising the induction did not intervene.

Five years later, none of those hurtful, undermining things were openly said or done. There had been a cultural change among donors, partners, and NGOs, and within Oxfam itself. It was no longer acceptable for staff to be openly derogatory about gender issues. By the time GADU was restructured for the first time in 1991, and I moved on, gender training was well established and Oxfam had tried out different kinds of gender training around the world; agreement had been reached to work towards introducing a gender policy to ensure that gender was seen as an organisational, not a GADU responsibility; gender work had been undertaken in many different field offices and some gender project staff had been recruited; and there were some women in senior management positions. GADU was active in gender networks within the organisation and outside it.

However, silent hostility and resistance to changes proposed by GADU continued and remained difficult to confront; the repeated yet often ignored or rejected demands for essential resources, for representation on key fora, for a voice in the organisation, for inclusion in decision-making, were testimony to that.

Working in GADU for five years was an experience of intense challenge and unhappiness; of enormous potential often unfulfilled. Initially, there was much open hostility from many staff members; later, we wasted a lot of time fighting for survival during constant restructuring. There was a lack of management support at critical times, and continued resistance at all levels to the radical demands that working on gender issues involves. Working in GADU was often very bitter: there was a sense of battling against the odds, of being out of kilter, of being marginal, of being resisted. While some changes in working practices and attitudes were evident within Oxfam, as well as outside, we always saw the potential to achieve so much more within an organisation that espoused equality, justice for the poor, and a voice for the disadvantaged. We were often bewildered in trying to understand where the blocks were coming from: it was easy, at times, to turn the failures in on ourselves, and ask whether we were too confrontational or radical. Did we demand too much? Perhaps if we had been more conciliatory, more compromising, more bland ... we might have achieved more. We were certainly angry about the injustices and pretences we saw on issues of race as well as gender. Yet the agenda was not feminist, and the changes we hoped for were not revolutionary.[7]

In trying to understand and untangle what was won and what was lost during those early years of the gender unit, I will trace the story through the lens of organisational change. There are some key issues which I think have relevance for a wider audience, for those trying to get gender recognised within their organisations as well as in their development and emergency work.

Organisational change

During the late 1980s, many NGOs in the UK started to undergo major restructuring; many, including Oxfam, brought in external consultants to help them to become more 'professional', more strategic, more competitive. The ideas brought in were largely drawn from business practice, the language was of 'positioning', focus, efficiency, effectiveness, and impact. While continuing to use the language of values and openness, learning and participation, the new organisational structures were hierarchical, power was increasingly vested in management, and performance was to be assessed by tangible results.

Why does this theme seem, in retrospect, so important to the progress of gender within Oxfam? Many efforts by NGOs to become more 'professional' used business methods which contradicted many of the values and goals they espoused, especially those of learning and promoting gender equity. As the ideologies moved away from 'accompaniment' (working with social movements and in solidarity) towards strategic planning, upward accountability,[8] and impact assessment with its short-term perspective, many realities about working with complex and slow social change became distorted or compressed.

With hindsight it is clear to me that the way in which GADU was set up, and its aspirations, rooted in a non-hierarchical, open, networking vision, were in contradiction to the organisational style subsequently adopted by Oxfam. Yet it was a vision that coincided with those of reflective and learning organisations and may have fitted better with the NGO rhetoric of participation, bottom-up approaches, and the 'new professionalism' espoused by Chambers[9] which are a very far cry from the corporate management structure of Oxfam today.

The early vision of the Gender and Development Unit

GADU was set up as a non-hierarchical co-operative, reporting directly to the head of the Overseas Division, and supported by an informal committee. The primary focus was on working with staff and partners across Africa, Asia, and Latin America, because major support for the unit's establishment had come from overseas offices, but there were also matters concerning Oxfam's head office, such as equal opportunities and setting up a workplace nursery.

A co-operative

The Gender and Development Unit was set up as a co-operative. The two programme staff were on equal grades and were to share the decision-making and running of the unit. Recruitment, budgets, and supervision of tasks were shared, and both staff had access to the Head of the Overseas Division.

This structure was important to GADU's founders who wanted the unit to break the mould of hierarchical, top-down working. This was a radical vision, drawn largely from work in Latin America, but over time this structure became increasingly contested. Oxfam underwent a series of restructurings, each of which marked an increasing formalisation of the organisation. A hierarchical structure became entrenched, decision-making teams became smaller and slowly grew more distant from the rest of the staff.

GADU lost the fight to remain a co-operative with a restructuring in 1991. There were probably many reasons for this: first, the external consultants, who had fixed ideas on how the organisation should be shaped, demanded it. While many staff agreed with their analysis of the problems, few accepted the proposed solutions, which were drawn less from Oxfam's own experience and understanding than from business management approaches. GADU was forced to become a hierarchy, a change which contained many of the seeds of its future demise.

Second, making a co-operative work effectively is difficult and demanding. Proper management support is needed to sustain this way of working, which was lacking in our case. The pressure and tensions that the staff experienced within Oxfam were played out within the unit and made working co-operatively problematic. These problems were not acknowledged by either management or personnel — instead, the model of working co-operatively itself was blamed.

Third, these internal disagreements raised wider problems for GADU staff, familiar to anyone working on challenging and 'oppositional' issues within organisations: the need to convince the constituency about the validity of the issue requires staff to present a united front to the organisation. In GADU, internal differences were hidden initially, for the sake of 'the cause'. When they were eventually aired and recognised by management, no training or advice was given. Instead, the unit's structure was blamed and the solution was to bring the unit into line with the new, hierarchical, streamlined management.[10] This pattern of ignoring internal difficulties in GADU, which started in the late 1980s, came to its final fruition in 1996 when the unit was merged with another team.

Direct access to decision-makers

The gender unit was established as an advisory unit. We had no management control or authority over staff in the rest of the division, no operational budget, and had to rely on our ability to persuade people to take the issues on board. This handicap was counterbalanced initially because staff reported directly to the head of the division. This was a crucial link, providing access to a senior decision-maker.

In the early days, unit staff were invited to meetings held by the director and senior managers within the Overseas Division, but during the progressive restructurings, this direct access was lost. Management theory demanded that no manager should manage a wide range of people, so the numbers of staff reporting to the Overseas Director were reduced. GADU was subsequently represented at decision-making meetings through its line manager. Over time, this post was held by different people, some of whom fought for unit positions, some of whom did not. The increasing hierarchy and exclusion from access to the centre of power was detrimental to organisational learning about gender, and meant that GADU's voice was mediated through a third party.

The GADU committee

The original GADU committee was of central importance to the unit. It provided real moral and intellectual support; the meetings were an opportunity to air issues, discuss problems, and explore ways forward. It was made up of staff from across the whole organisation who were interested in and supportive of working from a gender perspective; it included men as well as women, those with experience and those without. It was a regular but informal gathering, a grouping of like-minded people supporting GADU staff, and learning alongside them about how to work with gender issues.

When the focus of the unit narrowed to the work of the Overseas Division, the committee members felt, because of their massive workloads, that this should be reflected in its composition. Slowly, and perhaps inevitably, representation on the committee changed from those who were interested and committed to those who attended as formal representatives of their departments. While it continued to be an essential place for discussion, sharing, and sounding out ideas, and many of those who came were supportive and involved in gender issues in their work, the strength of the group was diminished.

Over time, the GADU committee faded altogether, partly because some members who were mandated to come or who had to be represented because of their position in the organisation were not interested, and partly because it was not part of the organogram in the new hierarchical structure of Oxfam. No one had attendance at GADU meetings listed in their job descriptions, and time was no longer available for a semi-informal grouping of people to share and reflect on gender issues. Not all GADU staff saw the role of the committee as positive as the organisation changed; they wanted to become part of the new, more streamlined structure, unfettered by inputs from a range of people outside the unit who were not gender specialists.

But in both its forms the committee was, from my perspective, invaluable. It provided warm company, a place to talk freely; it was a forum for sharing ideas and getting gender issues 'pushed out' into the wider organisation. In 1990s parlance, it was a good tool for 'mainstreaming' gender, for ensuring that at least one person in every department saw gender as relevant to their work. GADU's demise was sorely felt by many and contributed to the sense that gender was in danger of becoming ghettoised as the sole concern of a specialist team; it certainly diminished the cross-divisional learning and sharing around gender issues.

Focus on the field work

While in the original job description GADU was to cover every aspect of Oxfam's work, it was clear from its origins and its location in the Overseas Division that it was set up primarily to promote gender work in development, through working with staff and partners. That focus certainly dominated the early years of the unit, although much more time than was desirable was spent on internal bureaucratic and management issues in Oxford.

In addition to field visits, and running workshops and gender training around the world, one of the real strengths and innovations during the early years was the creation of the 'GADU Newspack'. The need for staff in different countries to share ideas, to get advice and support from others was so clear right from the start; the in-trays quickly piled up with questions, comments, experiences, and challenges. Staff were grappling with complex problems in widely differing cultural contexts, with few resources or precedents to guide them on how best to address gender relations. Some were learning lessons which were clearly relevant and valuable to others, and so the idea was born of developing a forum where ideas, lessons, and concerns could be shared between staff and partners across the world.

The GADU Newspack was designed as an informal 'publication' through which people could discuss issues of mutual interest. The articles were largely unedited, except for improving clarity, and staff or partners were encouraged to use their own words and idioms for expressing the lessons they wanted to share or the issues they wanted to raise. While working closely in this way with the field staff, the gender unit also ran gender seminars in Oxford, bringing speakers from academia and other NGOs. These talks were also included in the Newspack, sometimes in simplified language to ensure a wide audience, and tape recordings of seminars were sent to field offices.

The Newspack was produced by GADU six times a year and went out to every field office. It was a folder which contained this wide range of articles. The material was non-copyright and could be photocopied, and staff were encouraged to use it in any way they found appropriate and helpful in their work. Over time the volume of material increased and genuine debates started between staff in different offices and countries. The quality of the material included was unique: much of it was first-hand case material, written by people who had never written for publication before. Academics were forced to write in simple terms for this audience and so, slowly, an interesting synthesis of the theory and the practical developed. Out of the early packs came a book, *Changing Perceptions*.[11]

As Oxfam underwent major change as a result of the drive to 'professionalise', it wanted to reinforce and improve its standing as a market leader in the NGO sector. Pressures from within GADU — we felt the need to raise our profile within Oxfam and among other NGOs — as well as external pressures led to the demise of the GADU Newspack; it was replaced by a published journal. While the journal is successful and valid in its own right, the demise of the Newspack saw the end of an exciting experiment which was proving a valuable learning tool for gender issues across many NGOs who had started to request copies of the pack, Oxfam staff, and their partners. It was easily accessible and open to any kinds of contributions, including cartoons, pictures, and jokes, as well as articles and debates. It was unique within the organisation, and allowed a wide variety of opinions to go out unedited; it had a growing readership and a very diverse range of contributors.

Conclusions

My experience of working in GADU was a hard one. Looking back, I see that much of my energy and anger were misdirected, and my expectations unrealistically high. In so many ways, GADU was trying to move in a very different direction at the end of the 1980s from the wider organisation, which was increasingly under the influence of the business ideologies of the Thatcher era, by then permeating much of the NGO sector. While some things changed in a positive way, often mirroring changes taking place outside the organisation, many new barriers were erected in the name of 'professionalisation', 'accountability', and 'efficiency'.

While personal attitudes to gender mellowed, and some women started to find their voice within Oxfam and its development work, and although training gathered pace and some practices changed, many barriers to real change—which would have empowered women within the organisation and the development process — were erected. Although gender was officially integrated into Oxfam's thinking and ways of working through the adoption of an organisation-wide Gender Policy, many of the new procedures, ways of working, and demands of the evolving Oxfam were inimical to addressing issues of gender equity.

Oxfam continued to resist addressing concerns with the personal commitments of its staff: for example, beyond the provision of the nursery, issues of childcare did not enter the organisational culture. Women did not manage to penetrate the highest reaches of management during the restructuring; recruitment criteria still seemed to emphasise unbroken work histories, and the ability to work long hours and to travel freely. Within the new management structures, GADU had always been an advisory unit and remained marginal; as the hierarchy was expanded, it was pushed further away from centres of power and decision-making. It lost its voice within the Senior Management Team of the Overseas Division, after years of direct access to the Overseas Director.

Oxfam's growing concern with its public profile in the North, and with its role in advocacy forums in Europe and the USA, switched some of the attention away from the field workers; combined with the restructuring of the organisation into a more rigid hierarchy, this militated against several approaches which were key to promoting gender issues. GADU initially placed much stress on working primarily at field level, on working in a non-hierarchical way, and on working across the organisation through formal and informal groupings in order to promote learning and sharing between staff and partners actually working in development and emergencies. Restructuring removed many of those avenues. The increasing focus on results, on measurable impact, on visible achievements also hit hard at gender work. Gender relations are complex and embedded within cultures; change is often imperceptible, and may take years to come about. The requirement to document change over short periods undermines the long-term work that is essential for addressing gender inequalities.

Many lessons were learned during those early years about the importance of access to decision-making and the need for proper and consistent management support if gender is to be taken seriously within an organisation; about the necessary but limited role of policy in influencing practice; and about the value of networking. We learned in so many different, often painful, ways that gender is a personal as well as a development issue which is often challenging and threatening to some staff. We realised that working in ways conducive to women's needs and in ways which confront gender inequalities sits uneasily with the move to more hierarchical, business-like structures within the NGO sector. In addition, issues of gender, however packaged, are radical and thus do bring staff into conflict with the wider organisation, and often with the very power structures which promoted an overt commitment to gender in the first place.

The battles are long and hard: it is salutary to remember that during a major restructuring in 1993 Oxfam created five corporate director posts and appointed five men; when the British Government's Department for International Development restructured their top management in 1998, all but one woman were restructured out of the team. We have far to go within development organisations as well as on the ground to redress gender inequalities and ensure that the voices of women are heard. But surely one key role of a non-government agency is to take risks, to be pioneering, to develop structures and processes drawn from its own experience and values, not those of the wider society in which it is placed. It is the memory of the organisation's refusal to take real risks, to stand out against the dominant trends of the time, that still rankles after all these years.

About the author

Tina Wallace obtained her PhD from Makerere University in Kampala, Uganda, and taught in Nigeria. Returning to the UK after many years in Africa, she worked first with the World University Service and later with Oxfam, where she helped set up GADU and the Strategic Planning and Evaluation Unit. She currently teaches at the University of Birmingham and carries out consultancies and research with NGOs. Tina Wallace is co-author of *Changing Perceptions* (1991), Oxford: Oxfam.

Fairytales and feminism: Volunteering in the Gender Team

Alison Farrell

The issues explored in this article arise from my personal experience as a volunteer in Oxfam GB's Gender Team from 1993–94. I worked with the Gender Team on its advocacy agenda from early 1994 onwards and was contracted (and paid) from 1995–96. This period was dominated by the preparations for the UN Fourth World Conference on Women in Beijing, which I attended.

A fairy tale

Once upon a time there was a graduate. She had studied hard and gained her degree, and was cast out onto a dirt track which led to a place called 'career'. There, she took in the sights and sounds at the main market place, where big companies competed for graduates with their huge stands, glossy brochures, and big salaries. Having tried to accommodate the needs of these corporations, she said 'no' to this kind of career.

For her, success was not a pin-stripe suit, a house, and a car by the time she was 25 years old. How would she find the satisfaction she was looking for? How could she feel that she was adding, not taking away? How could she find a way of working which reflected her ethos and political convictions? Ah ha! The voluntary sector beckoned. Three months after graduation she found herself in Oxford, working as a volunteer in Oxfam's Gender Team, where a combination of common purpose and activism, cemented together by a feminist ethos, was the order of the day. Furthermore, the international character of the Gender Team gave a sense of belonging to something greater than the shores of the United Kingdom.

This is too rosy a picture, but it is not aimed at disguising hard work and struggle. The main premise of this article is that there are contradictions in the role of, and attitude to, volunteers in an international development organisation such as Oxfam. In taking my own example as a starting point, and looking at the political and social context within which I volunteered, two sets of closely related contradictions emerge. The first is the 'battle' between altruism and self interest, which centres on the question of why people volunteer, and how this is recognised by the organisations they work with. Volunteering is a political project in any context, involving altruism and a commitment to a common vision; but it also brings into stark relief the complexity of the relationships which develop around this political commitment, and the very pragmatic transactions that take place between volunteers and the organisations they work with.

The second aspect of volunteering I will explore in this article is the way in which feminism and a commitment to gender equality interact with volunteerism, in an era when both volunteerism as a political project, and feminism, are considered dead. Looking at the circumstances which would bring someone to Oxfam to volunteer, it does not seem to make sense that a young, feminist graduate would necessarily attach herself to an organisation like Oxfam. It would seem to make more sense that she find a place in a 'women's organisation', and head for segregation. Volunteering as a feminist in a development agency throws up the additional challenge of engaging with an essentially male-dominated world, making the political project of volunteering a feminist one as well. Volunteering as a feminist contributes not only to the vision of social justice, but also to the struggle for fundamental transformation of gender relations within the development process itself.

Volunteering as a political act

Volunteers come in all different shapes, sizes, and colours. Some work in shops, some work in the streets, some work in depots, and some work in offices. Some have money, some don't; some are men, most are women; some do it for years, some for only a few months; some want to gain experience, some have experience to share. It is very difficult to say what a volunteer looks like. Myself? I look like an educated, lower middle-class, white girl, with no 'overseas experience', yet keen to utilise the knowledge and skills gained at university to benefit more people than just myself. I also have the experience of volunteering for over 12 months.

Sometimes my way into Oxfam makes me look like a martyr, and sometimes it makes me look like a conniving schemer. Perhaps the most honest and easiest way of looking at it is to say that I am a pragmatist. Having demonstrated aptitude and skills as well as showing commitment and dedication, a number of short-term contracts were offered to me and I made the transition from volunteer to paid worker. In this way, volunteering was a way to enter into my chosen career — the commitment shown by volunteering was a necessary step to gain necessary 'credentials'. But the gap between volunteering and being a paid member of staff is smaller than one would imagine.

In many ways it is often most palatable to assume that volunteerism is a purely altruistic act, where reward and recompense are solely located in the act of giving time freely to a cause or organisation. Yet in giving time, skills, and effort, and in adding value to the work of an organisation, the reward is only partly that you are giving it free of charge; it is also the reward of being part of something political — the feeling of adding rather than taking away. The idea of commitment that is inherent in volunteerism brings up the issue that political conviction and social justice make volunteering more than just 'something to do'. In this way, volunteering is a political act.

Volunteers who work with Oxfam and its partner organisations undertake a variety of tasks, from running shops throughout the UK, to producing research in the Policy Department, to supporting community health-care programmes in Peru. All these very different, essential and related activities, are entered into with political motivation. Whether or not each individual volunteer perceives their contribution to Oxfam or other organisations as political is, in some ways, irrelevant — they are all committed to a vision of social justice and human well-being and give their time and skills to contribute to this vision. Volunteering is a political undertaking despite the fact that it does not always look or feel like it.

'Oh, which shop do you work in?'

The opportunities for young graduates whose ambition it is to work in a development agency are extremely limited. Development agencies have changed; the view of what constitutes development has changed. The value of motivated Northern individuals, straight from school or university, who volunteer to work abroad for agencies such as Voluntary Service Overseas (VSO) and Oxfam, has rightly been questioned. However, many young Northern people who want to enter the development sector are in a catch-22 situation — agencies want experience, yet the opportunities to gain that experience have dwindled.

Alternatives to entering the voluntary sector straight from university tend to require further study. Competition for research posts is high, and researchers must display many of the same qualities as volunteers: namely, a commitment to a particular field of work and readiness to face financial insecurity. As a result, volunteering is also a route into a working environment. Although the atmosphere and the expectations of volunteers are different, in some ways the pressure of work is greater in a charity than in a profit-oriented company, both for paid and unpaid staff. The personal and political investment necessary for working in the development field is very high. Oxfam relies on that commitment from both paid and unpaid workers. It trades on the idea that each person's work counts at an individual level and is valued at a much wider level.

Research has been carried out on how Oxfam's partners in the South work with volunteers, and particularly on the role of women in the provision of some essential services. However, very little research has been done from the perspective of volunteers on the role of the women and men who help run the network of shops in the UK, nor on that of numerous volunteers who work as campaigners and researchers (both at head office and throughout the UK). In many ways, volunteers do the 'reproductive' work which ensures that non-government organisations can operate effectively: they provide skills, time, and commitment with no monetary benefit (granted, there are schemes to ensure that the volunteer does not incur an economic cost for this). Yet as stated above, the transaction between volunteer and organisation is far more complicated than a straight-forward exchange of skills and labour in return for being part of a common cause. It can be a consciously chosen route into a highly competitive career.

However, in a context where the dominant culture defines people's value and status chiefly in terms of how much money they earn, the value of unpaid work in the voluntary sector is simply not understood or recognised, in many cases even by the agencies who are so reliant upon this work. Status in Oxfam and in the development sector as a whole still depends upon attaining certain positions within the organisation, with hierarchy based on grade and salary. These hierarchies are discussed elsewhere in this book,[12] but the important point here is that volunteers do not figure in this hierarchy, and that non-altruistic motives are not recognised in the rewards for volunteers, in terms of attaining some formal status. Patronage and informal relationships still account for volunteers' status. The contribution that volunteers make to organisations within the voluntary sector needs to be acknowledged in more systematic and creative ways.

Feminism in selfish times

Over the past few years, there has been an increasing number of news reports and articles about the political inertia that has beset British, and more broadly European, youth. A report produced by Demos (a think-tank based in the UK) in 1995 states that 'evidence seems to suggest that 18 to 34-year olds are apathetic and inward-looking: that those at the lower end of the range have not fully accepted the responsibilities of adulthood while those at the higher end of the range have become more selfish.'[13] Therefore, as a politically motivated, young, white, middle-class woman I am an oddity. I am a member of a generation of twenty-somethings who can barely remember life before Margaret Thatcher,[14] whose formative years were the boom years of the 1980s, and who left tertiary education heavily in debt to enter an extremely competitive job market. As a whole, the members of this — my — generation are supposed to be out for themselves, as though they had their social conscience removed at birth. We are portrayed in the media as a marauding collection of beer monsters with too much disposable income and a sense of priority which has no basis in reality. If British print and television journalists are to be believed, the Conservative Party's election victory in 1979 marked the death of political activism and the birth of apathy in the UK.

Coupled with this negative portrayal of European youth is the wholesale rejection of feminism in the 1990s. The term is rarely openly used to describe a set of political ideals, as is evident in this common remark: 'I am all for women's equality, but I am not a feminist'. Feminism is also no longer referred to as a political project in the mass media, who instead demonise women who still use the term—this again serves to alienate young women. Sometimes choosing *not* to say that you are a feminist, while following what would appear to be feminist principles, offers flexibility; and in many situations resisting association with one particular doctrine has its benefits. However, there is also the danger of losing a clear idea of what the issues are, and failing to respond to changing environments. If women are told often enough that a feminist agenda has achieved all that it can and that, if you are a Northern European woman, you have achieved equality with men, then there is a danger that much of what we have gained will be lost.

As a concept and a way of organising women, feminism almost fell off the agenda altogether with the so-called backlash against feminism. The backlash, which claims that the women's movement has achieved its goal equality of the sexes and that feminist ideology is now redundant, has been documented by Northern journalists throughout the 1980s and 1990s. It can be seen in the demonising of young single mothers in political and media discourse, in the portrayal of the single woman as a threat (in films such as *Basic Instinct* and *Fatal Attraction*), and in accusations that feminism and feminists are the cause of all political and social ills. This alienates many young women from engaging with feminist thinking or with the political project it sets out.[15]

Recent developments in British popular culture show the contradictory portrayal of women's role in British society today. The media have talked about the birth of the 'new lass' — confident young women who know what they want and how to get it (a pop-feminist model of women's equality). A 'new lass' can behave as badly as men and reject traditional femininity, while retaining her attractiveness to men as a central part of her identity. This image fits hand-in-glove with the media's portrayal of selfish youth and at the same time celebrates the death of feminism. The 'new lass' embodies the ideal of a post-feminist generation.

In the late 1990s, women display an ability to break many taboos which constrained previous generations; and we are rightly indebted to those women who fought for women's rights. But feminists of my generation (yes, they do exist) are caught between two stools. We are faced with a popular media representation of what it means to be a young woman today which, although it challenges gender stereotypes to a certain extent, actually centres on display and attitude. It is all show and little content, and fundamentally continues to reproduce a conventional concept of 'woman'. On the other hand, we are faced with older feminists who were there during the golden age of the protest marches. Some older feminists expect young women to treat them with reverence, and there are unspoken rules of engagement, which tell of deference and a need to be quiet. Young women's legitimacy as feminists is questioned, because we weren't there.[16]

Volunteering and feminism

If being a young feminist is difficult, working as a young feminist is even more challenging. For me, this challenge took on another dimension because my work takes place within a 'mainstream' development organisation.

The image and location of the Gender Team within Oxfam highlights some of difficulties of working as a feminist — paid or unpaid — within a mainstream development organisation. The way in which Oxfam has utilised 'gender' and 'feminism' to push forward the development debate and advance the understanding of complex issues of gender relations and gender inequalities for development organisations and government institutions is impressive. However, the challenge of furthering a feminist agenda, and working for social justice in a context where the predominant organisational culture is imbued with male-oriented concepts of development (however radical) is great. The suspicion of the 'otherness' of a gender perspective, among other organisational issues, produces a sense of embattledness which brings a team together in response to external forces, but also increases internal tensions related to having too much invested in a project and too narrow a support base.

There was a great sense of political commitment in the Gender Team. However, my status as a volunteer within the organisation as a whole was restricted because of my personal commitment to feminism. The image of a 'young feminist' is of a woman who is very serious, and politically correct in the extreme. This links in with the media images of the 12-headed monster that is a feminist. An organisation is, in many ways, a reflection of the society in which it operates: I had a sense of informal boundaries within the organisation, and a feeling of being enclosed and barricaded within the Gender Team, missing greater opportunities for transformation and political activity outside, in the wider organisation. The informal barriers between feminist volunteers and the rest of the organisation restrict access to patronage relationships and routes to higher status. The irony is that feminist volunteers find themselves excluded from the organisational hierarchy because of the very political commitment that brought them to Oxfam in the first place.

Conclusion

Volunteering is much more than just 'something to do'. Volunteering, in whatever capacity, in whatever role, is a political act. Even if a volunteer is maximising the opportunity to gain much-needed experience, by providing time to a development organisation 'freely',[17] the exchange of skills and commitment for experience has a political by-product. Volunteers' contributions add value to the work towards social justice.

Politics and feminism have not died. They have adopted different faces and different voices, and are sometimes not immediately visible. However, if we take our time, and resist the assertions of cultural commentators and media pundits, we can see that people are there fighting for social justice, in its broadest sense. They may not necessarily be linked by a common generation, but they are living in the same world and work within similar contexts.

About the author

Alison Farrell graduated with a degree in Geography in July 1993. She joined Oxfam's Gender Team as a full-time volunteer in October 1993. From January 1994 her work focused mainly on the Gender Team's advocacy project, preparing for the UN Fourth World Conference on Women in Beijing. She began her first paid contract with the team in January 1995, working full-time on the Beijing conference, which she attended in September 1995. After leaving the team in March 1996, she has now returned to Oxfam and works as one of the Gender and Learning Team's administrators.

Middle-aged man
seeks gender team

Chris Roche

If you don't want to read about the experience of a white middle-class, middle-aged, married man with two children, working on gender issues, skip this article. If you do, at least now you know where I am coming from! I have worked with colleagues engaging with gender issues for the past ten years, and during that time I have questioned and developed my understanding of and conviction about working on gender relations, and about those who promote gender equity.

Probably the most important events which changed my attitudes to gender were living with a polygamous family in a West African village for one year, and becoming a father. Until recently, I have never really deliberately interpreted and built upon these experiences, but now I am recalling them and analysing what shaped my idea of gender roles and relations. As a parent who would like to spend more time with his children, am I at a point of my life when it is in my interest to challenge traditional notions of what it is to be a man? If we can assume that at least some non-poor people are willing to make sacrifices in order to achieve economic and social justice for the poor (such as changing their life-style or paying higher taxes), why should we not assume that some men are willing to let go their privileged position in favour of gender equity? If I am willing to do so, what challenges lie ahead both for me and for the organisation I work in?

Gender issues and organisations

The relationship between the individual and the organisation is critical. Oxfam GB, like any organisation, is made up of staff with their own identities, interests, and opinions. Various aspects of these will dominate in various settings — gender, but also class, race, age, disability, and other dimensions of difference. However, many would argue that, at least at the apex of power, the dominant identity of most Northern NGOs such as Oxfam is white, middle class, and 'male'. This is not, of course, the only imbalance in organisational identity. White, middle-class, 'female' interests might dominate over, say, black, working-class, 'male' interests.

The first lesson that a man working on gender issues learns is that what he has to say is sometimes discounted. The first brush with such 'identity politics' was particularly upsetting because, in other places, my views have hitherto been listened to as a matter of course - even if it was because I was a man. It takes some time to learn what it is like to be excluded or ignored. It takes even longer before you wonder whether what you had to say before had any inherent value, or whether your gender simply made your views seem more coherent and more readily accepted, especially in an organisation that shares your identity.

Next I learned that trying to discuss with colleagues the importance of incorporating a social analysis into their work quickly induces a sort of 'gender deafness' and 'glazed-eye syndrome'. So whatever prior advantages I had as a man, for some the subject matter of my work seems to have made me less interesting, perhaps less coherent, and almost certainly more tedious. Those glazed eyes are not only male, indicating the complex relationship between personal identity and the organisation, often perceived as male-dominated, or having a male identity.

Men's influence on men should not be underestimated. As we see in public-policy advocacy, 'insider' strategies, i.e. using discrete private lobbying rather than public campaigning, are an important part of changing others' attitudes and behaviour.[18] Men have not yet been trained and used as gender advocates at Oxfam as women have, but this should be part of any transformation strategy. However, men who wish to undertake this role must accept that in the eyes of some, they can never win. If they succeed as gender advocates, this will simply confirm that the institution listens to men rather than women. If they fail, critics will say that they lack true commitment or conviction. Once again, this is a hard, but rewarding, lesson to learn for men who are used to being personally associated with success. It is also a good test of whether you are more concerned with getting good ideas adopted than with personal recognition!

Debate and dialogue

If we do want more men, and women, to act as advocates for gender equality, 'gender experts' must be more prepared to open up debates and to be challenged. Sometimes many men, and some women, in the organisation feel that they cannot really question or debate issues, because it will be seen as a lack of commitment to 'gender'. Staff in Oxfam mentioned this to me on a number of occasions before I joined — it is interesting that they felt more able to confide this to a man, even a man who works on gender. Equating commitment with the extent to which people do or do not understand notions of gender equality can lead to an uncritical, superficial acceptance of the 'right' views, opinions, and rhetoric. This is dangerous because people who do not fully understand ideas of gender equality are not necessarily resistant to them (although this may well also be the case); the ideas simply have not been adequately discussed, understood, and argued over. These people may therefore be surprised when they delve into feminist literature and discover that a lot of the questions they had, but did not dare ask — about men's role in society, about the relationship between gender and class or ethnicity, about whether there is one feminism or many, about whether the world would be a better or more equal place if it were run by women — are the subject of intense debate and argument.

There is a growing sense in the North that the world is more complex, diverse, and uncertain than we are often led to believe, and that well-known theories which explain the truth of the universe are in fact fallacies. As a consequence, any theory which claims a monopoly of knowledge or offers a single explanation for complex problems is increasingly viewed with suspicion or disbelief. Unfortunately, much of the discourse on gender has followed this trend in order, as Ruth Lister[19] puts it, to challenge male 'universalist' views and to uncloak the 'female non-citizen' beneath. But this necessary challenge to a 'false universalism' has now itself been questioned by those who no longer simply want to oppose 'male' universalism with 'female' universalism. These critics reject the single category 'women' and wish to define other dimensions of identity as equally, or more, important in various contexts.

In a development organisation such as Oxfam, a lack of debate and education on matters of gender equity and social diversity can result in people simply using the 'right' language for planning or evaluating programme work, instead of carrying out the necessary analysis of complex social relations and contextual difference. This has been evident in a number of country strategic plans, and the organisation has accepted such superficial usage of its Gender Policy. I fear that putting right the alleged absence of feminist language in Oxfam (suggested by Ines Smyth in this volume) may simply lead to further acceptance of certain words, but not to a greater insight into how women's status can be improved, and how this aim requires different strategies to be implemented in different places. Moreover, debates must also be grounded in a solid evaluation of case studies, so that the various strategies which are adopted to fulfil Oxfam's Gender Policy can be compared properly.

Open and honest debate at the organisational level should encourage men to gain more than a superficial commitment to gender issues. With a greater intellectual conviction of why and how gender equality can and should happen, men will not merely be encouraged to change their attitudes towards women and towards themselves (which we increasingly understand as necessary), but will build on this knowledge in their own lives. We can make allies among men who will then behave in a gender-sensitive way when 'unsupervised' and act as advocates for change among their colleagues, family, and friends.

The importance of communicating new ideas

Considering the above, it is perhaps all the more surprising that less effort goes into ensuring that the arguments for gender equity and the insights offered by feminist debate are clearly presented and debated, than into gender training (and other aspects of building capacity on gender issues). I am particularly surprised because those arguments seem to me so compelling, and the insights of some feminist analysis so exciting. This may sound like the typical reaction of a man who feels uneasy about exploring his own attitudes and behaviour, which forms an important part of gender training and other capacity-building initiatives. Personal exploration must be buttressed and complemented by intellectual argument, which will reinforce the attitudinal and behavioural change. Ines Smyth's article is partly right in asserting that it is important to open up the organisation to feminist ideas, but I feel that there is sometimes a danger of focusing on the language of feminism rather than the ideas and debates it describes.

Clearly there is a relationship between the words of transformation and the ideas of transformation. Failure to achieve change is often blamed not so much on the language, but on people's inability to understand or accept the ideas and concepts represented, particularly in the case of concepts that challenge the status quo of power relations. In this analysis, the failure to put new ideas into practice is blamed on those people who do to understand them, rather than on those people who communicate them inadequately. Part of adequate communication is being open to challenge and discussion. In Oxfam, some new or rediscovered concepts, such as social capital and civil society, have been subject to intense questioning, and the proponents of these ideas welcomed debate. However, there has been a lack of open discussion of gender theory. It seems that sometimes intellectual curiosity and challenge is acceptable for some things, but not for others.

This raises another question about Oxfam's organisational culture and the distribution of power. To what degree does the organisation encourage or discourage debate on gender issues, compared to other issues? To what extent are such debates limited to a small group of the converted, rather than addressing a wider audience? And to what extent does Oxfam encourage any debate on development when so much time is spent discussing internal procedures and processes? The changing organisational culture of development NGOs, which some would argue has been one of growing managerialism, leaves little space for thinking about our 'core business'. This imposes severe constraints on potential allies to enter into necessary debates on development, and gender issues in particular.

Exciting Ideas

So what exciting ideas does feminist thinking and analysis offer a man like me, working in an agency such as Oxfam?

Ideas about institutions and organisations

Naila Kabeer's Social Relations Approach[20] and Anne-Marie Goetz's writing on gender and institutions[21] provide particularly rich material for an agency endeavouring to link micro and macro processes of development, and influence the policies and practices of those institutions which perpetuate poverty and inequality. In addition, their work elucidates how organisations are at the same time the product of the society in which they are situated, as well as actors in reproducing that society. This helps us understand how male interests (or any other set of interests) become institutionalised, and how Oxfam must therefore transform itself if it is to maximise its impact on society. Kabeer's work in particular shows how important the household is, as it is at this level that broad social trends actually affect people's daily lives; more generally, the nature of family or household relations is a critical determinant of how societies function.

These are just two examples of the many authors who have contributed to our understanding of organisations and institutions, and whose work would be useful to a wider, non-specialist audience.

Ideas about the link between economic and social relations

The traditional divide between economics and social studies has been challenged by Nancy Folbre and Diane Elson, among others. Folbre's wonderful caricature of a debate between a Marxist economist, a neo-classical economist, and a feminist economist — which not only gives the reader a good insight into basic economic theories but also challenges some fundamental premises of both the 'left' and the 'right' — should be compulsory reading for all Oxfam programme managers.[22] Diane Elson's suggestions on how to ensure a sound integration of gender into macroeconomic analysis should form part of our strategic planning guidelines.[23]

Both authors challenge the established division between economic production, the domain of most economists, and social reproduction (put simply, how societies care for children and other dependants), which has been ignored by conventional economics. Folbre offers intriguing insights into how both of these are shaped by various interrelated interests, which compete and co-operate at different times. These interests exist and are played out at all levels: from the state to the household, and even at the individual level. I am thus an employee, a consumer, a manager, a father, and a middle-class white man all at the same time; different elements of my identity will predominate in different contexts.

Elson emphasises that there are efficiency as well as equity arguments for promoting women's status and empowerment. (In other words, gender equality is not only desirable for moral reasons, but also because it will enable women to contribute to economic development.) Like Folbre, Elson offers some explanation for why, if it is beneficial to society, gender inequality is still allowed to persist. The first, kinder, interpretation is that men do understand that short-term losses will lead to long-term gains. The second one concludes that it is in the interests of the powerful — usually men — to pay the price of lower efficiency in order to retain control.[24]

Men and masculinity

Not surprisingly, I find the recent interest in men and masculinity especially absorbing. A recent issue of *Gender and Development* (*GAD*) offers challenging ideas and insights which resonate strongly with my own experience. These include the suggestion that there are aspects about the male role which don't actually suit my personal preferences; that women as well as men may have good reasons to preserve the status quo in gender relations; that 'social fatherhood' (in other words, the part played by fathers in their children's social development) is an important role; that male violence, and the links between violence, the socialisation of boys and their livelihood options in particular, need greater study. I also welcome Sarah White's challenge of the caricature of the unhelpful man:

> 'Good girl / bad boy' stereotypes present women as resourceful and caring
> mothers, with men as relatively autonomous individualists, putting their own
> desires for drink and cigarettes before the family's needs. (White 1997, in *GAD*)[25]

Of course it is quite easy to agree with, and push for, changes that are in my interests and suit my preferences: less time at work equals more time at home with the kids; a better social environment means less worry about my and my family's security; improved government expenditure health and education services, paid for by progressive taxation, means lower potential expense for me; a higher number of women in the army, and there is less chance they might have to call up unfit 40-year-olds. There is therefore a comprehensive, important agenda for change which would further the interests of both women and men — and this agenda must be elaborated more thoroughly.

It is of course more difficult to accept the cost of realising those aspects of gender equity which challenge my own status or power, where it is not a 'win-win' situation. These range from the relatively simple — would I, and my two male colleagues, be prepared to use the toilet upstairs so that my 17 female colleagues, who now share one toilet, could convert the 'gents' to a 'ladies'? — to harder, usually more personal, questions about roles and responsibilities at home and at work. I also wonder whether I would be prepared to forego a promotion in order that the position would be won by a (gender-sensitive, or feminist) woman. These situations are less clear-cut, and involve considerable sacrifice of power and privilege.

Putting ideas into practice

Feminist authors provide ideas and perspectives that go to the heart of how societies and organisations function. Their work uncovers how seismic changes in societies, including industrialised societies, can occur without a single macroeconomic indicator picking up on them; how we raise and care for children; how and where men and women's gender interests may complement or compete with each other; and they analyse the complex interaction of economics, politics, and social institutions. However, these ideas and concepts are often cloaked in a form impenetrable to busy field workers and managers. They need translation into simpler language, but they also need to be transposed to people's own lives and experiences. As Becky Buell (quoted in Ines Smyth's contribution) suggests, the challenge is to use these concepts and insights in a way that is relevant to the specific context. The authors who have inspired me cannot answer, on my behalf or that of other men, the more difficult question on how we deal with our own power and privilege; but they can certainly provide food for thought.

Another challenge for development workers is to think more about how the lessons we learn from the women whom we encounter and work with around the world, whose daily struggles we witness, can be better synthesised and shared, and how they might bring about change. Thus we must bring together and link the insights gained from practice as well as from theory.

There is much to be done in interpreting gender concepts both 'up' (i.e. from practitioners) and 'down' (i.e. from theoreticians). Those working on gender issues in Oxfam must communicate in both directions if they are to add value in the process of sharing and generating knowledge. This is a difficult balancing act.

In addition, they must also balance the inflow of others' ideas into the organisation with Oxfam's sharing of its own experiences. It is all too easy either to be sucked into interminable internal processes or to abandon all hope of achieving organisational change and thus to only communicate externally. In our work on gender equality, where the relationship between an organisation and its environment is so critical (as Goetz and others have shown), operating both on the inside and the outside, in a complementary way, is critical.

Can NGOs achieve gender equity?

In summary, being a man working on issues of gender equity demands a thick skin; the courage to challenge and debate issues until you understand them; to study feminism and engage with feminist debates; and to be prepared to debate and argue with colleagues and friends. It also means working out how your personal interests are translated into organisational interests, and how your personal behaviour interacts with organisational culture. If we accept that most Northern NGOs are white, middle-class, and 'male' in identity, can we really expect these organisations to check their dominant interests in support of those who might undermine them? For an individual such as myself, whose personal identity seems well aligned with the dominant interests, I believe that this is difficult, but not impossible; for an organisation, it must be much harder. Perhaps the first step is to recognise that the organisation's normal practice, its 'default option', is always liable to favour dominant interests, and that the price of transformation is eternal vigilance.

About the author

Chris Roche is currently Team Leader of the Gender and Learning Team in Oxfam's Policy Department. Before joining Oxfam in 1994, he worked for the international NGO consortium ACORD for ten years, on the West Africa programme and setting up their Research and Policy Programme. Previously, Chris conducted research into the role of NGOs in Burkina Faso and was involved in the production of an *Atlas of Social Protest in the UK*.

Notes to section III

1 From Gabriel García Marquez (1996), *Chronicle of a Death Foretold*, Penguin.

2 Throughout this article I refer to Oxfam's Gender Unit by its original name, the Gender and Development Unit (GADU). Latterly, when 'teams' became popular in the new corporate deal, it was renamed the Gender Team.

3 'The process of understanding the gendered nature of organisations engages researchers in an "archaeological" investigation: it involves disinterring and reinterpreting histories, and scrutinising artifacts such as favoured concepts, terms of inclusion or exclusion, symbols of success or failure.' Anne-Marie Goetz (1997), *Getting Institutions Rights for Women in Development*, London: Zed Books.

4 Gita Sen and Caren Grown (1998), *Development, Crisis and Alternative Visions: Third World Women's Perspectives*, London: EarthScan.

5 Rounaq Jahan (1995), *The Elusive Agenda: Mainstreaming Women in Development*, London: Zed Books.

6 These are issues faced by many women in organisations around the world, where organisational demands fail to recognise let alone accommodate the needs of parents, but especially women in most cultures, to provide care for their children.

7 Other agencies were taking on gender issues at the same time and their experiences mirrored some of those in GADU. There is certainly a story to tell and research to be done comparing the different approaches. Did agencies that took a more conciliatory approach and saw gender as a technical issue and a way of improving project performance, rather than an issue of women's rise and gender equity, achieve more than GADU? What was lost by 'hiding' gender under broader issues of social development and what was lost by trying to get an organisation to accept that working from a gender perspective was more than making projects 'women friendly'?

8 The stakeholder rhetoric suggests that NGOs become accountable to people at all levels, but in practice lines of accountability have been drawn tighter and tighter to Trustees, donors and senior management, not to the people at community level.

9   Robert Chambers calls for a 'new professionalism' which involves humility, recognising the limits of outside experts, which listens and learns from people on the ground. This is the antithesis of hierarchical corporate management structures which are based on a 'professionalism' drawn not from NGO experiences but from the business sector.

10 It is my perception as an outsider that it was this same problem of being unwilling to resolve difficult issues within the unit that led to the managers closing GADU finally. This is of course highly contested within Oxfam.

11 Reference to Wallace, T. and March, C. (eds.) (1991), *Changing Perceptions*, Oxford: Oxfam.

12 See Wendy Carson's article in this volume.

13 Demos (1995), 'Freedom's Children', quoted in *The Guardian*, 'The Victory of Me over We', 28 February 1998.

14 British Prime Minister from 1979–90.

15 See among others, Faludi, S. (1992), *Backlash: The Undeclared War Against Women*, London: Vintage.

16 Wurtzel, E., 'Get A Life, Girls', in *The Guardian*, 10 August 1998.

17 That is to say with minimum economic cost to an organisation.

18 Iain Gray (1998), 'Trends in Advocacy', paper prepared for the Oxfam fundamental review.

19 Ruth Lister (1997), *Citizenship: feminist perspectives*, London: Macmillan.

20 Naila Kabeer (1994), *Reversed Realities*, London: Verso.

21 Anne-Marie Goetz, 'Institutionalising women's interests and gender-sensitive accountability', *Development Bulletin*, Vol. 26, No. 3.

22 Nancy Folbre (1994), *Who Pays for the Kids? Gender and the Structures of Constraints*, London: Routledge.

23 Diane Elson (1995), *Male Bias in the Development Process*, Manchester University Press.

24 Diane Elson (1997), *Gender-aware country economic reports: Concepts and sources*, Working Paper No. 1, Manchester University Press.

25 *Gender and Development*, Vol. 5, No.2, 1997.

IV

Working at different levels

Introduction to section IV

Multiple strategies, employed at various levels, are essential for the effective integration of a gender perspective into development work. There are many different levels at which gender issues are being addressed in Oxfam's work — from advocacy at the international level of the UN and the World Bank, to networking within and between regions, and national-level programme strategies. In addition to discussing these various kinds of work, articles in this section also explore what opportunities there are for links to be made between the different levels, and the importance of such linking, which enables like-minded organisations and individuals to achieve common goals by working together.

Kanchan Sinha's article focuses on Action for Gender Relations Asia (AGRA), an Oxfam GB staff network with branches in South and East Asia, which aims to share information, build capacity, and boost the morale of staff in relation to gender in development issues. Kanchan Sinha gives particular attention to suggestions of staff, revealed in a survey of AGRA's activities and impact, that the move to make gender issues the responsibility of managers may have undermined the momentum and enthusiasm for gender-sensitive work at the grassroots level, and the sense that gender-fair work is everyone's responsibility.

Between 1992–94, a major process of networking and dialogue between Oxfam GB's staff and partners, and representatives from the women's movement across the world, was in progress. The Women's Linking Project can be seen as a milestone along the road of putting Oxfam's Gender Policy into practice. However, it was much more than this: it was a brave attempt to abdicate power from Oxfam as an international funding NGO, in favour of an equal dialogue with women activists from the South. Co-ordinated by Oxfam's specialist gender unit, the Women's Linking Project was an ambitious, and risky, voyage into new ways of working. In her article, Candida March assesses some of the many challenges this innovative project presented for participants from South and North, and for Oxfam GB itself, and suggests possibilities presented by women linking together in pursuit of gender equality.

Like Candida March, Lina Abu-Habib and Omar Traboulsi in their article reflect on the importance of linking with and learning from feminist organisations from the South, in order to develop a regional programme which has a commitment to gender equality at its heart. Their story recounts how Oxfam GB's programme in the Middle East has been transformed as a result of a central commitment to developing regionally-coherent programmes, and a regional commitment to understanding the common issues facing women in the Maghreb area. The account brings out the importance of relationships between country or regional offices and Oxfam's head office.

In her article, Lucy Muyoyeta, who worked for Oxfam GB in Zambia, discusses the personal and professional gains and costs of attending large international fora and advocating for change, based on her experience of the Fourth World Conference on Women, held in Beijing in September 1995. She describes how she related her own work with Oxfam in Zambia, as well as her personal identity as a member of the Zambian women's movement, to various international debates, including the accountability of international financial institutions (IFIs). It was at the Beijing conference that the successful campaign 'Women's Eyes on the World Bank' was born, which involves women living in development countries in monitoring the activities of IFIs, and demanding transparency and accountability. Lydia Williams of Oxfam America discusses her organisation's involvement in this advocacy campaign. Women's Eyes has played a considerable role in ensuring that the World Bank turns rhetoric into reality regarding the adoption of a gender perspective into its activities. Oxfam America's involvement has also, in Lydia Williams' estimation, helped the organisation develop wider advocacy strategies on gender issues.

The Oxfam International network, developed during the 1990s, joins Oxfam GB with ten other like-minded organisations in an effort to increase their impact on poverty-alleviation and the promotion of justice. This strategy of working together as Oxfam International is referred to as 'harmonisation'. In their article, Ellen Sprenger of Novib (Netherlands) and Diane Biray Gregorio of Oxfam America examine the role of the inter-organisational Gender Working Group, which has set about integrating gender issues into the harmonisation process. In a separate article, Penny Plowman, an independent consultant formerly of Oxfam GB, and Josette Cole, who manages an Oxfam International fund for gender-related work in South Africa, describe some of the complex issues that have been encountered as harmonisation is implemented on the ground. It is part of the dizzying array of organisational changes taking place in different member organisations of Oxfam International, against the swiftly-changing political context of South Africa.

Regional cohesion and gender in the Middle East programme

Lina Abu-Habib and Omar Traboulsi

Introduction

Oxfam GB has been working in the Middle East since the mid-1950s. It funded numerous projects and programmes—in Egypt, Yemen, Palestine, Lebanon, and the Western Sahara — but until very recently there were no obvious thematic links between the activities funded in these countries. Recognising this lack of cohesion, Oxfam began to develop a strategic programme for the whole region in the early 1990s. Drawing on our experience of working for Oxfam in the Middle East, this article shows how Oxfam's process of regionalisation[1] has led to the creation of an innovative programme for the Middle East / Maghreb region, which has a primary focus on gender relations. We will look at some of the key moments in this process, and explore some of the opportunities and challenges for integrating a gender perspective into Oxfam's work in the region.

Both authors joined Oxfam GB in the late 1980s. At the time, setting up projects and programmes in the Middle East which specifically addressed gender inequalities depended very much on the interest and commitment of individual staff. This was in spite of the fact that Oxfam had been focusing explicitly on gender issues since 1985, when the Gender and Development Unit (GADU) was formed at head office in Oxford. Project documentation was mostly carried out in an *ad hoc* fashion, and did not require staff to tackle issues of gender relations. Managers who developed 'gender-blind' programmes were not penalised, and attempts to do otherwise were not rewarded. Oxfam was supporting many projects 'for women', so perhaps the case for shifting the focus of our work and investigating imbalances in gender relations was not seen as justifiable.

GADU did not immediately succeed in establishing effective links or systematic working relations with the Middle East desk in Oxford and the field offices. As a result, we felt on the margin of debates on gender issues within head office. This marginalisation may have been exacerbated by perceptions within Oxfam head office of the Middle East as an isolated, Muslim region which presented particular challenges to work on changing gender relations. Such perceptions typically result in rifts and lack of communication.

The lack of expertise, skills, and analytical capacity in the region was another factor which constrained the incorporation of gender concerns into the Middle East programme. In addition, and perhaps more importantly, the region presented itself as being preoccupied with more 'important' debates. At the time, these were related to conflict and to the nature and depth of relations with our local partner organisations. Moreover, resistance to work on gender issues was strong, both at management level on the Middle East desk at head office, as well as in country offices in the region. These are examples of typical views we encountered: 'Gender is a concept from the West'; 'It is not up to a foreign agency to get involved in issues relating to the local culture'; 'Women over here enjoy a lot of advantages'.

Setting priorities and creating a regional programme

In the early 1990s, two innovations prompted Oxfam's staff in the Middle East to initiate a systematic assessment and analysis of its programme in the region, rather than in individual countries. One was the introduction of 'strategic planning' to Oxfam; the other was the process of 'regionalisation' in its international programme. This aimed to bring about a region-wide understanding of poverty and marginalisation and the development of a coherent programme to address these. While regionalisation made it possible for us to take a broader view, to analyse the links between poverty, gender, and development in the Middle East, strategic planning offered an opportunity to use systematic (albeit embryonic) gender-analysis tools to do this.

Our second strategic-planning exercise, carried out in 1995, resulted in a more coherent analysis of the regional situation and our programme, as well as a realistic view of Oxfam's role and impact. Regional staff met three times in one year in order to draft our first strategic plan, with an important outcome: our attention centred on gender power relations, which cross-cut poverty and inequality throughout the region. Specifically, Oxfam's analysis of poverty in the

Middle East identified legal and other institutional forms of discrimination against women as some of the root causes of poverty and inequality. Oxfam also recognised the growing incidence and the various forms of violence against women as a powerful means of excluding and subordinating women.

During strategic planning, Oxfam's Gender Policy served as a general guiding framework. Finally, we identified 'addressing the imbalance in gender relations with particular stress on gender violence' as a main strategic aim for the region. However, in order to develop the programme in accordance with our strategic aim, we had to prioritise our main areas of intervention. We drew on the expertise of external and internal advisers, notably from the Gender Team in Oxford,[2] to further the analysis and assist in programme planning.

A number of events and initiatives facilitated this process. Regionalisation heralded new ways of thinking and working, within and beyond the organisation. Oxfam's Middle East programme became more integrated and communicated more effectively within the organisation. As a coherent entity, we were able to engage in debates and processes on gender issues taking place at Oxfam House, and in implementing the Gender Policy in the region. These improvements were also the result of staff changes, at management level, on the Middle East desk, of the region's participation and input into the Gender Implementation Workshop organised by the Gender Team in 1996, and of the secondment of Lina Abu-Habib, a member of the Lebanon programme, to the Gender Team. Not only did this develop her expertise on gender issues, but it also allowed the Middle East programme to engage actively in debates within Oxfam House.

Oxfam's relationships with partner organisations in the Middle East and Maghreb also changed quite considerably with regionalisation. Western aid agencies have often assumed that they should respect the so-called 'local culture'. In practice, this has meant that everything connected with local culture (and consequently with Islam, as the region is predominantly Muslim), was considered a 'no go' area. The development of regional programme priorities meant that relationships with partners were re-examined and the question raised of whether Oxfam should intervene in 'local culture'. The answer was yes: Oxfam expanded its work relationships considerably, and actively sought the views of women's groups and organisations, individual feminists and human rights activists, various NGOs, research and training institutes, and regional networks. Although this development did not include a withdrawal from many of our very close partnerships with grassroots groups and NGOs, many perceived it as a radical, not necessarily positive, change in Oxfam's ways of working.

In fact, relationships with local partner organisations in Lebanon had already been changing before regionalisation. From late 1994, the Middle East Desk took a leading role in introducing, supporting, and at times pushing for this reexamination and expansion of relationships, both in the field and at Oxfam House. One essential factor facilitating this change was the close working relationship with the Gender Team at Oxfam head office.[3]

A regional analysis of poverty, gender, and development

With regionalisation, Oxfam in the Middle East began to look at poverty and development in a different way. During the strategic planning process, external political, social, and economic trends were subjected to a gender analysis which used methods of institutional analysis, including the Social Relations Approach.[4] This analysis identified imbalances in gender relations as one of the main challenges for development processes and programmes. It also pointed to the fact that Oxfam's interventions in various parts of the region only claimed to respond to women's needs, but had no transformative agenda whatsoever.

In other words, if our projects aim to improve women's status at the community level only, with no intervention at other levels (such as the state), their overall impact will be negligible. For instance, if we teach women to sew, without intervening in the markets through which their products must be sold, then they will still suffer discrimination in the market and there will be no change in their status. Institutional analysis enabled us to make the links between discrimination at different levels. We examined the structural basis of problems such as domestic violence — as a result, we decided to focus our interventions on the 'Family Laws', laws which maintain the artificial distinction between public and private spheres.

In addition, a gender-aware local consultant was commissioned to write a general paper on poverty, gender, and development issues, which provided the regional team with a good baseline analysis.[5] Subsequent training workshops allowed the Middle East team to gain a fuller grasp of the Social Relations Approach, which can be used to assist an understanding of gender relations, and which has been used at all levels of analysis in the Middle East programme.

However, many have found this gender-sensitive analysis of poverty and development difficult to understand and absorb. Some felt that it was too threatening and judgmental, because it pointed to major gaps in Oxfam's past work, and to past interventions of doubtful quality. Our changing to this mode of analysis was difficult to accept, as it required questioning assumptions and prejudices. Some development practitioners found it hard to admit that the endless series of sewing courses for women which have been strongly argued for in the past were futile, in the sense that they had little, if any, impact on women's social and economic status.

Overcoming resistance

Some, both within and beyond Oxfam, have argued that the regionalisation process has negatively affected the Middle East/Maghreb programme. Within the organisation, there were a few raised eyebrows related to our work on gender inequalities. Here are two of the many comments made by staff at Oxfam House: 'Is Oxfam in the Middle East / Maghreb turning into a *feminist* organisation?' and 'I am not sure that advocacy on women and family laws is an appropriate response to issues of livelihood and poverty...'

The clear focus on gender has been developed with support from and through close links with feminist women's groups and networks in the region. Criticisms of such groups as Westernised, bourgeois, and removed from the grassroots were common in many countries that Oxfam works in, mainly arising from an inadequate understanding of poverty, gender and development, and the factors underlying male resistance to gender equality. In our opinion, this resistance can only be overcome by pointing out that in its official Gender Policy, Oxfam has a mandate to promote women's interests. The implementation of an organisational policy is not negotiable. Our solid regional analysis, which so clearly pointed to gender inequalities as a cross-cutting issue of concern, also helped to overcome resistance. It became obvious that any development programme which lacks a gender perspective can only produce an inadequate response to poverty.

How we got there: developing a focus on gender

Establishing links with regional feminist networks
Many have long scoffed at the idea of Oxfam establishing links with women's movements and groups in the Middle East / Maghreb region. The reasons put forward to justify this resistance were many. As mentioned above, activist women were generally perceived to be middle-class, educated, and often 'Westernised'. They were therefore seen to have few links with 'poor' women at the 'grassroots' level. The women's movements in the region were believed — in many cases rightly so — to be too fragmented and/ or politicised, and thus too risky to work with. (Oddly enough, such arguments did not hold in many other cases when Oxfam supported and funded NGOs whose leadership was by and large middle-class, 'Westernised', and/ or closely linked to political parties).

The role of feminist women activists and women's groups on the wider social and political scene was little appreciated, even misunderstood. In fact, there was a clear reluctance to engage in dialogue or collaborate with feminist groups, because some women's organisations perceived Oxfam's agenda as diametrically opposed to their own. However, this perception was slowly overcome by closer contacts, discussions, and exchanges with the representatives of various groups within the women's movement. While maintaining the individual identities of both Oxfam and the groups, it became clear that our concerns overlapped significantly.

The UN Fourth World Conference on Women in Beijing: An opportunity for reflection and action

The Fourth World Conference on Women, held in Beijing in September 1995, was a major landmark in building a gender-focused programme across the region. Unlike earlier world conferences on women such as Nairobi in 1985, the Beijing conference brought together a high number of NGOs and women's groups from the Middle East / Maghreb region, many of which had not formally existed ten years previously. Beijing was a catalyst for many activities within and across countries in this region, and helped create many alliances and networks. By choosing to engage in, support, and influence the preparations for Beijing, Oxfam's Middle East team took a strategic decision to engage in a region-wide process which had important long-term implications. In the case of Lebanon, for example, gender began to be effectively 'mainstreamed' within the programme.

A major initiative in this process was the identification, and subsequent support of, the Collectif Maghreb Egalité 95, a Maghrebian working group composed of 15 feminist activists and groups from Algeria, Morocco, and Tunisia. This group formed three years before the Beijing conference in order to undertake 'shadow preparations' (in parallel with the UN's work), particularly with regard to violations of women's rights in the three countries, including violence against women. The Collectif presented a shadow regional report to the United Nations, and drafted and proposed an alternative and egalitarian regional family code. Oxfam saw in this group a strategic partner for collaboration on gender work as well as an interesting forum for learning and exchange with other countries of the Middle East. The relationship with the Collectif Maghreb has developed to form an important axis of the current regional programme.

Violence against women: an increasingly prominent phenomenon

In June 1995, in the course of region-wide preparations for the Fourth World Conference on Women, a network of more than 20 NGOs (from Algeria, Tunisia, Morocco, Egypt, Jordan, Morocco, Syria, Mauritania, Iraq, and Palestine) convened the first Arab Women's Tribunal on Violence Against Women. Victims of violence testified for the first time on their personal experiences of domestic violence, incest, child abuse, forced feeding, female genital mutilation, crimes of honour, and so on. This was indeed the first public condemnation of all forms of violence against women which prevail in the region. The tribunal also clearly demonstrated that violence against women is a huge obstacle to development.

The public acknowledgement of this fact meant that a state of denial had to be challenged. For example, people in the region had to be made aware of the fact that, contrary to popular belief, female genital mutilation is a significant issue here; and the barrier between the 'private' and the 'public' sphere had to be broken down so that domestic violence is no longer seen as a personal, family issue. There is ample research documenting the extent of gender violence and its different manifestations. Such evidence supported our arguments that the regional programme should address the issue of violence against women, which then became a stand-alone regional objective. Oxfam has also taken an active role in supporting and encouraging innovative initiatives, both regional and country-based, which address various aspects of gender violence.

A new regional initiative

Oxfam's relationships with partners have changed considerably with the creation of a coherent, gender-focused regional programme. As a result of our developing relationships with women's groups and networks, we have emphasised regional exchanges and learning, and boosted our advocacy work through regional links.

In late 1997, following a regional gender-training workshop on gender analysis and planning organised by Oxfam, the workshop participants[6] met to discuss their needs regarding gender training and capacity-building. In order to break the isolation of women groups and networks, the project on 'regional linking, learning, and capacity-building on gender' was launched. Its member groups engage in regional and international debates and processes, disseminate and exchange information on gender work, thus maximising the impact of their advocacy work on gender issues. The network provides an open forum for ideas and points of view, and allows member groups to develop new resources on gender issues in the region. Although Oxfam functioned as the focal point and catalyst, the network is a collective creation, owned by its all members.

Conclusion

Oxfam GB is increasingly gaining a strong reputation in the Middle East/Maghreb region as an organisation seriously concerned with addressing unequal gender relations. This has come about gradually. Key factors in the success include Oxfam's close interaction with feminists, women's groups and NGOs, and the high quality of Oxfam's publications on gender issues, which add much to Oxfam's reputation and to the trust it enjoys of groups which it works with.

The Middle East team, like every other regional programme, have a responsibility to implement Oxfam's Gender Policy. Developing a regional programme with a focus on addressing gender inequalities is indeed possible and feasible. However, it is a process which involves the input and support of all the people who are part of Oxfam, and requires a clear, stated will on the part of the organisation's decision-makers. Such a commitment entails the provision of appropriate resources and the creation of mechanisms which will ensure that both Oxfam and its partners can regularly review and evaluate progress, and consider the way forward.

Although each region must develop its own specific plans for implementing the Gender Policy, its essence and its stated aims must be universally applied. Judging from our experience, the idea of 'adapting' the Gender Policy to fit the need of one particular cultural context merely serves to dilute it. Indeed, adapting a policy to fit one particular region can be used as a tactic for rendering the policy itself meaningless. To draw a parallel, 'adapting' Oxfam's Gender Policy to the Middle East region is like ratifying CEDAW[7] with reservations.[8]

Oxfam's Middle East/Maghreb programme is still in its early stages. Its focus on gender is developing fast; so is the expertise and experience gained. With continued monitoring of this programme's progress and committed fostering and support, it will sustain its distinctive nature and innovative work.

About the authors

Lina Abu-Habib is Lebanese. She has worked for Oxfam since 1989, with a focus on disability concerns. In 1995/96 she moved to Oxford to work with the Gender Team. Back in Beirut, she became Oxfam's Programme Co-ordinator in Lebanon as well as gender trainer and gender 'lead person' for Oxfam in the Middle East. Lina graduated in Public Health from the American University of Beirut and worked as a lecturer at this and other local universities. She is currently a freelance consultant, and is author of Oxfam's *Gender and Disability: Women's Experiences in the Middle East.*

Omar Traboulsi is Syrian and resides in Lebanon. An economics graduate from the American University of Beirut and the Université Saint Denis in Paris, he has worked with Oxfam since 1986: first as South Lebanon Programme Officer, then as Deputy Country Representative, and, since 1988, as Country Representative for Lebanon. In 1994 he moved to Oxford as Middle East Regional Manager. He returned to Beirut in 1996 as the Middle East/Maghreb Regional Representative. Before joining Oxfam, Omar was a journalist, writing for various economic and political newsletters in Lebanon.

The experience of Beijing from a Zambian perspective

Lucy Muyoyeta

Introduction

The Fourth World Conference on Women was held in Beijing, China, in September 1995. Alongside the inter-government conference, a separate venue was devoted to the NGO Forum, where 30,000 women and men from all over the world came together to 'Look at the World Through Women's Eyes'. This article is written in a very personal style, in order to emphasise not only my own commitment to women's struggles, but also to give expression to an experience that has affected both my personal and professional life.

My journey to the NGO Forum is rooted in the 1985 Third World Conference on Women in Nairobi. I did not attend this conference, but the preparations for Nairobi and my participation in the preliminary workshops sharpened my sense of gender oppression and injustices against women. This forms the background to my own commitment to women's struggles, and also to my work on gender issues within Oxfam GB. Ten years on, the learning I drew from the experience of participating in the Beijing conference has been born out of and contributed to all aspects of my identity as a Zambian woman committed to gender equity.

The 'Beijing process' in Zambia

Zambian women's preparations for Beijing were characterised by the consciousness that the activities leading up to the conference were as important as actually participating in it. We recognised that the Beijing conference was not the end of our efforts, but part of a momentum to promote structural change within Zambia, in which all Zambian women had a role to play and which must be continued after Beijing. Many different activities were organised which Oxfam participated in. A march through Lusaka was organised in August 1995 to publicise the Beijing conference within Zambia. The Oxfam office in Zambia marched in solidarity with the Zambian women's movement under our banner 'Together for Rights, Together Against Poverty'.

Oxfam's Zambia programme also supported the Zambian government in its preparations for the conference. The government committed itself to developing a platform of action to be incorporated into the regional and international platforms of action in Dakar and Beijing. To co-ordinate this, a National Preparatory Committee (NPC) was formed in January 1993. Oxfam was the only international agency invited to sit on the committee, in appreciation of the role we have played consistently in supporting the cause of women in Zambia.

This commitment to the cause of women is at the centre of our work on basic rights and poverty, and this was emphasised through our participation in various events leading up to Beijing. I represented Oxfam's Zambia team and our work on structural adjustment at a national-level workshop which was part of this process. Oxfam's work on structural adjustment has provided a focus for our advocacy objectives in Zambia. For me, a vital part of our commitment to working with a gender perspective is ensuring that our advocacy work promotes an understanding of the different effects of structural adjustment on women and men.

This area of macroeconomic change and the effects of structural adjustment on women therefore gave focus to my participation in the NGO Forum in China as a representative of Oxfam in Zambia. But I was also participating as a Zambian woman and an African feminist with a personal interest in supporting the struggle of women in Zambia for economic justice and equality.

Participating in Beijing: linking my agendas

I arrived in China on 25 August 1995. Arriving a few days early allowed me to become acquainted with the geography of the site for the NGO Forum, where I would spend most of my time. It was a huge area, and most delegates suffered the difficulties of finding their way around the site.

Arriving early also allowed me to 'touch base' with the Gender Team and other colleagues from Oxfam offices around the world. My participation in Beijing as the representative of the Zambia field office was at the Gender Team's request, who co-ordinated our participation in keeping with Oxfam GB's overall advocacy objectives. Mention must be made of the Gender Team's effort to trace the Oxfam participants and get some cohesion in the group. They must be commended for this, as communications were extremely difficult. But we struggled on and managed every other day to meet as the Oxfam group.

I was asked to make a presentation on the Zambian Oxfam team's advocacy work on Structural Adjustment Programmes (SAPs). This was an opportunity to develop our work on gender issues and SAPs, providing a wider scope for our advocacy work at the international level. But apart from this specific professional input, I was personally interested in following the theme of economic alternatives and supporting the Zambian delegation as much as I could.

On a personal level, I was happy to be at the NGO Forum to celebrate women's achievements. Women's achievements need to be celebrated, because in spite of the odds against us, still we achieve. Undoubtedly, the NGO Forum provided an opportunity to do so. From the splendour of the opening ceremony (which celebrated women's achievement in China and the world) to the many other art, music, and dance events that took place, to the colourful national costumes that were worn, there was no shortage of opportunities for celebration. Indeed we celebrated. Yet there is the sobering fact that the gains made by women and, indeed, by humanity have faced serious reversals in the last decade, as we grapple with all manner of forces acting against us, including economic crisis, growing poverty, militarisation, violence, and economic globalisation.

Beijing was also an opportunity for learning. There were perhaps too many opportunities, as it was difficult at certain times to make choices about which activity to participate in and which to forego. As can be imagined, activities of one's interest would sometimes be running at the same time in different venues.

Linking and learning — the personal and the professional

In my choice of workshops I made a decision to participate as much as possible in those organised by organisations and networks that I had previously not had much contact with. I wanted to gain new perspectives and ideas, both personally and professionally, on the issue of economic alternatives, but also expand my knowledge of organisations and networks working on similar issues.

Economic alternatives
A common thread running through the theme of economic alternatives is that the search for alternatives means a critical re-assessment and reshaping of economic theory and policy from a gender perspective (WIDE, August 1995). This is based on the idea that economics should serve people, rather than people serving economics. We need a new criterion for measuring success, which would

include the equitable distribution of resources within and across countries, between men and women, and between social classes. It would also reflect women's unpaid caring work in economic statistics such as GNP.

The search for alternatives is developing, although no single model has yet been produced (and perhaps the era of one economic model that everyone follows is/should be past). The main idea is that we must rethink our definition of what is economic (and therefore gets valued and paid for) and what is social (under-valued or not valued at all). Perhaps this is best articulated by the Wages for Housework campaign.[9] This idea of a completely alternative view of economics, with women at the centre of our understanding, could have exciting implications for organisations working in Zambia, such as Oxfam.

It is certainly important for women such as myself who challenge dominant and restrictive economic thinking in our own countries. In Zambia, women suffer disproportionately from the dominant understanding of economics, because of its conventional distinction between unpaid and paid work. However, we have begun to challenge this, for example by supporting widows' rights to inheritance. Whether their work is waged or unwaged, women make a contribution to the social reproduction of their families, which must be valued by ensuring that they have the right to inherit in case of the husband's death.

In thinking about Oxfam's work at the community level, questions regarding the exploitation of women's unpaid labour must be raised. The work that Oxfam supports promotes community participation. Community work is mostly done by women and is unpaid. Perhaps the clearest example is that of AIDS home care, where Zambia is recognised for its pioneering work. In particular, Chinkankata Mission Hospital in Zambia's Southern Province is widely acclaimed for its programme of home-based care for people suffering from AIDS. But while the programme is indeed very good for AIDS patients, it places those who care for the patients at home (mainly women) under huge additional strain.

Reflecting women's unpaid work in statistics is an important first step, but statistics on their own do not feed people nor save them from being over-worked. Within the context of Zambia, this question arises for me: how do we put new economic thinking into practice? The issue is somewhat different for richer countries because, given the political will, their states have the resources to do it. In our case, reflecting and valuing unpaid work is certainly a valid principle to aim for, but we must acknowledge that it will be a long struggle before this is accepted in our country. The struggle for us is hard enough, even for those widely accepted social-spending priorities like education and health.

I also believe that alternative economic models cannot emerge without serious thought about the level of consumption. Excessive materialism is exhibited not only in the rich Northern countries, but also among the elite of countries such as my own. The women's movement have not made sufficient linkages between their oppression, which is rooted in an unbalanced economic system, and our levels of consumption. For me, one of the least attractive aspects of the Beijing conference was the excessive materialism exhibited by many of the delegates. On the way back, when I saw the huge amount of shopping that women carried out of Beijing, I was reminded of Mahatma Gandhi's famous saying, which I paraphrase: 'It took the exploitation of half the world for a small island like England to develop, how many worlds would it take a country the size of India'.

Inter-generational dialogue

I heard a panel of older and younger women discuss inter-generational dialogue — another issue of great interest to me personally and to the Zambian women's movement — at the Beijing conference. The key question for me is how to strike a balance between celebrating older women's pioneering role and creating the space to allow younger women to grow into leadership roles. I must caution here that the issue is not a simplistic one of older women standing in the way of young women's advancement in the movement. Rather, the question is how the skills, knowledge, and experience of older women and the enthusiasm, idealism, and indeed the skills and knowledge of youth can best be used to strengthen the women's movement as a whole. Out of the experience in Beijing came just the same sentiment: the movement belongs to all, and we must harness our different strengths and not dwell on weaknesses.

I feel strongly that Oxfam's role is to support and not undermine the strong and effective leadership in the Zambian women's movement. Within the context of inter-generational dialogue, it is important that Oxfam is aware of the some of the sensitivities in the women's movement. Zambian women are concerned about one aspect of Oxfam's role at both the national and international level: that some individuals who are no longer very active in (and who contribute very little to) the national context, remain credible in international networks, often using their international contacts in ways that frustrate the work going on locally. This is an important point for Oxfam to be aware of and sensitive to, because we work both at local and international levels. We can then ensure that our actions give the necessary support at all times.

Making sense of Beijing

I was looking forward to creating alliances with other women at the Forum, with great expectations of the strength that both I and the Oxfam office in Zambia would gain from this. While it is difficult to talk concretely about having built coalitions and alliances at an individual level, the Forum certainly provided a chance to begin doing so. I identified some organisations whose work on alternative economics — my area of special interest — appeals to me; an important starting point.

However, the Forum's down side in this regard was its sheer size: 30,000 people are estimated to have participated. The huge numbers of people in each workshop hindered coalition-building in two ways: it was difficult to discuss issues in depth; and having met a person once, the chance of meeting again was slim.

After about three days of participating in workshops related to alternative economics and meeting with other people and organisations on this theme, it all became rather repetitive. My initial enthusiasm began to wane somewhat, and the dreary rainfall of course exacerbated this. With these feelings, I began to ask: What are we all here for? How does what I have done so far fit into the wider context of the official inter-government conference?

Sometimes it was difficult to see the link. A complicated system of caucusing has developed around UN conferences, which is difficult to understand by novices, such as myself. (I must also confess that I have an aversion to conferences in general, and bigger ones in particular.) I was later to discover that at Beijing, even without being an official conference participant, you were still able to make an input through the system of caucuses. You identify as many people as possible during workshops, from as many different countries as possible who share or sympathise with your concern. Then all of you endeavour to make this a concern of as many official country delegations as possible. The more countries voice a concern, the better its chance of making its way into the Platform of Action. There is, of course, a lot of compromising and, to some extent, dealing involved.

After Beijing

A major benefit of my participation in the Beijing Forum for the Oxfam office in Zambia is that we now have some direct knowledge of what UN conferences are like. We can therefore make better judgement about people we sponsor to attend these conferences, and brief them effectively.

The Zambian women's movement has returned from Beijing with incredible motivation and strength. A lot has since happened: collectively and individually, NGOs have organised report-back sessions for colleagues who did not participate in Beijing. They have held a visioning session which we did not attend, but reports reached us speaking of vibrancy, frankness, and a renewed strength. The National Women's Lobby Group organised a National Convention on the Role of Women in Politics, in which I participated, and which examined the

Beijing Platform of Action — especially those parts of relevance to the role of women in politics. A draft Charter of Women's Rights in Zambia, produced by the Women's Lobby, was also considered at this workshop. Within the context of Oxfam's lobbying on structural adjustment, we see a lot of scope for supporting work that is both an outcome and follow up of Beijing. The Beijing conference and the resulting document have provided a framework for the Zambian government's commitment to the cause of women, giving us a starting point from which women can campaign for their rights.

Conclusion

It is extremely difficult to try and capture something as large, diverse, and colourful as Beijing, with both its highs and lows. Nagging doubts remain about whether I have done justice to Beijing in this article. Since returning, I have been asked questions such as: What do you think of the Chinese people? What about the chaotic organisation of the conference we heard about? And what about all the excessive security measures? Really, in trying to report an event like Beijing one could go on; but I end here.

About the author

Lucy Muyoyeta is a Zambian. She worked for Oxfam for 12 and half years until May 1998. Her last post was as Oxfam's Acting Regional Representative for West Africa, but she has mostly worked in Zambia and Malawi. In her own right, Lucy Muyoyeta is a social activist on women's and basic human-rights issues, working on a voluntary basis with a number of Zambian organisations. Currently, she is a consultant for ActionAid.

Women's Eyes on the World Bank: Integrating gender equity into advocacy work

Lydia Williams

This article focuses on Oxfam America's experience in integrating a commitment to gender equity into our policy advocacy programme. In particular, it uses Oxfam America's role in the campaign Women's Eyes on the World Bank (US) as a case study to show how the agency has turned its commitment to women's empowerment and human rights into action.

The mission of Oxfam America

Oxfam America's mission is to create lasting solutions to hunger, poverty, and social injustice. Oxfam America has a three-pronged approach: support for development work of community-based partner organisations, policy advocacy, and education of the North American public about the issues faced by our partners. Rather than operating its own programmes, Oxfam America has always sought to build partnerships with community-based organisations. Partnership means more than just providing funding to local organisations; it means making a long-term commitment to organisations with whom we have developed reciprocally beneficial relations based on mutual respect, common goals, solidarity, and shared risk.

Central to Oxfam America's mission is a belief that poverty will be eradicated only with the removal of structural barriers — including gender discrimination — that deny people basic rights and access to the skills, resources, and power to become self-sufficient. Over the years, Oxfam America has funded organisations that seek to meet the practical needs of women such as credit, literacy training, and health education. But by listening to partners, the agency came to understand that gender equality would be realised only if the cultural, legal, and political systems that perpetuate women's inequality were broken. Thus, Oxfam America has tried to support organisations that attempt to meet women's 'strategic' needs, with efforts to transform gender relations and remove obstacles to women's equal access to productive resources and decision-making. This is done through funding and technical support for local initiatives for leadership development, consciousness-raising, awareness of gender violence, and, increasingly, policy advocacy at national level to protect women's rights through government intervention and legal reforms.

The link between grant-making in the South and policy advocacy in the North

As economic and political decision-making has become more globalised, advocates for sustainable development have realised that grant-making targeted at the local level is not enough. Support for grassroots strategies must be accompanied by action to influence actors who are often half-way around the world. Responding to structural adjustment programmes (SAPs) instigated by the International Monetary Fund and the World Bank is perhaps the most powerful example of the need for global action to transform systems of inequality. As SAPs began to take their toll in the 1980s, many of Oxfam America's partners mobilised against cuts in budgets and wages, deregulation and privatisation of state-owned industries, removal of subsidies and trade barriers, and other economic reforms that were hurting the poor. It was women who were often the harshest critics, arguing that, given their subordinate position in society, it was they who frequently paid the highest prices for adjustment, in the form of lower wages, heavier workloads, and rising rates of domestic violence.

Given the tremendous power of the US government in the international arena, Oxfam America has always felt a deep responsibility to speak out when US policies negatively affect its partners and their communities, from the Vietnam War, to military aid to El Salvador, to the politicisation of foreign assistance. Through encouragement from its partners, the agency has in recent years increased our ability to affect the policies of the United States and international institutions that affect people around the globe. Since the mid-1980s, Oxfam America's policy advocacy unit has grown from one to five people. In 1995, we opened a Washington DC office (in addition to the programme office in New York), staffed with two policy advocacy coordinators, including myself. This office affords us much better access to policy makers at the World Bank, the IMF, and the US government, and improves our collaboration with other NGOs also based in Washington DC. This proximity has provided an important tool in our advocacy work with these institutions.

Oxfam America defines policy advocacy as the implementation of a range of activities designed to change the actions of government institutions. Our advocacy takes many forms: some are direct, such as letter writing and face-to-face meetings with decision-makers within institutions we are trying to influence; some are indirect, such as research to document negative effects of a policy on partners and to make a case for an alternative approach, or education of the American public about the policy through our newsletter, public events, or use of the mass media.

While Oxfam takes its own independent positions on issues, its commitment to partnerships means that one of the most important functions of the Washington office is to amplify the voices of Southern civil-society groups. A key critique of SAPs is that these policies are designed without input or consent from civil society. A focus of our advocacy in Washington has been to establish formal mechanisms for input from civil society into the decision-making processes of our own government's foreign policy as well as those of the international institutions. The lobbying of Oxfam America staff is supplemented by the facilitation of occasional visits by partners who meet with Washington-based policy-makers, and constant information-sharing with partners. The value placed by Oxfam America on maintaining its independence and speaking out against the US government when necessary is illustrated by the agency's tradition of not accepting US government funds.

The Beijing conference as a catalyst for Oxfam America's gender-justice advocacy

The Fourth UN World Conference on Women in Beijing, 1995, provided a global Forum for women's groups and non-government organisations to bring concerns about the impact of SAPs to the international stage and advocate for change on a global level.[10] Oxfam America sponsored the participation of over a dozen female partners at Beijing, organised workshops on gender and the economy, and participated in the NGO Economic Caucus, which sought to influence the conference documents on economic issues affecting women.

This Economic Caucus became a catalyst for action by women to challenge the role of the World Bank in maintaining the status quo of women's subordination. Seizing on the opportunity presented by Bank President James Wolfensohn's enthusiastic participation in the conference, members of the Economic Caucus drafted a petition to be delivered to Wolfensohn and managed to gather the signatures of 1,000 NGO conference participants. The petition took the Bank to task for ignoring women's needs and demanded that the Bank take specific steps to bring its policies in line with the Beijing Platform for Action. These included efforts to engage grassroots women as full partners in the Bank's economic policy-making; mechanisms to institutionalise a gender perspective in Bank policies and programmes; increases in Bank investments designed to improve women's access to and control over productive assets and services, including health care, education, financial services, and land; and increases in the number and diversity of women in senior positions at the Bank.

Upon receiving the petition, James Wolfensohn pledged to engage in dialogue with women's groups to implement the petition's demands. To ensure that the demanded reforms would become a reality, Economic Caucus members launched the campaign known as Women's Eyes on the World Bank. Volunteers from each region agreed to act as focal points for organising to promote the campaign's goals within their countries and regions. While the campaign was conceived as an international effort, since the Beijing conference, chapters have emerged only in the United States and Latin America.

Member groups from seven countries in Latin America have begun to monitor the Bank's operations in their countries from a gender perspective, and a number of workshops have been organised to train women's groups in how to monitor Bank projects. In the United States, Oxfam America and a dozen Washington-based gender activists sought to establish a more formal structure for Women's Eyes in the months following Beijing. Seeing the campaign as an opportunity to complement the grassroots organising for economic justice of many of its partners, Oxfam America agreed to act as the focal point, and I volunteered to act as the convener of the US Chapter as part of my duties as an Oxfam America Advocacy Coordinator. In the US, a variety of NGOs with experience in monitoring the World Bank worked in collaboration with organisations with expertise in international women's issues. The campaign has benefited hugely from the different strengths that each member group brings.

The US chapter of the Women's Eyes campaign

Given our physical location, the United States chapter identified its primary function as that of monitoring the actions of the Bank's headquarters in order to implement the demands of the 'Beijing petition'. Soon after Beijing, the Bank announced the formation of an External Gender Consultative Group, which meets annually with Bank officials to discuss the Bank's progress on gender equity. Fourteen prominent feminist leaders from around the world serve on it.

With our proximity to the World Bank headquarters in Washington, DC, the US chapter of the Women's Eyes Campaign has been able to provide the Consultative Group (which includes a member of Oxfam America's Southern Africa team) with timely information about the status of gender-related issues within the Bank, as well as help in developing strategies to use the Group's annual meetings to win agreement from Bank management to move faster to mainstream gender concerns throughout the agency.

In addition to monitoring, we are also committed to direct lobbying of Washington-based World Bank officials to open up space for greater participation of grassroots women in Bank operations, and sharing information with networks that are concerned about gender and the World Bank.

Monitoring

Effective advocacy for change must be backed by solid documentation of the problem. Thus, Women's Eyes identified monitoring and documentation of what the Bank was actually doing with regard to gender as its first priority. In March 1996, the Bank released its first 'Progress Report on Gender', outlining in rather glowing terms its progress towards implementing each of the demands of the Beijing petition. Acknowledging that some progress had indeed been made, Women's Eyes nonetheless found the Bank's report to be over-optimistic about the agency's progress and determined that an independent analysis of the Bank's record was needed. A team of ten members of the US chapter embarked on a project to document the progress and problems of the Bank's gender policy.

The results of the survey were released in a October 1997 report, 'Gender Equity and the World Bank Group: A Post-Beijing Assessment'. The report — the most comprehensive external review of the Bank's gender policies — found that, while worthwhile initiatives have been launched, the Bank has yet to address concerns about gender equity systematically across the various sectors in which it operates, and continues to promote macroeconomic policies without regard to the gender implications of those policies and without women's participation. The report ended with 13 concrete recommendations to Bank management on how to better integrate gender equity into its operations.

Lobbying

Once the report was completed, it was distributed widely to Bank managers and staff responsible for gender. The report's recommendations then served as the campaign's lobbying agenda for the coming year. Women's Eyes members engaged in direct meetings with various World Bank managers, as well as the United States Executive Director to the World Bank, to press for action on the recommendations.

The US Executive Director to the World Bank has been both a target of our lobbying and an ally. Because the US holds a 17 per cent share of the votes on the World Bank board, maintaining a relationship with this office is very important. The US Director has been helpful in pushing a gender-equity agenda on the board, for example, by raising questions about gender when projects come up for consideration at board meetings.

Outreach

While monitoring and direct lobbying have been the key advocacy strategies of Women's Eyes, outreach to other NGOs has also been important in educating the broader NGO movement about the campaign, and demonstrating to the Bank that a wide range of civil-society organisations share the goals of Women's Eyes.

Use of the internet has been an important outreach tool. Women's Eyes has developed an e-mail 'listserve' through which information about World Bank gender policies is shared with broader NGO networks. Upon completing the October 1997 report, we used the listserve to invite NGOs around the world to endorse the report's recommendations. Over 300 gender advocates, development NGOs, environmental groups, women's groups, and other NGOs responded, and their names were signed to a letter to Mr Wolfensohn which was printed as an annex to the report. Presentations at NGO forums have also been successful in bringing other activists into the campaign. Women's Eyes has also made limited use of the mass media to get our message out to a wider audience.

Key signs of progress for Women's Eyes on the World Bank

While the Women's Eyes on the World Bank is just one strategy for change, a number of lessons can be drawn from the experience of the campaign. By employing a mix of advocacy strategies, ranging from research, direct lobbying of Bank officials, media, and outreach to the wider NGO community, Women's Eyes has been successful in pushing for a number of new initiatives at the Bank.

It is clear that Women's Eyes succeeded in using the Beijing conference to capture the attention of the Bank, particularly its president. While James Wolfensohn was taken aback by the criticism voiced by NGOs at Beijing, he moved quickly to create openings for dialogue with Bank staff at all levels, to improve the Bank's performance on gender. The campaign's strategy of 'constructive engagement' has resulted in fruitful debates about gender with the Bank.

By producing a solid report, which balanced acknowledgement of progress with a hard critique of the Bank's overall record, the campaign is taken seriously within the institution. In a seven-page letter responding to each of the findings and recommendations of the October 1997 report, the Vice President responsible for the Bank's gender policy, Masood Ahmed, called the document 'a valuable contribution to the Bank's efforts to mainstream gender' and agreed to work with Women's Eyes to implement the recommendations. Perhaps most significant is the fact that gender issues have caught the attention of the World Bank's Chief Economist, one of the most powerful members of Bank management, who has announced a major new research initiative on gender, called a Policy Research Report. This research is intended to establish a set of analytical underpinnings necessary to develop a Bank-wide conceptual framework for gender. Women's Eyes has acted quickly to seek agreement with Bank management to work with the Women's Eyes campaign to establish a consultative process for the development of the conceptual framework, engaging a broad array of gender advocates, grassroots women's groups, and academics from around the world.

In Latin America, the campaign is also producing promising results. As a result of aggressive lobbying, the Latin America chapter has won agreement by the Bank to increase the number of gender specialists in the region and to work with the campaign to conduct an in-depth analysis of the Bank's operations 'through a gender lens'. Collaborative action between Women's Eyes members has also succeeded in country-specific issues. For example, when members learned that the Bank's Mexico Country Assistance Strategy failed to integrate gender or women's participation in a meaningful way, over a dozen US and Mexican NGOs drafted a joint letter to the Bank's Mexico Country Director to complain. As a result, the Director has agreed to hold regular dialogue with Mexican women's groups to look for ways to improve the Bank's treatment of gender in future.

Challenges for Oxfam America and Women's Eyes

Support for partner advocacy for gender equity

One of the hard lessons of Women's Eyes on the World Bank, however, is the reality that there is a very limited number of Southern NGOs which are actively engaged in analysis, monitoring, and advocacy targeted at the Bank's policies on gender. This is evidenced by the failure of Women's Eyes to become established in Africa and Asia. As a result, many opportunities to influence Bank polices are missed. Several women leaders have told me that, while they understand the tremendous influence of the Bank in their country, faced with limited capacity and challenged by the need to focus on meeting women's basic needs and to react to actions by national and local governments, lobbying the Bank is a luxury they cannot afford. In addition, these groups often lack the technical expertise to take on a giant like the World Bank.

In the absence of strong, organised Southern monitoring and advocacy groupings, Northern NGOs and coalitions, including Women's Eyes, are open to criticism for being Northern-driven. For Oxfam America and Women's Eyes US one of the most important challenges is to make sure that we do not dominate the policy dialogue on gender and development, but promote space for marginalised groups in civil societies, including women, to take control over decisions that affect their lives. Given the nature of policy-making in Washington, where there are often very small windows of opportunity for influencing decisions, Washington-based NGOs frequently feel compelled to act quickly, with no time for careful consultation with partners. While Northern NGOs like Oxfam have a responsibility to challenge the international financial institutions, and to speak from our own our experiences, we must be clear that we do not speak 'on behalf of' Southern NGOs and must be prepared to step aside in the policy making arena and make room for our partners.

There are several ways in which donor organisations like Oxfam America can help accelerate the integration of grassroots women into policy-making fora. We should be prepared to offer a range of support for groups dedicated to women's empowerment, including capacity-building, leadership development, economic literacy, advocacy-skills building, as well as networking and sharing of information on advocacy strategies. Because information is power, donors should prioritise support for translation and dissemination of policy information, and for increased access of NGOs to the internet. Equally important is support for networking and sharing of innovative and successful advocacy strategies, such as the Women's Budget Project in South Africa, which analyses the national budget from a women's perspective and promotes women's spending priorities. Support for intensive training in advocacy, seminars on how to influence the World Bank, economic literacy training, and media-skills building are all important.

The experience of Women's Eyes on the World Bank demonstrates the potential impact of strong North-South coalitions to promote sustainable development on a global level. In the coming year, together with our Women's Eyes colleagues, Oxfam America hopes to focus more attention on creating synergy between our advocacy in Washington and our grant-making to partners in the South in the pursuit of a more global and effective movement for social and economic justice.

Incorporating a gender perspective into other advocacy initiatives

Another challenge is to ensure that gender considerations are fully integrated into all advocacy campaigns, rather than compartmentalising our gender work in the same way that we have accused the World Bank of doing.

All of the Oxfams and many of our partners have been mobilising for years for debt forgiveness. Oxfam International (of which Oxfam America is a member)[11] lobbied hard for the establishment in 1995 of the historic Highly Indebted Poor Country Initiative — which aims to reduce multilateral and bilateral debts of the poorest countries — and have monitored implementation of the agreement. While gender issues *per se* have not predominated in Oxfam's call for debt relief, we have had some success making the links between gender equity and debt relief. We must seek new ways to highlight the gender implications of the debt crisis and to build alliances with gender advocates, including members of the Women's Eyes on the World Bank campaign, in this effort.

While campaigning on World Bank reform must continue, Oxfam America and the broader NGO community must rise to the challenge of confronting other important actors in the global economy who affect poor women and men. Advocates in the North and South must build capacity to influence the macroeconomic policies of the IMF and press this enormously powerful body to be more accountable to citizens and more committed to equity. As private investment increasingly outstrips official aid in many parts of the world, Oxfam America must work to ensure that the globalisation of trade and investment protects the rights of marginalised populations, including women.

At Oxfam America, we must also continually ask ourselves whether we are practising what we preach. As we bang the drum about the Bank's need to mainstream concerns about gender equity throughout its operations, we must ask if we are succeeding in this regard within our own agency. While the agency may be recognised as a leader, it cannot rest on its laurels: we must ensure that gender equity been ingrained into our agency culture and personnel policies, so that Oxfam America staff receive sufficient training, and that accountability mechanisms are in place to ensure that gender and women's participation are fully integrated into all of our programme planning, implementation, and evaluation, and that mechanisms are in place for systematic consultation with partners across the continuum of our advocacy programme.

About the author

Lydia Williams is a Program Co-ordinator in the Advocacy Unit of Oxfam America based in Washington, DC. She serves as the lead advocate for OA on issues related to international financial institutions, including gender and development, debt relief for poor countries, and civil-society participation in policy-making. Lydia is currently the convener of the United States chapter of the Women's Eyes on the World Bank campaign and was recently appointed to the World Bank's External Gender Consultative Group.

Gender and diversity in Oxfam International

Ellen Sprenger and Diane Biray Gregorio

Introduction

Oxfam International (OI) is a network of 11 Oxfams working towards the eradication of poverty by addressing the structural causes of social and economic injustice. Founded in 1995, it is a network of like-minded affiliates in North America, Europe, and the Pacific Rim region[12] striving to increase efficiency, effectiveness and impact on the lives of poor communities through collaboration in areas such as long-term development, urgent humanitarian need, advocacy, public education campaigning, and fund-raising.

This article looks at the role of the Oxfam International Gender and Diversity Working Group (OIGDWG) in promoting the integration of a gender and diversity analysis and practice into OI's work.[13]

The foundations of a strategy

Even before Oxfam International was formally established, individuals working to advance gender equity in the various Oxfams had been exchanging materials, examples of best practice, and strategies. The founding of OI in 1995 allowed increased opportunities for linking and learning, including the formal establishment of the working group in 1996. The Working Group consists of representatives from each of the affiliates who are working for gender equity in their own organisations. In the first few years, the OIGDWG struggled to formulate an effective strategy for working together.

What kind of 'animal' is Oxfam International?

Before the working group could identify ways to facilitate change, we had to understand the large and complicated system that Oxfam International is. Who founded OI, and for what purpose? What are its values and beliefs? What are its structures and practices? What strategic opportunities does it provide? To what extent is management committed to gender equity and diversity?

In exploring these questions, the working group found that the character of OI could help advance a gender and diversity analysis and practice. OI's fundamental belief is that collaborative efforts contribute to improved efficiency and impact, both individually and collectively. We felt that, as a network, OI would be open to linking and learning about gender and diversity, especially as it increases the quality of our work as development agencies. The working group was asked to act as an advisory body to the OI programme directors' committee (PDC), an alliance which promised to be a powerful one, because the PDC is a respected, vocal, high-profile advocate and decision-making body within OI. Within the PDC, there is a critical mass of senior managers who are proactive and outspoken on issues of gender and diversity and thereby help greatly to establish credibility for these issues.[14] We concluded that this was a truly unique opportunity to help shape the work of the network at this early stage.

One factor that complicated the discussions about the OIGDWG's mandate and role was that each individual Oxfam is at a very different stage in its work on gender and diversity. Although all affiliates are in their own ways becoming more gender- and diversity-aware, there are significant differences in the levels of implementation, whether in the workplace or in their programme, advocacy, and fund-raising work. When positioning the 11 Oxfams on the continuum from gender-blind[15] to gender-aware[16] to gender-responsive,[17] we can conclude that all are recognising the importance of a gender analysis and can be classified as gender-aware. However, interpretations of the meaning and the consequences of a gender analysis differ considerably. On the issue of diversity, most Oxfams are in the early stages of deepening their own understanding of the issue; interventions primarily address recruitment and internal organisational culture. Due to these differences it was to be expected that the definition of quality in relation to both gender and diversity would be a point of debate and negotiation.

Another challenge informing the discussion of the OIGDWG's mandate and role was the range of its members' perceptions of their sphere of influence within their respective Oxfams. For some, the momentum generated by the working group would provide very useful leverage to promote progress on the issue within their Oxfams. For others, who are already engaged in major change processes, the challenge is more to determine how the OI work can complement and support these existing processes.

Clarifying the working group's mandate and role

Once the working group had a better sense of the 'landscape' of OI, we began to discuss our mandate and role. The programme directors had given the OIGDWG a broad mandate: to provide them with proposals to ensure the integration of gender perspectives into OI collaborative activities. Acknowledging the limitations of staff and resources, we felt that more clarity and focus were necessary. We asked ourselves the following questions: Where would the group's efforts have most leverage and long-term impact? What activities would allow deeper mainstreaming of gender issues into the work of OI? Where was the energy and attention of senior management? Where was there already strong support for gender? What could this group realistically propose and carry out? And, last but not least, how could the activities of OI at an international level help to advance ongoing learning and improved performance within each Oxfam and its work? Gender and diversity policies and practices could not be confined to programmes only—this was both an issue of principle (to practise what you preach) and quality.

Statement of common purpose: building a common vision

In order to unify the efforts of the Oxfam International affiliates, a Statement of Common Purpose on Gender and Diversity was drafted as part of the first OI strategic plan (1996–98), in the form of a single statement that 'gender inequalities and other diversity issues will be addressed in [Oxfam International] actions and programs'. In 1997 this statement was further elaborated to also include individual Oxfams' internal policies and practices and areas for action. While the various Oxfams were at different stages of implementation, we were surprisingly consonant when it came to outlining the ultimate desired outcomes of our work in these areas. This is evident in the statement, which was approved as an official OI working principle.[18] The following are excerpts from that statement.

> OI is committed to equal rights and opportunities in our work and in our workplace, and a belief that quality is enhanced when individuals of different gender and different backgrounds are engaged in decision-making processes.

> In striving to achieve diversity and equal opportunity it is recognised that disadvantaged groups, such as women, start from very different and unequal positions in society relative to others. Therefore actions to redress this inequality include proactive measures and other practices where equal rights and opportunities are the goal, and which seek to end discrimination on the basis of gender, race, religion, age, ethnicity, sexual preference, or disability.

> Oxfam International pursues diversity and equal rights and opportunities in three related ways. First of all, its activities (marketing, advocacy, program work, fund-raising, and education) are designed to promote pluralistic and just

societies around the world and to increase the opportunities available to historically disadvantaged groups. Second, recognising that without internal diversity Oxfam International member Oxfams are constrained in their ability to achieve excellence in their individual and collaborative activities, therefore they strive for broad representation in their own boards and staffing compositions. Finally, the Oxfam International member Oxfams seek to encourage the same diversity in board and staff composition, and activities of all counterparts.

While appropriate strategies must necessarily vary according to the particular constraints and possibilities present in different societies, Oxfam International member Oxfams are committed to working with each other and with counterparts to promote these efforts and to ensure their success.

Undoubtedly, much more discussion will take place about how to interpret and implement the statement. These debates will reflect the diverse organisational cultures, approaches, and traditions as well as political and strategic interpretations of our role as change agents within our Oxfams.

Establishing a role: strategists, not watchdogs

Given this mandate, the OIGDWG then reflected on the role that we should play in supporting the implementation of this common purpose. It emerged very clearly that the members of the working group were not going to act as watchdogs, policing the entire scope of OI activities. Not only would that be impossible, due to time and staffing constraints, but it would also go against the principle that every individual and programme is responsible for working on gender and diversity. Instead of imposing activities to make Oxfams more gender- and diversity-responsive, we would aim to inform the heart of OI decision-making from the outset.

In order to act strategically and move the basis for the gender debate from a small group of individuals to one shared by all staff members, we needed a tool for systematically assessing the state of affairs; for identifying areas of strength and areas in need of improvement; and for creating a framework to generate learning and share best practices within both the Oxfams and across the network.

This mechanism needed to be based on a set of principles for improving quality, identifying critical quality areas, and achieving agreement on indicators and variables, while acknowledging and allowing for differences among affiliates. The next stage would be to assess each Oxfam's performance by gathering information from multiple sources, and involving reflection, discussion, and learning among staff members. One of our longer-term goals is a comparative analysis of the relative strengths and weaknesses of each of the Oxfams and presentation of the main findings; this includes the idea of lateral accountability and open discussion among OI management in the form of peer review.

Managers must take responsibility for implementing the recommendations and measures for each Oxfam and at the level of OI collaboration.

Ideally this mechanism, also called competitive benchmarking, should be repeated over time. Also, the critical quality areas identified need to be reviewed and reflected upon at a regular basis. With this in mind, the OIGDWG created the 'gender and diversity mapping tool'. At the time of writing, the Oxfams have gone through one mapping cycle, with a second one on its way.

Lessons from the first gender and diversity mapping cycle

The gender and diversity mapping tool consists of a series of strategic questions arranged under six rubrics. These categories encompass all aspects of member Oxfams' work, both internal and external: policies and procedures; human resources; organisational culture; programme learning, networking, and external relations; media, communications, and fund-raising; and OI collaboration.

In 1996–97, the OIGDWG conducted the first cycle of the mapping exercise. Even at this initial stage, the tool has helped OI to establish a baseline for future comparisons. Although each affiliate is in its own way becoming more gender- and diversity-responsive, the exercise helped us to identify areas for individual and collective improvement. The following are examples of the comparative data generated by this first mapping exercise.

Allocation of Financial Resources:

- Five Oxfams apply gender criteria to their funding decisions: three do so on a rather *ad hoc* basis and two more systematically. Almost all of the Oxfams use checklists or guiding questions in approval, monitoring, and/or evaluation processes. The use of those checklists seems to depend on individual initiative.
- Four Oxfams make explicit efforts to allocate funds, provide other forms of support to, and form alliances with women's organisations.

Staffing and organisational culture:

- While men still hold the majority of decision-making positions (for example, all Executive Directors are men), women are well represented in most of the Oxfams. Most report an increase in the number of women at decision-making levels; for example, 60 per cent of the Programme Directors are women.
- Data on staff diversity is limited across the Oxfams, mostly due to a lack of systemised record-keeping. Most of the data relates to ethnicity, but such information has limited comparability, in part because definitions of ethnicity and what would constitute ethnic heterogeneity varies in local contexts.

- Five Oxfams have affirmative action and/or equal opportunity policies for women and peoples of diverse backgrounds. Three other Oxfams have more limited policies; one Oxfam is developing them; and only one recorded no policies in these areas.
- All Oxfams make efforts to promote women and diversity-friendly working environments, ranging from attempts to use non-sexist language to complaint and/or sexual harassment procedures (six Oxfams). Two Oxfams point to implicit organisational norms (such as having to be 'on call' because meetings are scheduled without notice, or the expectation to be flexible and work overtime) which limit or negate the expressed intent of encouraging progressive ways of working, such as flexi-time and other family-friendly measures. Other Oxfams record information about extensive efforts in field offices to adapt work and travel schedules to take into account women's family responsibilities and to address traditional norms about women's roles (which discourage women from working and/or travelling).

Capacity-building, training, learning, and networking:

- In six Oxfams, internal capacity-building and training are being promoted and seem fairly well institutionalised. Where it is not promoted (four Oxfams), it appears that capacity-building and training on gender-awareness is extremely limited or non-existent.
- All Oxfams are involved in sharing learning and networking with partner organisations and also facilitate such processes among counterparts. One Oxfam, for instance, initiated communication/information networks for East and South Asia in which many other Oxfams have participated over the years. Other examples include a shared involvement in lobbying activities, for example on the Convention to Eliminate all Forms of Discrimination against Women, or on the occasion of the Fourth World Conference on Women.

Fund-raising and educational campaigns:

- Data clearly shows that women's visibility in fund-raising and education has increased steadily. However, the integration of gender analysis in fund-raising is problematic, partly because existing tools for fund-raising encourage the simplification of complex issues and are analysed on the basis of their 'saleability'. Conveying complex issues of power relations remains a big challenge.

In most Oxfams, the data-gathering was a consultative process, involving reflection and discussion with those responsible for decision-making and implementation. Several working group members have reported that the exercise helped to create new momentum for advancing gender equity in a number of ways. For example, one Oxfam reported that the mapping resulted in the development of a policy on gender. In another Oxfam, the exercise led to special efforts of affirmative action for women, resulting in the recruitment of a woman manager.

After the first year's experience, the OIGDWG refined the questionnaire as well as the gender-mapping methodology. For instance, working group members noticed that the time allocated for the first round of mapping had been limited. In planning the second annual mapping cycle, we made it a high priority to provide ample time to encourage reflection and discussion.

Although the working group was successful in generating and comparing data on gender and diversity, we have yet to realise the more ambitious goal of the mapping exercise: the promotion of lateral accountability and the institutionalisation of the recommendations.

Challenges for the future

Small Oxfams, large Oxfams: What is useful and achievable?

Member Oxfams vary greatly in terms of budget, and have different capacities to staff OI collaborative activities. Smaller Oxfams may only have a single person assigned to cover several of the OI focal areas, whereas larger Oxfams are able to dedicate one or more full-time staff members to OI activities. As a result, there is a constant tension and negotiation about what is useful and achievable.

The gender- and diversity-mapping exercise is an example of an OI activity which is considered valuable, but which represents a significant investment of time. Ultimately, each Oxfam will have to make its own trade-offs. Whether working in smaller or larger Oxfams, working group members observed that this tension is minimised when the areas covered in the mapping tool closely match the ongoing change processes within the Oxfam, or when the change agent uses the tool strategically to create new momentum and excitement for learning.

Global information technology: potential and constraints

As with any group attempting to work across continents and time zones, communication is paramount. The OIGDWG was among the first OI working groups to establish an e-mail mailing list in 1996. However, this electronic communication tool is by no means without its difficulties. In the beginning, many working group members were unfamiliar with the use of e-mail, and a third did not have their own address. Technical problems also hampered the process. Due to collaborative efforts between the Oxfams, most of these technical problems have been solved, and staff members in general have become much more comfortable with e-mail. This has greatly improved communications among working group members, but e-mailing seems to work best between people who already know and understand each other, to follow up on the implementation of agreements which were reached face-to-face. This is especially the case in situations where participants are from different cultural backgrounds and have different communication styles, so multi-layered interactions are still very much needed.

Moving from mapping to benchmarking

Perhaps the biggest challenge for the OIGDWG in improving our approach to gender and diversity, is making the transition from merely mapping our progress to benchmarking Oxfams against each other and perhaps against other NGOs. The ultimate aim of benchmarking is to raise OI's overall performance by encouraging all Oxfams to move towards the highest standards of best practice. This transition represents several challenges for OI.

Accountability and competition for quality as welcome traits. The mapping exercise is valuable tool for quality improvement within OI only to the extent that leadership is willing to hold each other accountable. This is of course related to the extent that the OI affiliates are open to discuss their strengths and weaknesses. This is easier said than done, as such openness requires a sense of trust and an ability to give and accept constructive criticism, both of which require time and investment in relationships to develop. The role of the leadership in modeling these behaviours becomes paramount. In making the transition from mapping to benchmarking, we also need to welcome a certain level of friendly competition to encourage each other towards higher performance. As NGOs, the idea of competition carries many negative connotations. However, in the case of benchmarking, competition in a benign form is a necessary aspect of encouraging higher standards.

Identification of critical quality areas. Because the Oxfams are at different stages in the implementation of gender and diversity perspectives, and have different priorities, agreeing on specific areas for quality improvement has proven to be a great challenge. Also, the mapping tool in its current form looks primarily at whether technical procedures and regulations are in place (such as the existence of policies, criteria for funding, the occurrence of networking and capacity-building, or the availability of gender-disaggregated data). What the tool fails to cover are the organisational dynamics required to make those technical measures work. These dynamics include the role of management; the level of participation in an organisation; staff attitude; organisational culture and the organisation's willingness to learn from others, to be transparent, and to be self-critical. The experience of the OIGDWG seems to indicate that quality in the field of gender and diversity is more appropriately seen as a constantly evolving continuum, rather than as a static definition of minimum standards or procedures.

Availability of reliable data: with whom do we benchmark? As we found in the first cycle of the mapping exercise, one of the key constraints on comparative analysis is the availability of reliable data, especially regarding programme impact. Most of the smaller Oxfams lacked systems for collecting gender-disaggregated and diversity-relevant data. Improving information systems thus becomes an important element of benchmarking. Moving beyond the Oxfam network, ultimately the OIGDWG would like to benchmark member Oxfams' performance against other NGOs internationally. Which organisations would be appropriate to benchmark against? What characteristics would make the comparison relevant?

Computer programmes: new modalities for benchmarking. As we become more sophisticated in our mapping and benchmarking, there may be innovative ways to collect data, both on more technical aspects of an organisation (the 'hardware' of an organisation) and on the factors and variables that enable these procedures and mechanisms to work (the 'software' of an organisation). Some Oxfams and consultancies are experimenting with the use of computer programmes for organisational self-assessments. The potential to apply this technology to the work on gender and diversity benchmarking is an exciting one: such an interactive tool will generate comparative data on both the 'hardware' and 'software' of organisations, and it can be used by each of the individual Oxfams to formulate practical, tailor-made guidelines and proposals for improved quality.

Evolving role of the change agent. The role of the change agent, especially that of the working group members, will also shift. Moving from mapping to benchmarking will require less emphasis on putting gender and diversity on the agenda, and more emphasis on organisational self-assessment and formulating proposals for doing things differently.

Conclusion

It is still too early to predict the impact of the OIGDWG's work on Oxfam International. Although the working group has only been active for two years, we believe that several aspects of our work have broader relevance for other networks, international and otherwise. One strong lesson is the importance of conducting an analysis of factors and an emphasis on variables conducive to advancing gender and diversity. A collective organisational culture based on transparency, self-criticism and openness has proven to be very important for the success of the working group. We hope that the strengthening of this culture within OI will create an increasingly favourable environment for challenging and encouraging each other towards higher-quality performance.

The OIGDWG's experience also teaches the importance of an alliance between an expert group and key decision-makers in promoting change. There are many examples of networks where expert groups on gender or diversity spend most of their time 'watchdogging' and fixing, but ultimately failing to contribute to gender equity and diversity. In this case, the working group was given the space to work at the heart of OI decision-making. As a result, we could build a tool which, once it is fully matured and institutionalised, will be sustainable and self-generating.

On the one hand, the OIGDWG has made an important start in systematically promoting gender and diversity within OI. On the other hand, there are still many areas for improvement. The reality remains that, despite the advances made, women and people of diverse backgrounds throughout the world are still over-represented among the poorest of the poor and under-represented at decision-making levels. The challenges which Oxfam International faces are reflective of the task facing organisations everywhere that strive for the promotion and respect of human rights. The challenge is great, but the vision is inspiring: to build, throughout our Oxfams and as a network, a global humanitarian response to poverty and injustice, and to do so in a way that results in equal rights and opportunities for all segments of the world's population.

About the authors

Ellen Sprenger and Diane Biray Gregorio are both members of the Oxfam International Working Group on Gender and Diversity.

Ellen Sprenger works with Novib as a senior policy adviser. Her areas of expertise include organisational development, the role of the change agent, leadership development, and monitoring and evaluation. She was co-ordinator of the Oxfam International Working Group on Gender and Diversity 1996–98, and is co-author of the book *Gender and Organisational Change: Bridging the Gap between Policy and Practice* (Macdonald, Sprenger, Dubel, 1997, KIT Press).

Diane Biray Gregorio is the Program and Organisational Development Adviser in the Learning and Technical Support Unit at Oxfam America. Her areas of special focus include gender, human rights, and development finance.

Harmonising gender and development: The GAD fund in South Africa

Penny Plowman and Josette Cole[19]

Introduction

This article reflects on a joint initiative by Oxfam Canada and Novib in South Africa, the Gender and Development (GAD) fund. This positive collaboration between two Oxfams has some useful lessons for the wider task of building a gender perspective into Oxfam International (OI).[20] Although the GAD fund has made important contributions, its institutional and programme experience remains marginal to current OI debates and processes. We hope that this article can contribute to the current debates on integrating gender into all OI programming.

The broader context for this article is the process known as 'Oxfam harmonisation' which Oxfam GB initiated in 1990. It aims to find new ways in which the member organisations of OI can work together more effectively and efficiently to end world poverty and injustice. As the different Oxfams have explored new ways of working together, they have developed a range of models. It is clear that there is no one blue-print for how we collaborate. We approach the issue from an analysis of how best to integrate a gender perspective into development work. This leads us into the now familiar debates about 'separate' versus 'integrated' gender approaches. We believe that the development of a gender framework for the whole of OI needs to take into account both approaches. However, by setting up a separate GAD fund, without an overall gender framework for OI in South Africa, there is a danger that gender will remain marginalised. People tend to assume that because there is a GAD fund, member Oxfams are integrating gender into their programmes. This is problematic, because the commitment to development with gender justice demands much more.

Gender issues in South Africa

The GAD fund, which was initiated in early 1996, must be understood in the context of South Africa's democratic transition. The fund's short history coincides with the establishment of a much more visible and vibrant institutional base for emerging women's and gender issues in South Africa. It operates within the contradictory transitional context where the principles of basic needs and gender equity, enshrined in the new South African constitution and in the government's Reconstruction and Development Programmes (RDP), exist alongside the tough structural-adjustment imperatives of the government's GEAR strategy (Growth, Employment, and Redistribution).

During 1994–96, while the government struggled to establish new policy and institutional frameworks, in the end failing to meet the delivery targets it set itself in 1994, South Africans experienced a number of different social trends. These included escalating violence against women and children and rising poverty, but also the increased political representation of women and the establishment of new statutory bodies (the Office on the Status of Women, the Commission of Gender Equality, and Gender Desks in some ministries and local councils). All of this has contributed in some way to placing gender issues (practical and strategic) more squarely on the South African political and development agenda.

Within the development sector, gender issues have certainly gained a higher profile in the last few years. Combined with the window of opportunity in the South African context, this has assisted the Oxfams' work in developing gender programmes. However, it must also be said that for all the politically correct rhetoric, gender analysis continues to be sidelined. Building gender awareness is a good starting point, but the integration of a gender perspective into all aspects of development theory and practice requires much more than this.

Before reflecting on the GAD fund in more detail, it is useful to look at the different approaches to gender in the three main international Oxfams working in South Africa: Oxfam Canada, Novib, and Oxfam GB.

Similarities and differences in three Oxfams' approaches to gender

An in-depth analysis of the Oxfam programmes by Penny Plowman (October 1995) showed that although there were some differences in gender programmes, there was a great deal to gain from a joint approach to gender and development. While the original concept was a 'pilot', and quite limited in its vision (only two Oxfams joined at the beginning), it was believed that it had the potential to grow.

Novib and Oxfam Canada's concept for establishing a joint gender and development funding mechanism (the GAD fund) came about in the mid-1990s, a time when a number of other processes were taking place simultaneously within different Oxfams. These included restructuring in a number of Oxfams, debates between its members on how to turn the theory of 'harmonisation' into practice in the field, and the development of different institutional strategies on how to address gender at a programme level.

Since the early 1990s the three Oxfams have been developing their own gender programmes; support to women's organisations (for example, those working on women and violence) and gender training for project partners have been common objectives. However, different strategies were developed to meet these objectives. Novib and Oxfam Canada set up separate women and gender programmes, whilst Oxfam GB integrated support for gender issues into its main programme. Moreover, in addition to funding, each Oxfam has developed a range of other support strategies. These have included exchange visits (with Oxfam Canada and Novib); in the case of Oxfam GB, a programme officer worked for a South African national network against violence against women.

There have also been a number of different responses in the area of gender training, including support for local gender trainers through a gender-training network, and building local gender-training units in educational institutions (Oxfam Canada). A more hands-on approach was a donor-initiated and supported gender network set up by Novib, which involved six project partners.

The GAD fund: Working on the margins

The GAD fund started with a limited funding base and modest objectives. Its institutional structure was also lean, with a part-time co-ordinator and a small co-ordinating committee. The programme's focus in 1996 was on women and violence, women and finance, gender training, and on strengthening women's organisations. This focus was broad enough to capture and respond to the gender-specific issues emerging out of South Africa's democratic transition. The GAD fund was also flexible enough to respond to other priorities as they became clear, including HIV/AIDS. The GAD fund has also been part of an exciting new development in South Africa, the establishment of the Donor Network for Women (DNW), which began as a loose network of women programme officers from Northern NGOs working on gender and development in South Africa. These women came together on an ad hoc basis to discuss and review respective project proposals and new developments on gender issues in South Africa. The DNW now meets every two months, and has developed a joint activity plan for 1998.[21]

Although the GAD fund was set up primarily as a new funding conduit for two Oxfams (with the view that other Oxfams could join), both Oxfam Canada and Novib believed that the pilot fund should provide access to new kinds of projects. This is exactly what the fund has achieved; but as it has developed, we believe it can play a much bigger role in the Oxfam 'harmonisation' process.

It has become clear in the fund's relatively short history that certain trends are emerging in South Africa. For example, the increasing number of initiatives which address the issue of women and violence highlights the way it cuts across boundaries. Violence against women and children cannot be neatly boxed into the 'women's sector'; it affects every aspect of development. Similarly, trends in HIV/AIDS, and awareness of how it affects women and men differently, must be understood in the broadest development terms. Therefore OI programmes in housing, land, and urban development must each be imbued with a gender analysis rooted in the South African context. It is our view that the GAD fund could assist a great deal in conceptualising and implementing OI programmes. Both organisations and individuals involved in the fund represent an important knowledge base, which can provide a deeper understanding of the broader environment and how it affects women and men differently.

However, the kinds of initiatives which the GAD fund has been involved in remain relatively marginal to other gender processes taking place in the OI 'family'. These include Novib's parallel GAD initiatives taking place in South Africa; strategic thinking on OI harmonisation; and gender initiatives taking place in the Northern offices of the different Oxfams, including Novib and Oxfam Canada.[22] Practitioners in the field, including gender-sensitive development practitioners in South Africa, seem to be unable to find points of entry into current OI debates and discussion. We remain unsure of who makes decisions, of where power lies. This is not something peculiar to the gender programme, but it raises important questions about how and with whom communication takes place.

Although we are aware that there are many interesting and important opportunities to debate these issues in the North (for example, through the OI gender and diversity group[23]), we know of no institutional mechanism that can bring us together. We have yet to agree on a strategic gender and development framework that can guide and inspire us in our work in the North and the South. Because of this, none of us can ensure that gender concerns do not slip off the OI agenda — we in the South have concerns that they may.

OI's apparent inability, thus far, to strategically assess and make use of its own institutional and human resources, is worrying. It has resulted for example, in a set of sectoral reviews which failed to come up with any serious gender analysis and strategies. While these reviews are now being revised, it is questionable how feasible it is to inject a gender analysis as an afterthought. We believe that it must be carried out from the beginning. These fundamental gaps in thinking remain, despite years of work and experience in OI on mainstreaming gender at institutional and programme levels. It is therefore clear that there is a lack of understanding about how a gender perspective can be applied to programme planning and implementation.

The starting point is a much more serious look at how a gender perspective can be built into the whole of the OI programme in South Africa. It is clear that this is not going to happen by osmosis: a framework must be set up and adhered to, and effective links must be made between North and South, in order to share and build on our different models and approaches. At the same time we cannot assume that there is a shared understanding about what gender and development means. Raising gender awareness at a personal level is the key, because only then can links be made at a programming level. At the same time, we need to institutionalise gender in all OI programmes, South and North. This is not solely the responsibility of women who are passionate about the issues; it is everyone's, men's and women's.

Conclusions

Translating the guiding principles of 'harmonisation' into practice has been extremely challenging and difficult. At a Novib meeting of South African project partners, the question was raised: 'Are the time, effort, money, and resources going into harmonisation really worth it? Why not just carry on giving us the money from the individual Oxfams?' This sense of doubt is shared by many of us who are involved in a process which does seem very complicated and painfully slow.

What is the value of harmonisation? The Oxfam International Advocacy Office in Washington is an excellent example of increased co-operation making sense. The power of OI as opposed to individual Oxfams, has been much more effective in lobbying the World Bank and the IMF on critical global concerns, such as world debt, poverty, and structural adjustment policies. However, the assumption is that 'harmonisation' means common programme areas and shared development approaches. This has had to be thoroughly examined: although everyone works under the same Oxfam banner, there are many differences in terms of programme content and management structures. The process of harmonisation has opened up a myriad of consultative processes in which, for the first time, people who representing Oxfams from different cultures and contexts have had to share information about their programmes in a formal, structured way. This has not been easy, and it has taken time. As in any change process, this has meant confronting difficult issues of power and control as well as building trust. It was to be expected that a change process of such complexity and scale would inevitably result in some disharmony as well as harmony.

At an operational level, albeit in a limited way, the GAD fund has begun to set the agenda on 'harmonisation' in the field. It provides a flexible, cost-effective and, responsive, mechanism for Novib and Oxfam Canada to address emerging gender and development initiatives in South Africa. The GAD fund's ability to respond strategically to emerging gender issues and needs (institutional and project-related) is not only due to its institutional flexibility. It emerges out of a context where the kinds of issues which it was designed to address became more visible, and were accompanied by increasing political commitment to address issues of gender inequality. With limited resources and limited institutional support from the North, the fund has been able to establish a potential way forward for OI programme collaboration in the field.

At the same time this experience, together with other lessons emerging out of the OI 'harmonisation' process, challenges us to address gender relations at a number of different levels — personal, institutional, and in the development and implementation of programmes. We need to understand the difficulties in trying to build a gender perspective into all aspects of OI and its programmes in South Africa. Why do people find it so difficult to integrate a gender perspective into programme planning beyond the GAD fund? Is it a lack of understanding of what needs to be changed and how, or is it a lack of commitment at a deeper personal level to bring about an end to gender inequalities? The experience in South Africa forces us to confront a key question: how do we design a strategic gender framework and implementation plan which can begin to institutionalise gender principles across OI, North and South? At the same time it is clear that this in itself is not enough — it must be accompanied by a personal commitment to a development agenda within a framework of gender justice.

About the authors

Penny Plowman is a development consultant, working with NGOs and international funding agencies in gender and organisational change. She carried out the feasibility study for the Oxfam International GAD fund, and was the NOVIB representative on the committee for the first year.

Josette Cole is the GAD fund co-ordinator and works with members of Oxfam International as a freelance consultant. Her special interest is in gender and development.

Gender means doing things differently: Lessons from Oxfam's Women's Linking Project

Candida March

This article focuses on some of the learning points arising from Oxfam's Women's Linking Project (WLP), which ran from 1992 to 1994. Effective work on gender issues requires doing things very differently from conventional, mainstream ways of working. While this point is echoed by many of the contributors to this book, it was also a message that came with almost overwhelming clarity from the participants of the WLP.

The WLP was an ambitious and trail-blazing project, designed and co-ordinated by Oxfam GB's Gender Team (formerly GADU) as a key activity for Oxfam in the run-up to the Fourth UN Conference on Women, held in Beijing in 1995. It was part of a NGO process of enabling Southern women's voices to be heard in international forums; it was also part of an internal agenda within Oxfam, aiming to support gender work and to influence development policy and practice. The WLP ran virtually concurrently with the process of writing and agreeing Oxfam's formal Gender Policy, which had started in 1991 with a two-year consultation within Oxfam, and culminated in May 1993 with the ratification of the policy by Oxfam's trustees.

This article draws on my experience as the second co-ordinator, after Dimza Pityana, of the WLP, and on the review of the WLP carried out by De Beuk in 1994. Not only the tangible outputs and achievements of the WLP, but the actual process of the project, with its associated intangible outcomes of capacity-building and building solidarity, have valuable lessons to offer to Oxfam and other Northern funding agencies which aim to contribute to gender-equitable development. In the discussion which follows, I have therefore chosen to focus on the lessons to be learned from the project's methodology.[24]

Setting the scene

A central aim of the WLP was to stimulate linking and networking between women working on gender issues within and outside Oxfam, as an important first step in building mutual understanding and shared strategies. The project aimed to bring different constituencies together and begin to break down the barriers between North and South, between regions, between funding agency and women's organisations, between practitioner, activist, and academic, between feminist and mainstream. Those of us involved in planning and implementation were convinced that such a process is crucial to strengthening the momentum for development that promotes gender equity.

When the WLP began in 1992, Oxfam worked in over 70 countries world-wide. In our country programmes, work on gender issues varied enormously. In terms of quality, while some offices had put tremendous energy into working for gender equity, and many had valuable experience to share and were exploring new ideas and strategies, others had few reference points and were looking for support.

There was also considerable variation between country offices in their allocation of responsibility for gender issues. In some programmes, whole teams had taken responsibility for ensuring gender-fair development; in some, managers were actively promoting it. In others, gender issues were one of many responsibilities for a delegated project officer; or a project officer was appointed with a special remit to promote gender equality. The experience of gender-specialist project officers was patchy: many felt isolated within the team, some faced open hostility. In Asia, the Action for Gender Relations in Asia (AGRA) network was initially established as a support mechanism for staff, but became a key channel for work on gender and induction of new staff into gender analysis and concepts. In Africa, a network never got off the ground, so individual project officers were dependent on their managers for support. Many project officers reported that their gender-related activities seemed to be seen as peripheral to the office's main programme. They felt unable to influence central policy-making structures at Oxfam, since they felt excluded in terms of position and subject matter, and frequently language as well. It was clear that Oxfam's gender work could only become more effective and central when the position of those working on gender issues in international offices was strengthened, and their isolation reduced.

We in the Gender Team also wanted the WLP to be a catalyst for bringing staff from the country programmes into closer contact with women's organisations in North and South, with the international women's movement, and with feminist organisations. The build-up to the Beijing conference meant that it was particularly important that Southern organisations promoting gender awareness were supported in creating their own lobbying strategies. In some regions where Oxfam worked, the women's movement was nascent or weak; in others, there were organisations working at the cutting edge of policy and practice on women's rights, building on years of experience with a depth of understanding and analysis of the issues and ways of working that development organisations, still fairly new to working on 'women in development' and 'gender' issues, could rarely emulate. In a few Oxfam country offices, links with the women's movement were strong and mutually supportive, but in the majority of offices, women's organisations with a rights-based as opposed to needs-based, analysis were seen as outside the orbit of legitimate development: they were labelled too feminist, too urban, or too middle-class. Links with research institutions and resource centres focusing on women's issues also tended to be poor.

Related to the aim of increasing contact between overseas staff and the women's movement was that of strengthening ties between the Gender Team itself, situated in the Oxford head office, and women's organisations in both South and North. It was extremely difficult for us, at the time, to have direct contact with Southern women's groups, because such contact had to be brokered by hierarchical 'line management', stretching from Oxford, through our regional desks, to the country offices, before Southern organisations could be approached. Meanwhile, although we were linked with women's organisations in the UK which worked on international development issues, our relations with women's organisations working on UK and Irish issues were limited by the Gender Team's positioning and role as an advisory unit within Oxfam's International Division.[25]

From the outset, we recognised the incredible diversity of all our colleagues working on gender issues. We wanted the process of working together in the WLP to an affirmative and strengthening one, while offering challenges at an appropriate level. We were aware of the difficulties of crossing geographical and hierarchical distances, but we hoped that the process of working together through the WLP would forge a shared analysis that could be used to promote better work on gender, grounded in the experience of Oxfam and its partners, and influenced by Southern feminist analyses. Within this analysis, we aimed to compile a set of recommendations useful to all working on gender issues within Oxfam's orbit: recommendations that would contribute to developing gender-fair policies and programmes that would be sensitive to Southern women's interests.

Methodology[26]

The WLP initiated two processes. The first was a process of linking between Southern women's organisations, Oxfam staff, and UK-based women's groups. At the start of the WLP, eight Southern women visited over 20 UK organisations, including women's refuges, local-government information centres, and development agencies in March 1992. The process then led to four regional meetings at the end of 1993 in Africa, Asia, and Latin America, giving women's organisations and Oxfam partners the opportunity to share their work, their aims and hopes, and make recommendations for change. Ten regional meeting representatives attended a global meeting and an international conference for Oxfam staff and partners. Both of these were held in Thailand in February 1994.

The second process in the WLP was a review by Oxfam of its development practice. All participating Oxfam country offices were asked to review their gender work to date and the external context of their work from a gender perspective. In addition, they were asked to contribute a case study to the conference in Thailand, sharing lessons they had learned and their ideas on 'best practice' on gender work in their part of the programme. At the Thailand conference, 109 participants met to share their experiences, discuss best practice, assess Oxfam's work from the perspective of Southern women, and to make recommendations to Oxfam and like-minded agencies. Participants comprised gender project officers and other staff from country offices, staff and senior managers from Oxfam House, staff from sister agencies, resource people and delegates from Southern organisations. The conference drew on the insights not only of those present, but on seven world-renowned activists and researchers, who were asked to write key-note papers on their areas of expertise, to be used as a stimulus to discussion at the international conference.

Three models of change management

De Beuk's evaluation of the WLP usefully identified three models of change management. The first is the top-down approach: it holds that change is a rational, analytic process (De Beuk 1995, 44), involving pre-planning with clear objectives. Many working in Oxfam in the early 1990s perceived the organisation to be relying increasingly on this form of management, although in some respects the senior managers adopted a converse attitude of *laissez-faire*. This combination was particularly problematic in terms of trying to increase awareness of gender, which has both personal and political elements; where resistance to change can be so very strong. The second model of change identified in the evaluation saw change as a political process: 'The organisation consists of several parties with their own interests, who act politically and tactically in order to serve their own interests' (ibid., p.44). Finally, De Beuk argued that 'between these two extremes there is a third view, in which the objectives of the organisation are clear, and in which these objectives are translated to every level in the organisation. The different stakeholders in the organisation have their own interests, and they integrate these in the objectives' (ibid.). In this view, 'not only the objectives, but also the process are important parts of the strategy of change' (ibid.). This third model poses the general direction or framework and then facilitates and supports people to meet these objectives. Key to this is respecting different ways of doing things, and making the shift from prescription to participation. The project team's role then becomes that of levelling differences of opinion, building consensus, and facilitating change. De Beuk viewed the WLP as fitting into this third category, as a political process with clear objectives.

The challenges of the project methodology

Setting a general direction

As the De Beuk evaluation pointed out, process-orientated projects can be non-linear and difficult to plan. The WLP aimed to initiate dialogue between women from different constituencies on gender issues and identify ways in which we could work together for change. It pushed into uncharted territory. The WLP had a set of questions which themselves were open to being questioned, and which could not be answered until a later stage of the project. We recognised that one may enter dialogue with a particular aim, but that any successful dialogue means treating this aim flexibly. Dialogue is a continuous process, whose timetable and outcomes cannot be firmly predicted. It was important that the process should be shaped by the participation of the various interest groups. This needs a lot of time for debate, for reflection and realignment, for reviewing progress, re-checking the validity of initial assumptions, and changing strategies.

We also had another set of realities to deal with in the design of the WLP. We were working within an institutional context that limited the extent of mutual decision-making and designing. For example, proposals for methodology needed to be firm enough to allow for funding decisions to be made and resources allocated, and sufficiently well-formed to give participants and observers confidence in the project. We had to provide enough shape for people to decide whether they actually wanted to participate, and in what form; once we had made this clear, there were high risks associated with changing the proposal. The investment of time and energy needed to manage such a process was easy to underestimate, especially when planning across continents, cultures, languages, and hierarchical divides. Our success at consensus-building around objectives and strategies varied. One attempt to plan the project jointly with a core group of women from Southern organisations failed after all involved had put a lot of effort into it. This was very distressing for all involved.

In an organisation which was used to receiving messages in one of two forms (top-down instruction from the head office, or a *laissez-faire* support for the status quo), the more flexible methodology of the WLP was sometimes confusing for people. As the subsequent evaluation indicated, some participants felt over-directed and controlled, while others were uneasy, fearing that if they took up the challenge to do things their way, the WLP, or the Gender Team which was steering it, might then deem it 'wrong'. De Beuk's evaluation commented that such a project needed 'to respect people doing things in ways which are not its ways, as long as they led to the joint objectives … to shift from prescription to participation is a process as well and takes again time and effort.' (De Beuk 1995, p.47). Although this principle was extremely important, there were in practice many discussions and internal tensions within the Gender Team about what did constitute working towards the joint objectives, and how much diversity of approach we could really accommodate.

Even when we had been very clear about the boundaries, we needed to be open to being challenged like this. For instance, the regional meetings were intended as an opportunity for women from Southern organisations to meet to identify their priorities, and create their own strategies. It was not envisaged that Oxfam staff should take part. A general framework for the regional meetings was set, comprising clear criteria for participation, and guiding aims for the meetings. In addition a very non-directive facilitator's guide was written. The host offices were invited to choose external facilitators. The Latin America team considered the proposals, and felt that they wanted to change the profile of participants for their regional meeting, so that it was jointly for Oxfam staff and Southern women's organisations. We then had to debate the issues with them, and investigate whether this could still work in the overall co-ordinated efforts. It was decided that it could, and the meeting was extremely rewarding, starting some very interesting joint activities which had real momentum.

Complexities and 'mixed messages'

Projects like the WLP deal with change, which implies complexities and contra-dictions. These lead to 'mixed messages' which are difficult to deal with, and can cause a lot of tension; yet, according to De Beuk, they are part and parcel of the third view of change. Where these messages can be untangled through further thought, attention must be given to ensure that this actually occurs. We learned that where this cannot happen straight away, instead of trying to claim coherence, it is important to admit openly that the messages are mixed, to accept the fact, and to allow time and energy for debating the problems. Where possible, it is impor-tant to make the various actors' priorities and assumptions explicit, and to define the boundaries that determine each actor's freedom to challenge the process.

The regional meetings required us to put a lot of thought into 'unmixing' messages. While, as stated above, these meetings were intended as an opportunity for women from Southern organisations to prioritise and devise strategies for change, at the same time, participants were invited to spend time considering what Oxfam in particular should be doing to support their efforts further. It was important to identify that there was a potential tension between the two messages. After debate and discussion with the core group who were steering the planning of the meetings, we agreed that the priority at the regional meetings was to ensure that the participants had freedom to use the opportunity as they saw fit. To support this end, they were led by Southern facilitators who were external to Oxfam. In making this decision, we had to be prepared to accept the possibility that making recommendations to Oxfam would not be seen by the participants as an appropriate thing to do.

Process and outcome

Those of us involved in planning the WLP aimed for both 'hard', visible outputs (for example, in the form of case studies or recommendations to Oxfam), and 'soft', intangible outputs (for example, increased cross-regional learning and support) throughout the process of the project. The key was to find the appropriate balance at each stage of the project between planning for hard outputs, and building a process which encouraged and supported participants to take on the aims of the project and work with these themselves, in their own way.

An example of how we tried to balance tangible and intangible outcomes is the way in which in-country reviews of programme work and case studies of best practice were conceptualised in the project. These were seen not only as the basis of learning and creating best practice, but also as support to enable staff in our country programmes to build their own capacity to work on gender issues. The methodology for the case studies and reviews was designed in the hope that both new and seasoned 'gender campaigners' would benefit from the exercise. Each would have a chance to reflect and research, to be stretched in a way that suited their own professional development. The De Beuk evaluation found that this aim had been met on the whole: most of the country offices reported that doing the reviews had been very helpful. However, we were very aware in the planning that a natural consequence of this process would be that the reviews and case studies would be subjective and of variable quality, which would make it harder to to meet an aim of creating a unified output, since the information given in them could not easily be compared or drawn together.

At the regional meetings we invited the representatives from Southern organisations to recommend ways in which funding agencies could contribute to furthering North-South co-operation. By asking women who had a relationship with our country offices, we were looking for greater accountability on the part of our field offices, who would be expected to respond to the recommendations and put some of them into action. In addition, although a unified set of guidelines would be useful for centralised processes, we were also acutely aware that gender issues vary greatly in different contexts. It was important that the process strengthened a contextual understanding as well.

Working with difference and power differentials

The central rationale for the WLP was that dialogue was needed between different constituencies working on women's issues, to tap into the huge potential for mutual learning and support. The WLP was notable for the rich variety of perspectives, experiences, and beliefs held by its participants. Participants from both inside and outside Oxfam represented so many different nationalities, languages, cultural contexts, constituencies, and working styles that it was essential to see diversity of identity as a key to the project.

But this meant dialogue across power divides: funding agencies and Southern organisations; men and women; people from the South and North; different races and religions; Oxfam corporate management and project officers. For many involved in the project, dialogue across these power divides was very new and uncomfortable. There was a legacy of misunderstandings, or even mutual mistrust. To enter into dialogue means to face the mistrust, the differences, and the challenges: to discover areas where it is not possible to work together as well as areas where co-operation is possible. It is not cosy, nor predictable.

An awareness of these issues informed the planning of the project. For example, not only did the facilitators at the global meeting and international conference themselves each come from different cultures, but they were all skilled in managing diversity. This led to a conference methodology which used a range of techniques to encourage participants to step outside their experience, to expand their own willingness to respect other's learning processes, and their willingness to learn from each other and to discuss their own values. Techniques such as role plays, personal testimonies, and mixed group discussions were all used to facilitate opportunities for participation through listening and speaking, giving power to all to join in in their own way, in their own time. (For a full account of the methodology of the international conference, see Suarez 1994.)

In every activity and communication, we had to try to create a feeling of the project as a neutral borderland between established territories. Each individual and constituency needed to feel that their views were validated, in order to be able to listen to others without becoming defensive, or to revise long-held beliefs and strategies if needed. Even with forethought, we in the WLP sometimes did not achieve the right balance, which brought feelings of suspicion, anger, or misunderstanding to the surface. At times, we were over-keen to get agreement in order to achieve a concrete result, and so pushed too hard.

In addition, there were apparent disparities of power, given the fact that the project was co-ordinated by the Gender Team at head office, and set within a Northern funding agency. In retrospect I think the Gender Team needed to communicate more about the role of the team in co-ordinating the WLP, about our perspectives as well as the project itself. In particular, we needed to be clear about the tensions between the relative powerlessness of the Gender Team as an advisory unit (which did not have management status) and the fact that we were located at the centre of a Northern funding agency. It was the latter which tended to dominate the perceptions of the country offices and Southern organisations.

Constraints on openness

This last point brings me to the final set of issues concerning transparency. For the the WLP's potential to be fully realised, I felt that we needed to be very open about the difficult issues we encountered: failures, weaknesses, uncertainties, and unresolved issues. But the very learning and openness that I wanted to promote created difficulties. Tina Wallace confirms in her article in this book that this issue is familiar to anyone who works on challenging issues within organisations. For us in the WLP, there were a number of easily identifiable reasons for the difficulty:

The project's very size and high profile were part of its strength: involving people who would not otherwise be involved, giving a sense of momentum for change, creating a strong message. However, it also increased the pressure to be seen to be right. We felt we needed to 'talk' up the project to the organisation, in order to secure funding for the project and follow-up, and increase the chances of having the work of all the men and women involved taken seriously.

Confidence in sharing failures needs an environment which encourages and supports risk-taking and genuine learning, and which honours lessons learned from failure of innovative approaches as much as those learned from success.

In order to distil many of the lessons learned, we needed time for reflection on such intense processes after the event, and then we needed time to promote those lessons. For this, considerable follow-up was needed.

Evaluating projects focusing on 'process'

The WLP evaluation stated: 'to do justice to the WLP strategy a new, more dynamic view on measuring the output of this project has to be developed ...' (De Beuk, p.48). A theme throughout work on gender issues (repeated in many of the articles in this book) is the need to measure the impact of development projects.

While the impact of any particular development intervention is extremely hard to measure, social development is particularly slow, complex, and difficult to analyse. Consequently, pushing for the production of short-term, tangible measurements as an essential part of impact assessment can have very negative effects on interventions which aim to do the lengthy work of changing gender relations.

Due to the long-term nature of social development, projects like the WLP should perhaps be evaluated several times after the project's official ending, in addition to monitoring during the project's life. Without this type of measurement, how can we judge the effectiveness of such processes, of networking and linking, of starting dialogue and building staff capacity? However, with so many urgent demands on the funds available for development which are administered by organisations such as Oxfam, it takes a very serious commitment to and belief in the value of the project to agree a continuing evaluation of a project which has no current life (even where this evaluation can be embedded in an existing process such as strategic planning).

Who defines the criteria for evaluation?

Who determines the criteria for evaluation, and how? Focusing a project on linking people to exchange information and strategise is a long-term investment in building capacity and in empowerment, rather than a direct 'tool' of development which will deliver tangible results in a measured period. Such projects are an investment in the future. De Beuk suggested that in order to assess the impact of the WLP, success criteria identified by different participants of the WLP should be used as the starting point. In this way, the method of impact assessment would reflect the commitment to enabling participants to determine their own goals: 'one of the basics of the WLP is that it is important to work from a basis of strengthening institutions, and the position of women in them. This means to facilitate and not to impose. To do this, Oxfam needs to have respect for, and pay attention to, helping people to secure their own goals' (De Beuk 1995, 48).

Handing over responsibility to participants to determine success against their own indicators is, of course, particularly challenging if the funders are unsure about the participants' indicators of success. For example, the De Beuk evaluation showed that the solidarity provided within the WLP for many project officers was highly valued by them, but much less valued by top decision-makers. More generally, those involved in the WLP at all levels within Oxfam felt that it succeeded in strengthening voices that were marginal to Oxfam. These voices called for change, and were in many ways challenging the decisions of senior managers in Oxfam. Should Oxfam count that as a success? The more that an issue like women's subordination highlights needs that are misunderstood by decision-makers or viewed as of marginal importance, the more acute this problem becomes.

Evaluating innovation and risk-taking

The WLP moved into many uncharted areas for Oxfam, and combined many accepted ways of working. An important lesson is that, in addition to measuring the outcomes of a project, development workers need to consider how to evaluate the cost of innovation and risk-taking. This would identify the time, cost, and energy spent on a project that is exploring new or difficult issues, and introducing untried procedures. The WLP was a pioneer project in terms of fostering information-sharing and learning across the regions where Oxfam works, rather than channelling information up to head office and down into another region. As these new ways of working become more accepted within Oxfam, procedures will develop to facilitate them, a body of experience will be accumulated, and cross-regional learning will become easier to understand for participants.

Also to be evaluated would be the time, cost, and energy needed for working 'against the grain', in terms of overcoming resistance to certain types of change. As the different stages of the WLP got underway, an enormous amount of the gender Team's energy and resources was used in this way.

> To make a project like the WLP a success, support and co-operation within the already existing organisation is imperative. However, this same organisation often experiences innovative projects as threatening and as criticism upon their own work. When the topic is gender, people become defensive even more quickly. The innovation is seen as not only criticism upon their work, but also against their whole person … In gender projects, the same struggle has to be fought for over and over, every step of the way. (De Beuk 1995, p.52)

Resistance to change is inherent in any organisation. Before an organisation or the individuals in it will shift certain beliefs, it seems that much energy is expended without achieving any apparent change. But where a critical momentum is gained, there will be a dramatic shift, and what was formerly counter to the culture is suddenly accepted as common sense. Issues such as opposition to violence against women, and the need for cross-regional learning appear to have begun to make that essential shift within Oxfam. How can we measure the degree to which the WLP, which championed those causes among others, contributed to that shift?

Conclusion

'Changes in an organisation are generally about one or more of the following issues: methods and means; strategy and goals; culture and ideology; and identity' (De Beuk, p43). The WLP worked for change across all these fronts. It was about building on the diversity of experience, identity, and perception that makes up the context in which we work. The project was about learning and linking across hierarchies and geographical boundaries. It was a project which emphasised process as much as outputs, at a time when there was increased emphasis on short-term, visible achievements. It reached out to new constituencies for development agencies: feminist organisations and women's movements; groups often viewed with open animosity. It explored new forms of North-South co-operation, part-nership, and horizontal accountability (particularly to Southern organisations). It was an attempt to empower and give a platform to the marginalised, and strengthen the impact of groups and ways of thinking that had little leverage on Oxfam's learning or policy-making fora. It explored issues such as women's human rights, women's reproductive rights, and violence against women, at a time when they were still not accepted by many as legitimate development issues.

The evaluation stated that the strategy of the project was innovative and challenging for Oxfam and clearly contributed to its formulated objectives. So not only do messages, outputs and achievements of the project have importance, but the strengths and weaknesses of the project itself offer an enormous amount of institutional learning about processes within agencies like Oxfam in general, and about the process of challenging unequal gender relations.

About the author

Candida March read engineering at university and trained as a manager. She joined Oxfam's Gender and Development Unit in 1989, and worked in a number of jobs: editor, writer, researcher, gender adviser, and co-ordinator of the Women's Linking Project. She now combines freelance work on gender and development with facilitating and managing change in a health and safety company. She is co-author of *A Guide to Gender-Analysis Frameworks* (1999, Oxford: Oxfam).

References

De Beuk (1995), 'An evaluation of the Oxfam Women's Linking Project (WLP): An important step in the process' (written by Dorien de Wit), internal document, Oxfam.

Suarez, M. (1994), 'Treading new paths: the methodology of the Women Linking for Change Conference', in *Gender and Development*, Vol. 2, No. 3.

Reardon, G. (1995), *Power and Process: A Report from the Women Linking for Change Conference*, Thailand, Oxford: Oxfam.

O'Connell, H. (1994), *Dedicated Lives*, Oxford: Oxfam.

Participation and management in South Asia: Gender transformation in the AGRA South network[27]

Kanchan Sinha

Introduction

There have been, broadly speaking, two separate 'streams' through which Oxfam GB has undertaken its internal gender sensitisation. The first may be called the 'participatory stream', in which attempts were made to involve the staff and create an environment in which our objectives to address gender concerns could be achieved through participatory fora and networks, such as Action for Gender Relations Asia (AGRA), which have enabled staff to debate the issues. The other 'stream' could be called the 'management stream', denoting the integration of goals which incorporate gender concerns, and the institution of appropriate practices into line-managers' responsibilities. Both streams are inter-related and complementary, and both are necessary. While both are to be credited with remarkable successes, each has run into its own set of barriers and constraints. I cannot undertake a comprehensive review of the entire experience in this article. Instead I will be selective, and focus on staff perceptions of some of the main problems which have emerged. Most of these focus on the management stream.

AGRA is a central component of the democratic and participatory stream of work on gender in Asia. It began in 1986 as a grassroots network, run by and for Oxfam staff working on gender issues. All staff members of Oxfam in the Asia regional offices are automatically members of AGRA. AGRA's aims are to foster equal relations between men and women within Oxfam; within Oxfam regional offices in Asia; and in the communities with whom Oxfam works. Its intention has been to provide a broad-based forum to address gender issues. Activities have included information-sharing and staff development through thematic work-shops, opportunities for networking, and documentation on gender issues. In 1988, AGRA was divided into AGRA East (for staff in East Asia) and AGRA South (for those in South Asia),[28] mainly to reduce technical difficulties such as travel.

Like AGRA itself, this article has its origin in the participatory stream. It is based on the findings of a research survey which was conducted among Oxfam staff as part of the restructuring of AGRA South. Restructuring AGRA South was first discussed in 1995, because the group felt that it was losing steam and needed rejuvenation. Oxfam GB's shift to a decentralised organisational structure provided further impetus for change from the management stream. A comprehensive survey of the entire AGRA South membership in India was undertaken in 1997.[29] This gave us a picture of how Oxfam staff in India viewed gender issues. Through a detailed questionnaire and discussion meetings in all the regional offices in India, issues such as Oxfam's Gender Policy and its implementation, processes to internalise gender analysis, the role of AGRA South, and the interface between AGRA South and Oxfam's management, were discussed. The questions were broad, and the discussions were allowed to flow freely.

The discussions were the most effective part of the survey, because (after some prodding) they brought the real issues into sharp focus. One-to-one discussions with those who were willing were particularly important, and in a number of cases provided insights that were impossible to obtain during group discussions. The whole process, which required 15 days of 'quality time' spread over little more than a month, was a revealing experience. The findings of this research survey were not confined to the experience of AGRA South: many of the issues raised related more widely to the issues of management and participation, and I will focus on these in the following.

The flip side of mainstreaming gender

Staff recalled that there was a time, not so long ago, when gender issues were peripheral concerns, and talk of gender analysis was more likely to invite an amused response, if not outright ridicule. How things have changed! Gender inequalities are now a 'mainstream' issue which no one in Oxfam, or indeed the development sector, can ignore. The survey confirmed that everyone approaches the issue of gender with due care and attention, and speaks about it in a politically correct manner. This transformation in behaviour has come about through a complex and multi-faceted process, which has unfolded through many twists and turns. Formulating Oxfam's corporate Gender Policy, and setting in motion mechanisms to implement and internalise it, have resulted in successes which are commonly acknowledged, not least in this book.

There is, however, a flip side. Paradoxically, our survey findings point to a widespread feeling among staff in India that the situation on the ground may have worsened in many respects. This apparent contradiction has disappointed those members of staff who invested time and energy to ensure that gender concerns were fully integrated into the organisation. In a number of instances, the gender activists who took part in the India survey (who were often the 'gender lead persons' of respective AGRA chapters) expressed their dissatisfaction with the prevailing atmosphere. Gender policies and implementation strategies have sometimes resulted in a formalised commitment to address gender concerns, flaunted without being internalised or put into day-to-day practice. While at the grassroots, 'gender' was now a much better-known and commonly used word, some felt that there was hardly any improvement in the way the actual issues are addressed. Added to this, they perceived a diminished interest in the affairs of AGRA South. The survey findings particularly highlighted a feeling among staff that at managerial levels, concern about with gender issues was not translated into actual practice.

In course of the research survey, many among the staff reminisced about the 1980s and early 1990s, when they said debates on gender issues had been more lively, involving, and practical, including diverse aspects of life and work. There used to be attempts to integrate the relatives of staff into the discussions. There used to be meetings and get-togethers. Of course, staff also remembered other less positive aspects: many a time, advocates of gender concerns were ridiculed or ignored, while the attempts to bring family and household matters into the discussions on gender issues sometimes caused friction. But overall, staff remembered lively concern, informality, and spontaneous activism, which had a positive impact. They felt that AGRA had played a very important role in fostering an atmosphere which encouraged informal modes of gender activism and interaction. In one of the offices, for example, a male staff member mentioned a woman project officer who had shown care and concern for his wife, and had made sure that she attended the family get-togethers of the staff and felt at ease.

Staff involved in the survey felt that this contrasted with the current situation. Now, Gender-Policy implementation is the responsibility of line management: it is part of evaluations and performance reviews, and managers are accountable to their managers. As the implementation has become more mechanistic, the process is being perceived as over-bureaucratised. The survey found that, as a result, staff have tended to dissociate themselves from responsibility for implementing the policy. Women staff, who have suffered and continue to suffer on account of gender inequity and insensitivity, feel frustrated because they perceive that conditions are hardly changing. Oxfam's policies and systems have succeeded in making gender relations a subject on which most people try to speak correctly, but they say that this has sometimes resulted in driving the real problems underground. Staff committed to addressing gender issues in their work and in the workplace feel pressurised and vulnerable to rumours, and are resentful because their expectations are unmet. Some other staff members, particularly at lower grades, feel that one more weapon has been placed in the hands of managers, which can be used against them. Some male staff have a growing sense of resentment that a process of reverse discrimination has begun against them. There is muted, resentful talk of gender sensitivity being traded for incompetence, and of people being appointed to coveted posts just because they wear sarees or skirts, so that Oxfam can display its gender sensitivity through its employment statistics.

Oxfam's programme work, too — namely the relationship with its partners and their joint intervention on the development scene — is not free from such paradoxes. The research survey reported that as Oxfam's emphasis on addressing gender issues in development projects has become well-known, the partner organisations' leadership have quickly adapted by formally proclaiming their gender sensitivity, and changing the organisational structure. It seems that such gender sensitivity has become a practical imperative for those who have to run NGOs and hunt for funds. The situation on the ground, however, is changing relatively slowly, and there is growing cynicism among staff in partner organisations, particularly women.

To manage or to lead?

The above should not be taken to imply that participants in the AGRA South survey in India felt that Oxfam should not have formulated a Gender Policy, or that the line management should not have been entrusted with the responsibility to implement it. Both these decisions have had a very positive impact on the way in which gender issues are addressed within Oxfam. I have deliberately chosen in this article to focus on some of the more negative aspects of this process, and examine their specific sources.

At least one of the major sources of contradiction highlighted in our survey is not related to gender issues alone: this is the perceived gap between management and programme staff, which seems to be rooted in doubt about the changing nature of Oxfam as an organisation. In common with other international funding agencies, over the past decade, Oxfam has put a higher premium on efficiency, which some staff fear may discount or de-emphasise the value of grassroots activism and participation. There is no simple answer to how this fear has come about, but certain contributing factors are clear enough and were highlighted in the research survey. It is common sense that it is not possible to preach to others what one does not practise oneself. Although terms such as corporate management, business plans, and so on are prevalent within Oxfam, it is far from being a regular kind of corporation. Altruistic goals cannot be pursued by the same methods which are employed in the pursuit of profits and self-interest. Managers in organisations such as Oxfam must be leaders, committed to the value-system and the goals of the organisation.

In course of conducting the AGRA South survey in India, I came across numerous examples where mistrust between managers and their staff, fuelled by perceptions of differences between stated values and actual behaviour, seemed to have harmed the promotion of the Gender Policy.

Another lesson from the survey was that a manager's inaction where action is required can also be extremely damaging. In any kind of organisation, but particularly in organisations like Oxfam, complaints which are brought to the managers of any form or degree of sexual harassment, must be cleared up in a clean, transparent, and just manner. If such a matter is not dealt with, the office atmosphere is harmed for a long time: the parties concerned either have to resign and leave, or continue to face each other in an atmosphere of animosity, prejudice, and hypocrisy. It is worth noting that although there undoubtedly have been instances of sexual harassment, even if mild ones in many people's opinion, there has not been, according to the responses to our survey, a single example of transparent punishment and reprimand.

Face to face with reality 'on the ground'

One of the major findings of our survey points towards a particularly painful aspect of reality 'on the ground'. Often, the instances of gender-related insensitivity or misconduct reported in the survey come from staff at lower levels of the organisation, who do not work directly on Oxfam's programme. In some ways, it is simpler to deal with the case of a manager or a senior staff member who displays insensitivity to gender issues. We all reflect the values of surrounding society, and the working atmosphere in organisations like Oxfam, in spite of the shortcomings one often points out, is like an island of relative sensitivity and awareness. Peculiar problems seem to arise at the interface of such organisations and the surrounding society.

One instance may be mentioned to illustrate this kind of problem. The survey meeting in one of the offices was effectively held up for half a day because one of the participants insisted that first the word 'gender' must be explained to him, and that a vernacular equivalent must be provided. On the face of it, this may appear a perfectly legitimate and honest demand. But it was clear enough that things were not that simple. This person went on to be the most vocal participant in the meeting, dominating everyone else and heaping ridicule on 'urban, woolly-headed, liberal gender-mongers' who would never understand the culture and traditions of the people. He made frequent references to the 'foolishness' and 'naïvety' of two female project officers and some gender trainers. While ostensibly sounding earthy and pragmatic, he seemed to me to be putting up a resolute defence of his own gender insensitivity.

It is difficult to deal with such problems, and more so for a foreign funding agency working in a society where it has to pay special attention to popular sensitivities. This difficulty, however, should not stop us from acknowledging the problem. Only after this may understanding follow, and a thoughtful approach may emerge which can help in planning effective interventions. If we ignore reality and indulge in wishful thinking, problems only get further complicated.

Gender rights and affirmative action

During the research, some examples of unexpected effects of the Gender Policy were cited. One question that arose in a number of contexts was whether the facilities and concessions provided to women staff on account of their needs as mothers and carers for their families do actually meet their desired objectives. As stated earlier, all of us live in societies where gender issues remain largely unaddressed. If a woman faces discrimination and exploitation in her household, how can Oxfam ensure as her employer that facilities and concessions offered to her on grounds of her gender identity do not benefit the perpetrators of gender inequality in such households? One participant in the survey raised the question of 'paternity leave'. If the man gets paternity leave as a right, but is of no help to his wife in this period, can it be said to have served a useful purpose? Other examples were cited, including the the case of nuclear families where both husband and wife work, and are conscious and vocal about their rights concerning gender issues. There was a view that the burden of running their household (taking care of their children and so on) should not be transferred indirectly to their workplace. What was coming through loud and clear from such examples was the fact that if the question of gender equity needs to be considered in an unselfish and enlightened manner. If the prevailing conditions in wider society are not taken into account, Oxfam and other similar organisations will carry the burden of gender insensitivity and gender-blindness alone, and may end up being exploited by those who assert their rights in a self-centred manner.

Concluding remarks

I have pointed out some of the complexities of gender transformation in an organisation such as Oxfam. As stated previously, I do not purport to have given a comprehensive review of Oxfam's experience of gender issues — which is far from being a tale merely of difficulties and limitations.

I have concentrated on four aspects of the findings of the AGRA survey of Oxfam's India staff. First, with gender equity emerging as a universally recognised concern within Oxfam, a flip-side has also begun to appear, endangering the cause with dilution, resistance, and subversion. Second, staff have moved from considering gender issues as their concern via participation, to a somewhat one-sided reliance on the 'management stream' for achieving gender objectives. This carries with it severe limitations and constraints, and I suggest that there are lessons here for both managers and staff. Implementation of the Gender Policy through line management must be accompanied and complemented by efforts to release the creative energies of the 'participatory stream', through democratic structures like AGRA. Third, the complex interface between organisations like Oxfam and surrounding societies, particularly in the Third World, must be mapped carefully in order to devise effective strategies for intervention. Finally, it is my view that women in organisations like Oxfam need to pursue an enlightened course and refrain from narrow and self-centred assertion of their rights as mothers and carers, in the interest of the larger cause. Otherwise, the counter-winds of resistance and subversion will gain strength.

I can inform the reader that the process of restructuring AGRA South, of which this research survey was a part, has yet to reach a successful conclusion. The challenge before managers is to take the initiative and assume leadership by empowering and strengthening the 'participatory stream; if this eventually limits managers' own rights and responsibilities, that should be taken as its success and as a desired and happy outcome.

About the author

Kanchan Sinha joined Oxfam GB in 1993 and is its Regional Representative in North India, based at Lucknow. She is also the co-ordinator of AGRA South. She has been active in the women's movement in India since 1984, working for a number of women's organisations in Gujarat and Uttar Pradesh. She holds a PhD in Philosophy and has taught at Gorakhpur University, India; from 1978–79, Kanchan was a Research Associate at Boston University, USA.

Notes to section IV

1 'Regionalisation' is a process of decentralisation, in which decision-making power is devolved from Oxfam House to the regional offices. In this article, the process of regionalisation refers to the shift in Oxfam's ways of working from a country-based approach to one which encompasses a wider geopolitical region (in this case, the Middle East/Maghreb) and focuses on clear issues which cut across the region.

2 Formerly known as the Gender and Development Unit (GADU), and currently referred to as the Gender and Learning Team (GALT).

3 This close working relationship has weakened as a new structure has emerged at Oxfam's head office, in which advisors no longer have specific responsibility for a region. This has resulted in the loss of commitment and support which was such a vital part of the transformation which has taken place in the Middle East programme.

4 The Social Relations Approach, developed in Naila Kabeer (1994), *Reversed Realities: Gender Hierarchies in Development Thought*, London: Verso.

5 See A. Ammaoui, 'Overview of Middle East/Maghreb region', paper prepared for the Middle East Regional Conference, December 1995.

6 Representing women's groups and NGOs from Lebanon, Iraq, Egypt, Algeria, and Morocco.

7 The UN Convention on the Elimination of All Forms of Discrimination Against Women (1979).

8 To ratify a convention with 'reservations' is to agree to abide by the convention with the exception of certain clauses or sections that a government finds disagreeable — a tactic often used by resistant governments to render the convention meaningless and impossible to implement.

9 See Sue Smith's contribution to this book, 'Making Visible the Invisible', for further discussion of this.

10 For a further discussion of Beijing as a forum at which many concerns were discussed, please see the article by Lucy Muyoyeta in this volume.

11 For further discussion of Oxfam International, please see Ellen Sprenger and Diane Biray Gregorio's article in this volume.

12 As of mid-1998, the following Oxfams are affiliates: Community Aid Abroad (Australia), Intermón (Spain), Novib (the Netherlands), Oxfam America (United States), Oxfam Belgium, Oxfam Canada, Oxfam Hong Kong, Oxfam New Zealand, Oxfam Great Britain, Oxfam Ireland and Oxfam Quebec. Special focal areas include: programme harmonisation in a select number of countries and regions; humanitarian assistance and emergency relief; international advocacy; joint marketing and media strategies and the piloting of information technologies. In an effort to be truly international, OI is seeking to include affiliates from the global South.

13 With 'diverse backgrounds' we mean people who have unequal and disadvantaged positions in society on the basis of sex, race, age, religion, ethnicity, sexual preference, physical ability, or other. Although the OI group agreed that diversity is a significant issue, it also pointed out that to address diversity properly requires a base of knowledge which sometimes (but not always) coincides with gender expertise. The working group adopted the issue of diversity, but at the same time emphasised the need for individual Oxfams to explore the issue.

14 The OI decision-making body to which the working group on gender and diversity reports is also the OI body with the largest number of women. Although it is difficult to prove, it would be very interesting to find out whether there is indeed a relationship between quantity — the number of women in a group, and quality — the proactive role this group plays in promoting gender equity and diversity in OI.

15 Gender-blind: an organisation with no recognition of gender differentials; where assumptions include biases in favour of existing gender relations; in which hardly any change, or learning, is taking place.

16 Gender-aware: an organisation where there is some awareness of gender issues and commitment to include women's needs and priorities into analysis, planning, and programming; but which lacks systematic implementation; where a process of change and learning is taking place, but is limited to a small group of people.

17 Gender-responsive: an organisation whose interventions intend to transform existing distributions to create a more balanced relationship between women and men; an organisation which can show evidence of good gender practice; where a process of institutional learning and change is taking place.

18 As endorsed by the OI Programme Directors (Brussels, 13–17 October 1997) and Executive Directors (The Hague, 30–31 October 1997).

19 The authors work in the field of organisational change and development, with a specific focus on women and gender issues. This article provides an opportunity for both practitioners to reflect on their experiences of working

on the development and implementation of a joint fund, the Gender and Development (GAD) fund, supported by Oxfam Canada and Novib. The views expressed in this article are based on the experiences of the two authors and are not the official views of Oxfam Canada and Novib.

20 For more on Oxfam International and its member organisations, see Ellen Sprenger and Diane Biray Gregorio in this volume. See also note 12.

21 The DNW currently consists of representatives from: FORD, C.S. Mott Foundation, Interfund, Oxfam Canada-Novib (via the GAD fund), the Transitional National Development Trust, the Open Society Foundation and the British Council.

22 Where linkages have been made (visits of the GAD fund co-ordinator to Oxfam Canada and Oxfam GB) these have been initiated from the South and not vice versa.

23 See Ellen Sprenger and Diane Biray Gregorio in this volume.

24 The results, messages and outcomes of the project are written up elsewhere: see references at the end of the article.

25 At the time of writing, this situation has changed, because Oxfam GB now has an anti-poverty programme in the UK (see Geraldine Terry's article in this volume).

26 The methodology of the WLP is described more fully in 'Women linking for change: Oxfam's Women's Linking Project' in *Focus on Gender* Vol. 2, No. 3, 1994, Oxfam (UK/I).

27 AGRA: Action for Gender Relations in Asia, an Oxfam staff network.

28 Within South Asia, AGRA has chapters in Afghanistan, Bangladesh, India, Nepal, Pakistan, and Sri Lanka. Within India there are nine chapters, one in each office of Oxfam's programme in India.

29 The survey is intended to reach the entire membership of AGRA South, but has so far been completed only in India and later in Nepal.

V

Building capacity

Introduction to section V

The importance of building staff capacity to work on gender issues, which includes training, learning from experience, and sharing good practice, is addressed in this section. Jan Seed was employed within Oxfam GB's specialist gender unit at head office as a gender trainer, soon after it was set up. In her article, she records the early successes and failures of gender training as a means of integrating gender into the organisation's life and work. In Oxfam at that time, as in many other 'mainstream' development organisations, training was seen by senior managers as a trouble-free, technical 'fix' which would be readily taken up by all, as a one-stop method of integrating gender. In their article, Fenella Porter and Ines Smyth bring the debate on the use of gender training up-to-date, concluding that it must be part of a broader strategy for organisational transformation.

Publications like this one are a key part of this broader strategy, offering a method of sharing good practice and learning points with other organisations and individuals working towards similar goals. In her article, Caroline Sweetman looks at publishing as a feminist strategy, emphasising how publishing about women and gender issues must be seen as both an outcome, and a process of empowerment in itself. Publications also play a role in advocating gender-sensitive development practice: Deborah Eade's article looks at the challenges involved in re-writing Oxfam GB's definitive *Handbook of Development and Relief* from an unambiguous gender perspective, and argues that all too often, integrating a gender analysis into development policy and practice is seen as an optional add-on.

Sue Smith looks at the importance of documentation and communication, and her own role as 'resources officer' in Oxfam GB's specialist gender unit. Her article reflects the importance of documentation, resource centres, and networking to the development of women's movements world-wide, valuing, recording, and sharing their own knowledge and experience outside the mainstream.

In her article, Rajni Khanna looks at staff development, stressing the value of developing knowledge and experience on gender issues. She records the effect that a postgraduate course on gender analysis has had on her work, and on her role as a manager in an Oxfam GB country office.

From the slipstream to the mainstream: Incorporating gender into *The Oxfam Handbook of Development and Relief*

Deborah Eade

Oxfam's publishing on development and humanitarian issues is a means of distilling and communicating its experience and concerns. The prime aim is to influence thinking and practice within the professional development community in its broadest sense. 'Going public' also exposes Oxfam to the external scrutiny and judgement that form part of its wider accountability to its 'stakeholders'. And internally, the publishing programme represents a major link in the institutional learning cycle, serving to crystallise critical lessons so that these feed into subsequent work.

What is often overlooked, however, is that the very act of writing is a collective learning process, particularly in a Northern funding agency. First, because its experience does not truly 'belong' to Oxfam or to any other outsider, but rather to the people and organisations in whose lives it has intervened. Second, because any institutional wisdom is a product of the work and thinking not of individuals but of generations of colleagues and counterparts worldwide. And third, because the process of drafting and peer-review itself encourages discussion and analysis: 'learning organisations' should create an environment in which their members can both give and receive constructive criticism.

Producing a publication also forces an organisation to confront its own inconsistencies and woolly thinking. Differences of approach can easily be tolerated, overlooked, or concealed when an organisation works in over 70 countries around the world. Open debate on such matters reflects a healthy state of affairs — and can make for a lively book. But what if the discrepancies reveal serious gaps between rhetoric and reality, between policy and practice? What if an organisation says that it believes and does one thing, while its staff actually believe and do something quite different — and not only different, but in implicit or open defiance of policy? What if it just doesn't know whether it is really doing what it says it wants to do, and has no reliable way of finding out? True, organisations such as Oxfam generally produce books only on those subjects in which they feel confident. Nevertheless, the process of writing inevitably contributes to policy development even on 'safe' topics, if only because it forces the issue in certain areas.

In late 1991, Suzanne Williams and I took over responsibility for co-editing *The Oxfam Handbook of Development and Relief*, a revised edition of Oxfam's 1985 flagship publication, *The Field Directors' Handbook*. Work had commenced some six months before, and we were taken on simply to wrap up the process so that the book could come out during Oxfam's 50th anniversary celebrations in 1992. We were keen to embrace the challenge. Suzanne, a feminist anthropologist with extensive experience in Southern Africa and Latin America, had written the section on women in the earlier *Handbook*, and was the intellectual author of Oxfam's Gender and Development Unit (GADU). When our job-share began, she was also about to start work on *The Oxfam Gender Training Manual*. I too had worked for Oxfam in Mexico and Central America throughout most of the 1980s, though somewhat as a closet feminist.[1] The right to 'come out' on gender issues was, therefore, an immense relief and a chance to revisit my own experiences in a more up-front way. The wish to produce a *Handbook* which was firmly grounded in gender analysis — and which would make this accessible to colleagues and counterparts alike — was our main reason for getting involved in the project. Oxfam's Gender Policy soon promised to make such commitment a matter of professional duty, albeit a very pleasant one.

In the event, as we shall see, things were to turn out very differently. Instead of editing existing work, we ended up writing virtually the entire book from scratch. Placing limits on the extra time and resources required became our managers' over-riding concern, even, as we found, at the expense of jettisoning the commitment to ensure that the *Handbook* was fully in line with Oxfam's Gender Policy.

External reviews of the *Handbook* have consistently praised its success in demonstrating the relevance of gender analysis to all aspects of development and humanitarian work. Ironically, however, in spite of its ground-breaking attempt to take gender analysis as its point of departure, the *Handbook* is not generally seen or presented as one of Oxfam's gender titles. What follows is a reflection on our experience of co-authoring this triple-decker monster — not on the relentless struggles of trying to do so in the midst of constant restructuring within Oxfam's International Division over the 1991–94 period, but on the problems we encountered in ensuring that gender was properly 'mainstreamed' throughout the book. This experience throws light on the specialisation versus mainstreaming debate, and demonstrates that practice and policy will reflect each other only if a large and constant investment is made in ensuring that they do.

First, some history

1985 marked a watershed in Oxfam's history. After 40 years, it had decided to put money behind its belief that gender power relations were the key to much of the poverty, distress, and suffering that it sought to relieve. Oxfam had become convinced, largely through the determination of a group of (mainly) women staff, that social and economic injustice could not be understood without taking into account the relations between men and women; and that these relations were themselves the cause of much avoidable human misery, pain, and oppression. The Gender and Development Unit (GADU) was established to spearhead Oxfam's work and thinking in this area, to publish on gender issues, and to be a focal point for work with others who shared these concerns.

The year of GADU's birth also saw the much upgraded edition of what was soon to be acclaimed as 'the bible of development' and Oxfam's best-seller, *The Field Directors' Handbook: An Oxfam Manual for Development Workers.* Having started out in the 1970s as a loose-leaf internal policies and procedures manual, this edition was billed as Oxfam's comprehensive and authoritative account of its views on development and relief work, from its distinctive viewpoint as a British NGO largely involved in funding (and sometimes implementing) development projects and emergency relief programmes in developing countries.

Looking back, one might be forgiven for thinking that GADU and *The Field Directors' Handbook* had emerged from different organisations, or at least that they represented different (even divergent) epochs in Oxfam's evolution. In a sense, a reference book necessarily looks backwards as well as forwards; it is a reflection of an organisation's past (including its myths about itself) as much as a statement about its future directions (and its fantasies about these!). And since change may be very rapid in some areas, parts of such an all-encompassing account will inevitably appear outdated even as the book is going to press. Leaving such 'health warnings' aside, however, the conceptual framework that gave rise to GADU is broadly incompatible with the 1985 *Handbook's* focus on 'priority groups' such as 'women, children, disabled people', and 'ethnic groups'. A gender analysis first of all looks at the social construction and meaning of male and female, and at the ways in which these are expressed in the daily lives of men and women both within their own societies and globally. It thus stresses the impossibility of isolating 'groups' from their context, and treating these as homogeneous 'targets' for assistance. And, as all international aid agencies (should) know, the achievement of social and economic justice demands that contexts and social relations, can, do — and must — change.

'Genderising' the *Field Directors' Handbook*

The terms of reference for updating Oxfam's 1985 publication were 'to revise *The Field Directors' Handbook* taking into account new information, experiences and thinking relevant to the relief and development work of Oxfam and other agencies' (internal document, c. July 1990). For instance, it was envisaged that new or expanded sections should include topics such as human rights, armed conflict, 'the elderly', HIV/AIDS and reproductive health, environmental issues, urbanisation, income-generation and sustainable livelihoods, strategic planning, evaluation, information technology, advocacy and lobbying, alternative trade, and so on. These were to be slotted into the existing framework of chapters on Field Methodologies, Social Development, Economic Development, Agriculture, Health, and Disasters. Some rewriting of the chapter on Priority Groups was anticipated, to take into account Oxfam's 'new thinking on gender'. To assist in this, the budget included the handsome sum of £1,000 to 'genderise [*sic*] the *Handbook*'.

This inoffensive-sounding shorthand is in fact highly revealing of how gender analysis is largely perceived as an optional extra within most aid agencies. 'Genderisation' essentially means just tinkering in the margins of a text (or institution) that remains otherwise intact. In our own experience, incorporating a gender perspective on development and humanitarian relief issues may mean turning our previous assumptions on their head. Certainly, it means (re)examining how social identities are constructed, in order better to understand the processes that result in the systematic oppression of women. This allows us to understand from a gender perspective broad issues such as violence, globalisation, new communication technologies, the role of the state, or human rights; and to know the relative strengths and pitfalls associated with supporting certain kinds of work or organisation.

Oxfam's Gender Policy, finally approved in 1993, stated that

[l]ack of understanding on the part of governments, multilateral agencies and NGOs of the different impact of development aid on men and women, has led, in many cases, to a further marginalisation of women from traditional decision-making structures, displaced them from their economic activities and ignored their valuable knowledge and contribution to development. Development aid is less effective when women are not participating on an equal footing.

Merely adhering to the principle of 'first, do no harm' demands a detailed picture of the situation of women and girls relative to that of men and boys. There is obviously more to this than simply tagging 'and women' to the end of every paragraph in order to 'genderise' the preceding content. Indeed, Oxfam's Gender Policy emphasises ensuring that women can — and will — benefit from its interventions, rather than assuming that 'no news is good news'. This means refraining from supporting projects or organisations that cannot provide such assurance.

The original idea had been that the new sections for the revised *Handbook* should be drafted by Oxfam's own specialist advisers (and by outsiders in subjects where Oxfam had no in-depth knowledge, such as children, disability, and elderly people). It was then to be knocked into shape by the editors. This was to ensure that the published work properly represent Oxfam's current thinking and practice, and so be genuinely 'owned' by the organisation. The fact that few of these specialists possessed the necessary research and writing skills, much less the time or support to develop them, is not my concern here. People who do not write for a living seldom appreciate how long it takes to research, write, and revise their material to publication standard; and the process was not helped in this case by the fact that many of the staff concerned were facing the prospect of redundancy.[2]

The underlying problem, however, is one that no amount of tinkering with the structures will address. It became depressingly clear as we went through the motions of commissioning material for the *Handbook* that for most senior staff in Oxfam, 'gender' was at best an afterthought; for many, it was simply not an issue at all. Thus, we received manuscripts on sanitation in refugee camps stating that up to one-third of the refugee population are likely to be adult women — but without any mention of the implications of the fact that women and adolescent girls also menstruate! Or a draft chapter on health might include an excellent section on women's reproductive health, while being otherwise virtually gender-blind — as though 'gender relations' were a special subject, rather than an analysis (and commitment) that will necessarily shape the organisation's agenda and priorities. Gender, it seemed, could be dealt with only if people deliberately put on a 'gender hat'. Otherwise, it was simply forgotten. The challenge of mainstreaming gender analysis is, then, to ensure that 'the gender hat' fits everyone, and that it is routinely worn.

Who wears the 'gender hat'?

This is not to suggest that external writers showed any greater understanding of gender issues, unless they were themselves 'gender experts'. That is why Oxfam's 'gender titles' are so important in the development literature. Nor, broadly speaking, were colleagues overtly hostile to gender analysis, or to tackling the oppression of women (as long as this was seen as a problem 'out there' in the South, rather than 'here' in the office or at home). The real problem was that they simply didn't know how to relate their knowledge of Oxfam's Gender Policy to their own thinking and practice. In other words, although Oxfam had 'signed up' to a Gender Policy, programme staff generally had little or no idea of how to translate it into their everyday work and lives. Most were all too happy to 'pass the buck' to us. 'Yes, you're right. I hadn't seen it that way. I haven't got time to do anything on it, so just make whatever changes you think are necessary', was a typical 'constructive' response. Yet these very people were responsible either for giving technical policy advice (be it on computer management or health education) to Oxfam's staff and counterparts in the South, or for assessing and approving grant proposals, and in some cases for designing and managing vast operational programmes.

Our own research was hampered by the fact that Oxfam's files on project grants generally offered little or no insight into how the work that it was funding (or undertaking) would affect gender power relations; or even into the different ways in which women and men might be affected by it. Like children, older people, and those with disabilities, women were to be found only in projects focusing exclusively on them, as though normal societies were made up of males aged between 18 and 55 years.

More disturbing still, an informed understanding of gender issues and a commitment to addressing gender-related injustice appeared to be in inverse proportion to status and, therefore, decision-making power. Staff lower in Oxfam GB's hierarchy (and often on the periphery of the institutional structure, such as women project officers) may have a hard-hitting, precise picture of the issues and priorities on the ground. But by the time this is transmitted through the bureaucracy, much of the 'punch' may have been lost. With very few exceptions, senior managers had done little more than attend their mandatory gender-training sessions some years before. Without an iron discipline and commitment, their heavy workloads and responsibilities made any additional reading or thinking time an impossible dream.

This left us in the paradoxical position of both rejecting colleagues' work as not up-to-scratch (hardly the best way to foster learning), and 'holding the line' on Oxfam's Gender Policy against the seeming indifference (or ignorance) of those charged with ensuring its implementation. And all this in the face of constant concerns that the writing process was taking too long, and the cost exceeding our budget. Had the policy issue in question been one of clear-cut rules — whether Oxfam funds child-sponsorship programmes, for instance (it doesn't) — there would have been no pressure whatsoever to withdraw from the official position. But gender analysis involves judgements about what is or is not important, what is and is not negotiable, and interpretations of diverse realities and perspectives. It is about the quality of an agency's analysis and ways of working, and how far it is prepared to water down its commitment to its declared beliefs. Social change does not lend itself to easy definitions of what constitute minimum standards of performance. When the dimensions of gender injustice are so immense, who can say what is 'enough', and if so, for whom and for what?

'Ownership' and exclusion: Some lessons about the Gender Policy

The tremendous difficulties we experienced in trying to 'mainstream' gender issues through editing and rewriting the flagship publication of an organisation committed to addressing gender discrimination and injustice, give some major insights regarding organisational policy and practice in the debate over specialisation versus mainstreaming.

Policy is not the same as consensus

A regulatory framework is a necessary, but not a sufficient, condition for influencing the attitudes, understanding, and behaviour of management and staff. Arguably, the process of generating the consensus behind Oxfam's Gender Policy was as valuable—if not more so—than the formal outcome. It still remains by far the most participatory policy-formulation process in the organisation's history (Wallace 1998). For those who were involved, the battle (and it was a battle) was often inspiring, and offered a way to integrate our professional, personal, and political identities. The hope of achievement gave the energy to fight on; while the links with women's struggles worldwide were themselves exhilarating.

But this focus on achieving tangible gains entails risks. While the Policy was being fought for, its supporters had to invest time and intellectual energy in establishing and maintaining an institution-wide consensus on it. Now it is part of the organisational 'furniture', it is easy just to pay lip-service to its substance: familiarity may not always breed contempt, but it certainly leads to complacency. Having the Gender Policy ought to mean that we need no longer have to fight old battles. However, the difficulties we confronted in producing the *Handbook* suggest that having a policy that is only half-understood and half-heartedly implemented is very likely to lead to its attrition, unless we keep fighting the corner and develop the Policy further. The challenge today is to create ways to generate the same sense of ownership among those who have inherited the Policy which came from struggling to get it adopted in the first place.

(Dis)empowering the non-specialist

One of the saddest experiences in writing the *Handbook* was to witness the unintended effects of making gender a specialist concern. On the one hand, in-depth knowledge was locked into a small (though often beleaguered) group, to which only a chosen few outsiders were admitted. A specialist unit serves as a vital peer-group, giving support to its members when they need it. However, it is also part ivory tower and part ghetto, while often perceived by those who are excluded as an élite members-only club.

The effects on non-specialists were twofold. First, any knowledge or expertise not emanating from or controlled by GADU was easily viewed as potentially threatening to (or, rather, by) those within it. Second, involvement by GADU in mainstream affairs could be seen as a form of interference, whether through co-option or censorship. This made it hard for potential allies to share their own understanding and experience of working on gender-related issues in a spirit of confidence or trust. And it made it easy for those who were not much bothered about gender anyway to turn their backs on the whole business.

That said, without a specialist grouping to be its 'eyes and ears' on the outside world, an organisation risks becoming doctrinaire or outdated, unable to deal maturely with genuine intellectual challenges or to seize new opportunities. Specialist knowledge does have a place within an agency like Oxfam; and specialists need the support and challenge of a peer-group. This is especially so in areas in which thinking and fashions move very fast — whether micro-enterprise development, capacity-building, or gender. The risk of making everyone equally responsible for an area of analysis (as opposed to more narrowly technical subjects such as medicine) is that the analysis itself becomes dissipated. But specialists can find themselves absorbing the generalists' responsibilities.

The *Handbook* illustrates the paradox. It remains the only book of its kind to have mainstreamed gender so comprehensively. But this was achieved not by getting it written by 'non-specialists' from within Oxfam's mainstream, but by committed feminist practitioners and writers who had a firm grounding in gender and development issues, a broad knowledge of Oxfam, and who could jointly draw on some 20 years' experience of working in countries as different as Namibia and Nicaragua. The in-house gender specialists understandably declined to be involved in 'genderising' the *Handbook*, limiting their input to offering critiques on a few draft sections. The reasons were partly historical (restructuring, personality clashes, lack of time, and so on); but also had to do with the petty rivalries that are fostered by an organisational structure which expects the gender specialists (along with the other advisory staff) to try to exert authority but without the resources or status to do so. This is, in a nutshell, why *The Oxfam Handbook of Development and Relief* was never owned as a 'gender title'.

Training alone does not change hearts and minds

In producing the *Handbook*, we dealt with no one who had not undergone at least one day's in-house gender training. Indeed, the consensus-building for Oxfam's Gender Policy had involved compulsory and voluntary training sessions for all managerial and advisory staff. As we found, however, it is one thing in a training workshop to recite the difference between sex and gender, or to disaggregate socio-economic data; it is quite another for an individual to incorporate such analysis into their daily work. This is especially true if doing so will lead to conflict, to challenging the decisions and priorities of peers and seniors, or to having to re-think one's own assumptions. Training is not the same as managerial back-up, and is largely meaningless without it. Commitment must be demonstrated from the top down.[3]

Mainstreaming without investing in a comprehensive training programme is a recipe for disaster in terms of ensuring that there is a solid cadre of staff who are well informed about gender issues, speak a common language, and so can take forward the Gender Policy. Further, to be effective, training needs to be reinforced throughout each individual's career, especially during periods of high staff turnover, or when organisational restructuring can result in a loss of momentum (to say nothing of institutional memory). It also needs to evolve with new thinking and experience. When the bulk of the gender training was undertaken, feminism, patriarchy, or masculinity were not part of Oxfam's vocabulary — and post-feminism had never even been dreamed of (except perhaps as something to look forward to in a post-patriarchal paradise!). Similarly, the experience of ten or more years of working from a gender perspective has exposed Oxfam to many different strands of feminist analysis from the South. How can this be heard if there is no identifiable 'place' to take it?

Getting recruitment right

It became very clear in the course of producing the *Handbook* that senior programme staff had been appointed without the supposedly mandatory 'awareness of gender issues and a commitment to Oxfam's Gender Policy'. In conjunction with the Equal Opportunities Policy, this clause had been intended to rule out unfair recruitment and promotion practices; and to ensure that all staff shared a common set of values concerning gender issues. But policy and practice diverge significantly in this area.

Leaving aside for a moment the question of how one measures such aware-ness, a major problem is that managers who themselves lack a firm understanding of gender issues are ill-placed to assess candidates against this criterion, or to review the performance of existing staff. Putting a gender 'expert' on the selection panel usually generates resistance, because their role is perceived as one of 'policing' the manager and challenging her or his competence. It can also cause resentment as the manager is let off the hook by dumping responsibility for screening candidates onto the gender expert. In practice, the only jobs for which a commitment to gender analysis has ever been a central criterion (even to the exclusion of other important skills) have been those of 'gender experts'. Again, this risks treating specialist staff as the organisation's fig-leaf — just enough to cover potential embarrassment, but little more.

It is well recognised that 30 per cent female staffing at all levels represents a critical mass in terms of ensuring that an organisation does not slip back into 'patriarchal mode' (UNDP 1995). It is not that men cannot defend the organisation's policies on gender equity; but we must recognise that in practice they usually don't, or won't (Longwe 1997). The same obviously holds true for any other sector that is disadvantaged in relation to the dominant group (in this case, white, educated, middle-class British men). The only way to tackle this is to take affirmative action that will enable such people to seize the opportunities available to them on fair terms — although it is no good having level playing fields if the outsiders are playing hockey while the insiders are in a rugger scrum.

Slipstream or mainstream?

Our experience in trying mainstream gender in the *Handbook* suggests that to see the organisational options in dichotomous terms is extremely unhelpful. It is not a case of either specialisation or mainstreaming gender. We patently need both — partly to balance the disadvantages of each approach, but also because this is the only way an organisation can maintain its analytical vitality while inviting everyone to play their part in contributing to a deeper understanding of the role(s) that they and the agency should play.

Second, it shows that the writing process can and should enable a 'learning organisation' to align its self-image with its reflection. Basing our work on Oxfam's Gender Policy, we sought to show the true dimensions of what it had taken on, so that the *Handbook* should act as a public benchmark for its performance.

Third, it shows that discrepancies between rhetoric and practice are like cracks through which moisture will seep into an organisation's foundations, causing the whole edifice to subside. Policies and procedures provide important regulatory frameworks; but they will be constantly undermined if they are not translated into real, tangible changes in the working environment. An organisation with a poor record on health and safety will command little respect in the field of health education. Similarly, in the case of gender, there is a practical and above all a moral need to ensure that an agency's own employment practices are consistent with its co-operation policies. This will not happen simply by an act of will; and it cannot happen without investing resources into areas such as flexible employment (such as job-shares or job-swaps), practical support for staff with caring responsibilities, affirmative action to address disadvantage, an attitude of zero tolerance for sexual and racial harassment, and so on.

But the overriding lesson is that only when it is really prepared to take on the full consequences of its commitment to gender justice, can an organisation risk 'mainstreaming' gender without selling its integrity down the river.

About the author

Deborah Eade worked throughout the 1980s in Oxfam's Regional Office for Mexico and Central America. Since 1991 she has been Editor of the international quarterly *Development in Practice*. She is co-author of *The Oxfam Handbook of Development and Relief* and author of *Capacity-building: A people-centred approach to development* (Oxfam, 1997).

References

Eade, Deborah and Williams, Suzanne (1995), *The Oxfam Handbook of Development and Relief*, Oxford: Oxfam.

Eade, D. and Williams, S. (1996, rev.), 'The Oxfam Handbook of Development and Relief: Review of a Process', unpublished report, Oxfam.

Longwe, Sara Hlupekile (1997), 'The evaporation of gender policies in the patriarchal cooking pot', *Development in Practice*, Vol. 7, No. 2.

Oxfam UK/I, 'Gender and Development: Oxfam's policy for its programme', internal paper (see Appendix).

Pratt, Brian and Boyden, Jo (eds.) (1985), *The Field Directors' Handbook: An Oxfam Manual for Development Workers*, Oxford: Oxfam and OUP.

UNDP (1995), *Human Development Report 1995*, New York and Oxford: OUP.

Wallace, Tina (1998), 'Institutionalising gender in UK NGOs', *Development in Practice*, Vol. 8, No. 2.

Williams, Suzanne with Seed, J. and Mwau, A. (1994), *The Oxfam Gender Training Manual*, Oxford: Oxfam.

The 'cutting edge' of practice? Publishing, gender, and diversity in Oxfam GB

Caroline Sweetman

Depending on one's location (both physical and mental), publishing has many different images and associations. Some consider it an activity undertaken by academics and grammarians, who are far removed from the economic, social, and political realities of life outside the editor's office. For others (including many feminists working in women's resource centres, publishing companies, and NGOs throughout the world) publishing is a significant form of political activity. It aims to encourage writers to value their own knowledge, democratise information, and inspire both writers and readers to future action. Oxfam GB's continuing commitment to publishing as a part of its development programme encourages those of us who share this view that the importance of publishing as a way of promoting development and justice is recognised by the organisation.

Apart from producing tangible outcomes, publishing can be a development — and feminist — process in its own right. Since the start of Oxfam's formal engagement with women's rights during the 1980s, a commitment to publishing women's knowledge and promoting women in development has been seen as an integral part of this work. This means not only publishing books on gender-related issues and ensuring that all our books are informed by a gender analysis, but also promoting women as writers. At its best, our publishing is participatory, enabling, and can effect social change — not only outside Oxfam, but within the organisation itself. How far does Oxfam's publishing fall short of this ideal, and what insights does a concern for issues of gender and diversity offer for improving what we do?

In this article, I have chosen to focus on two sets of unresolved dilemmas which I think our organisational commitment to feminist goals (in the 1993 Gender Policy) raises for our publishing. The first of these is how we balance our desire to publish books which are worthwhile contributions to debates about feminism and women's visions of development taking place outside the organisation, with the commitment to reflecting Oxfam's programme in our publishing, and sharing our knowledge gained through practice. Oxfam is not always working at the 'cutting edge of practice' on gender issues. The second set of dilemmas is about the process of publishing: how, as feminists, can I and my colleagues balance a commitment to diversity among our authors, and in particular to publishing the perspectives of Southern women, with the reality of the organisation? Oxfam GB is a British-based NGO which currently publishes only in English; and we have a mandate to reflect Oxfam's programme reality — where decision-makers and opinion-formers at high levels are predominantly Northern men.

Publishing as an outcome

Other articles in this collection discuss the successes and failures in introducing a gender perspective into different parts of Oxfam's work. In publishing, the creation of a list of 'gender-specialist' books has been successful in developmental (and commercial) terms; the list is perhaps the best advocate that Oxfam has, bearing witness to its commitment to putting resources into promoting women's rights in development. It is, indeed, widely acknowledged in Oxfam that the organisation's enviable reputation for its gender work is in large part due to its publications on gender issues. However, this success is only part of the story. Attempts to 'mainstream' a gender perspective into the rest of our substantial publications output are still imperfect, since our publishing reflects the wider reality of Oxfam's development programme.

Gender-specialist publications: The 'cutting edge' of practice?

From 1985, the Gender and Development Unit (GADU), and later the Gender Team, were chiefly responsible for persuading Oxfam to produce a series of specialist books on gender-related topics. This continues to form a key part of our publications list, with some 125 titles in print. Our book publishing has tended to reflected the 'state of the art' within our own programme; it has often shared practice which was well ahead of the work of other Northern-based development organisations. Debates on gender-related issues between practitioners around the world have been faithfully reflected in terms of Oxfam's own experience.

In 1991, *Changing Perceptions* collated the views of development academics, feminist activists, and development workers into a book of 'think-pieces' on key aspects of women's marginalisation from the market, the state, and development projects. Three years later, reflecting the enormous faith placed in training as a means of solving the problem of blindness to gender power relations within organisations and the communities they exist in, the *Oxfam Gender Training Manual* was published to huge acclaim. The manual, which has become Oxfam Publications' biggest single income-earner, is a vast resource, drawing on the experience of many Southern and Northern trainers. It provides development workers with pre-tested exercises for training sessions to raise awareness of women's marginalisation through gender-discriminatory power relations.

I joined Oxfam in late 1993 as the first permanent editor of our journal for policy-makers, practitioners, and researchers, and as an adviser on gender-specialist publications. Then entitled *Focus on Gender*, the journal had started earlier that year. Soon after my arrival, it was re-launched as *Gender and Development*. It had started (as Tina Wallace discusses in her article) as the GADU Newspack, a thematic, *ad-hoc* collection of think-pieces, written by Oxfam staff working on gender issues and like-minded colleagues in partner organisations.

Staff in the Gender Team at that time had a strong belief in the positive role of publishing in 'progressing' gender within an organisation such as Oxfam, drawing strength from the external women's movement through stimulating debates, and promoting women's involvement in shaping these debates by paying attention to whose voices are heard through our publications. In 1993, the Gender Team had decided that turning its newspack into a formal publication would enable it to reach a wider audience. Moreover, the 'professionalisation' of it as a journal would enable Oxfam to use it as a tool for advocating change on feminist lines with NGOs, UN agencies, and national governments.

The shift from 'grey literature' to formal publication as a journal, disseminated by an external distributor of academic journals, had not really been thought through. There were many questions to think about: who was the journal intended for? Which parts of the audience would be lost in making it a formal publication? Would the conventional readership of journals find the ideas in it challenging enough? At my job interview, I was asked how I could ensure that the journal was useful for both high-level policy-makers and 'grassroots women'. I probably wasn't the only candidate who told them that it couldn't be done! Language and literacy are the two most obvious barriers to prevent Oxfam's central Publications Team in Britain from publishing resources for women living in poverty in various developing-country contexts.

After two sets of interviews, I secured the job, because I presented a publishing proposal for the journal suggesting that the primary readership — and 'writership' — should be development policy-makers, practitioners, and researchers. I argued that the market niche that the journal would fit into was, in marketing terms, the 'cutting edge of practice'. We would invite outstanding activists, development workers, and academics from Northern and Southern contexts to become members of an editorial advisory group. We would retain the thematic focus of the journal, in line with making a commitment to producing a stand-alone resource, with articles addressing different aspects of a hot topic. Since its relaunch, the journal has flourished, publishing issues on topics well-known to gender and development workers, such as the environment and violence against women; but it has also moved to new fields, publishing an issue on men and masculinity from a feminist perspective in 1997. The journal aims to combine factual rigour with accessibility, and is an example of part of our publishing programme where the aim is to question gender and development practice — in both development work and research — through sharing innovative and unfamiliar ideas which offer creative challenges to orthodoxy.

Our publications are part of the public face of Oxfam, and play a key role in advocacy and profile-raising with other organisations; they provide a record of our work, which forms a basis for lobbying for change on the world stage. A recognition of this leads, of course, to a sense of divided loyalties for a feminist like myself working on our publishing programme. All our work, publishing included, should transform the institutions, including Oxfam, which define 'development' themselves, so that their work can benefit women equally with men. No part of our work should become a smoke-screen concealing the difficulties which all organisations have in taking on a gender perspective. However, it could be argued that this is exactly what has happened with the *Gender Training Manual*, which has become famous world-wide and has made many believe that Oxfam is an organisation whose work is exemplary from a gender perspective. It would be ironic indeed if, through excellence in our gender-specialist publications, we take the pressure off Oxfam to strive for excellence in its other activities.

'Mainstreaming' gender into our publications: Is honesty the best policy?

The record is less good in attempts to ensure that all the books we publish reflect a gender perspective which will promote best practice in development. A key aspect of our publishing should surely be an honest assessment of experience, making us accountable to those who have a stake in our activities: the women and men of the communities in which we work, our donors, and the organisations with whom we have links in practical work, research, and advocacy. The activity of writing should provide an opportunity for over-loaded development workers to reflect honestly on what they have been doing; and on the successes and failures of plans which have sometimes borne fruit and sometimes gone badly awry.

However, if our publications faithfully reflect the multiple realities of Oxfam's programme — where gender work is good in parts — we may no longer have a publishing programme on gender-related topics that we can be proud of, and which contributes to gender-fair development in itself.

As Deborah Eade's article suggests, writing for publication is (perhaps too often) the process through which policy is formalised; commitments are set down in black and white, and diverse views on particular issues are identified as such and either set down as a dialogue, or distinguished between and the favoured one selected. Far from simply reflecting our policies, the act of publishing may act less as a mirror than as a lamp, casting a light on a hitherto shadowy area where gaps or anomalies in our policy lie: these gaps must be bridged during the discipline imposed by the writing process. Soon after I joined Oxfam, I experienced a case in point, when the need to formalise Oxfam's line on abortion arose in response to the inclusion of an article on that topic in an issue of the journal *Gender and Development* focusing on population and reproductive rights.

Publishing as a process: Gender, diversity, and 'other voices'

The second set of dilemmas I wish to address concerns who writes our books. Oxfam's understanding of poverty sees it as more than economic deprivation, but as concerned with political and social marginalisation. Its work therefore focuses on promoting the empowerment of groups in society, including women, whose interests have been overlooked by the powerful. Voicelessness in public fora is a central characteristic of marginalisation. In this respect, Oxfam's vision of what we want our publications to achieve is shared by others involved in publishing in the UK voluntary sector, and in politically-motivated publishing in other thematic and geographical contexts, including feminist publishing in the North and South.

The central insight here is that it is impossible to look at gender without considering other aspects of people's identities which prevent them finding a 'space' to speak. A central strategy of the women's movement in North America and Europe has been to challenge the idea that knowledge and scholarship are male preserves. Feminist publishing seeks to promote women's writing and to record their experience and knowledge; it provides women with a space — in both its abstract and physical senses — in which these activities can occur. Feminist publishing also tries to present the result in a form which enables the maximum number of readers to have access to it. For many publishers, including Oxfam, this means not only a commitment to making the material physically available on a printed page or a computer screen, but also to rendering material accessible through clear language and a rejection of unnecessary professional and theoretical jargon which often excludes the very people whose experience it discusses.

Moving on a step from this, Southern feminists have challenged the right of Northern feminists to present their views as representative of 'women in general'. Gender issues are often the way in to considering other aspects of identity, including race and disability. Southern feminists, for example Chandra Mohanty, have argued that race and gender cannot be separated due to a colonial and post-colonial history in which formal publishing has represented Northern women and ignored the existence of Southern feminists (Mohanty 1988)[4]. In a short policy statement on gender offered to potential writers of our publications, we state that we currently see gender analysis as a route into a wider analysis of social relations. It is certainly time to put these words into action with regard to choice of authors for our books. A 60:40 male:female ratio among our writers in 1995 has moved steadily to a 50:50 split in 1998. However, the split between writers from the North and writers from the South[5] is 92:8 per cent.

How can our publishing move from this appaling imbalance to become a process in which Southern as well as Northern staff can participate, reflecting Oxfam's commitment to encouraging diversity among its staff and in the perspectives applied to its work? Such statistics are, unfortunately, easily explained by Oxfam's organisational culture. In principle, anyone in Oxfam can suggest an idea for a publication, or become a writer; however, as ever, the geographical location of staff and the nature of their jobs are two determining factors which militate against Southern staff writing for publication. It is most likely that staff who receive information flows about different parts of our work worldwide are located at head office. And all too often, those who are valued as having worthwhile knowledge to share, and who are able to allocate time to writing in an organisation where everyone has conflicting priorities and little time for reading, writing, and learning, are not likely to be from the South, and least likely to be Southern women. In her article in this collection, Wendy Carson provides compelling evidence of the lack of time in the lives of women working for Oxfam, juggling with a double workload and constantly faced with the need to prove that they are as good as the men.

Both Wendy Carson's and Lina Abu-Habib's contributions to this book point out the complex power dynamics which result in most senior posts being held by Northern women and men, while the top positions are all occupied by white middle-class men. Writers tend to inhabit the middle levels of advisory and management work; they have substantial experience of working in international contexts, where expatriate aid workers are big fish in small ponds. Self-confidence develops more easily for these international workers who become acclimatised to 'speaking the right language' in different cultural contexts. These are the staff who are most likely to be confident that they have something worthwhile to say; they may also be able to negotiate time off for writing.

We have started to work on ways of promoting the participation in writing of Southern women (and men). Over the past few years, time and energy has been put into a number of different experiments to develop publications in an unconventional fashion. The first of these is to produce books which are multi-authored and edited in a very flexible and intensive way, providing support to authors who have not previously published. Short articles are less time-consuming and thus less intimidating to write (and read!); the writers also stand more chance of being supported by their managers if the undertaking is not too outfacing. In 1998, we published our first book on the Middle East, *Gender and Disability in the Middle East*. Edited by Lina Abu-Habib, who was at the time on secondment in Oxford from her position in Oxfam's Lebanon office, the book is a collection of short analytical articles written by Middle Eastern development workers, many of whom are disabled and all of whom are women. Lina and I worked hard to develop the articles from tentative first drafts, discovering what was new and different in each and encouraging the writers to bring out these points in their first drafts. Lina herself was on maternity leave during the editing process, and I used to visit her at home and plan the book while one of us held the baby. The extra time it takes to get the right, rather than the best-placed, writers and editors is considerable—but worth it. My main learning point was, however, that a baby cannot be factored into a publishing timetable!

The journal *Gender and Development* is edited in the same way, featuring the experience of development workers, working with them to build confidence that their ideas are publishable. This is one of my favourite parts of the job: finding the time and mental space to reflect on their work and pulling out the interesting analysis, is an empowering task to do. The finished result — an article in a reputable journal which is read throughout the world—is a tangible sign of a lot of invisible realisation of the value of the work which many writers have never had time to stop to consider before.

A final way of ensuring that our publications are as close as possible to the experience of the women (and men) in communities with whom development organisations work is to ensure accessibility of language. Often, we become used to talking in impenetrable jargon in our working environment; in the case of journals, we may be tempted to publish work from researchers whose ideas are expressed in forms which 'colonise' the experience of women and men in developing countries, by using language impenetrable to development workers who may be interested in the issues and concepts of the research. A degree of jargon is permissible among peers in any profession; but, for example, using the word 'gender' as a stand-alone is not only incorrect English but is also a hostage to fortune in that it means everything and nothing.

Academics are also commissioned to write for the journal *Gender and Development*. Within the women's movement, there have long been fruitful alliances between academics and non-academics. In line with this, academics published in the journal are encouraged to write in a way which is of use to the maximum number of policy-makers and practitioners, some of whom may not have had access to higher education. This means avoiding the familiar language of academia, and expressing key ideas in language which is free of unnecessary jargon. Working with academics to ensure this shift in style is often more demanding — in tact and time — than supporting the community workers who thought they couldn't write.

Finally, the critical issue of language remains unresolved in an organisation where the costs of translation and marketing mean that we do not produce publications in languages other than English, although we encourage organisations in other countries to translate and publish our books, and spend considerable time facilitating this process. By pursuing this way of working, we hope to help to build the capacity of publishers and NGOs in the countries in which we work.

Conclusion

For some, publishing is seen more properly as an outcome of policy discussions which have already happened. But for those of us who work on issues which have been taken on incompletely or incoherently by our organisation, the discipline and rigour required by writing offers an opportunity to identify gaps in our practice and our analysis, which policy-makers are obliged to address if the publication is to be produced. As noted more fully in the Introduction to this book, its production has in itself been intended to be a significant part of the long process of integrating a gender perspective into every aspect of Oxfam's work and into the organisation's culture. While we in the Publications Team must continue to find ways of ensuring that all our publications are informed by an understanding of how women's and men's gender identity interacts with other aspects of their personalities and circumstances to determine their access to resources and power, those responsible for managing our international programme ultimately have the power to determine whether this is an artificial 'add-on' at publishing time, or something which is naturally reflected in publications promoting good — i.e. gender-sensitive — development policy and practice.

About the author

Caroline Sweetman is Editor of Oxfam's journal *Gender and Development* and adviser on gender issues in Oxfam's Publications Team. From 1988–92 Caroline worked in Lesotho, launching and co-editing a feminist popular magazine project funded by UNICEF. She has a MA in Gender Analysis in Development Studies and is currently doing doctoral research on gender, health, and violence in Ethiopia.

Making visible the invisible: The work of the gender resources centre

Sue Smith

Introduction

A Resources Officer post has existed since the early days of Oxfam's Gender and Development Unit in the 1980s. The job was to collect, disseminate, and communicate information about gender and development. When I started in 1990, I inherited a small collection of lovingly classified boxes of leaflets, unpublished papers, and magazines. We had a card box of contacts and correspondence with activists in and outside Oxfam, and a handful of books. Publishing on gender and development, now central to development courses world-wide, was only just beginning.

My previous job was advertising for peace — so I had already faced the struggle to win a space in the mainstream. I knew what the boxes were for. I recognised the vision of the founders. They saw that, until it was part of development thinking that gender roles are created by society, not natural, and that gendered power relations are at the root of poverty and inequality, progress would be slow. Their inspiration was Latin American feminism, where documentation centres played a key role in supporting and recording the struggles of the women's movement. All this could be found in the boxes that I inherited. Documentation, and the Resources Officer role, were to play a key part in consciousness-raising in Oxfam.

'The story of hunting has not yet been told by the lions'

Telling the story of the marginalised requires a commitment to telling stories from another point of view, one which may need to struggle for legitimacy, for the right to be heard, and then for the mainstream space to ensure that it is heard. The struggle for a place in the mainstream can be illustrated by the Wages for Housework campaign, which began in 1972. These campaigners were seen at the time as a wild bunch of extreme left-wing feminists, pushing an agenda that had no hope of acceptance in mainstream economics. Their message was that women's reproductive work in the household should be valued in the same way as employment in the workplace, and should be counted and recognised in official statistics on the productivity of nations.

By 1995, the tide was turning. The UNDP Human Development Report valued women's unwaged work at $11 trillion, and the value of a UK housewife at £600 per week. Such a notion would not have gained respectability without years of campaigning and research to find ways in which statistics could be gathered. Oxfam has played a small part, by supporting participants from a bonded labour organisation in India, and a South African woman, at conferences run by Wages for Housework, as well as working within the global network, the Alliance for Economic Alternatives, to get the issue included in the Platform for Action at the UN Conference on Women in Beijing in 1995.

Similar resistance and struggle were encountered during the early days of gender and development. Suzanne Williams, the first paid worker in GADU, expresses something of the need for pioneering conviction when she says,

> I remember being genuinely, and perhaps ingenuously, astonished by the extent of the resistance … and the suspicion which GADU generated. 'And what are the ladies plotting today?' was a drearily familiar taunt flung in at my office door.[6]

It is the documentarists who keep the records of these struggles, the research, and the campaigns to change things. When the ideas are accepted into the mainstream, they can surrender the job to librarians. Then the lions in the African proverb have told their story, and it has been heard by the hunters.

Grey literature: documenting activism

One of the central pillars of the gender resource centre in Oxfam has been the collection, classification, and dissemination of grey literature. But what is it? And why is it important? Any political or social movement that challenges the mainstream, whether for peace, civil rights, or women's liberation, has to be documented. And that means grey literature. It means keeping the leaflets, the newsletters, the magazines, the campaigning strategies, the press statements, the newspaper cuttings, the workshop reports. The books and journals come later, when academic or political respectability have been achieved. Grey literature has little perceived market value. It is used at first only by the committed, the activists, and later, the researchers. But later, it is the gold dust for publications. Without the materials for gender training, and the reports of workshops, there would have been no *Oxfam Gender Training Manual*, which is now one of Oxfam's most successful publications. Without the GADU Newspack, there would have been no *Changing Perceptions*, one of the first publications on gender and development.

To begin with, the Oxfam gender resources library was mostly a collection of what others had done, and how they did it. This inspired and informed those who had a vision of what the gender perspective could do for Oxfam's work, and slowly it became a record of what Oxfam itself had done. So the resource centre kept a record of how women had fought battles and sometimes won, sometimes lost, as well as how Oxfam itself was changing.

To librarians grey literature often represents a difficulty. It has no ISBN identification, often no clear authorship, or even a date. It is hard to classify, and seems of doubtful value. It is often classified as 'ephemera'. It is no accident that many of the feminist resource centres have had to develop their own classification systems, as traditional hierarchies simply will not fit. Although Oxfam has devised its own library classification system to fit its development work, integrating the gender perspective was a challenge. 'Gender issues' is a subsection of *social development*, along with 'training' and 'the elderly'. As a perspective it is now classified throughout the Oxfam system in *economics* or *statistics, disasters* or *dysentery, multilaterals* or *mother and child health*. What we publish has to fit marketing categories in a way that cannot easily reflect the fertile area of interface between activism, academia, and campaigning. We still try to squeeze the large foot into the glass slipper, and still cannot put an ISBN on the unorthodox. The attitude that damns grey literature as ephemera still persists in the world of orthodox learning and study.

Filling in the cracks: the role of translation

If the gender perspective is to be central to Oxfam's development work, then the tools we use should be translated into as many different languages as possible. Only in this way can Oxfam's programme officers reach out to their partners and beneficiaries, who rarely speak English. It is well known that the women who are the beneficiaries of Oxfam's support often do not communicate in the colonial languages. Despite the official commitments to diversity, translation of materials is rarely seen as a top priority. What kind of a message do we give if we don't turn that commitment into reality?

Nevertheless, we know that through the determination of programme staff, the *Oxfam Gender Training Manual* has been translated into Spanish, French, and

Arabic. Parts have been translated into Portuguese, Russian, Indonesian, Chinese, as well as many other local languages, some of which we know about, many of which we don't. It is something Oxfam can be proud of, but each time, managers have to be convinced, resources have to be protected against apparently more pressing priorities. And how do you translate concepts like gender? Part of the Resources Officer role is to record and use the experience of the translators, for future use. As well as the struggle for the right word or phrase to express the subtleties of gender relations, the task may need to transform the structure of the language itself. An Oxfam worker described the impact of gender awareness on Spanish speakers:

> It is interesting to see how this surge in the women's and feminist movement has had an impact on language. Spanish has a masculine bias in its grammatical structure, so girls and boys, for example, as just niños, the masculine form of the word. In recent years, most people within social movements, the mass media and even politicians will say niños y niñas, hombres y mujeres … Now it is common in the region to use the @ to resolve this problem in writing: niñ@s, compañer@s.[7]

Networking — who does it and what is it?

The Resources Officer is also a networker. This role has been significant in enabling Oxfam to develop its relationships and offer support and commitment, to carry out joint work with women's organisations and networks, without undue pressure for short-term results, and at some distance from the pressure of the funder/funded relationship.

For example, part of the Resources Officer role has been to produce an Oxfam newsletter, Links, three times a year. Staff are encouraged to write brief articles about their practical experiences, good and bad, in trying to integrate a gender perspective into Oxfam's programme. The emphasis is on regular exchange of practical tools. In some cases, writing for the newsletter has given project officers the confidence to go on to more sustained writing for wider dissemination and formal publication. Links is distributed together with the Oxfam journal Gender and Development, reaching a wide audience of practitioners and academics, and also has its own mailing list of Oxfam staff, partners, and other interested individuals and organisations all over the world.

Networking involves more than relationships with organisations external to Oxfam. One of the most significant networking relationships is an internal Oxfam staff network in south and southeast Asia, Action for Gender Relations in Asia (AGRA),[8] which promotes and strengthens the skills and commitment of project officers and their managers on gender issues. The role of the Resources

Officer in supporting and promoting this network has been critical in providing continuity and internal publicity for what it tries to do, in a number of ways. For each yearly meeting on a theme chosen by the participants, the Resources Officer in Oxford and the core group planning the next AGRA meeting have pooled information on the chosen theme. From Oxford, we can provide materials from other regions, or with global perspectives, built up over a long period as a result of the documentation role. As part of the yearly workshop, participants commit themselves to practical follow-up in their daily work. The material collected goes to create a set of papers to prepare participants for the meeting, and to strengthen follow-up through annotated lists of further materials and references. The Resources Officer has frequently taken the responsibility for production and dissemination of the workshop report within Oxfam and wider. These reports, in addition to recording the workshop, are much in demand as state-of-the-art collections of key resources on the themes, and some have been published later as Oxfam discussion papers.

Support to field offices: A key role

The job of the resources officer was, and still is, to support those working at the sharp end: the programme staff who face the real challenges of integrating a gender perspective in their work. The resource support role includes putting them in touch with people doing similar work, so they can compare ways of working. There is on-going mutual support between staff in the field offices and the Resources Officer — questions, requests for papers and information, and informal exchanges of ideas. The link with the Resources Officer has often operated as a safe channel in which staff find it is possible to ask basic questions which they feel unable to raise with their managers, and to ask for materials that build their skills in a gradual way as part of their everyday work.

Case study: Gender in the Middle East

Oxfam's work in the Middle East provides a good example of successful resource support on gender. The recipe has several ingredients. First is long-term commitment by management to tackling gender inequality in the region, as the basis for effective work on poverty. The second is a keen awareness of the opportunities offered by resource support. The third is an appreciation of how such support can strengthen the chances of developing regional expertise. The fourth is using the opportunities offered by an Oxford-based post with global access.

Isolation from the chance to learn and develop is often keenly felt in Oxfam's international offices, and the Middle East team has kept in regular contact with the Resources Officer.[9] Often this is the only active form of collaboration on programme development with other offices and with Oxford. Information is exchanged about broader campaigns for women's rights in the Middle East and the Maghreb; about resource centres in the area, about research completed and in progress, about global movements and networking which need a voice in the region. Names and addresses of key contacts change hands; a directory of regional organisations and their work is in progress. Resources have been found for translation of key materials into Arabic: the *Gender Training Manual*, a book on gender and disability in the region, and the Links newsletter. They will reach a wide audience in the region and get feedback from the NGO, government, and multilateral sectors to fine-tune the tools themselves for the future. The Oxfam Middle East office is building up its own resource library on gender in the region, supplemented by copies of all Oxfam's own materials and workshop reports. The idea of appointing a staff member to work on gender issues is under discussion.

From this solid foundation of information exchange and reinforcement, Oxfam is gaining respect for its commitment to gender. It can build on this. At a recent gender workshop for Oxfam partners from four Middle Eastern countries and campaigning organisations from North Africa, plans were made for a wider network.

Conclusion

To small, cash-strapped organisations, struggling from one year's funding to the next, the fact that Oxfam commits its resources to long-term support on gender is of lasting significance. They know they can call on someone with the remit to give time and space to ferreting out the latest statistics and research projects, and telling them who's moved on to where, from the database. It is invisible work, but after more than ten years there are many who know of Oxfam's commitment and use the resources it offers. And so the invisible becomes increasingly visible and valuable.

About the author

Sue Smith has been working as Resources Officer on gender and development since 1990. She manages the Gender and Learning Team library, edits the Links newsletter, and is responsible for the team's communication and information support work. In previous lives she was a lecturer in further education, trainer, teacher, and peace worker. She has two adult sons and lives in Oxford. Now they are grown she has time for other things — like Morris dancing!

A history of gender training in Oxfam

Jan Seed

Introduction

By 1985, at the time of the Third UN conference on women in Nairobi, it had become increasingly clear that development was leaving women out or, in many cases, actually making things worse for them. Even projects specifically targeted at women could leave them with more work to do, and no extra money within their control. Development agencies were concerned about this, both from an efficiency perspective, and a moral one. The problem was identified as one of lack of information and understanding among development practitioners, rather than one of patriarchy. Gender training came to be seen as the solution — if only planners and development practitioners could be fully 'gender-aware', then projects could be planned which would benefit women as well as men.

There have been many successes in gender training, yet its effectiveness is limited unless it is part of an on-going process. Individual lessons learned in training must be fully incorporated into an organisation's policy, practices, procedures, and structure. Gender trainers have consistently stressed this point, for example, Field (1988),[10] Seed (1989 and 1991),[11] and Poats and Russo (1991)[12]. However, in practice this advice has often been ignored. Furthermore, if gender training is seen as solely a 'technical solution' it will also be inadequate. Gender relations are intricately connected to the personal and political identities of individuals, and training must be allowed to address this in order to be successful.

This article outlines my own experience of gender training as Oxfam's full-time gender trainer from 1988 to 1991, and attempts to draw out some of the lessons from that period.

The history of gender training

From 1985, gender training began to emerge. In the USA, a group from the Harvard Institute for International Development devised a training method based on case studies (Overholt et al. 1985)[13]. Trainees analyse projects for their differential impact on participants with regard to sex and age, creating profiles of activities, and of access to and control of resources. In the UK, the Gender Planning method developed by Caroline Moser (1986, 1993)[14] uses the organisations' own projects as case studies, analysing them to identify which roles and needs of women they address, and which policy approach they use.

Other methods, such as checklists, had been used to further gender awareness in the planning and evaluation of projects, but these have suffered from being both too long (too time-consuming and difficult to complete) and too short (leaving out questions relevant to specific situations). The advantage of both the Harvard and Moser methods was that they provided simple frameworks which could produce detailed information pertinent to many different communities and projects. Another advantage for some development organisations was that they appeared to be value-free and not feminist. These methods could be used to present gender analysis as a technical solution, without necessarily engaging with personal or political issues, and without challenging male power.

Gender training in Oxfam was based on a wider range of experience of popular education, awareness-raising, and group work, as well as gender-training methods. Paulo Freire (1972)[15] pioneered the use of participatory learning, based on people's own experiences, to raise awareness of social injustice, and to enable people to create their own solutions. Women's groups in Latin America and India aimed to increase women's awareness of their situation, and to enable them to overcome the limitations of narrow sex-role stereotyping within a patriarchal system. Followers of these approaches disliked the use of such terms as 'training' and 'targeting', and instead stressed the importance of connection and collective reflections. They linked the issue of gender with that of caste and class, and worked from the personal to the political.

Another influence on Oxfam's gender training was the increasing trend towards equal-opportunities and anti-racism training, based on the idea that it was the 'oppressor' groups who needed to have their awareness raised, as well as, or instead of the oppressed groups who were only too aware (see Katz 1978)[16]. In Oxfam, as in many organisations, equal-opportunities training included some aspects of awareness-raising, but was far more concerned with obtaining non-discriminatory behaviour in the work place simply to ensure compliance with the Equal Opportunities Policy, developed in 1983. This was more along the lines of a 'technical solution', and hardly transformational in style.

Strategies and methods

I was appointed to the position of full-time gender trainer in Oxfam in 1988. My role, among other things, was to facilitate training of all project-related staff in the International Division. It was originally envisaged that everyone in the organisation would be trained and would then 'have' gender awareness, and thus further training would be redundant. In practice, things were slightly different. There was a high turnover of staff, partly due to the fact that most field staff were on short-term contracts. It also became very apparent that more than just gender awareness, or a gender analysis of projects was needed.

Gender training was to be spread to the rest of the organisation, including the field offices, through training of gender trainers at workshops. The first of these was held in India in 1991.[17] Things did not exactly follow the plan here either, as it turned out to be the only one of its kind. I stopped working as gender trainer soon afterwards, and the responsibility for training was distributed among other staff. At present, the responsibility for implementing Oxfam's Gender Policy rests with the line managers. All the more reason, one might think, for gender training to be kept up for this group. Yet the gender training which was being carried out centrally at Oxfam House ceased after 1991.

The gender-training method that was developed in Oxfam incorporates the gender analysis into a process that includes awareness-raising and plans for action. We believed strongly that the training should be as accessible as possible to a wide a range of people, including development practitioners who might have less experience of formal education, and whose first language might not be English. Participatory methods were chosen as the most appropriate for adult learning, and exercises devised which would introduce concepts in an enjoyable way (see *The Oxfam Gender Training Manual*)[18].

In whichever country the training workshops took place, it was important to have at least one co-trainer from that region, and if men were being trained it was often preferable to include a man in the team. Like all participatory training, it needed to start from the participants' own experiences and understanding, and case studies and activities were devised from project visits and interviews. In field-based training, there was also a need to include sessions on the practicalities of working in a gender-sensitive way, such as how to listen to women, and how to work with men to encourage them to 'allow' their women to participate. In many countries, project support staff were included in gender training. This appeared to be counter to the usual Western good training principles of targeting training to those who needed it. However, field staff argued that project partners would come into contact with administrators, drivers, and so on, and if they were hostile to the notions of gender awareness, this could be counter-productive.

However, training by itself can never be enough: it must be part of an organisational strategy of transformation which incorporates a gender analysis into all policy, procedures, and practice. When I first began work as a gender trainer in Oxfam, the Gender Policy was still being developed, and the project application documents made no mention of women or gender issues. Both these are now in place, and gender is certainly a concept which Oxfam staff are now familiar with, yet it seems that not everyone always includes considerations of gender equality in their work.

There may be many reasons for this. Even to develop a fairly simple skill there are many stages from learning about it to doing it automatically. For a potentially threatening topic such as gender awareness, there may be many more stages to go through. The individual needs to have the continuing motivation, and constant practice of thinking and acting in gender-aware ways. For this to happen, gender awareness must be structurally integrated into the organisation itself, as well as its work. It may be personally and professionally easier for some people not to question the existing gender power balance in their own lives and work, and they may use various forms of bureaucratic resistance in order to avoid this (Longwe 1989)[19]. But this level of transformation in individuals and in organisations is absolutely necessary if gender training is to have any perceptible impact.

Linking the personal and the professional

In international field offices, gender relations within the office and even within the home, were seen as relevant to gender training, and in many cases as crucial to a proper integration of gender considerations into the programme work. This was in stark contrast to the situation in the UK head office. The difference may have been partly due to differences in ideology, to the fact that many people working in field offices felt closer to the development process, and perhaps to the fact that there was no explicit equal opportunities programme in field offices where these matters might be dealt with. This affected how participants reacted to training courses — in the UK people tended not to discuss their personal lives, or see it as relevant. It is not easy to challenge perceptions of gender and change gender practices, and people need to be motivated to do so. A continuing theme in gender work is the importance of personal interest and motivation.

The importance of the key individual

The Gender and Development Unit (GADU) at Oxfam House was part of a strategy, common in many large organisations at the time, to have dedicated units or workers with responsibility for gender. Women / gender project officers in the international (field) offices were part of the same strategy. However, there was some disquiet that this effectively let the other staff 'off the hook'.

In Kenya, a project officer was appointed with particular responsibility for, and interest in, gender training. She facilitated many gender-training workshops for staff, partners, and even grassroots groups, which have not been continued since she left Oxfam. It was decided that the next project officer should provide more general development and support work. Unfortunately, it is very difficult in practice for a general project officer to have the considerable time which is needed to organise and run training courses, and it is unlikely that this will happen unless the individual has the skills and interest and is allowed to prioritise training.

Certain individuals have had a big influence on gender training, and gender work in general, even where they did not have any formal responsibility for it. Requests for gender training had to come from the field offices; therefore, those field directors who did not want gender training did not get it, and this situation continues. It was recognised that some senior staff in the field would act as 'gate-keepers', deciding how much information was allowed to come through from GADU. One regional manager indicated to me that it would be physically dangerous for him to do any gender work at all in a certain country. Some months later, I was very surprised when a woman project officer from that country came into the GADU library, and enthusiastically perusing the shelves bemoaned the fact that such things were unavailable to her, as she would like to use them in her work. She was equally surprised when I told her that I had the impression that gender work was not possible in her country, and wondered where on earth I could have got such a strange idea from!

Oxfam's Gender Policy and the shift of responsibility for its implementation to line managers rather than dedicated individuals, was intended to help integrate gender into all Oxfam's work. However, even now, the attitudes of individual managers seem to be crucial in determining the range and quality of gender work, and whether or not gender training takes place.

Some burning issues

In any gender-training workshops there were some issues which would be a source of lively debate. Outside the UK, there was often a need to spend longer discussing certain topics, such as defining and understanding 'gender', which was often seen as an alien and imposed word and concept (although in the early days, 'gender' was also a new concept to many in the UK).

A related and constant theme in gender-training sessions is the issue of cultural sensitivity. However, this is in fact an issue in any kind of development work. There is always a danger of donor organisations with power and wealth imposing, or seeming to impose, their agendas on their recipient 'partners'. This is a real concern, which we always tried to address in the gender-training workshops. Some people felt personally threatened by ideas about gender and invoked the issue of cultural sensitivity, when perhaps the perceived loss of male power was more relevant.

Gender training touches the identity and personal lives, as well as the working practices, of everyone. Gender equity is not an issue which people can usually feel neutral about, and sometimes there are real conflicts of interest, although we always tried to focus on the real human benefits to everyone, of a more just society and more efficient development work.

Another 'hot potato' in the workshops was the issue of feminism.[20] Some field staff thought that 'gender' was a movement, and opinions varied as to whether they wanted to be part of it. In the workshops we had many different reactions. The workshop with partners in Kenya was particularly interesting and rewarding, because there were many who had never been exposed to ideas of gender awareness, and found them something of a revelation. This was often most clearly demonstrated when gender training linked personal issues with gender analysis. The '24-hour day' activity in the Moser method compares the activities of women and men during a day, showing that women do more work than men. Some men, particularly those who perhaps knew that their own wives worked so many more hours than they did, while they themselves did no housework, found this a very difficult exercise. However, others were genuinely surprised, and wanted to change things — demonstrating the transformative potential of gender training.

Conclusion

The success of gender training in practice depends to a large extent on external factors — including the attitudes and priorities of those in power within organisations. Training should be part of an overall strategy, which includes changes to working procedures and practices, and changes in personnel or responsibilities of personnel within an organisation. This has been said many times, and some organisations have made changes. Yet there is often organisational and personal resistance to radical change.

'The personal is political', states the feminist slogan. Sometimes gender training has ignored both these aspects and tried to steer a safe and non-confrontational course. But it is not possible to conduct gender training as a technical issue, introduced in a vacuum. My experience clearly brought out the importance of linking personal and political aspects to professional training on gender analysis. Even where gender training does not explicitly make the links, it throws into question a central part of everyone's identity, and of every society. Some have argued that their personal lives or political beliefs are nothing to do with their employer and do not reflect on their work practices. But as one male project officer said, 'Oxfam is encouraging men to take their share of the family responsibilities, but at the same time as an employer it is sending me out on project visits, so I hardly ever see my family.' This is a sentiment which will surely strike a chord with many people, and which brings out exactly the kinds of contradictions in people's work and personal lives that an integrated strategy of gender training can help to address.

About the author

Jan Seed worked as a gender trainer for Oxfam from 1988–91, and co-authored *The Oxfam Gender Training Manual.* She also contributed to *The Oxfam Handbook on Relief and Development.* Prior to this, she worked as a trainer/ development worker in Zambia. She has taught evening classes, and has run various training courses for community groups in Britain. Jan has worked extensively on equal opportunities issues, and co-authored *Missing Links*, a training manual on racism, power, and responsibility in development. In 1991, while working for Oxfam, Jan developed ME.

Academic reality:
From theory to practice

Rajni Khanna

Introduction

After working as a development professional for a number of years, I attended a two-month course on 'Women, Men and Development' at the Institute of Development Studies (IDS), University of Sussex, UK in 1996. This article relates how I applied the theoretical insights gained during the IDS course to my work with Oxfam India, both in terms of its organisational and programme aspects. It raises some key issues based on my experience, and the lessons which I brought away from an academic training.

This course represented a milestone in my understanding of gender analysis. It enabled me to gain an insight into gender theory, and apply its concepts to the day-to-day reality of development work. This understanding has been useful in developing gender-aware approaches to programme-planning and in implementing gender-sensitive development strategies. Moreover, academic study made me challenge my attitudes and ideas and helped me to reconceptualise and develop a new perspective on gender. It raised critical questions in my mind as to whether gender was a technical or social issue, and whether it included a political agenda for bringing about social change.

However, as a development practitioner, I was also able to bring to the course my professional experience and understanding of development, including an understanding of the reality of gender relations in a specific context. I had understood for a long time that women, just as men, are not a homogeneous category, that they differ on the basis of class, caste, age, religion, and education, and that they have different needs and interests. I was well aware of patriarchy and women's subordination, because I had experienced it and seen it all around me. The course allowed me to view this reality through a conceptual lens. I began to see that gender inequality went beyond male power and privilege to uncover the institutional sites where these inequalities were produced and reproduced. I learned more about women's subordination in the context of power relations, gender roles and relations, and appreciated how central gender is in constructing the identity of individuals.

Gender and development in Oxfam

There are multiple perspectives on the concept of gender within Oxfam in India. People ascribe different meanings and ideologies to it. For some it is another name for women, for others it means the representation of women at different levels in our organisation, for still others it is about culture and diversity, about relationships between men and women, about identity, and about power.

Oxfam GB's Gender Policy, although well conceived, has not been clearly and uniformly understood. Some see it as a 'top-down' agenda, difficult to interpret, and without a clear implementation strategy.[21] Moreover, the policy's interpretation is often ambiguous — especially in terms of its transformative potential. How does the policy address issues of power and gender relations within the organisation, and how are these translated into action? What are the structural and cultural issues for an organisation that is going through a fundamental process of change?

Barriers to creating a gender-sensitive development organisation

Organisations represent the link between the macro and the micro level, policy and practice, between production and reproduction, and the private and the public domain. An organisation's culture is also gendered, illustrated by the beliefs about, values of, and attitudes to women and men in the organisation, and by how space and time is structured in terms of work patterns, work hours, the approach to work, and the relationship between public and private life. An analysis of the rules, norms and practices through which an organisation constructs gender relations and hierarchies helps to uncover the underlying ideology of the organisation.[22]

Oxfam in India has an Equal Opportunities Policy, and women are beginning to gain previously 'male' positions of responsibility. However, there are still very few women in management positions. Although Oxfam in India has made serious attempts to recruit women, little progress has been made in changing the organisation's management profile. At a recent interview for a senior position, not a single woman appeared, although there is clearly no dearth of women development professionals in India! Such a situation raises questions about how organisational hierarchies, and positions within those hierarchies, respond to an analysis of gender roles and expectations in wider society. Even if a job is presented as gender-neutral, it does have a gender bias because women and men enter the organisation on unequal terms. In India, men have greater cultural rights to autonomy, social freedom, and mobility outside the home than women. Women's domestic responsibilities, and their culturally and socially specified roles, hinder them from entering into and fully participating in an organisation, unless they receive support to overcome such barriers. Moreover, a gender division of labour in society (for example, a 'natural' split between productive and reproductive roles)[23] means that women's roles and positions in organisations are equally determined by the assumption that women are good at certain tasks, but not at others. This has consequences for the allocation of power, which is also unequally allocated on the basis of 'men's' or 'women's' work.

Women's spaces, men's spaces

Particular theories have been useful to me in understanding the way in which organisations reflect gender divisions and inequalities in wider society. Anne-Marie Goetz's theory of gendered time and space helps to explain organisational transformation. She argues that physical space reflects not only men's physical but also their social freedom. For example, men are able to travel long distances on their own; they can establish a clear division between private and public space, because they often do not have the same domestic or child-care responsibilities as women. The gendered dimension of time is seen in the structure and pattern of the working day, and also in the way in which careers dominate people's life-cycles. Yet an organisation can be managed in such a way which allows the full participation of all, and takes into account women's needs and interests.

For Oxfam in India, such theories are reality: work consistently takes precedence over domestic and reproductive responsibilities. Work has become an extremely important aspect of life, both in terms of the amount of time staff spend in the workplace and in terms of what it means to them, given their commitment to the organisation and a shared ideology. Women and men working in a development organisation often have little time for domestic responsibilities and consistently face the stress of being separated from their families. Many women development workers put off marriage, child-birth, and child-rearing responsibilities: work is so central to their lives, the hours are long and erratic, they are absent from home for long periods of time due to extensive travel, and so on. Single women relocating for their work often suffer a significant loss of security and support, which is normally provided by the family. What can a development organisation do to bridge the divide between work and life?

Since a lot of our time is spent at work, we have tried to create a 'woman-friendly' workplace and conditions. The work environment is kept informal, warm, and friendly, and everyone is encouraged to work in a supportive way. We have adopted a work culture which takes account of family needs, with flexible hours of work so that staff can accommodate their domestic responsibilities. Staff sometimes work from home or take a few days off after spending a weekend in the field to spend time with their families. Travel schedules are planned with staff members' child-care and family responsibilities in mind.

Although we have tried to structure time and space at work in a manner that breaks down the division between productive and reproductive spheres, we are still facing a dilemma: how far should an organisation go in compensating for the constraints which women face in their private lives? It is possible for sensitively structured time and space at work to be manipulated and abused. However, even more fundamental than the way in which structures are managed, is the issue of power distribution within the organisation.

Power and gender equity in organisations

Another academic concept which I found useful to apply to Oxfam's work in India is Lukes's theory of power, which helps to interpret how women are situated in an organisation's power structures.[24] Luke distinguishes between 'power to', 'power over', and 'power within'. 'Power to' is analysed in terms of individual freedom to make decisions about issues where conflict is likely. 'Power over' moves from the individual to the institution, which exerts power through its rules and practices. 'Power within' is concerned with socially structured and culturally shaped behaviour in which power is distributed more equally and openly, for example in horizontal power structures.

We have attempted to incorporate this theoretical concept of power by adopting a democratic and participatory culture, where all staff have a say in decisions taken. Although roles of hierarchical power exist, the hierarchy is underplayed. We delegate authority and responsibility as far down the management line as possible, and staff are encouraged to take decisions without having to check with their managers. Of course this requires transparent guidelines for decision-making. In this way, staff grow in their roles with renewed commitment. Thus a different and useful method of exercising power can be conceptualised, in which power can be distributed and built on evenly.

To further develop this way of working, we experimented during my absence from the office, by giving management responsibility to a team of one administrative and one programme staff. These staff members have now had an opportunity to get hands-on experience in management. More generally, women members of staff have been provided with management training to strengthen their capacity to take up senior functions.

By and large, the women who work for Oxfam in India have been given opportunity and space to grow. As a result, they are becoming strong, articulate, and confident. However, men feel threatened sometimes — especially when women become powerful. They feel that there is a reverse discrimination against men in the organisation, which contradicts social reality.[25] It is clear that by concentrating on women in our organisation, we are maintaining the Women in Development (WID) approach, which tends to treat them as a separate group and fails to address the relationship between women and men. Questions concerning masculinity, male identity, and changing gender relations within the organisation must be understood and addressed before we can truly implement a gender and development strategy as part of our organisational culture.

Only when all Oxfam staff accept gender equity, will it become a reality. Working towards gender justice requires a personal commitment. Staff have undergone gender-awareness training to make them sensitive to gender inequality, and there has been a shift from having a gender 'lead person' and gender specialists (usually women), to making gender the responsibility of all the staff (men as well as women). In other words, we are making efforts to 'mainstream' gender. The challenge here is not to choose either a specialist or a generalist implementation strategy, but to constantly enhance staff capacity in order to incorporate a gender perspective into all our work.

However, training alone is not enough. Other strategies of capacity-building must be adopted, which may be less formal and rely far more on day-to-day interactions and relationships. In our work, we pay a lot of attention to breaking down the barrier between the private and public domains, and discuss informally our attitudes to gender at home and in the workplace. This is crucial: values of gender equity imposed on staff through a management line may be useful, but have their limitations. It is important that staff feel a commitment to values of gender equity, because it is they who can bring about or impede change. (It is often assumed that women are more sensitive to gender issues than men, but this is not always the case.) Transforming gender relations within an organisation is essentially about changing everyone's attitudes and behaviours. These are the real challenges before us as a team.

Perspectives on partnership and partner organisations

The concept of participation and partnership in development work also has implications for greater gender equity in such relationships. This involves making it possible for women and women's realities to be more visible, and better understood. While we were attempting to establish a gendered culture within Oxfam, our partner organisations, with whom we carry out programme work, by and large still have male leaders, and a patriarchal structure and culture. I feel that gender equity cannot be imposed on partner organisations. Development agencies such as Oxfam must be aware of local sensitivities, and change must be internalised through continuous interaction and support. Theories and methods of participation have been particularly useful in promoting gender equity in partnership with Indian organisations.

The kind of interaction and support that I can give relies very much on how partner organisations perceive my role as a woman manager. With professional organisations and women-headed organisations, a rapport is easily established, and we talk about various issues comfortably and openly. However, the male heads of small grassroots groups, who themselves belong to the local feudalistic communities which have entrenched patriarchal systems, I am often perceived as a woman outsider, from a different caste, and from an urban background. I have made enormous efforts to break down these barriers through constant contact, interaction, and learning – the keys to participation and partnership.

Integrating gender analysis at the programme level

We have made a shift from a Women in Development (WID) to a Gender and Development (GAD) perspective in our programmes. Our previous emphasis on working on gender issues with women only has broadened; we now try to include both men and women. However, while focusing on women, men, and the social relationships between them, we do keep sight of the fact that it is women who suffer most from inequality and disadvantage. We have started to target 'male attitudes' in order to bring about sustained changes in gender power relations.

We have successfully used conceptual frameworks as tools for gender analysis. Gender-planning frameworks have been useful in critically reviewing existing projects and in identifying development interventions which address both women's and men's needs. The Moser Framework, for example, provides a tool for analysing gender roles, practical and strategic gender needs, and for developing efficient and equitable approaches to gender and development. Analytical tools can be used to determine the gender division of labour and the distribution of resources between women and men, as well as to identify which women's needs and interests are different from men's. For example, we now analyse a development intervention to see whether it simply meets women's practical needs (those which they face because of their social position and as a consequence of the tasks which are socially assigned to them, such as provision of food, water, health-care, and child-care). If a project is conceived as a longer-term commitment we might design it to address women's strategic interests (those interests which would alter women's position vis-à-vis men) using gender-planning frameworks. We now assess our projects for their potential to transform gender roles and relationships, and to challenge women's subordination. This involves engaging further with social issues which perpetuate gender inequality such as child marriage, girls' education, and infanticide.

Conceptual frameworks are necessary and useful tools in gender analysis, and improvements have been made in programme planning. But by themselves, these frameworks are not sufficient for the successful incorporation of a gender perspective into Oxfam's programmes in India. Improved staff development and capacity, the internalisation of gender values by all staff, and a consistent commitment, are central to achieving a gender-sensitive organisation. All these depend far less on analysis and programme planning than on the organisation itself.

Conclusion

Working towards gender equity is a slow process. It is my belief that there is a strong need for theory to underpin practice, in order to take this process forward and ensure its success. Tinkering with procedures is not adequate to address issues of power relations in the structure and culture of an organisation, which are embedded in the broader context of society and reflects its gender inequality. There are no ready solutions, only many challenges and opportunities in moving towards gender equity and social transformation, both within an organisation and society at large.

We need to work in partnership with field practitioners, who have different identities and ideologies, so that we can move towards a common goal. Knowledge and experience must go both ways: practical experience from the field must inform theory, and vice versa. Just as frameworks for gender planning are a necessary but not sufficient part of incorporating a gender perspective into development work, so academic courses are an important part of understanding gender concepts and theories; but they are not sufficient to produce an implementation of gender analysis in practice. My experience of the 'Women,

Men and Development' course at IDS has confirmed and challenged many of the lessons I learned from my work in the field. Attending an academic course gave me the time and space to grasp concepts and theories of gender and development, which I have tried to reflect upon and apply to the realities in the field. A course does not provide you with ready answers, but it does help you to challenge your assumptions and sharpen your analysis. Theories of gender and development cannot be simply applied; all theory must be interpreted and grounded in social reality. There is no substitute for experience, commitment, and an understanding of the situation of the people with whom you are working.

About the author

Rajni Khanna has many years of experience as a development professional. She worked as Oxfam's Regional Representative in India. As a manager of the Western India programme, which covers Gujarat and Rajasthan, she has provided strategic directions for programme development. She is now Oxfam GB's Country Representative in Yemen. Rajni Khanna attended an academic course on 'Women, Men and Development' at the Institute of Development Studies, University of Sussex, UK in 1996.

Gender training for policy implementers: Only a partial solution

Fenella Porter and Ines Smyth

The theory and practice of development have faced challenges over the years, and among the voices which have contributed to this have been those demanding gender equity. The promise of a fundamental transformation of gender inequalities, both in society at large and in development institutions, is not yet realised or perhaps not fully realisable. Development institutions differ very widely in the extent to which they are committed to gender equity, what that commitment entails, and the means they propose to adopt in order to achieve related goals.

Gender training is often advocated as an answer to these questions. It is sometimes presented as the technical solution to the stubborn refusal of development policies and projects to become 'gendered'. More fundamentally, it is also presented as a way to address the root causes of systematic inequalities between women and men in the development process. This perception mirrors 'human capital' theories in management, which claim that training of women can redress their under-representation. At the opposite end of the spectrum lies an understanding based on Freireian ideas of learning as a process of self-awareness leading to social mobilisation. Such a view fits well with many feminist principles:

> Gender training is a tool, a strategy, a space for reflection, a site of debate and possibly of struggle. Training is a transformative process: it aims to increase knowledge and to develop understanding as a way to change behaviour, and to offer new skills with which to do this. (MacDonald 1994, p.32)

This article specifically addresses the significance of gender training for 'development practitioners' or 'implementers': those working within the context of a development programme or project in a particular national context. Oxfam staff at this level are often national staff and therefore represent the culture in which they are living and working, as well as those of Oxfam. Gender training must be fully informed by and relate to the reality of implementers' lives and work. The way in which implementers experience gender relations, and their ability to understand and implement work for gender equality, are controlled not only by the complexity of their context, but also by their hierarchical position within it.

There are evident limitations in a view of gender training as merely the acquisition of skills and as a 'quick-fix' solution. More recently, consensus has been built around the institutional aspects of gender issues in development. The realisation that 'institutions are gendered' (Goetz 1995) has led to the conclusion that development organisations cannot achieve gender fairness in their work unless they fundamentally change their own structures, practices, and culture.

These two elements form the focus of this article:[26] contextualising gender training for development practitioners, and the potential of gender training as a transformative tool within institutions.

Gender training in Oxfam head office

Oxfam, like most international NGOs, aspires to be a 'learning' organisation. Learning is understood as the cycle through which planned activities produce information on their nature and impact; these are in turn analysed to influence the new cycle of action and learning (Howes and Roche 1996). To what extent is staff training part of this commitment to learning in Oxfam? Until the early 1990s, the Training Department delivered a range of mandatory and optional courses open to all staff. They included courses on gender and development, and gender and communications. Since the restructuring of the Oxfam's training services, training has been provided through each separate division of the organisation, according to its needs and priorities. The Learning and Development Team of the Human Resources Department, established in 1996 in the International Division, stresses the importance of individual learning, and of individual responsibility for organisational learning.

However, with the abolition of the Training Department, there is no form of gender training available centrally in Oxfam. The one remaining course open to all staff which has a gender component is the 'Knowledge of Oxfam' course for new staff and volunteers in the UK, which includes a one-hour session on Oxfam's gender and development work.

Although training is only one avenue to learning, it could be argued that the decision to decentralise training has weakened Oxfam's ability to use formal training as part of a broader learning strategy. The disappearance of the gender-specific courses has deprived Oxfam of a valuable method of building the competence of its staff to implement the Gender Policy. The reduction of training on gender to a one-hour slot is also a signal to new staff of the secondary importance which the organisation attributes both to gender issues and to the awareness and skills necessary to operate effectively as a development worker.

Gender training in the field context

It is important to clarify here what we mean by 'context'. Gender training for implementers is at the interface between a development organisation and a local context. Implementation staff are required to understand concepts of gender as these relate to their work, but also as they relate to their personal and cultural context. It is vital that gender training is presented in such a way as to make sure that 'gender relations' are understood not as foreign and imposed concepts, but as important social relations which affect not only their work but their lives.

Local trainers are a vital link with the field context, both in order to relate concepts of gender to it, and to build local capacity to support work for gender equality. Alongside this, the presence of a trainer or co-trainer from the 'central' office of the organisation can help to position gender issues as an integral concern of the organisation. The use of local trainers and co-trainers in Oxfam is both widespread and very varied. In many field offices, gender training is carried out with local gender trainers, and Oxfam staff have taken on the role of gender trainer themselves, working with local counterparts.

However, gender trainers represent not only a context, but also a hierarchical position within that context. The trainer's age and sex will, in many cases, dictate her or his position within a hierarchy, and may influence the effectiveness of the training. Many development organisations (including Oxfam) have appointed gender advisers or officers to carry out training.[27] Although these roles enable staff to develop the training over time, they have not been roles of particular authority or power. Despite the considerable success so far (mainly thanks to the commitment and vision of individuals), gender training and commitment to gender equality have not yet been systematically endowed with authority within Oxfam.

Another important element in ensuring the success of gender training is the manner in which it is presented. The principles of pedagogy concern *how* people learn, as opposed to *what* people learn. There is little written on the pedagogy of teaching the various gender 'frameworks'[28] which have become widely used in development contexts. In general the 'framework' being taught (i.e. what is being taught) is often assumed to be the same as the pedagogy (i.e. how it is being taught). This leads to misunderstandings about frameworks, and how they can be used. Frameworks are only tools, and a particular framework can be used with different pedagogies, and applied in varied contexts. Above all, frameworks are not the answer to the challenges of carrying out gender-sensitive work.

> Frameworks are seductively universal, presented as providing universally applicable tools. Experience has shown, however, that they are not universal and cannot be universally applied. (ODA 1996)

Practitioners often understand this. For example, participants in the Oxfam South Sudan training observed:

> The discussion highlighted that in using such frameworks it is important to be aware of their limitations. These are important considerations, given the uncritical way in which these frameworks are often proposed ... most seriously they run the risk of being equated with the long-term work of developing and implementing appropriate gender strategies. (Smyth 1997)

Developing gender-training material for specific contexts ensures that the material reflects the dynamic nature of the contexts in which practitioners to work. This is a constant creative process, and much exchange of learning can take place between gender trainers and development agencies as the material develops. *The Oxfam Gender Training Manual* is widely used at the present and, more importantly, the translations which so far have been made (in Spanish, French, Portuguese, and Arabic) have offered the opportunity of adapting the material to different regional contexts.

One of the limitations of the present gender training is that there is a distinct shortage of material that is produced from gender training courses or workshops. For example, there is little material available centrally on the gender training that Oxfam project officers carry out with partner organisations. If an organisation is to learn and develop further strategies of gender training, documentation of gender training is essential — including the recording of failure. Existing documentation of gender training will seldom include any notion of failure. Although failure may be shared internally and informally, this discourages a wider sharing of experiences and longer-term development of the training itself.

Finally, it is important to address some of the problems and resistance that are often encountered in gender training. Many difficulties that arise in gender training are a consequence of trainees' personal resistance to concepts of gender. There may be emotional reactions from men and women who have much invested in the patriarchal system, the legitimacy of which is being questioned in the process of gender training. Resistance will inevitably restrict participants' understanding of gender, and when participants do not fully understand the main concepts, they cannot understand where they fit into their work.

Key concepts in gender analysis have often been developed in cultures different from those of the trainees, thus giving rise to resistance. Underlying this difficulty is the fundamental question: *what concept of gender should we expect people to understand?* Practitioners are fearful that their legitimacy within the community will be negatively affected by their espousal of gender concerns that have been developed in another culture.

> One of the principal fears that participants have about dealing with gender issues in their work is that gender is an imposed agenda and one which may create dangers for the programme and for individual staff members when promoting this agenda in the local community. (El Bushra 1996, p. 4)

Language barriers can create problems. This is because training at the implementation level is often targeted at people whose first language is not English (or another European language). There is a real lack of training material in local languages, and this compounds difficulties with conceptual understanding:

> Workshops and related activities conducted in a multi-lingual environment always present difficulties of communication ... the question of language and communication should be explicitly addressed in all programme activities. (Smyth 1997)

Gender training for field staff can also pose logistical problems. Field-level training might take place in relatively isolated areas, with poor infrastructure; participants may have problems in getting there. Logistical problems do not affect men and women in identical ways. If gender training intends to give a clear message about gender relations, awareness of the constraints on the trainees' productive and reproductive lives must be incorporated in the training itself. The idea of 'gendered time and space' has clear implications for the way in which gender training is organised, as well as for the way in which gender concerns are integrated into development projects.[29]

Gender training as a transformative tool

Success in relating concepts of gender to complex contexts is an important step towards ensuring the positive impact of gender training. However, it is only a partial solution. In order to increase the capacity of staff to implement gender-fair programmes and projects, gender training must go further, and become part of a more fundamental strategy of personal and organisational transformation. Oxfam's basic gender training is based on a personal approach:

> Awareness-raising ... addresses attitudes, perceptions and beliefs; unless people are sensitive to gender inequalities, gender analysis training is unlikely in the long

run to change planning and practice in development and relief agencies' work. We believe that unless people's emotions are touched, and their practices in their personal lives are brought into the discussion, there is a risk that gender awareness will remain merely an intellectual construct, and will be limited in its power to bring about meaningful social change. (Williams 1994, pp. viii–ix)

Only after this personal exploration of the issues do most workshops analyse the projects from which the participants are drawn, and develop relevant tools and skills (Williams 1994). This kind of training can be threatening, because it challenges basic assumptions that are part of people's sense of their own identity. But if it is facilitated carefully, it can be a non-confrontational process of discovery, with the participants themselves bringing out otherwise difficult elements of gender relations, as shown by the following comments:

The role-play generated a lot of discussion … the other issue … which aroused a lot of comment was … the gender perspective with regard to leadership, particularly as the elders were not only talking on behalf of the women but were also talking as if the men were a homogeneous group … It was generally felt that the workshop had been useful, interesting and challenging. (Walker 1993)

When gender training is seen by development organisations as only a set of skills for planning, implementation, or evaluation, it will very seldom reflect back on the working relationships within the organisation itself:

Gender and Development (GAD) policy initiatives have, at least in principle, been accepted by the development establishment, yet the fact that social institutions and development organisations continue to produce gendered outcomes which can be constraining or outright disadvantageous for women means that we must interrogate patterns of administration and rule from a feminist perspective, and insist on accountability to women as a serious issue in development management and politics. (Goetz 1995, p.1)

Equality in working relationships has for some years now been governed by an equal-opportunities policy. Employers who have a stated commitment to social justice, as do organisations working for development, have an obligation to take equal-opportunities initiatives seriously. These policies concern not only recruitment, promotion, training opportunities, and physical facilities, but also the establishment of a physical environment free from sexual harassment, and a work culture which allows both men and women to contribute fruitfully.

Questions such as where does Oxfam's stated principles on gender stand in relation to the proposed strategies for promoting diversity and its policy of equal opportunities need to be clarified to pave the way for interventions necessary for the implementation of the gender policy. (Rahman 1997, p.6)

The Oxfam Equal Opportunities Policy (established in the late 1980s) applies to the whole organisation.[30] Oxfam also has a Gender Policy (established in 1993). The two policies are structurally connected, and between them there is considerable transforming potential for both the organisation and its work. But this connection is at best unclear and certainly not brought out in gender training. Oxfam's gender training has, like that of other development organisations, concentrated on programme and project work, not on its internal functioning as an organisation. This reinforces the separation between the gender policy and the Equal Opportunities policy: the latter being more focused on management issues, monitored by personnel and central human-resources departments; and the Gender Policy being more focused on programme issues, monitored by desk and field staff in the International Division.

Conclusion

Implementers occupy a crucial place in the development process. Their position is at the interface of the development organisation and the local context. Training strategies (among other initiatives designed to increase the capacity of staff to carry out gender-equitable work) for policy implementers therefore need to reflect their positioning in this complex and sometimes conflicting reality. Further to this, implementers are positioned hierarchically within both the local context and the organisational context. Gender training should always aim to relate to the opportunities and limitations that are presented by the trainees' hierarchical positioning.

Gender training for implementers can increase the capacity of organisations to address gender concerns in their work. However, if gender training is seen only in terms of access to technical skills, the concepts and tools will be misunderstood and ineffective.

Gender training without transformational potential is still only a partial solution. The transformative potential of gender training lies in its personal and political nature, affecting as it does personal perspectives and questioning as it does fundamental social relations. Denial of these elements of gender training leaves it with a lack of political clout and relegates it to a status alongside other 'technical' interventions.

Above all, we need to ensure that a commitment to gender equality is institutionalised into all structures of the organisation. Training as a part of this institutionalisation can contribute a great deal to building the capacity of development organisations to carry out transformative work.

About the authors

Ines Smyth is a social anthropologist with a PhD from University College London. She has taught development studies in several academic insitutions, before joining Oxfam GB in 1996. Her areas of expertise and interests are gender theory, gender and industrialisation, and reproductive rights. Among her most recent publications is *Searching for Security: The Impact on Women of Economic Transformations* (edited with Isa Baud), 1997, London: Routledge.

Fenella Porter is a gender and development specialist, with experience in East Africa, and in advocacy and networking at the international level. She has worked in the Policy Department of Oxfam GB for two years, focusing on the institutionalisation of gender analysis into development policies and programmes. She is the author of several articles on gender training, gender and social exclusion, and the role of women's organisations in development.

References

El Bushra, J. (1996), 'Gender training in ACORD: progress report and critical assessment', RAPP, ACORD.

Goetz, A.-M. (ed.) (1995), 'Getting institutions right for women', *IDS Bulletin*, Vol. 6, No. 3.

Howes and Roche (1996) 'How NGOs Learn: The case of Oxfam UK and Ireland', internal paper, Oxfam.

Kabeer, N. (1994), *Reversed Realities*, London: Verso.

MacDonald, M. (ed.) (1994), *Gender Planning in Development Agencies: Meeting the Challenge*, Oxford: Oxfam.

March, C., Mukhopadhyay, M., Smyth, I. (eds.) (1999), *A Guide to Gender-Analysis Frameworks*, Oxford: Oxfam.

ODA (1996), 'Towards the Design of a Post-Beijing Training Strategy', report of workshop (4 March 1996).

Rahman, T. (1997), 'Draft Concept Paper on the Mapping of Gender Policy Implementation in Oxfam', internal paper.

Smyth, I. (1997), 'Gender in South Sudan: the Personal, the Practical and the Political', report of an Oxfam workshop (4–9 February 1997).

Sweetman, C. (ed.) (1997), 'Organisational Culture', *Gender and Development*, Vol. 5, No. 1.

Walker, B. (1993), 'Gender Workshop Report, Addis Ababa, 26–28 January 1993'.

Williams, S. (ed.) with Seed, J. and Mwau, A. (1994), *The Oxfam Gender Training Manual*, Oxford: Oxfam.

Notes to section V

1 Please see Ines Smyth's article, 'A rose by any other name', in this volume for a discussion of this.

2 Over ten specialist staff in areas such as public health, evaluation, or agronomy, and who collectively represented a vast body of knowledge and experience of Oxfam's work worldwide, were either made redundant or left Oxfam over an 18-month period. This is over and above normal staff turnover and 'natural wastage'. No organisation can survive such a haemorrhage without major blood transfusions and a long period of intensive care!

3 One of the side-effects of prolonged restructuring was that the *Handbook* became seen as a finite project rather than as part of a longer-term process that would have included training in its use, and so ensured that it would provide a common starting-point in the major strategic planning exercise that commenced in 1994.

4 Mohanty, C. (1988), 'Under Western Eyes: Feminist Scholarship and Colonial Discourses', *Feminist Review*, Vol. 30, pp.61–88.

5 We know that this split is simplistic and fails to reflect the academic/non-academic distinction among others.

6 Links newsletter on change agents, October 1996.

7 Becky Buell, Oxfam, personal communication, 1997.

8 See also Kanchan Sinha's contribution to this volume.

9 See Lina Abu-Habib's and Omar Traboulsi's contribution for a more detailed discussion of the Middle East programme.

10 Field, Sukey, 'Gender Awareness Training', National Women's Network Newsletter, 1988.

11 Seed, J. (1989), 'East Africa Gender Training Workshop', unpublished report, Oxfam; and Seed, J. (1991), 'Gender Training', GADU Newspack No.14, Oxfam.

12 Poats, S.V. and Russo, S.L. (1991), 'Training in WID/Gender analysis in agricultural development', an extract from 'Training in Women in Development/Gender Analysis in Agricultural Development: a Review of Experiences and Lessons Learned', Working Paper Series No.5 (FAO), reprinted in GADU Newspack No.14, Oxfam.

13 Overholt,C., Anderson, M.B., Cloud, K. and Austin, J.E. (1985), *Gender Roles in Development Projects: A Case Book*, West Hartford: Kumarian Press.

14 Moser, C. and Levy, C. (1986), 'A theory and methodology of gender planning: Meeting women's practical and strategic needs', DPU Gender and Planning Working Paper No.11, London: University College.

15 Freire,P. (1972), *Pedagogy of the Oppressed*, Middlesex: Penguin Books.

16 Katz, J.H. (1978), *White Awareness: Handbook for Anti-Racism Training*, Norman: University of Oklahoma Press.

17 Varghese, S. and Seed, J. (1991), 'Training of Gender Trainers Workshop', unpublished report, Oxfam.

18 Williams, S., Seed, J. and Mwau, A. (1994) *The Oxfam Gender Training Manual*, Oxford: Oxfam.

19 Longwe, S.H. (1989), 'Supporting Women's Development in the Third World', in GADU Newspack No. 13, Oxfam. Forms of bureaucratic resistance include: diluting women's development to mean women's welfare; shelving projects (justified in terms of practicalities or timing); paying lip-service only; compartmentalising (making women's development the sole responsibility of one under-funded department); and tokenism.

20 See also Ines Smyth's article in this volume.

21 See Kanchan Sinha's contribution to this volume.

22 This has been explained as an archaeology of organisational culture, examined in Goetz, A.-M. (1998), *Getting Institutions Right for Women*.

23 See Wendy Carson's contribution to this volume.

24 Stephen Lukes (1974), *Power: A Radical View*, London: Macmillan.

25 See Kanchan Sinha's contribution to this volume.

26 The original paper from which this article is drawn was prepared for the UK Government's Department for International Development (DFID), and used multiple examples from DFID and other development institutions. This article uses more selective examples from Oxfam's own experience, drawing specifically on the implications for gender training and capacity-building at the implementation level of the field offices.

27 Oxfam's Gender and Development Unit (GADU) included an in-house gender trainer from 1989 to 1991 .

28 'An analytical framework sets out different categories of elements/factors to be considered in any analysis: it draws attention to the key issues that have to be explored. A framework may outline a broad set of beliefs and goals, or it may be more prescriptive and give a set of tools and procedures.' (March 1999)

29 Goetz, in Sweetman (1997).

30 But in field offices, local national law mitigates them.

Appendix:
Gender and development —
Oxfam's policy for its programme

Agreed by Oxfam Council on 16th May 1993

Women are half the world's population, yet they do two-thirds of the worlds work, earn one-tenth of the world's income, and own less than one-hundredth of the world's property. (UN 1985)

Poverty and gender: Why Oxfam is concerned

Oxfam's mandate is to combat poverty, distress and suffering, and to educate the public about the root causes of these problems. While there are some aspects of poverty and exploitation which are shared by women and men, many aspects are different. Women are poorer than men and face social and cultural discrimination on the grounds of sex. This affects every aspect of their life, including development. Oxfam must both analyse and address these differences if it is to be successful in its development practice.

Today there is a growing awareness of women's absolute and relative poverty and inequality all over the world. In spite of the significant efforts of many national governments and at international level, the situation of women has worsened. The feminisation of poverty has accelerated in the last decade and further increased women's dependence and vulnerability.

The present social and economic crisis has had devastating effects on the Third World poor and these have been particularly adverse on women. Cuts in public expenditure, coupled with discrimination in employment practices, have led to more female unemployment. Falling commodity prices have forced the intensification of cash cropping, resulting in more manual work for women without an increase in their pay. Structural adjustment policies, particularly cuts in subsidies on drinking water, food, health, education and transport, have had a disproportionate effect on women. Widespread armed and ethnic conflict have a gender dimension. Women and their children form the majority of refugees or displaced populations, and the proportion of woman-maintained households in turbulent situations has increased. In addition, women in conflict situations suffer abuses such as sexual assault and other forms of exploitation not experienced by men.

The growing environmental destruction has multiple repercussions for women. Increasingly they are unable to fulfil their responsibilities for providing fuel, wood, and water for family needs. Urbanisation has cut women off from traditional support systems. Industrialisation in factories with poor safety regulations has exposed women to hazardous substances, dangerous equipment and dangerous processes. In many areas of the world the spread of AIDS is particularly affecting women because of their role as mothers and carers and also as sufferers.

Lack of understanding on the part of governments, multilateral agencies and NGOs of the different impact of development aid on men and women, has led, in many cases, to a further marginalisation of women from traditional decision-making structures, displaced them from their economic activities and ignored their valuable knowledge and contribution to development. Development aid is less effective when women are not participating on an equal footing.

Apart from adverse macro socio-economic conditions, women and girls have to contend with aggression and discrimination in their own local contexts due to the patriarchal structure of most societies. In many regions of the world they suffer violence that breaches their human rights: physical abuse, rape, sexual assault, female infanticide, 'honour killings', 'dowry murder' at the hands of family members, and other forms of aggression related to cultural customs and practices. To cite a few examples, discrimination is expressed in preference for male children, and in double standards in nutritional patterns and education. In the public sphere, religious and cultural intolerance in many societies restricts the movement of women and limits their control over their own lives.

Women are not a homogeneous group and their lives vary depending on where they live as well as their age, social class, ethnic origin, and religion. Nevertheless there are some common elements which hold for most women and which Oxfam recognises as important to understand and to address in the development process:
• In all societies men and women have different responsibilities for the survival and development of the community. However, within the existing division of labour, responsibility for maintaining human resources falls largely on women's shoulders. Gathering fuel and water, processing food, caring for children, nursing the sick, and managing the household is heavy and time-consuming. This is widely seen as a woman's role, and is economically unrecognised.

- Women have less access to power, wealth, and resources and are less likely to own land or property. In most cases they have inferior status both legally and culturally. They have less access to education and training, and to paid employment. They are less likely to be represented in decision-making bodies and their voices are less likely to be heard. Frequently they have no control over their own bodies and fertility.
- Violence against women constitutes an infringement of basic human rights, undermines their self-determination and their ability to participate fully in and to benefit from development.
- Faced with many forms of discrimination, many women are challenging the patriarchal or male-dominated structures of their societies — either through organised groups or networks or through individual actions that defy the system.
- Balancing the unequal power relations between men and women cannot be done in isolation. For the development process to be gender-fair, changes will have to take place in the economic, political, social, and cultural spheres.

Oxfam believes that unless gender-related inequalities are addressed it will not be possible to achieve sustainable development and alleviate poverty.

In Oxfam's experience gender-related oppression varies according to context, as do women's opportunities for involvement in development. Therefore, Oxfam's responses to the above issues will be sensitive to local circumstances and respect the pace, capacity, and strategies of local women for change.

Oxfam's work on gender and the need for policy

Oxfam addresses many of these problems by working towards meeting women's immediate and long term needs in mixed or women-only projects. Oxfam has taken positive action to counterbalance gender discrimination in development and so ensure that its programme reaches women — the poorest and most disadvantaged in most communities.

The Gender and Development Unit was created in 1985 to develop a gender perspective in Oxfam's work. Since then Oxfam has promoted gender training for its staff and partners, facilitated exchanges and provided financial support and accompaniment to women's groups and networks working for change. Other activities have included the appointment of gender experts and consultants for field research, evaluation and project development; discussions on gender with partners; and the development of criteria for programme evaluations and project appraisal. Documentation of Oxfam's experience in gender work through reports, manuals, and books has contributed to the debate in the North and the South and provided platforms for Southern practitioners. Increasingly, gender considerations are used in the recruitment and selection of staff. Oxfam has taken an active role in advocating gender-focused policy changes with bilateral and multilateral agencies and is trying to ensure the full integration of gender into all its lobbying and communications work.

However, in spite of this awareness and positive action, the lack of a corporate policy has made it difficult to close the gap between principles and practice and to ensure an integration of gender into the work of different parts of the organisation. A corporate policy is seen as the next essential step in Oxfam's commitment to gender — to ensure the issues are fully integrated into its programme and management, and to give Oxfam a coherent and consistent framework against which objectives can be measured and poor performance rectified.

Oxfam's vision and experience of gender has developed as a result of constant interaction between staff, project partners and other NGOs in the South and the North. It has been inspired by the struggles of Southern women's movements, individual men and women and by the real changes taking place in villages and communities where Oxfam works. Because gender relations are dynamic, Oxfam's vision and policy cannot be static; adjustments and changes may be required over time.

Oxfam also recognises the constraints faced by different divisions in their responsibility for implementation. Therefore, the policy promotes a creative look at ways of overcoming these constraints.

Oxfam's gender and development policy

Principles

'Oxfam believes in the essential dignity of people and their capacity to overcome the problems or pressures which can crush or exploit them.' Oxfam's principles apply across the gender divide — to allow women as well as men their essential dignity, and to work with women and men in its emergency and relief programmes in overcoming the pressures which exploit them. To achieve this, gender relations need to be transformed.

Oxfam's focus is on gender, rather than on women, to ensure that changing women's status is the responsibility of both sexes. It acknowledges that development affects men and women differently and that it has an impact on relations between men and women. A focus on gender is required to ensure that women's needs (set in the broader context of class, ethnicity, race and religion) do not continue to be ignored.

Women are poor because their lack of material wealth is compounded by a lack of access to power, skills, and resources. Fully integrating gender into

Oxfam's programme should tackle the causes of women's poverty and promote justice to the advantage of women as well as men. Because women are in a subordinate position, special efforts and resources are required to promote their full and active participation in Oxfam's work and to make them equal partners in the fulfilment of Oxfam's mandate. To achieve this Oxfam will try as far as possible to give women the opportunity to formulate their own priorities and to work with men in addressing the status quo.

Objectives

Oxfam will work towards ensuring that its development and relief programmes will make the lives of women better. It is committed to:
- developing positive action to promote the full participation and empowerment of women in existing and future programmes so as to ensure that Oxfam's programme benefits men and women equally;
- confronting the social and ideological barriers to women's participation and encouraging initiatives to improve their status including basic rights;
- promoting independent access for women to key resources (e.g., land, employment), services, and facilities;
- recognising and helping women exercise their rights over their bodies and protection from violence;
- ensuring that all programme work in the UK/Ireland takes gender considerations into account and, wherever appropriate, to promoting initiatives with a gender focus.

Strategy

Overseas programme—Oxfam will achieve its objectives by:

a) ensuring that all emergency and development responses incorporate a gender perspective in assessment, planning, implementation and evaluation;

b) promoting women's access to basic needs, knowledge, education, new skills, and actively encouraging their participation in decision-making;

c) supporting the development of women's self confidence; strengthening women's organisations/groups, promoting dialogue, and networking;

d) continuing to support and strengthen links between women's groups and organisations nationally and internationally to enhance mutual understanding and solidarity for action;

e) continuing to expand Oxfam's knowledge of and commitment to gender issues, through research, documentation, publishing, institutional learning and work on global themes;

f) including a gender perspective in all lobbying and communications work;

g) strengthening the lobbying of bilateral and multilateral agencies on gender issues; promoting advocacy work in coordination with networks and organisations in the North and the South including institutional support for international gender-focused lobbying networks;

UK and Ireland programme—Through the work of the Marketing and the Trading Divisions, Oxfam will:

h) apply gender considerations and sensitivity to all Oxfam's materials for the UK/I public;

i) where appropriate, communicate the essential role played by women in all aspects of development. This means highlighting Oxfam's work on gender, communicating the contribution women give to development, and encouraging international links with women's groups and organisations;

j) wherever possible, present positive images from a gender perspective by written, verbal and visual means, and try to counterbalance dominant and stereotyped images of women provided by the media and other agencies;

Management—Through its management and policy implementation, Oxfam will:

k) raise issues with men and women, sensitising them to gender needs and involving them actively in supporting gender equality;

l) promote the understanding and commitment of Oxfam staff to ensuring policy implementation through gender training of all programme staff;

m) use gender-awareness and understanding as criteria for recruitment and selection of overseas and UK/I programme staff; promote women to decision-making positions at all levels; and strengthen commitment to Oxfam's Equal Opportunities Policy;

n) develop guidelines and procedures for implementation and monitoring by managers in all relevant divisions with measurable objectives, targets, and time-tables;

o) ensure that staff are given the resources for implementing policy;

p) establish a structure for updating and monitoring the policy within agreed time frames, and integrate this structure into the organisational strategic plan;

q) make information available to Oxfam's trustees and keep them regularly informed about the progress of implementation and monitoring of the gender policy;

r) ensure that staff, partners, and volunteers in the UK/I and overseas are aware of the existence of the policy by communicating it in accessible ways;

s) ensure that managers are responsible and accountable for the implementation of policy;

t) set a timetable for policy implementation and ensure that staff adhere to it.